Applied Architecture Patterns on the Microsoft Platform

An in-depth, scenario-driven approach to architecting systems using Microsoft technologies

Richard Seroter

Ewan Fairweather

Stephen W. Thomas

Mike Sexton

Rama Ramani

BIRMINGHAM - MUMBAI

Applied Architecture Patterns on the Microsoft Platform

First published: September 2010

Production Reference: 1020910

Published by Packt Publishing Ltd.
32 Lincoln Road
Olton
Birmingham, B27 6PA, UK.

ISBN 978-1-849680-54-7

www.packtpub.com

Cover Image by Sandeep Babu (sandyjb@gmail.com)

Credits

Foreword

To understand is to perceive patterns.

-Isaiah Berlin

Architecting a good software solution is in many ways very much like the art of cooking a great meal. Just like a chef needs to have a broad knowledge of various ingredients that go into a meal, an architect needs to have a broad understanding of potential technologies and tools that he would need for a software solution. Just like a good chef masters the techniques of combining his raw ingredients into a delicious course, a good architect should know when and how to use and blend various software components to come up with elegant and efficient solutions. Just like a chef's work is confined by physical conditions and customer requirements, so is the work of a software architect. Both need the right kind of discipline and structure to cope with external constraints. So knowledge, experience, discipline, and structure are critical, but as any good chef or architect will tell you, the art of cooking or architecting requires something extra, and that is creativity. To put it simply in the words of the author John Updike:

> *Any activity becomes creative when the doer cares about doing it right, or better.*

The book you are holding is a good example of the outcome of such creativity. I personally know the authors to be very experienced and knowledgeable on the topics they write — yet, it is a way they have chosen to distill their experience and know-how that make this book a very valuable resource for any software architect. Artfully transforming use-cases and requirements into recognizable patterns while discussing alternative architectures for implementing these patterns, this book provides you with an effective framework to handle the complexities of modern distributed applications.

Unlike cooking, where the basic raw ingredients do not change as much or as often over time, dealing with software architecture involves constant and frequent changes. New paradigms and methodologies for developing and delivering software solutions are constantly evolving. Innovative new technologies, some with overlapping capabilities, are introduced at an increasing pace into an already crowded marketplace. Making sense out of this dynamic and sometimes confusing domain, even when focusing only on Microsoft technologies, is quite a challenge. A great team of contributors was assembled to tackle the job. Together, they have produced an appealing guide by discussing a collection of common architectural patterns in software development and their implementation using Microsoft technologies.

This may seem like a book of "recipes" devised by a team of highly qualified "software chefs", but this is where again the analogy falls short: in the world of software, things are a more complex. In many cases, you'll find that you need to treat these recipes as the basis to build on. You will need to step into the role of the "chef" and start "cooking" your own solution by combining patterns or adjusting the suggested solutions to fit into your project's specific needs. Happy "software cooking"!

Ofer Ashkenazi
Senior Technical Product Manager
Microsoft

About the Authors

Richard Seroter is a solutions architect for an industry-leading biotechnology company, a Microsoft MVP for BizTalk Server, and a Microsoft Connected Technology Advisor. He has spent the majority of his career consulting customers as they plan and implement their enterprise software solutions. Richard first worked for two global IT consulting firms, which gave him exposure to a diverse range of industries, technologies, and business challenges. Richard then joined Microsoft as a SOA/BPM technology specialist where his sole objective was to educate and collaborate with customers as they considered, designed, and architected BizTalk solutions. One of those customers liked him enough to bring him onboard, full time, as an architect after they committed to using BizTalk Server as their enterprise service bus. Once the BizTalk environment was successfully established, Richard transitioned into a solutions architect role where he now helps identify enterprise best practices and applies good architectural principles to a wide set of IT initiatives.

Richard is the author of the book *SOA Patterns with BizTalk Server 2009* (Packt Publishing), released in April 2009. Richard maintains a semi-popular blog of his exploits, pitfalls, and musings with BizTalk Server and enterprise architecture at `http://seroter.wordpress.com`.

I want to thank my gifted co-authors and technical reviewer who brought an insightful amount of experience and knowledge to this project. I also have to thank my wonderful co-workers whose architectural brilliance constantly inspires and challenges me. Finally, thanks to my family for their support on this project. My dog, Watson, unexpectedly offered to proofread my chapters, and I eagerly accepted his invitation. Thanks buddy. But this book is for my son Noah who makes me want to be a better man.

Ewan Fairweather has worked for Microsoft for six years. He currently works as a program manager in the Business Platform Division on the Customer Advisory Team (CAT) working on large scale integration and OLTP SQL applications. Prior to this, Ewan spent three years working for Microsoft UK, in the Premier Field Engineering team where he worked with enterprise customers, helping them maintain and optimize their BizTalk applications. This included working in a dedicated capacity on some of the world's largest BizTalk deployments, predominantly within financial services. Ewan co-authored the successful *Professional BizTalk Server 2006* (Wrox, 2007) and has written many white papers for Microsoft including the *Microsoft BizTalk Server Performance Optimization Guide*, which is available on the Microsoft Developers Network (MSDN) website. Prior to joining Microsoft, Ewan worked as a Cisco Certified Academy Instructor (CCAI) for a regional training organization, delivering advanced routing and networking courses. Ewan holds a bachelor's degree in computing with management from the University of Leeds. Apart from work, Ewan's hobbies include reading and going to the gym. He has also recently found a fond interest for Jiu Jitsu. Ewan maintains his blog at `http://blogs.msdn.com/ewanf`.

Mum, Dad thanks for always believing in me, Shona and Kieran, and giving us the strength to do whatever we set our minds on.

Stephen W. Thomas is an independent consultant specializing in BizTalk Server and other Microsoft Server technologies including Workflow and AppFabric. He has been working with BizTalk for over eight years. For the past six years, Stephen has been recognized as a Microsoft Most Valuable Professional (MVP) in BizTalk Server. In addition to being an MVP, Stephen is a Microsoft Connected Technology Advisor.

Stephen has done consulting work for numerous clients including many in the Fortune 500. Stephen runs the BizTalk community site `http://www.BizTalkGurus.com`. The site offers a community forum, over 50 BizTalk samples, various how-to videos, and Stephen's blog. Stephen has presented at several Microsoft TechEd events, multiple SOA Conferences, and various user groups.

I would like to thank my loving wife, Angel, who has supported me over the many months of working on this book and to the new little BizTalkGuru scheduled to arrive in February 2011. I would also like to remember my furry babies Kendall and Jordan who lost out on valuable play time as I was working on sample code.

Stunningly handsome, yet surprisingly humble, **Mike Sexton** spent the first ten years of his career as a public defender in New York. Upon learning the discrepancies between his salary and the salary of newly minted college graduates working in IT, he had an epiphany and immediately learned how to program database applications. He has designed and built database applications for 12 years in both SQL Server and Oracle-based systems; he has published in SQL Server Magazine and blogs on a semi-regular basis. He currently works for Avanade, the premier integrator of Microsoft technologies in the enterprise. Mike's role as a database architect has him traveling the USA, bestowing his database wisdom on the less fortunate. Mike can be found with a gorgeous blonde on his arm, living the high life in Colorado.

I would like to thank my wife of 25 years for not giving in to the numerous temptations to murder me that I have provided over the years. I would also like to thank the management of Avanade for their patience and support while writing this book.

Rama Ramani has built experience, over the last decade, in enterprise server products across databases, RFID middleware, and application server caching technologies. The roles have ranged from systems programming, feature PM in product teams, and now as part of the Customer Advisory Team working with some of the largest customer deployments. He has a bachelors degree in computer science from the University of Madras and a masters degree in computer science from the University of Florida.

In this free time, he likes to read books or watch motivational videos on leadership and entrepreneurship.

I would like to acknowledge my co-authors for their excellent teamwork in getting this book to fruition. I would like to thank my wife for letting me spend some of the weekends and evenings alone, working on the book. Finally, I would like to thank my parents, who have been a great source of inspiration and for providing me with excellent education.

About the Reviewer

Yossi Dahan has been involved in professional software development for 13 years. Starting with the development of e-commerce systems for companies worldwide, he soon faced challenges involved in creating systems with complex business processes and both in-house and third party integration requirements. Drawn by these challenges, Yossi has decided to focus in these areas and so, since 2000, has been working almost exclusively on projects with significant BPM and EAI aspects.

In 2005, Yossi had founded Sabra Ltd in the UK. Created specifically to help organizations build better business processes and integration solutions, Sabra has worked with enterprises of all sizes, all over the UK, helping them architect, design, and build BPM and EAI solutions using Microsoft technologies.

Sabra also works to build in-house capabilities for its customers' training and mentoring teams; on design, development, and operations of complex systems, arming them with its experience gained through many projects, well-proven patterns, and best practices picked up in their field.

I'd like to thank the authors for asking me to review this book, I was flattered by their trust in me on this product of their hard work, and for the opportunity to learn so much in the process; this exercise has certainly been (as book writing/reviewing often is) thought provoking.

Of course I thank Iva, my wife, for dealing with long evenings of solitude while I worked on the chapters of this book and for putting up with my constant whining about missing my deadlines.

Last, I'd like to thank Packt, and in particular, Shubhanjan Chatterjee, for all the help during the whole process and for accepting my excuses for not meeting my deadlines.

Table of Contents

Preface

Back in May 2009, I had a lengthy chat with Ewan Fairweather who was a technical reviewer on my first book. We talked about the host of products that Microsoft had either released or planned to release, and how it seemed increasingly difficult for an architect to keep up with such a constant stream of new offerings. It's one thing to read a press release or a whitepaper and get the marketing spin on a product, but it's something else to truly grasp their ideal use cases and challenges. Ewan and I agreed that it would be a useful exercise to try to craft around a dozen enterprise IT use cases and evaluate which Microsoft product is truly the best fit for each scenario. Thus, a book idea was born.

To make an educated choice on which product should form the foundation of your solution architecture, you need to have an accurate picture of the strengths and weaknesses of the product, as well as see it in action. In this book, we will give you a solid overview of the core technologies in the Microsoft application platform, evaluate a range of business problems, and use a consistent decision-making process to choose the right technology to implement a solution and actually build the solution using the ideal product.

I started down a path of creating a fancy flowchart which, based on a distinct set of choices, could direct you to a proper Microsoft application platform technology. However, decisions about the core technology of a solution cannot be driven from a single fork of a flowchart. How do you realistically eliminate a product from consideration by asking a single question such as "is batch processing needed?" Decision point? There are a myriad of additional factors to consider prior to eliminating BizTalk Server or embracing SQL Server Integration Services for batch processing, for instance. Instead of a single, rigid decision matrix or single flowchart, we chose to create a decision framework that takes into account the essential areas of interest when comparing a product against the needs of your project.

In the first part of the book, we do a short dive into the core technologies demonstrated in the book. These "primers" provide a background about WCF/WF, Windows Server AppFabric, BizTalk Server, SQL Server, and the Windows Azure platform. Each primer will tell you a bit about what a product is for and how to use it. You should then have enough working knowledge to thoroughly digest the rest of the book.

The rest of the chapters follow a specific structure. Each chapter starts with the description of a fictional, but realistic, customer use case. We then offer some background on the customer and find out about the problem they wish to solve. Following the use case, you will find an evaluation of the type of pattern that best fits the customer's requirements. We then consider and evaluate multiple solutions against our decision framework. After the best choice is made, the remainder of the chapter describes the actual construction of a solution.

I have put together a great team of authors that bring a diverse set of experiences with the Microsoft platform stack. We started our effort with extensive discussions about common problems we come across on projects and which topics might be of most interest to our readers. We ended this first phase of evaluation with dozens of pattern candidates, and through prioritization, bartering, and a little pleading, we finally narrowed it down to the thirteen you find here. There are clearly many many more "common" problems that we all encounter each day, but we hoped to identify ones where the product choices weren't always clear.

The biggest challenge with a book like this is balancing the inherent bias that we technologists have towards products that we are most familiar with. It is apt then, that this is the same problem that architects and developers regularly have on their own projects. For example, if you are a SQL Server specialist, then most problems look like they can be solved with a SQL Server-based solution. Much like good project teams where multiple viewpoints can help create the appropriate solution architecture, our authors constantly challenged each other to ensure that expertise in one area did not cloud our judgment in another.

What this book covers

Chapter 1, *Solution Decision Framework,* outlines where to locate solution requirements and how to consistently evaluate key dimensions of a solution prior to selecting an underlying technology.

Chapter 2, *Windows Communication Foundation and Windows Workflow 4.0 Primer,* provides a background about WCF/WF technologies and typical scenarios to use WCF and Windows Workflow.

Chapter 3, *Windows Server AppFabric Primer,* explains the capabilities of Windows Server AppFabric and its components.

Chapter 4, *BizTalk Server Primer,* describes what BizTalk Server is, when to use it, and how to build a simple solution.

Chapter 5, *SQL Server and Data Integration Tools Primer,* contains a broad overview of the SQL Server products that address data integration and data management.

Chapter 6, *Windows Azure Platform Primer,* has an introduction into Microsoft cloud technologies including Windows Azure, SQL Azure and Windows Azure Platform AppFabric.

Chapter 7, *Simple Workflow,* covers a use case that involves aggregating data from multiple sources and presenting a unified response.

Chapter 8, *Content-Based Routing,* looks at how to effectively transmit data to multiple systems that perform similar functions.

Chapter 9, *Publish-Subscribe,* addresses a scenario where a message must be reliably sent to multiple endpoints.

Chapter 10, *Repair/Resubmit with Human Workflow,* builds a process for easy human interaction with failed messages inside a system.

Chapter 11, *Remote Message Broadcasting,* demonstrates a scenario where traditional polling solution is augmented to support real-time updates.

Chapter 12, *Debatching Bulk Data,* explains how to take giant sets of data and insert them into databases for analysis.

Chapter 13, *Complex Event Processing,* addresses website click stream analysis and creating actionable business events.

Chapter 14, *Cross-Organizational Supply Chain,* demonstrates how to build a supply chain solution to integrate systems in a purchase order scenario.

Chapter 15, *Multiple Master Synchronization,* covers methods for arriving at a single version of truth from multiple, often conflicting master data sources.

Chapter 16, *Rapid Flexible Scalability,* looks at creating temporary environments that can be easily created and contracted as needed.

Chapter 17, *Low Latency Request-Reply,* contains a retail scenario where high performing query services are established.

Chapter 18, *Handling Large Session and Reference Data,* discusses usage of distributed caching to scale large workloads in web applications.

Chapter 19, *Website Load Burst and Failover,* looks at leveraging the Windows Azure platform's elastic resources and high service level for building a low cost solution.

Chapter 20, *Wrap Up,* is a brief summary of the key points addressed in the book.

What you need for this book

The following software products are used in this book:

- BizTalk Server 2010 and ESB Toolkit 2.1
- .NET Framework 4.0 (which includes Windows Communication Foundation and Windows Workflow Foundation)
- SQL Server 2008 R2
- StreamInsight 1.0
- Windows Server AppFabric
- Windows Azure Platform
- Visual Studio 2010

Who this book is for

This book is for the busy architect, developer, or manager who needs to advance their knowledge of the Microsoft application platform space. If you last evaluated the Microsoft platform offerings in 2009, then you are woefully out-of-date. Don't worry, it happens to the best of us. I'd like to hope that flipping through this book will increase your confidence when trying to figure out a consistent way to choose which Microsoft product to use.

If you are a developer looking to transfer your skills into architecture, then this book can help you take a big-picture approach to pattern detection in use cases and apply a broad range of evaluation criteria to product selection. Alternately, you may just want to get a short primer on the latest Microsoft technology.

Conventions

In this book, you will find a number of styles of text that distinguish between different kinds of information. Here are some examples of these styles, and an explanation of their meaning.

Code words in text are shown as follows: "Data is stored in the custom region `June6_UserReviews` of the `ReviewsCache`".

A block of code is set as follows:

```
SyncOrchestrator orchestrator = new SyncOrchestrator();
orchestrator.LocalProvider = source;
orchestrator.RemoteProvider = destination;
orchestrator.Direction = SyncDirectionOrder.UploadAndDownload;
//bidirectional sync
orchestrator.Synchronize();
```

When we wish to draw your attention to a particular part of a code block, the relevant lines or items are set in bold:

```
SEND ON CONVERSATION @RecvReqDlgHandle
  MESSAGE TYPE [//SOAbook/SampleQueue/ReplyMessage]
  (@ReplyMsg);

END CONVERSATION @RecvReqDlgHandle;
END

SELECT @ReplyMsg AS SentReplyMsg;

COMMIT TRANSACTION;
GO
```

Any command-line input or output is written as follows:

```
sn -k biztalk.snk
```

New terms and **important words** are shown in bold. Words that you see on the screen, in menus or dialog boxes for example, appear in the text like this: "Right-click on the BizTalk project and select **Properties**".

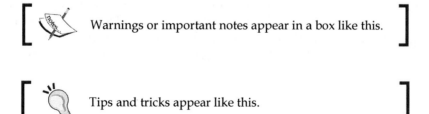

Warnings or important notes appear in a box like this.

Tips and tricks appear like this.

Reader feedback

Feedback from our readers is always welcome. Let us know what you think about this book—what you liked or may have disliked. Reader feedback is important for us to develop titles that you really get the most out of.

To send us general feedback, simply send an e-mail to feedback@packtpub.com, and mention the book title via the subject of your message.

If there is a book that you need and would like to see us publish, please send us a note in the **SUGGEST A TITLE** form on www.packtpub.com or e-mail suggest@packtpub.com.

If there is a topic that you have expertise in and you are interested in either writing or contributing to a book on, see our author guide on www.packtpub.com/authors.

Customer support

Now that you are the proud owner of a Packt book, we have a number of things to help you to get the most from your purchase.

Downloading the example code for this book

You can download the example code files for all Packt books you have purchased from your account at http://www.PacktPub.com. If you purchased this book elsewhere, you can visit http://www.PacktPub.com/support and register to have the files e-mailed directly to you.

Errata

Although we have taken every care to ensure the accuracy of our content, mistakes do happen. If you find a mistake in one of our books—maybe a mistake in the text or the code—we would be grateful if you would report this to us. By doing so, you can save other readers from frustration and help us improve subsequent versions of this book. If you find any errata, please report them by visiting http://www.packtpub.com/support, selecting your book, clicking on the **errata submission form** link, and entering the details of your errata. Once your errata are verified, your submission will be accepted and the errata will be uploaded on our website, or added to any list of existing errata, under the Errata section of that title. Any existing errata can be viewed by selecting your title from http://www.packtpub.com/support.

Piracy

Piracy of copyright material on the Internet is an ongoing problem across all media. At Packt, we take the protection of our copyright and licenses very seriously. If you come across any illegal copies of our works, in any form, on the Internet, please provide us with the location address or website name immediately so that we can pursue a remedy.

Please contact us at `copyright@packtpub.com` with a link to the suspected pirated material.

We appreciate your help in protecting our authors, and our ability to bring you valuable content.

Questions

You can contact us at `questions@packtpub.com` if you are having a problem with any aspect of the book, and we will do our best to address it.

Solution Decision Framework

Decisions, decisions, decisions. Each and every day, architects and developers make choices, which range from where to store configuration data to whether their solution calls for real-time messaging or batch processing. Each selection brings with it a host of side effects that impact the solution's maintainability, security, performance, speed of development, and more.

Two significant aspects of any architecture decision are: what should be done and how should you do it. The focus of this chapter is to provide advice on the latter by outlining a thought process for making sound decisions. Do you need to deploy your servers globally or in one location? Should the solution employ an asynchronous communication pattern for data processing? These are just examples of solution aspects that result from an architectural analysis of the requirements. This chapter contains a framework to help you determine which architecture quality attributes you should evaluate for your solution. We will leverage this framework in subsequent chapters as we evaluate business problems and choose the Microsoft technology that best matches the requirements of the solution.

In this chapter you will learn the following:

- The value of having a consistent, reusable decision framework
- Where to find the input information for your decisions
- How to organize your architectural assessment of the requirements

The need for a decision framework

There is no substitute for the hands-on experience of designing and building software solutions. The key is how you take what you have learned in each situation and apply these principles and lessons to subsequent projects. Recording and maturing a reusable set of decision criteria goes a long way towards establishing personal confidence in our architectural decisions. Each project should not be a blank slate. Rather, we should be leveraging our experiences and the experiences of others and reuse them so that we can surface key issues, prioritize our feature set, and establish which trade-offs we will need to make early on. While we cannot know every detail or requirement before starting to craft a solution, we must still make critical decisions that have significant impact on the direction of the solution architecture. This is all the more a reason to make consistent, well thought-out decisions.

There is nothing magical about a decision framework. In our case, the recommendation is to do the following:

- Gather all the facts that you can. See the next section (*Sources of Input to the Framework*) for ideas on where to obtain the data points necessary to make informed decisions.

- Look for the *hard* architectural decisions. What is the big picture? What are the critical aspects that we need to tackle right away? An example of this is determining whether or not your strategy is to copy data between systems, do real-time lookups, or leverage a shared data source. Broad data-sharing patterns shape how you build your system and this is an example of a weighty decision that impacts how we lay out the rest of the solution.

- Capture and evaluate alternatives. It has been said that "if you only have one solution to a problem, then you are not thinking hard enough". Every significant decision point should have multiple possible alternatives that reflect the interests of the project or organization as a whole.

- Weigh the strategic importance of feature requests. All desired solution capabilities are not created equal. If I work in an environment where we have limited in-house development resources and place a premium on system maintainability, then I will value products with standard support tools over products that have a more robust, but custom feature set. Amplify what the solution must do and avoid being distracted by "nice to have" capabilities.

The list of solution criteria we have in this chapter is by no means exhaustive. Instead, it is meant to provide a baseline for you to customize with your own experiences and organizational priorities. Following a framework strategy of "gather information, inspect for impact, assess alternatives, and weigh importance" will help you become successful regardless of how big or small your specific list of solution criteria is.

Sources of input to the framework

Where do we get the data points necessary to make informed architectural decisions? There are four key sources that will shape our understanding of the business problem: functional requirements, non-functional requirements, derived requirements, and organizational direction.

Functional requirements

The functional requirements of a solution dictate what the resulting system should be able to do and include scenarios that summarize the user's expected experience with the system. Functional requirements could address the type of data entities the system interacts with, how the system behaves when a user needs to invoke a particular calculation, or the order of steps to complete a business process. Functional requirements are typically gathered by a business analyst and are crucial in determining how a system should be architected. A software solution is worthless if it is architected beautifully but does not meet the business need. Staying focused on our client needs will ensure that we build a practical and architecturally responsible solution.

In order to ensure that our functional requirements help and do not hurt our effort to architect a solution, we must remain diligent and not allow system requirements to masquerade as business requirements. For instance, if we see a business requirement that says that customer profile information from System A should be copied via file transfer every night to System B, then that should raise a red flag. That business requirement is dictating system design and does not answer what the business need actually is. The proper business requirement would be "The system shall enable users of System B to view up-to-date customer information originating from System A". As architects, we can choose multiple implementation solutions (for example: shared database, data transfer, real time lookups) that can both satisfy that requirement and fit into the overall design patterns we have laid out for the project. While there may be relevant reasons for technical requirements (for example, security constraints) to get included as functional requirements, often these technical requirements are better stated as non-functional requirements.

Non-functional requirements

Wikipedia describes non-functional requirements in this way:

> *A non-functional requirement is a requirement that specifies criteria that can be used to judge the operation of a system, rather than specific behaviors. This should be contrasted with functional requirements that define specific behavior or functions.*

`http://en.wikipedia.org/wiki/Non-functional_requirements` as on 10/2009.

So unlike functional requirements, which dictate system behavior, non-functional requirements stay focused on how the system needs to operate. There are multiple dimensions to look at when evaluating system operations including maintainability, security, compliance, availability, and exception management. A business or system analyst typically uses a pre-defined list of questions to interview stakeholders and identify non-functional requirements. Questions such as "How many users will the system support?", "What is the sensitivity of the data stored by the system?", "What are the regular hours of operation for the system?", "What is the acceptable latency of a user request?", and "What are the disaster recovery expectations?", will all provide insight into how to best architect our solution. It should be noted, however, that it is often the responsibility of the analyst to translate the sometimes technical, non-functional requirements into more business-relevant questions. For instance, I would not ask my client to spell out their explicit disaster recovery needs (for example recovery point objective, recovery time objective, site configurations), but rather, I would focus on questions addressing business continuity and backup procedures and extract the disaster recovery needs from their answers.

Derived requirements

We sometimes forget about the requirements that are not explicitly stated but can be uncovered through the functional and non-functional requirements. Derived requirements are implied requirements and do not come directly from our users. These are the things that go unstated (or even forgotten about), yet still belong in the registry of requirements for the solution. For instance, we may receive functional requirements that state a need to capture key data points and progress indicators during each stage of a long-running workflow process. While no reporting interface was requested by the users, we realize after reading this requirement that the users will need some way to visualize the progress of a given workflow and thus we see a derived requirement for a report. Or we have a business requirement dictating that the solution run on mobile devices but no indication of the required phone platforms, so we may derive the platform requirement based on the types of phones issued by our company. Once we identify the derived requirements, we can assess them with appropriate stakeholders and use them as yet another input to our decision making.

Organization direction

Last, but not least, we need to take broader organizational goals into account when capturing solution attributes that drive architecture. Project architecture decisions should not be made in a vacuum. While I may be able to flip a coin to decide between two perfectly viable ways to expose a web service interface for a given project, I should always be considering enterprise standards and practices when making my selections.

For instance, you may work for a company which has a strict "build instead of buy" strategy for software because of the high caliber of on-staff developers and a consistent need to deeply customize any commercial product. If that is the case, I may have a soft requirement to choose the framework technology over the more rigid commercial product.

Solution decisions also must take into account the short term and long term investments of an organization. Am I basing my solution on a technology that is under consideration for deprecation? Do we have the staff on hand with expertise in a particular product? These are valid considerations that can sway us from a seemingly ideal technology to an alternate choice.

Deciding upon your architecture strategy

Once the core requirements are set forth, we as architects can begin to craft the major patterns that make up the solution architecture. It would be a grave mistake to jump directly from requirements gathering to a product selection. You would never say "BizTalk is the choice for all our solutions", unless you were clinically insane or ate paint chips as a child. Likewise, it would be foolish to jump immediately to a custom solution unless you had evaluated and eliminated packaged applications as a viable choice. Your architecture strategy should be driven by a full assessment of the architecture quality attributes required by your solution.

Turning requirements into patterns is beyond the scope of this book. That said, there are key aspects you need to decide upon before choosing a particular product for implementation. These areas of focus may include:

- How is data shared? In real time or via batch processing? Is data copied between systems or should we use a shared database?
- Does the system do most work synchronously or asynchronously?
- How do users interact with the system? Via services, mobile devices, command line?

- Is a centralized workflow needed to span the applications that comprise the system, or is distributed logic with queue-based transport the best choice?

- Should the application be deployed in one location, multiple locations, or in the cloud?

- Does the solution require a single security domain or is identity federation needed?

- What types of **service level agreements** (**SLAs**) are expected by the client and can I capture relevant measurement data?

The framework described next can help you capture the data points necessary to answer these questions and choose the right product to solve your business problem.

Framework dimensions

Our evaluation criteria have been segmented into four central categories:

1. **Solution design**: This area focuses on dimensions that shape the broad design patterns that make up our solution.

2. **Solution development**: This topic addresses what it will take to construct the solution.

3. **Solution operations**: Here we highlight factors that influence how the solution will be maintained after it has been built.

4. **Organizational considerations**: These are facets of the solution that take enterprise standards and organization direction into account.

Each category contains a set of criteria along with a description of what those criteria help identify.

Solution design aspects

In this section, we look at characteristics relevant to the overarching design of a solution. Once again, this list isn't exhaustive but it should provide you with a framework for thinking and steer you towards a particular implementation technology.

These data integration considerations touch upon a variety of needs in data sharing scenarios including how you receive data, how much of it you process, and what quality assurances are necessary.

Data integration considerations	
Software criteria	**Description**
Supports high volumes of data	Can a heavy throughput of data reliably flow through the software? While this characteristic is often dependent on other criteria mentioned below (for example: load balancing, latency), it should be a known aspect of any software solution. "High volume" may also be a subjective description. In some organizations, a high volume of data is thousands of records per day, whereas other organizations expect thousands of records per minute.
Handles large individual data sets	The raw size of a data set can greatly influence which software solution you select. Some products are tuned to process small data blocks: while others hungrily tackle megabytes, gigabytes, and terabytes of data all at once. If a particular software package is a perfect match for a solution except for its inability to process thousands of records at once, then maybe we can revisit the data processing requirements and bite off smaller chunks of data.
Offers guaranteed, at-least-once delivery	Reliable delivery is frequently a requirement of messaging solutions, but sometimes, this is a nice-to-have instead of must-have. If a particular piece of data does not reach a destination, can it be sent again from the source? For instance, few request/response query operations require guaranteed delivery since transmission failures can be instantly retried. Asynchronous operations are more directly associated with guaranteed delivery. Also, guaranteeing once-only delivery is something that has to be explicitly designed for. While some tools do support this, this is also where we can architect an idempotent interface where we can send data over and over again, without negatively impacting the data context.
Able to access a wide variety of data repositories	A thorough analysis of the data requirements will surface the range of data sources that our solution needs to leverage. Our chosen software platform should be able to easily interact with the full spectrum of data sources that make up our solution architecture.

Data integration considerations

Software criteria	Description
Able to access a wide variety of target system APIs	Much like the preceding criteria, we need to uncover which systems we need to interact with and determine whether a given software product is capable of consuming the interface offered by the dependent system. This could be a web service interface, native interface, or a protocol interface such as MSMQ.
Works with batches of data	We looked at large data sets and this criterion is an extension of that. Regardless of the batch size, we need to know if a particular software platform can easily unpack a collection of data records and process them individually. Sometimes, records are batched out of convenience to reduce network traffic and sometimes they are batched because the records are all part of a related transaction. Ideally, our software platform can treat a batch of data differently depending on this distinction.
Accepts real-time data input	The timeliness of data processing is a foundational aspect of most solutions. If we are building an application that demands a real-time (that is, not batch) interface, then we have clear choices as to which type of product to leverage.
Offers data quality features (de-duplication, format standardization)	When sharing data between systems, we may need to apply a series of data quality rules that cleanse and improve the integrity of the data. This could involve removing incomplete data, eliminating duplicate records, enriching the data with information from external sources, and standardizing data field formats such as phone number.

Security is often one of those things that we cannot compromise during application design. We may have to comply not only with organizational standards, but those of regulatory bodies. Here are some criteria that touch on user profiles, data in transit, and data at rest.

Security considerations

Software criteria	Description
Enables enterprise-wide and cross-organization users to access the application	It is important to know if the product can support enterprise directories for authentication and authorization so that we can establish reusable security groups and wide access.
Includes Single Sign-On capabilities	If your solution demands access to systems and repositories that span security domains, then having an **SSO** product available will be a lifesaver. A strong SSO product will enable you to securely map credentials from one domain to another and seamlessly access cross-domain resources.
Offers range of authentication mechanisms to invoke operations	This applies to items at an API level or even access to the application itself. If we need to be able to authenticate users against a default Windows domain, or also need alternate ways to prove identity (for example: certificates, HTTP basic authentication) then we have to choose a product with this capability baked in.
Provides authorization controls to invoke operations	Ideally, there is at least a coarse set of knobs that we can fiddle with in a software package, which allow us to restrict capabilities by the role of the user. Some software packages may allow granular access only through customization.
Provides authentication and authorization options for securing administrative aspects of application	Depending on the scope of your solution, you may need to provision administrative functions to distinct sets of users. For instance, you might have one set of users who can administer the entire application, while others can only modify specific settings. If your solution demands this, you will need to consider this capability in the available software packages.
Has compartmentalized components with independent security boundaries	One way to reduce the attack surface of a solution is to partition not only the application tiers, but also the modules within a given tier. A component that requires elevated permissions could be isolated on one server while other components running with least privilege can execute on additional servers.

Security considerations	
Software criteria	**Description**
Enables secure storage of configuration or reference values	When we extract volatile data values from code and store them in external configuration repositories, we make our code easier to maintain. However, these pieces of data may contain sensitive information such as passwords and connection strings. Whether embedded in the code or stored in a configuration repository, this data should be encrypted or isolated from prying eyes.

The project's need for exception handling can often be evaluated late in a delivery cycle, which is unfortunate. This is one of those areas to ask our clients about early on and get an understanding of the business need when system, data, or logical errors arise. Based on the expected types and volume of errors, we may lean one way or another on which product to leverage.

Error handling considerations	
Software criteria	**Description**
Failures within the system are captured in predictable way	Even the best of us write code that fails. What we hope to have is a software platform that enables a graceful handling of exceptions occurring in native components, custom components or infrastructure. If the product relies on a database to operate, what happens if the database temporarily goes offline? Or, what if you deploy custom code to the application and an uncaught exception flows up to the application? Knowing how a product handles failure goes a long way in understanding how to build for exceptions and prepare future solution administrators.
There are limited single points of failure	We all hope to build solutions that do not have any one component that can bring the entire system down. When we look at underlying platform products, we need to understand where things can go wrong and which components can or cannot survive a failure.
Failures in dependent systems are handled consistently	When we built systems that rely on other systems, we must prepare for the event when those dependent systems become unavailable. How does a particular software product resolve downstream failures?

Error handling considerations

Software criteria	Description
Includes facilities to monitor the system and configure alerts	If a product does not offer a management dashboard itself, hopefully it should minimally provide an instrumentation layer that enterprise monitoring tools can tap into so as to actively track the health of the application.

There are always a few uncategorized design aspects that touch upon how a solution can be designed to be maintainable and best leverage existing enterprise investments. Here we have a few items that address loose coupling of components, how operations can execute, and establishing transactions across system boundaries.

General design considerations

Software criteria	Description
Includes a modular set of components with a clear separation of concerns	Software products are at their best when they have clearly defined modules that work both independently and seamlessly with each other. When looking at your solution requirements, you may see aspects that are a perfect match for components of one product while other aspects are ideal for another. If those products are built well, then leveraging the best of each should be possible. Having modular components also means that changes can be made to one component without being forced to deploy or test all of the other ones.
Has functional flexibility and can be built for change	Sometimes a solution satisfies a very fixed need with static business rules and firm interfaces. However, that scenario appears to be an exception rather than a rule. If our solution requirements outline a very dynamic business space where interfaces may undergo change or business logic is susceptible to update, then we need a software product that can accommodate such demands.
Leverages asynchronous model for processing	Asynchronous processing allows us to execute operations without forcing the initiator to wait for a response. This is valuable for long-running processes, activities that can be handled at a later time, or broadcasting data to an unknown number of interested parties.

General design considerations	
Software criteria	**Description**
Is capable of enlisting both local and distributed transactions	If our solution requirements call for us to synchronize the update to multiple repositories then we have to make sure our software is capable of participating in transactions that potentially span application boundaries.

Solution delivery aspects

The big picture solution aspects cannot be the sole factor in choosing a particular implementation technology. We must also seriously consider how well the technology aids in the rapid and successful implementation of our architecture blueprint. A product that looks perfect from a design perspective may introduce an unnecessary burden on the implementation team.

First off, we should look at our development resources and consider if the technology at hand is something that existing .NET or SQL Server developers can quickly adopt, and what sort of physical environments are needed to perform development. While BizTalk Server is a mature product, it can still be difficult to find top-notch talent in the open market. For new products like Windows Server AppFabric and Windows Azure, there is an obvious gap in the marketplace until these offerings become more commonplace and skills can be developed. Consider whether you need, product expertise or have the internal skill set available to grow the expertise in house.

Resource considerations	
Software criteria	**Description**
Skilled developers can be acquired for this technology	This criterion relates to both in-house developers and contract developers. Do we have the resources within the organization and are they even available to work on this solution? If the answer to either question is no, then how easily can we get external expertise?
If a new technology for the organization, the skill can be picked up by existing developers	Many of the products in Microsoft's application platform have similar development paradigms. Someone with expertise in the .NET Framework could quickly understand the development process for products like Windows Communication Foundation or StreamInsight.

Resource considerations

Software criteria	Description
Solution components can be run on a standard developer workstation	Most software can be installed on a typical developer computer but we should know early on if we require centralized server software, virtual machines, or 64-bit hardware.

Once we evaluate the compatibility of products with our resource demands, we can look at how well a technology helps us actually build the solution we want. This includes topics such as the richness of the development toolset, maturity of the community ecosystem, and the existence of solid test and automation capabilities.

Construction considerations

Software criteria	Description
Robust set of tools / IDEs available to construct the solution	New technologies typically have development and administrative tooling that is fairly basic. It seems that the priority of the software vendor is on the underlying component maturity and tooling is not a primary concern on the initial release. That said, the proposed solution may not require significant coding and thus advanced tooling is ideal, but not required.
Rich ecosystem of plug-ins, community code, tutorials and blogs to help developers	When building solutions on a given product we always hope to follow best practices and leverage lessons learned by others. This is where established, mature technologies have advantages over newer, less investigated ones.
Written in an expressive language that accomplishes tasks in limited lines of code	Ideally, developers do not have to spend a majority of time writing excessive lines of code to complete simple tasks.
Integrates with a variety of source control systems	A software solution can be comprised of code, configuration files, scripts, images, and a host of other artifacts. We should understand how to collect all of the solution artifacts and centrally manage them in a durable source control system.
Allows developers to build and execute thorough unit tests	The cost of testing and bug fixes goes up as a project progresses towards completion. A software product should enable straightforward unit testing of each component.
Can be set up to run in an automated build environment	A solution may be made up of a number of software packages and components, so automating the regular solution built during construction can free up resources to focus on more strategic tasks.

Solution operation aspects

Even after we have satisfied our design and implementation needs, we absolutely must consider the operational aspects of the proposed solution. Although the project delivery team inevitably moves on to other work after a successful deployment, the actual solution may remain in a production state for years on end. If we have a grand architecture that was constructed cleanly, but is an absolute nightmare to maintain, then we have not delivered a successful project. In fact, many of these operational concerns actually directly affect our original solution design. These factors, which are often gathered through the non-functional requirements, have a noticeable effect on the architecture of the system.

Performance considerations address various topics ranging from application business process performance to data volume and latency.

Performance considerations

Software criteria	Description
Key Performance Indicators (KPIs) can be captured and monitored	KPIs could relate to the business capabilities built into the application or KPIs could refer to the performance of the application itself. If the business client wants to monitor the efficiencies of their processes, then we will want to choose a product that lets us easily capture and modify key business metrics.
Can produce sub-second latency for both simple and complex request/ reply operations	Latency requirements will factor into the overall design of the solution, but this also relates to the operations of the solution. Can performance be tuned in the production infrastructure?
Predictable behavior during both standard and non-standard volumes of data	Many integration solutions have to deal with spikes in data processing load at both regular and unexpected intervals. If this is possible in your environment, then you want to make sure that the software can gracefully handle floods of data without crashing.

The availability needs of the client have direct impacts on which product we should choose. How mission-critical is the application? Can we afford for the system to be down for a significant amount of time? What is the consequence if we lose some data when recovering the application? Honest answers to these questions, which typically mean fighting the urge to over-inflate the importance of a given application, will help us direct appropriate attention to availability attributes.

Availability considerations

Software criteria	Description
Natively includes load balancing capabilities	You may not need the software to contain its own load balancing mechanism if you have existing infrastructure to distribute work among machines. However, if you are dealing with a high volume environment with many long running processes, you may benefit from a technology that efficiently leverages the available resources across software nodes.
Can systematically fail over to other active servers	This also is a factor in solution design. While it may be quite useful to leverage a software platform that automatically switches execution to additional nodes when a given node fails, we may also want to define a stateless design. If we limit the state that each node must maintain, then we limit points of failure and can embrace automatic node switching.
Includes data backup routines	We may have to back up application data persisted in the software or back up the artifacts and metadata that comprise the software solution.
Support zero message loss in the product or through storage mirroring	If a software product stores application data (even while in transit), then there may be a business requirement to avoid any data loss in the event of system failure. Accomplishing this can be challenging, so we need to determine the real need and see if the software platform can accommodate this.

The day-in-the-life maintenance of an application is not the most exciting thing to mull over during project planning, but paying attention to this aspect is the greatest gift you can give to a system administrator. What are some of the general things you can do to make the maintenance of this application as straightforward as possible? We must consider the tools we provide, the way we have separated our components, and the means for making incremental changes to the application over time.

General operation considerations

Software criteria	Description
Rich set of support tools and interfaces	Strong administrative tools could be graphical in nature or through a well-defined programmatic interface. We may not want to teach administrators a brand new tool, but rather leverage existing skill sets or enterprise configuration tools. This would factor in to our product choice.
Clear strategy for versioning system components	If a product is built with a clear separation of concerns, it will be easier to make isolated changes. That said, if a solution is expected to undergo regular changes then we have to fully grasp the ways to consistently deploy new versions.
Defined extensibility points	Extensibility can be built both into the software itself and into the system built on top of the software.
Built-in instrumentation and tracing	Many organizations have existing application monitoring tools and it is important to find out if a particular software package can feed its data and system events into such tools.

Organizational aspects

You would think that after you took your project's design, development, and operations into account you have done proper due-diligence prior to architecting a solution. However, a good solutions architect always keeps an eye on organization strategy to make sure that what they are proposing for an isolated solution is in line with the broad vision of the company.

Here are a few things to consider when switching perspective from a project-centric viewpoint to an enterprise one.

Organization considerations

Software criteria	Description
Is sufficient for both temporary solutions and long-lived solutions	Sometimes we build solutions that are meant to temporarily solve a given problem. Maybe the organization is planning a massive system upgrade but needs an intermediate solution to a particular pain point. Conversely, we may be designing a solution that is expected to remain in operation for 4 to 6 years. If we look at the planned lifespan of the solution, this can help us decide which product offers the lowest total cost of ownership over that duration.
Includes support from Microsoft for solutions implemented with product	Product support is a critical component of enterprise systems. When you build a solution on top of a packaged application, you often get more vendor support than when you build a solution on a base framework.
Leverages existing software investments within the organization	These existing investments could be in employees or other software packages. Does the product use an underlying database technology already deployed at the organization? Or, is it an additional module of a product already in heavy use?
Limited impact on budget as introduction of this technology can be built upon existing environments	This relates to the prior criteria. The cost of software that underlies a solution is frequently a factor in product selection and ideally we can share existing infrastructure.
Complies with "buy vs. build" strategy of the organization	If you have an expert staff of developers on site and frequently find yourself customizing packaged products, then your organization may prefer building solutions vs. restricting themselves to packaged products. On the other hand, if an organization prefers to fit their needs into the capabilities of package applications so as to reduce ownership cost and accelerate development, then a heavier evaluation weighting should go to products with fixed boundaries and limited customization options.

Organization considerations

Software criteria	Description
Matches the risk tolerance of the organization	Some companies love being early adopters of technology and getting the chance to take advantage of the latest products and capabilities. For such companies, the risks of deploying new technologies are outweighed by the business benefits those technologies offer. However, other companies have a "service pack 1" mentality where only mature products are introduced into the organization landscape.
Provides sufficient speed to market for new solutions	We cannot make a blanket statement that building solutions with "Product X" is faster than building with "Product Y." This all depends on the solution. That said, we want to evaluate our candidate software choices by looking at which software allows us to build (and change!) a given solution as quickly as possible.

Applying the framework

So what do we do with all this information? In each of the "pattern chapters" of this book you will find us using this framework to evaluate the use case at hand and proposing viable candidate architectures. We will have multiple candidate architectures for each scenario and based on which underlying product is the best fit, go down the path of explaining that specific solution.

So how do we determine the best fit? As we evaluate each candidate architecture, we'll be considering the preceding questions and determining if the product that underlies our solution meets the majority of the criteria for the use case. Using the next representation, we'll grade each candidate architecture in the four major decision framework categories. The architecture that is most compatible with the use case objectives will win.

Design	Delivery	Operations	Organization

Summary

A common methodology for evaluating solution requirements against product capabilities will go a long way towards producing consistent, reliable results. Instead of being biased towards one product for every solution, or simply being unaware of a better match in another software offering, we can select the best software depending on its key capabilities for our client's solution.

In the next set of chapters, we'll introduce you to these core Microsoft application platform technologies and give you a taste as to what they are good at. While these primers are no more than cursory introductions to products, they should give you the background necessary to understand their ideal usage scenarios, strengths, and weaknesses.

2

Windows Communication Foundation and Windows Workflow 4.0 Primer

Windows Communication Foundation (WCF) and **Windows Workflow Foundation (WF)** were first introduced with the release of the .NET Framework 3.0 in November 2006. The goal of WCF was to introduce a framework that aids in building distributed applications that leverages web services, MSMQ interfaces, and remoting with a consistent, service-oriented, communication platform. This platform abstracts the communication details (including transport, encoding, encryption, and authentication) from implementation logic. Because of this abstraction, we can often modify service behavior through configuration changes without impacting existing logic or compiled code. WCF controls WS-* implementation, distributed transactions, security, and serialization in a manageable fashion, and in a way that is relatively consistent across service platforms. With Windows Workflow, the concept of designer-based workflow was brought to the mass developer audience. This allowed for a drag-and-drop based coding experience within the confines of the well known Visual Studio designer.

The developer adoption of WCF as a replacement for traditional web services was widespread while, in contrast, WF lacked a robust hosting environment and failed to impress in terms of out-of-the-box features. With the release 3.5 and 3.5 SP1 of the .NET framework, new features like **workflow services** (exposing Workflows as WCF services), basic correlation, and persistence were added and brought more attention specifically to workflow. This also increased the number of possible use cases, but still lacked a real attention-grabbing feature or a scalable hosting environment.

Many questions about the advantages of Workflow have disappeared with the recent release of the .NET 4.0 framework. Streamlined, model-driven workflow development is now at the reach of the mass developer market, reducing the need for complex custom-coded solutions for workflow scenarios. Now is the time to take a first look at Workflow or re-evaluate this platform, as considerable improvements have been made to increase both functionality and usability. Windows Workflow is now mainstream.

In this chapter, we will discuss the following topics:

- The basics of Windows Communication Foundation and Windows Workflow Foundation
- What is new with WCF and Workflow in the .NET 4.0 release
- The typical scenarios to use WCF and Workflow
- A Windows Workflow exposed as a WCF Service

What does this technology do?

While the common goal of WCF and WF was to provide a starting framework for developers working on custom solutions, the specific implementation scenarios for each are very different.

Distributed systems have distinct problems. *Distributed*, by definition means *spread-out*; in a programming sense distributed means spread-out but also cross system and even cross platform. Distributed systems are different from typical standalone applications in that they need to interact with other systems in order to function. This brings new challenges including: how these systems communicate, how security is enforced, and what happens if the system is down, just to name a few. The goal of Windows Communication Foundation is to simplify this process. WCF is just that, a foundation for communication, typically for distributed systems. The goal is to provide a configuration-based approach for systems to communicate with each other under a common framework, which once learned, will allow a developer to streamline communication in order to focus on the implementation logic. WCF provides a framework for developers to leverage specific framework elements inside a service configuration file and keep their accomplish common tasks like security and data transport. This is made possible by leveraging the framework built into the .NET 3.0 and higher framework. Using the framework greatly reduces the amount of custom coding needed for common tasks, while providing the ability to extend on the framework when needed to cover additional scenarios. As later .NET releases have been made, more features have become available in the framework thus, extending the reach of WCF.

While the power of WCF is increasing and basic scenario implementation is being simplified, the basic fundamentals of WCF remain the same since it was first released. The basics of WCF configuration are the ABCs:

1. **Address**: When a WCF service is running, this is the destination it will listen on for inbound requests. This location is created and monitored by the host process that is running the WCF Service. Typically this is IIS or a custom-built windows service.

2. **Binding**: Binding represents how the service will talk with outside systems in terms of transport, security, protocol, and other options. Inside the bindings, behaviors are defined that govern what will happen to the data once it is received. This could involve how to serialize the data, how to decrypt or encrypt it, or perform any other logic that is needed once the information is received into the service. While this is configuration-based to enable these features, the code to do it is not. In the bindings, we reference either framework assemblies or custom-written .NET code. The binding just outlines what code to use at runtime.

3. **Contract**: The contract outlines the exchange pattern and specifically, what data the service will exchange. It lists the available operations of the service and outlines the type of exchange.

These are the three cornerstones of WCF. They highlight how to interact with the outside world and are independent of the implementation logic of the service. Once this is mastered, the pattern is consistent for any WCF-based interface.

Windows Workflow Foundation (WF) was introduced at the same time as WCF. The purpose of WF was to solve a very different problem than WCF. WF is designed to easily enable workflow-based applications inside Windows. Workflows are typically thought of as a sequential control flow model with one task after another followed in order. WF can support the sequential task model as well as more complex state machine (pre-.NET 4.0) and a Flowchart (.NET 4.0) control models. The **State Machine Workflow** contains event-based flow control, based on the state of the workflow allowing moving from one execution block to another and back again. The **Flow Chart Workflow** is used to define a static, non-sequential process flow.

Modeling applications as a workflow using a supplied framework has several advantages. They are outlined in the following list:

- **Designer-based problem solving**: The designer inside Visual Studio provides a common platform for workflow development. This allows virtually anyone who knows WF to be able to read and understand any workflow process. As the model is graphical, the learning curve is easier in order to accomplish otherwise complex tasks.

- **Consistent approach to solving a problem**: Once a specific workflow or custom activity is written, it can be leveraged again if the implementation is the same. What makes this different from a custom-coded solution is that the developer needs to know very little about the solution in order to understand its use as workflow is a **UI**-based model.

- **Leverage the framework**: Using workflow and the supplied activities lowers the amount of custom code, reduces the time to market, and streamlines the testing process as much of the code is build into the .NET Framework.

- **Workflow services**: Workflows can be exposed as WCF Services. This combines the power and flexibility of WCF with the features of WF.

While it is always possible to custom code any solution coded in Windows Workflow, these advantages should outweigh those of a custom C# or VB.NET solution.

In the past, the existence of a supportable, scalable host for workflow was an issue. With .NET 4.0, significant enhancements have been made to the Windows Application Server Role to enable scalable WCF and workflow hosting. This is known as **Windows Server AppFabric** and will be covered in more detail in *Chapter 3, Windows Server AppFabric Primer*.

 David Chappell's Whitepaper is a good resource for more information on Windows Workflow. It can be found here:

`http://www.davidchappell.com/TheWorkflowWay--Chappell.pdf`

Highlights of the latest release

With significant investments made in the area of workflow, the following impressive changes outlined were drastically needed to increase adoption. If you have looked at Workflow in the past, the .NET 4.0 Workflow release bears little resemblance to past releases. With dramatic change comes the obvious pitfall of backward compatibility.

Windows Communication Foundation enhancements

The following enhancements are made to WCF in the .NET 4.0 release:

- **Easier configuration**: Developers do not like to spend time learning and setting up configuration. In WCF 4.0, default values can be set allowing services to be run without any service-specific confirmation files.
- **Content-based routing service**: WCF now has the ability to route inbound requests though information in the **SOAP** header or actual data inside the message, based on an **XPath** expression. In addition to this basic routing, error handling has the ability to send requests to alternative destinations in the event of a communication issue.
- **Enhanced MSMQ channel**: The MSMQ channel supports peek-and-lock functionality allowing a WCF process to lock a message, read it, and place it back onto the queue in the event that it cannot be processed. This is important when working with some workflow scenarios.
- **WS-Discovery**: Support for ad hoc discovery through a UDP multi-cast channel on a local subnet or proxy-managed discovery on a large network.
- **Greater REST support**: Support for HTTP caching and HTTP error handling.

Windows Workflow Foundation enhancements

The following enhancements are made to WF in the .NET 4.0 release:

- **Workflow service improvements**: Workflow services are workflows exposed as a **WCF service**. These services are typically long running and durable in nature. Workflow services have undergone major improvement in the .NET 4.0 release. Improvements have been made in the following areas:
  - New messaging activities to send and receive messages into and out of workflows, all leveraging WCF under the covers.
  - Transaction support allowing transactions to flow into workflows.
  - Correlation of messages in long-running workflow and between workflows, now supports both protocol-based and content-based routing.
  - Add Service Reference now generates a typed custom workflow activity allowing for a drag-and-drop designer experience for calling external services.

- **Declarative Model**: Workflows, including workflow services, can now be completely written in **Extensible Application Markup Language (XAML)**. XAML can then either be compiled into a typed assembly or executed as XAML.

- **Flowchart flow style**: A new style of workflow has been introduced called the **Flowchart**. This allows for a non-sequential, flow-control design experience.

- **Simplified persistence**: Workflow state can be persisted to a SQL store of choice, allowing for instance management and durable delays. Workflows can be stopped, started, suspended, resumed, or terminated while leveraging the durable delay workflows, which can react to time-based events.

- **Enhanced library**: Past releases of Workflow saw only a handful of out-of-the-box activities. With the .NET 4.0 release, developers now have a rich set of activities to leverage. Some of the new highlights include activities for transactions, data access, flow control (such as `Do-While`, `For-Each`), parallel execution, persistence, and error handling (including `Try-Catch`).

- **Removed state machine support**: Support for building state machines has not been carried over to the initial .NET 4.0 release of Workflow. This is being considered for a later release and in the meantime, the Flowchart workflow should be used to model this behavior.

- **Overall designer experience**: The workflow authoring experience inside Visual Studio has improved greatly with support for **IntelliSense** — the addition of workflow Variables, Arguments and Imports tab, enhanced bread crumb support, and overall performance improvements.

Enhancements to both technologies

The following enhancements are made to WCF and WF in the .NET 4.0 release:

- **Event Tracing for Windows (ETW) events**: Event Tracing for Windows is known as ETW. It is a highly efficient, kernel-level, windows operating tracing API. It can be turned on and off (early) giving developers the ability to troubleshoot WCF and WF issues with greater ease. Workflow and WCF now support tracing using ETW.

- **Performance Counter improvements**: The use of performance counts in the past .NET releases came at the cost of system performance. Improvements have been made in this area to limit the impact of collecting data via performance counters.

Typical use cases

Windows Communication Foundation and Windows Workflow Foundation follow different use case scenarios, but both share the fact that they are frameworks. Both WCF and Workflow are used as part of a custom-built solution. While some third-party vendors leverage and re-host these technologies, the use cases outlined here assume that these technologies are going to be used as the foundation of a new application. Use cases fit into one of these three categories: WCF, WF, and WF Services.

Windows Communication Foundation use cases

Windows Communication Foundation is striving to become the implementation framework of choice for distributed service-based scenarios. Examples include a company implementing a company-wide **Service-Oriented Architecture (SOA)** to offer enterprise services for tasks such as tax calculations, shipping quotes, or inventory checks. Using WCF is about approaching different distributed scenarios in a standardized way, increasing supportability, maintainability, and reducing time to market.

The WCF-based solution offers complete flexibility in the communication patterns used on all services, given the configuration-based approach. This would allow the same service implementation to be used on a client desktop—with no encryption, inside the network with encryption, or over the internet—totally secured, all with no changes to the service code. This is drastically different from a traditional ASMX service that relies heavily on IIS or an application written for .NET Remoting. While WCF Services are commonly hosted inside IIS, this is not a requirement.

Windows Workflow Foundation use cases

Windows Workflow Foundation provides a foundation for building workflow-based processes through a rich, designer experience. With a robust designer experience, it provides a model-driven approach towards workflow development. While nearly anything built inside the workflow could be custom coded in raw .NET, the goal is to make the experience simpler, repeatable, and quicker than using raw .NET. The designer experience is typically hosted inside Visual Studio, but it can be hosted inside custom applications as well, allowing Independent Software Vendors (ISVs) the ability to build on top of the workflow foundation.

Workflow processes are usually long running processes that interact with different internal or external systems and sometimes require human intervention to approve or reject specific steps in the process. Some typical workflow processes include a new hire process, outlining a document review process, and aggregating external service calls into a single process. These three workflows could be built using Windows Workflow and then hosted inside a custom .NET application, SharePoint, or simply a console application. This abstracts the core workflow logic from the hosting application. As Workflow is a foundation, other applications can build on top of it to leverage the existing workflow functionality. New features in the Windows Application Server Role known as AppFabric will add another hosting option for workflows, providing greater insight into the running mechanics of the workflows themselves.

Example solution

To get you up and running with workflow services, let's set up a simple example. This will be a Windows Workflow that is exposed as a WCF service. This example will use Visual Studio to host the workflow and expose WCF endpoints. The service will accept a simple string and return an updated string.

1. Create the new project inside Visual Studio 2010.
    ° Go to **File | New Project**.
    ° Select **Workflow** on the tab on the right under **Visual C#**.
    ° Select the **WCF Workflow Service Application** project type.
    ° Name it to IntroToWFService.
    ° Click on **OK**.

This will create a blank project and solution. `Service1.xamlx` is the base workflow service file created with the project.

2. Create local variables to store the inbound text and set the outbound text of the service.

   ° Click on the Sequence shape to ensure it is the active window.

   ° Click on the **Variables** tab on the bottom left.

   ° Add a variable named `InternalInputText` of type `String` to store the original inbound text.

   ° Add a variable named `InternalOutputText` of type `String` to create the response string to be returned from the service.

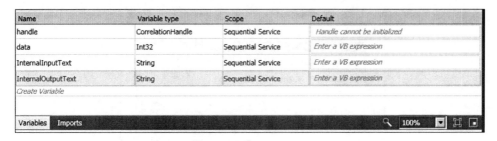

3. Define the Request and Response Contract because this is how this service talks to the outside world.

   ° On the ReceiveRequest shape, Click on **View Message**.

   ° Select **Parameters**.

   ° Add a new parameter named `InputText` as type `String` and assign it to `InternalInputText`.

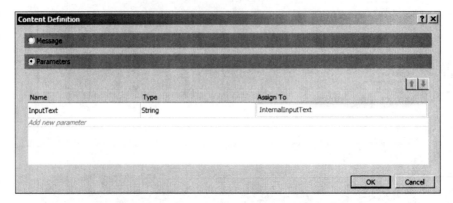

   ° Click on **OK**.

   ° Do the same for `SendResponse` but name the parameter to `OutputText` and set it to a value of `InternalOutputText`.

4. Set the output text. This step will create the output variable the service will return.

   ° Drag an Assign shape from the **Primitives** section of the toolbox onto the surface between the **ReceiveRequest** and the **SendResponse** shapes.

   ° In the **To** box, set the value to `InternalOutputText`.

   ° In the **Enter the VB expression** box type the following: `"You said"` & `InternalInputText` as shown in the screenshot.

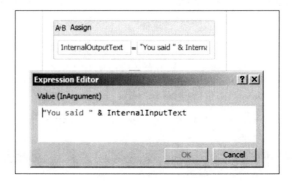

5. Build, run, and test the project.

    ° Press *F5* to build and run the project in debug mode; Visual Studio will show the **Directory Listing** of the project running on port `1110`.

    ° Click on `Service1.xamlx` when the page loads to view the service details.

    ° Open `WcfTestClient.exe` located at: `C:\Program Files\ Microsoft Visual Studio 10.0\Common7\IDE\`.

    ° Right-click on **My Service Projects** and add the newly started service. The default address should be `http:// localhost:1110/Service1.xamlx`. This is the address the workflow service is listening on and a request should be sent to.

    ° Double-click on **GetDate()**.

    ° Set the **Value** field to: `Test Message`.

    ° Click on **Invoke**.

    ° This should return the response: "**You said Test Message**".

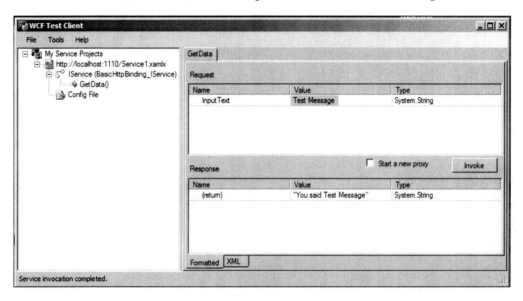

The above sample is an example of a simple workflow service. Once the framework is in place for receiving and sending the request and response data, the internal implementation can be easily changed by dragging new shapes into the surface. This can allow the implementation logic to be changed without impacting the exposed contract.

Summary

In this chapter, we took a look at the ABCs of WCF along with some basics of WCF and Workflow. We briefly reviewed the new features in WCF and Workflow that are available in the .NET 4.0 release. Lastly, we saw a workflow service in action in a simple request-response scenario. Further chapters will explore the hosting of WCF and workflow solutions, and dive deeper into the best use scenarios of these frameworks.

3
Windows Server AppFabric Primer

An application server hosts business logic (applications or services) in a multitier architecture and provides a rich set of capabilities for building robust, high-performing solutions. From an end-user standpoint, an application server needs to satisfy a set of criteria such as offering a highly available hosting environment for web and desktop applications, enabling durable storage through technologies such as message queues or databases, and providing enterprise monitoring and management infrastructure. In addition, the platform should provide an easy development and deployment framework so that the application server is compelling enough for a user.

Today, Windows Server provides several rich capabilities, some of which have already been mentioned above. Recently, Microsoft strengthened the Windows application server offering by making available a set of key enhancements which will provide unified hosting and monitoring for WCF and WF applications. In addition to this capability (known during its pre-release cycle as *Dublin*), the new application server will provide a distributed cache, originally codenamed Velocity. The distributed cache feature provides a performance benefit (latency and throughput) to applications by caching different .NET types and reducing the load on the data tier. Collectively, these new capabilities for Windows Server platform are known as **Windows Server AppFabric**.

With the introduction of Windows Server 2008, Microsoft introduced a new feature called **Server Manager**. Server Manager enables easy setup and configuration of a Windows Server 2008 machine through quick provisioning for the target purpose — be it that of a domain controller, a Web Server, DNS Server, an Application Server, or any of its other out-of-the-box roles. The idea of role-based server configuration is nothing more than just simplifying the setup of a server to perform complex tasks by aligning Windows' features together into understandable groupings. The new enhancements to Windows Server will be packaged as an update to the Windows application server Role.

This primer will focus on Windows Server AppFabric and the enhancements being made to the Windows application server role as part of the .NET 4.0 release.

What does this technology do?

In addition to being an operating system platform, Windows Server provides features such as **Microsoft Message Queuing (MSMQ)**, **Microsoft Distributed Transaction Coordinator (MSDTC)**, and **Internet Information Services (IIS)** for hosting ASP.NET applications and performance counters that monitor infrastructure; all of which make it easy to host web, desktop services and applications. The WCF framework is slowly becoming the de facto technology for distributed applications. Windows Workflow Foundation (WF), as a technology, enables automating long running processes, which could involve human and software interaction. Both WCF and WF have undergone improvements in the 4.0 release of the .NET Framework.

At its core, Windows Server is Microsoft's application server. Windows Server runs applications like IIS, custom .NET components, and Web Services. When adding the existing application server role inside Windows Server, the .NET Framework is added with the option to also install IIS. The intent of this role is to run custom applications containing .NET, WCF, WF, and WPF (Windows Presentation Foundation) code, run distributed services, interact with queues, and perform other typically distributed tasks across multiple servers. The initial server role on a Windows Server machine is somewhat limited. Prior to this release, it only provides basic hosting for WCF services inside IIS with limited tracking, monitoring, and management functionality. WF applications receive even less attention. To run a WF application, the user must define their own host, which may run inside IIS or as a part of a custom Windows service. Enabling the basic application server role's tracking options requires extensive knowledge of WCF and WF configuration files. In addition, the tracking models are different from WCF and WF, making knowledge of both essential in running complex systems.

With the .NET Framework 4.0 release, significant enhancements have been made to the framework to support enhanced tracking, monitoring, and management. To capitalize on these enhancements, Microsoft has built tooling and components to a Windows application role known as AppFabric. These enhancements include updates to the following core areas, as they relate to WCF and WF applications:

- Administration
- Scripting
- Hosting
- Monitoring
- Persistence

While these enhancements are targeted toward .NET 4.0-based applications, .NET 3.0 and 3.5 WCF and WF applications can run in this host as well albeit with some limitations.

Windows Server AppFabric core components

This section is split into two key topics—Application-server hosting and monitoring, and distributed cache.

Application-server hosting and monitoring

Windows Server AppFabric is a set of integrated technologies that makes it easier to build, scale, and manage web and composite applications that run on IIS. As outlined before, this adds key features in five areas. The following diagram gives a visual view of these outlined enhancements:

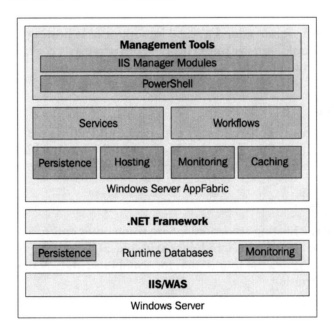

Details on each of these are further outlined.

Control

Windows Server AppFabric adds plug-ins into IIS to allow for control of WCF and WF applications in the same way as one controls websites today. With these controls, the following tasks are now easily exposed:

- Importing and exporting an application
- Stopping and restarting an application
- Turning the tracking on and off
- Setting up custom tracking profiles

Scripting

Windows Server AppFabric allows PowerShell integration of all commands seen in the UI. This is perfect for scripting of deployment and for ISVs that want to place commands into existing applications.

Hosting

Windows Server AppFabric added a scalable, supportable hosting environment to the Windows application server role. This host can serve as a container for WCF and WF applications written in .NET 4.0.

Monitoring

Monitoring has a greatly enhanced user experience and allows easy access to tracked data. This feature allows for various levels of out-of-the-box tracking on WCF and WF applications as well as creation of custom tracking profiles.

Persistence

Along with the basic hosting environment are some other enterprise-ready features made possible from a shared data store like SQL Server Express. With this persistence store, we have the foundation for scalability, high availability, instance re-start, and basic routing.

Distributed cache

With the advent of applications built for cloud scale, more data is accessed and consumed by applications. Further, usage of various smart mobile devices running these applications has surfaced bottlenecks in the mid-tier and/or database-tier.

One popular solution to this problem is the usage of distributed caching technologies, which provide a centralized store, elastic scale-out capabilities, and high availability with low response times even with increasing workloads. **Windows Server AppFabric Cache** is Microsoft's entry into the distributed cache market. It is an explicit, scalable, distributed, and in-memory application cache that can improve performance and scaling of .NET applications.

After installing and configuring the cache feature into a set of machines, the combined memory across all servers is made available as a unified cache. The set of servers now constitutes a cache cluster and can be used by application servers or web servers running on different machines to read or store items in the cache cluster. These application and web servers may also be referred to as cache-enabled applications or simply **cache clients**. These cache clients use a set of key-value pair based APIs to store and retrieve items from the cache. The stored value must either be a serializable .NET type or a byte array. The serialization happens at the cache-client side using the `NetDataContractSerializer` object, and the data is then sent over the wire and stored in the cache servers.

Internally, the **cache cluster** design uses a partitioned hashing algorithm by which various cached items are partitioned based on the "key" and stored on separate cache servers. The mapping information between the key and the actual cache servers containing the "value" is maintained in a routing table that is available to the cache client at connection time. When an item needs to be retrieved, cache clients hash the key value, look up the routing table, and contact the particular cache server. **High Availability (HA)** is provided as a configuration knob, where a secondary replica will be stored in another cache server. This is used for failover scenarios when the cache server holding the primary replica may go down. In a HA configuration, when an update is made to the primary cache server, the update must also be propagated synchronously to the secondary cache server, thereby increasing the latency. Depending on the data criticality in the workload, HA can be enabled selectively.

For example, one common problem when managing session state in ASP.NET is protection against state-server machine failures. Given that this session data does not need persistence but needs to be highly available, it can be stored in the cache cluster with HA enabled. Additionally, as the session data is now in a central cache cluster, users can connect to any web server (cache client) and have access to the session data. Thus, this avoids any sticky routing issues (a requirement to connect to the same web server where the session state is maintained).

One key benefit when using the distributed cache is being able to scale across several cache server nodes. Underneath, the distributed cache has a fabric layer used for data partitioning, rebalancing when nodes go down or are added, and replication in HA configuration. This layer is shared with the **SQL Azure** infrastructure, which scales to several nodes in the cloud.

The distributed cache feature has the following three sub-features:

- Caching services
- Cache client
- Cache administration

While installing the features, the cache client and cache service are a part of **Runtime Features** while the cache administration-based PowerShell V2 is a part of **Administration Tools**.

The caching service requires Microsoft .NET framework 4.0. The cache client can be compiled using Microsoft .NET framework 4.0 or 3.5 SP1.

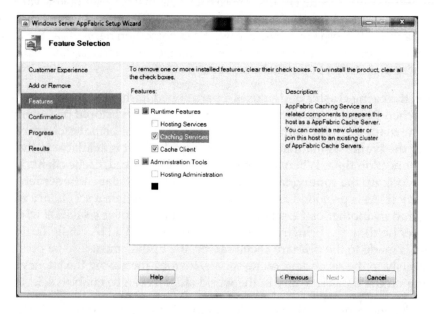

For example, on server machines A, B, and C, one could install and configure the cache service making them each individually a cache host. Here, the term **cache host** refers to the cache host Windows service. This process runs under the **NetworkService account**. This selection will install the AppFabric Caching Service and the required set of DLLs on the machine.

From a terminology standpoint, AppFabric Caching Service is referred to as the cache host and the servers A, B, and C are the cache servers. Cache servers can be physical machines or run on virtualized environments. Together, all these cache servers form a distributed cache cluster. The memory from all these cache servers will constitute the total memory available to cache-enabled applications. In order to make sure that the cluster is healthy, typical cluster management functionality can be performed by special cache hosts called **lead hosts**. These nodes, in addition to servicing data requests, also do a quorum heartbeat functionality—they check the health of their neighbors (normal cache hosts) and report back to the cluster manager, which is a component that runs on one of the cache servers.

The configuration information for the cluster can be maintained in SQL Server or in an XML file stored in a shared folder. When using SQL Server as the configuration store, the responsibility of lead hosts for cluster management is done by SQL Server. In such a configuration, SQL Server will manage the quorum and the cache hosts can focus on servicing the data requests. The concept of lead hosts is only required when an XML file is used as a configuration store.

An IT pro can use the administration tool to manage the cluster. This mode installs a set of PowerShell commandlets to start, stop, and configure the cache cluster. The cluster uses domain-based security for authentication. By default, security is enabled at transport-level with encryption on, which will affect performance.

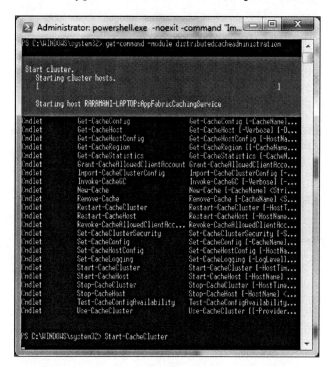

Applications accessing the cache cluster have to install the cache client sub-feature, reference the DLL(s), and rebuild the application. In addition, the client application needs to make some changes to `app.config` or `web.config`, by providing the list of cache servers and in the case of web applications, also change the ASP.NET session provider.

```
<configuration>
<!--configSections must be the FIRST element-->
  <configSections>
<!-- required to read the <dataCacheClient> element -->
    <section name="dataCacheClient"
      type="Microsoft.ApplicationServer.Caching.
              DataCacheClientSection,
      Microsoft.ApplicationServer.Caching.Core, Version=1.0.0.0,
      Culture=neutral, PublicKeyToken=31bf3856ad364e35"
      allowLocation="true"
      allowDefinition="Everywhere"/>
  </configSections>
  <dataCacheClient requestTimeout="15000" channelOpenTimeout="3000"
    maxConnectionsToServer="1">
    <localCache isEnabled="true" sync="TimeoutBased" ttlValue="300"
      objectCount="10000"/>
    <clientNotification pollInterval="300" maxQueueLength="10000"/>
    <hosts>
      <host name="CacheServer1" cachePort="22233"/>
      <host name="CacheServer2" cachePort="22233"/>
    </hosts>
    <securityProperties mode="Transport"
      protectionLevel="EncryptAndSign"/>
    <transportProperties connectionBufferSize="131072"
      maxBufferPoolSize="268435456" maxBufferSize="8388608"
      maxOutputDelay="2" channelInitializationTimeout="60000"
      receiveTimeout="600000"/>
  </dataCacheClient>
</configuration>
```

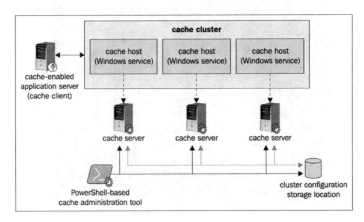

Here are a set of caching concepts and constructs that are important to understand:

Named cache

A named cache is a logical container, which an application can use to store objects. A named cache will span across all the machines in the cluster. The data units for each named cache are managed as partitions, which are then distributed across all the cache servers in the cluster. There is a "default" named cache. Named caches can only be created and configured from the admin tool. There are a set of explicit configurable policy settings that can be defined for named caches.

Region

A region is a container within a named cache that can be used by applications. Regions allow usage of bulk API, so that applications can get several objects as part of a single API call. Thus, this construct can be used for the "co-location" of related objects. For example, on a blog's discussion website there may be a need to show the topic objects and the related user-comments objects on a page load. There can be a region that is created for each day and the related objects stored within it. When the web page loads, it can invoke a single bulk API and get all the objects, improving the page-load response time. Also, objects within a region can be tagged and enumerated using these tags. For example, various blog articles can be tagged based on their user rating and the application can invoke all the "5 star" tagged articles.

Expiration

Objects in a named cache can have a lifetime expiry after which they can be deleted from the cache. Expiry is a configuration setting that can be maintained at a named cache. In addition, applications can also explicitly specify the expiry interval when storing objects.

Eviction

Eviction happens when there is memory pressure on the cache node, and this is done using the **least recently used (LRU)** scheme. Thresholds, or watermarks, are enforced to make sure that memory usage is buttoned-up across all cache hosts in the cluster. Initially, the expired objects are removed when a low watermark is reached. If the memory consumption still increases, and exceeds the high watermark threshold, objects are removed until the consumption goes back down to the low watermark. In cases when the available memory goes very low (less than 10%), the cache servers have a throttling behavior to reject writes until the memory gets back to normal state.

Local cache

Local cache is a feature that allows objects to be stored at the client side as a part of the application memory space. This is useful when there is a lot of repeated access of the same items. When storing in local cache, objects don't have to undergo the serialization and deserialization penalty. Local cache can be enabled by configuration or by code.

```
<!-- local cache enabled -->
<localCache isEnabled="true" sync="TimeoutBased" ttlValue="300"
  objectCount="10000"/>

//configure client with local cache enabled
int objectcount = 1000;
TimeSpan timeout = new TimeSpan(0, 0, 60);
DataCacheLocalCacheProperties localCacheSettings = new
    DataCacheLocalCacheProperties(objectcount, timeout,
    DataCacheLocalCacheInvalidationPolicy.NotificationBased);
long queuelength = 1000;
TimeSpan pollingInterval = new TimeSpan(0,0, 60);
DataCacheNotificationProperties notifySettings = new
    DataCacheNotificationProperties(queuelength, pollingInterval);
DataCacheFactoryConfiguration dcfc = new
                                    DataCacheFactoryConfiguration();
dcfc.LocalCacheProperties = localCacheSettings;
dcfc.NotificationProperties = notifySettings;
dcf = new DataCacheFactory(dcfc);
```

If local cache is enabled before retrieving cached objects from a cache host, the cache client application first checks whether the object exists locally. If it exists, the object is returned immediately to the application. If not, the object is fetched from the cache host and then stored in a deserialized form in the local cache.

There are two types of invalidation for local cache: timeout-based invalidation and notification-based invalidation. When the local cache is configured for timeout-based invalidation, the object is removed after the time interval expires. In case of notification-based invalidation, the application has a thread that polls the cache servers for any changes. If a particular item has changed, the local cache copy is invalidated. So the next access of the key will go to the cache tier to get the updated item value, which will then be be stored in local cache. The polling interval for synchronization can be configured.

The following figure illustrates cache clustering across cache hosts:

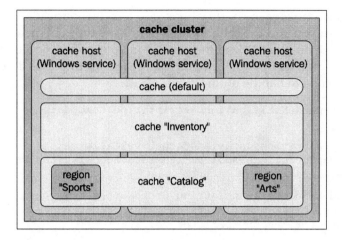

High availability

This is one of the policy settings that can be enabled at a named cache level. By default, this is turned off. This allows two copies of data to be stored in different cache servers, thus helping in failover scenarios. As the named cache data units (partitions) are striped across all the cache servers in the cluster, in HA mode, duplicate replicas are also striped to ensure that the primary and secondary are on different cache servers. It is important to note that there is no notion of a single secondary cache server and all cache servers will be primary for certain data and secondary replicas for others. In a virtualized environment, it is important to ensure that the various VMs are not on the same physical machine in a HA configuration.

 AppFabric Cache is an explicit in-memory cache. Configuring in HA mode protects cached objects when a single server goes down, but in case of multiple servers going down, there may be data loss. The cache is not durable and hence, the application has to explicitly persist it in a durable store such as SQL Server.

Cache notifications

Notifications are a mechanism by which cache applications can register for key-value pair changes in the cache cluster. For example, in a social networking application, once a user logs in, the friend list, status, latest news feed, photo albums, and the like may need to be refreshed immediately. In order to implement this, a set of services may register for the `login` event in `Users` named cache and populate the other named caches with relevant data from the backend.

To receive asynchronous cache notifications, add a cache notification callback to your application. When you add the callback, you define the types of cache operations that trigger a cache notification and the method in your application that will be called when the specified operations occur. Here are a set of things that need to be implemented in code to handle notifications:

```
private DataCacheNotificationDescriptor ndItemUpdateOps;

ndItemUpdateOps =
    cacheAccess.reviewscache.AddCacheLevelCallback(
      DataCacheOperations.AddItem | DataCacheOperations.ReplaceItem,
      handleCallBack);

public void handleCallBack(string CacheName, string RegionName,
    string Key, DataCacheItemVersion version, DataCacheOperations ops,
    DataCacheNotificationDescriptor nd)
{
    // Logic to handle after receiving the call back.
}
```

Typical use cases

These are a few scenarios for each technology that demonstrate its best fit in a solution.

Windows Server AppFabric hosting and monitoring

The hosting and monitoring enhancements will cover a wide range of use cases with most uses not utilizing all the features. By far, the most common use case is that this is a robust, scalable, and supportable host for WCF and WF applications.

In addition to the host itself, we also have a management tool for supporting the host. This would be a part of any hosting solution. Monitoring can be configured at different levels based on requirements. In addition, custom monitoring of specific data elements inside the solutions can be configured and persisted to a database.

Some examples include hosting a .NET 4.0 Workflow service for signing up a new customer to a website, tracking the number of orders that get processed through the system per day, and viewing the number of applications in a workflow process that are in a specific state.

Features are added to the particular solution as requirements of the solution expand.

Windows Server AppFabric cache

The data access patterns can be broadly classified as reference (read only), activity (single user read-write), or resource (multiple users read and write) data.

For example, the Books catalog on Amazon's website or your network list in LinkedIn is reference data. Such data does not change often and will be used by several clients accessing the website. Explicitly caching the data allows the system to respond faster and alleviates the load on the backend database server.

Activity data is tracking a single user's session activities: for example, a shopping cart for Walmart online, or a vehicle insurance computation from Progressive Direct. The web application in this scenario needs to respond really fast to the user changes as well as track the activities maintaining the session state. The user session might timeout and reconnect; refreshing the activities from the previous session enables a "stateless" web server to suddenly present user state.

Resource data scenarios are shared across a set of users where read, write, and updates are allowed. Imagine a travel portal such as Orbitz, which sells airplane tickets, where the tickets resource is shared and the system constantly makes changes to the resource, based on transactional activities in the system.

Windows Server AppFabric cache is a distributed, explicit cache that allows applications to store data in a dedicated chunk of memory. The objects continue to stay in memory and are not impacted upon by the usage of other applications. A caching tier such as this can also be used to store intermediate results based on computations and can be used directly from the application tier.

Typical scenarios

The following scenarios outline some uses of Windows Server AppFabric caching:

- ASP.NET session state management
- Caching large reference data sets for application objects reducing stress on backend databases or web services
- Intermediate results repository for high-end computations used by distributed applications
- Improving application latency by allowing it to scale for large numbers of users

In order to leverage caching, .NET applications require code changes and recompilation. In case of ASP.NET applications that need to use the cache for session state management, just modifying `web.config` may be enough. It is recommended to maintain cache-cluster host information and local cache settings in configuration to ease deployment.

Example solution

Let us look at a couple of quick solutions that demonstrate the capabilities of
Windows Server AppFabric.

AppFabric hosting and monitoring

AppFabric is an excellent host for .NET 4 Workflow services providing simple
hosting and monitoring. In *Chapter 2, Windows Communication Foundation and
Windows Workflow 4.0 Primer*, a simple Workflow Service was created. Now, we'll
take that service and host it inside IIS and monitor it using the new
monitoring features.

1. Open the `AppliedArchitecture.Chapter3.Monitoring.sln` project from
    the `<Installation Directory>\Chapter3\Begin` folder. This is the same
    solution used in the previous chapter.

2. Set the workflow project to use IIS for hosting by selecting the project,
    right-click on `Chapter3.IntroToWFService`, and select **Properties**.

3. Select the **Web** tab. Under **Servers**, select the **Use Local IIS Web server**.
    Leave the default address and click on **Create Virtual Directory** as shown
    in the next screenshot:

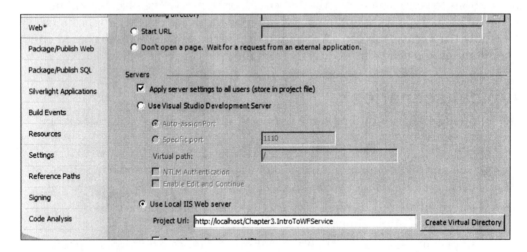

4. Save the project and build it inside Visual Studio.

5. Open **IIS Manger**. Find the project under the virtual directory that was
    previously created. Notice the three new administrator icons available
    under **AppFabric**.

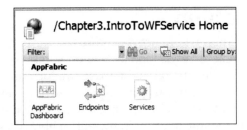

6. Open `WcfTestClient.exe` located at: `C:\Program Files\Microsoft Visual Studio 10.0\Common7\IDE\`.

7. Right-click on **My Service Projects** and add the newly deployed service. The default address should be `http://localhost/Chapter3.IntroToWFService/Service1.xamlx`. This is the address the workflow service is listening on and where a request should be sent to.

8. Run a few messages though the system. Click on the **AppFabric Dashboard** inside **IIS Manger**. This is the main dashboard page for AppFabric monitoring and tracking. This outlines **Persisted WF Instances**, **WCF Call History**, and **WF Instance History** over a configurable interval. As this service was a Workflow Service, items will show up under the **WCF Call History** and **WF Instance History**. Note that no additional configuration was needed in order to get this working—it just worked.

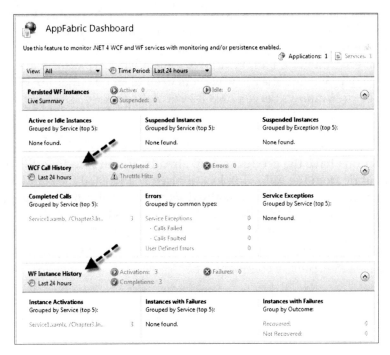

AppFabric caching

Consider a library application where users can browse for books using the author or title, read or update book reviews, look at new book releases, and then check out a particular book they like. The book database catalog has more than 100,000 entries and at any time, the system can have 100 concurrent users using the system across all locations. From a terminal in any of the library locations, users can use the application to review the information in the entire library's internal network. Each user will browse through an application running on the local terminal that communicates with a central WCF service, which will handle all the distributed cache interactions. The central service will be running on a Windows Server box in the library's data center.

 Just to simplify the solution, we will use a Windows Forms application interacting directly with the cache service via the cache utilities class.

Setup

A project solution `AppliedArchitecture.Chapter3.CachingPrimer` has been created in the `<Installation Directory>\Chapter3\Begin` folder. This solution contains two Windows Form applications that use the distributed cache.

Before beginning the lab, you must have Windows Server AppFabric Cache service and the client and admin feature installed and configured on your machine. The pre-requisites for configuring the cache features are .NET 4 RTM and PowerShell v2. In a development environment, both Windows 7 and Vista OS platform are supported. For production deployment, the cache servers need to be on either the Windows Server 2008 SP2 or Windows Server 2008 R2 OS platform.

Steps

1. If you don't have the product set up already, install Windows Server AppFabric from the following location. You can install the standalone cache feature or check the download section from this link: `http://www. microsoft.com/downloads/en/results.aspx?freetext=Windows+Server +AppFabricanddisplaylang=enandstype=s_basic`.

2. Start the Cache Administration Windows PowerShell tool and run the `Start-cachecluster` commandlet.

3. Using the same administration tool, create the following named caches—`CatalogDataCache` and `ReviewsCache` by first using the new-cache ReviewsCache -NotificationsEnabled true commandlet and then the new-cache `CatalogDataCache` commandlet.

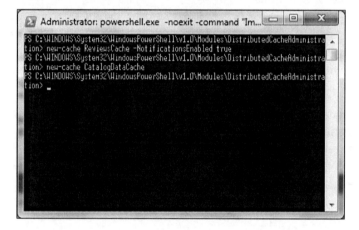

4. Launch Visual Studio.NET 2010 and open `AppliedArchitecture.` `Chapter3.CachingPrimer.sln` from the `<Installation Directory>\` `Chapter18\Begin` folder. You should see two Windows Form applications.

5. WinForm application 1 has the browse logic to see user review comments and can also let users add review comments for a particular book.

6. WinForm application 2 registers for cache-level notifications and displays an output whenever a user adds a particular comment.

7. Add a reference to the `Microsoft.ApplicationServer.Caching.Client` and `Microsoft.ApplicationServer.Caching.Core` DLLs.

8. Modify the `app.config` file to add the AppFabric `dataCacheClient` related sections.

9. Add a new .NET class `CacheUtils.cs` to contain all the cache-specific interaction and at the beginning, add the following set of `using` statements:

```
using System;
using System.Collections.Generic;
using System.Linq;
using System.Web;
using Microsoft.ApplicationServer.Caching;
```

10. Declare the following set of variables:

```
// channel factory that uses net.tcp binding
private static DataCacheFactory dcf;
// handle to named caches
public DataCache catalogcache, reviewscache;
public bool useCache = false;
private static readonly string CATALOG_CACHE = "CatalogDataCache";
private static readonly string REVIEWS_CACHE = "ReviewsCache";
private static int bookId;
private static readonly string REGION_NAME = "June6_UserReviews";
```

11. In the `Setup()` method, add the code to set up the channel for communicating with the cache servers and for creating the region within the Reviews named cache.

```
public void Setup()
{
  try
  {
    if (dcf == null)
    {
// Instantiation will setup connections to all cache servers
specified in <hosts> section in app.config
      dcf = new DataCacheFactory();
    }
    catalogcache = dcf.GetCache(CATALOG_CACHE);
    reviewscache = dcf.GetCache(REVIEWS_CACHE);
    LoadBookData();
    CreateRegion(REGION_NAME);
    useCache = true;
  }
  catch (DataCacheException dcexp)
  {
    useCache = false;
```

```
    }
  }
  public void CreateRegion(string regionName)
  {
    try
    {
      bool created = reviewscache.CreateRegion(regionName);
    }
    catch (DataCacheException dce)
    {
    }
  }
```

12. Add two internal classes for storing books and user comments.

```
[Serializable]
class BookInfo
{
  private string BookName;
  private string ISBN;
  private string AuthorName;
  public BookInfo(string bname, string isbn, string authors)
  {
    BookName = bname;
    ISBN = isbn;
    AuthorName = authors;
  }
  public string GetDesc()
  {
    return BookName + " " + ISBN + " " + AuthorName;
  }
  public string GetShortDesc()
  {
    return ISBN;
  }
}

[Serializable]
class UserReviews
{
  private string UserName;
  private string Comment;
```

```
      private string ISBN;
      public UserReviews(string user, string comment, string isbn)
      {
        UserName = user;
        Comment = comment;
        ISBN = isbn;
      }
      public string GetShortDesc()
      {
        return Comment + " - " + UserName;
      }
    }
```

13. Add the method to load some test data. This can be replaced by reading a set of database tables that represent the catalog data.

14. Add the methods to retrieve and store user comments.

```
    public ArrayList GetUserComments(string ISBN)
    {
      try
      {
        ArrayList output = new ArrayList();
        List<DataCacheTag> tags = new List<DataCacheTag>();
        tags.Add(new DataCacheTag(ISBN));
        IEnumerable<KeyValuePair<string, object>> comments =
          reviewscache.GetObjectsByAnyTag(tags, REGION_NAME);

        foreach (KeyValuePair<string, object> comment in comments)
        {
          output.Add( (UserReviews) comment.Value);
        }

        return output;
      }
      catch (DataCacheException dce)
      {
        return null;
      }
    }
    public void StoreUserComment(string ISBN, string user, string
                                                            comment)
    {
      try
      {
```

```
        UserReviews review = new UserReviews(user, comment, ISBN);
        List<DataCacheTag> tags = new List<DataCacheTag>();
        tags.Add(new DataCacheTag(ISBN));
        string key = user + Guid.NewGuid().ToString();
        reviewscache.Put(key, review, tags, REGION_NAME);
    }
    catch (DataCacheException dce)
    {
    }
  }
}
```

15. In `Form2.cs`, add the logic to register for notifications.

```
static CacheUtils cacheAccess;
private DataCacheNotificationDescriptor ndItemUpdateOps;
private static readonly string REVIEWS_CACHE = "ReviewsCache";
private static readonly string REGION_NAME = "June6_UserReviews";
public Form2()
{
  InitializeComponent();
  cacheAccess = new CacheUtils();
}
private void Form2_Load(object sender, EventArgs e)
{
  cacheAccess.Setup();
  NotifyFromReviewsCache();
}
public void NotifyFromReviewsCache()
{
  // ndItemUpdateOps =
cacheAccess.reviewscache.AddRegionLevelCallback(REGION_NAME,
DataCacheOperations.AddItem, handleCallBack);

  ndItemUpdateOps =
    cacheAccess.reviewscache.AddCacheLevelCallback(
      DataCacheOperations.AddItem | DataCacheOperations.
      ReplaceItem, handleCallBack);
}
public void handleCallBack(string CacheName, string RegionName,
  string Key, DataCacheItemVersion version, DataCacheOperations
ops,
```

```
        DataCacheNotificationDescriptor nd)
{
  if (CacheName.Equals(REVIEWS_CACHE))
  {
    if (listBox1.InvokeRequired)
    {
      string notification = String.Format("Review comment added at
      {0}. To view, use KEY as {1}",
      DateTime.Now.ToShortTimeString(), Key);
      listBox1.Invoke(new MethodInvoker(delegate {
        listBox1.Items.Add(notification); }));
    }
  }
}
```

16. In `Form1.cs,` add the logic to load the listbox and then add the logic in the button-click events to invoke `GetUserComments` and `StoreUserComment`. Also within the `load()` method, instantiate `Form2.cs` and invoke the `Show()` method on that instance.

17. Build and run the application.

18. Enter a set of user comments and then click to store the comments. This data is stored in the custom region `June6_UserReviews` of the `ReviewsCache`.

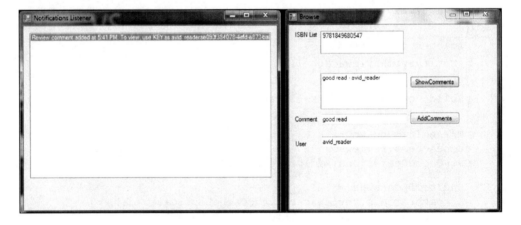

19. You can monitor the cache statistics from the admin tool.

Summary

With Windows Server AppFabric, now customers have richer features to leverage WCF, WF, and distributed cache features as part of their solution. Some of the challenges around hosting and monitoring of such custom applications are now made easier by hosting in the application server. The distributed cache feature provides a centralized store, elastic scale-out capabilities, highly available with low response times even with increasing workloads. As we look towards the future, this provides a good foothold to enhance the capabilities of the Windows application server.

Summary

4
BizTalk Server Primer

This chapter is intended to provide people who specialize in technologies like SQL Server or perhaps, general .NET development with an understanding of what BizTalk is, how it works, and also gives you an idea of how to write your first application.

If you have worked with BizTalk Server for many years, written pipeline components, developed custom adapters on the old and new framework, then before delving into the later chapters please flick over and briefly look at the roadmap information to ensure there is nothing new that you've missed.

Heterogeneous systems

Every IT department of any reasonable size that I have seen has used systems from at least two separate vendors. In this heterogeneous world, there are a number of challenges that I consistently see customers facing:

- Incompatible data formats:
    - X12 850, EDIFACT ORDRSP, IDOC 850 are all used to represent purchase orders, but they look very different and represent content in different ways

- Incompatible system metadata:
    - SAP Repository, Siebel, SQL schema, developer's diagrams
    - Metadata is scattered around systems with no consistent story for discovery and representation

- Incompatible wire formats:
  - ° Transport and application specific protocols: HTTP, SFTP, HTTPS, MSMQ, IBM MQSeries, SAP — IDoc, RFC, BAPI, and SAP DB

- Incompatible message exchange protocols:
  - ° SWIFT versus FIX, X12 versus EDIFACT, EDIINT, RNIF, BTF 2.0
  - ° All have different reliability protocols that need to be supported

- Weak process visibility:
  - ° How do I see what is going on?

What does BizTalk Server do?

Most Microsoft products provide some feature/functionality in the mindset of internal Microsoft people and customers alike. Microsoft Exchange Server owns e-mail, SQL Server owns the data tier, and IIS is Microsoft's web hosting solution. BizTalk Server is Microsoft's premium enterprise integration solution. In few words, it provides the ability to connect these disparate heterogeneous systems (entities) together. To provide full system integration, which goes beyond just data connectivity, **adapters** provide wire-level connectivity, and message transformation used for data. A robust **Orchestration engine** enables complex events and process workloads to be handled. BizTalk also provides the ability to expose and consume services, monitor the end-to-end process flow (providing visibility into the process), and since 2006, the 2006 R2 release has introduced RFID connectivity. **Entities** may be a device (in the case of RFID), a system within the same department, organization, or a service that a partner firm has exposed.

Can't we just use Web Services or WCF?

This is perhaps the most common question I hear. WCF is Microsoft's unified programming model for building service-oriented applications. It is fully interoperable with a number of different web service protocols as defined by the WS-* specifications. This means that it is interoperable with line-of-business (LOB) systems from vendors who adhere to the standards. This removes a large number of barriers to implementing a service-oriented approach within an organization. This can be used to provide intra and inter-organizational connectivity. However, there are still a number of challenges and factors that need to be considered. Following are the key factors I consider when working with customers:

- **Wire formats**: The number and complexity of different applications that you need to connect to is a key factor. BizTalk provides extensive connectivity with 25 out-of-the-box adapters and has more available in the adapter pack and from third-party vendors. A majority of these are now built on top of the **WCF LOB Adapter SDK**, so they can be utilized from any .NET application. This means that either BizTalk Server could be used, or the WCF Adapters could be used outside of BizTalk Server within a LOB system, in another host such as AppFabric, or within your own custom application host.

- **Data formats**: There is still no such thing as a common XML purchase order format across all systems. Therefore message transformation is required. This is often the most challenging requirement; different LOB vendor systems tend to have a different way of modeling and storing organizational metadata such as customer information and PO format. It is very rare to find a common XML message format that is used across all systems within an organization. In addition to this, LOB systems are subject to upgrade, change of version, and so on, all of which can impact the model they use. This is compounded by the fact that an organization may decide to change the attributes of metadata that have modeled the LOB app. If a tight coupling is built between each LOB system, it is important to consider the work that needs to be done, should a change on either system occur. In particular, you should pay attention to schema and model changes and consider the amount of development work that this will require.

  BizTalk Server provides a Mapper, which can be used to handle flat files and XML-based formats. In the EAI scenario, this can be used to map between the LOB system models that are used. BizTalk is specifically designed to deal with existing interface transports and data models. By leveraging this, you can minimize the change that needs to be performed to the LOB system. In many cases, due to its powerful transformation capabilities BizTalk can interact with existing APIs that are exposed with no change required to the end system.

- **Process management**: WCF provides separation of contract (functionality) and data transport (binding). This provides wire connectivity, but a service host is still needed to manage the durability, provide tooling, scale out, and so on. BizTalk provides this and other building blocks that can be utilized in your application.

Long running transactions pose another problem. Certain updates to organizational information may occur over a period of time, for instance to change a customer's bank address; the change may be initiated but it may be in a pending state until appropriate copies of documentation have been received by e-mail post. In this scenario, if the change does not complete for any reason, it's important that all the systems involved be able to rollback to a consistent state. BizTalk provides a compensation capability, which enables this to be performed across many disparate systems.

In summary, in order to meet business requirements, solutions need to provide version control, the ability to roll out different versions with little or no downtime, deal with long running services, and have robust instrumentation and tooling. BizTalk provides a rich host that has these capabilities. It is important to consider how this will be implemented if you decide to perform your own integrations or utilize another host such as Windows Server AppFabric.

Typical BizTalk use cases

BizTalk Server is typically used to solve problems in four main areas: EAI, B2B, BPA, and ESB.

Enterprise Application Integration (EAI)

The modern enterprise is often littered with the spaghetti of proprietary interfaces, which cannot natively communicate with each other due to incompatible platforms, data formats, and security policies. This can pose challenges for normal business activity. For example, when a new employee starts, a record for them needs to be created in the HR system and an order for a laptop may need to be placed in the ERP system. An account may need to be created for them in the CRM system with their appropriate level of access. To avoid doing this manually, one could write a small application that has all the built-in logic necessary to connect to these disparate systems. Or perhaps, the HR system has an extension module that allows you to use some programming language to build the logic in there. Over time, however, as the system scales, a durable host needs to be developed to run this custom integration code. Tight coupling between systems means that any changes will often break the custom integration layer in several systems and require changes in them. A former manager of mine used to say that "the devil is in the detail" with integration work. Unfortunately, this custom point-to-point approach often results in a scene like the next diagram; managing these proprietary interfaces can inhibit an organization from seeking a service-oriented approach towards system integration.

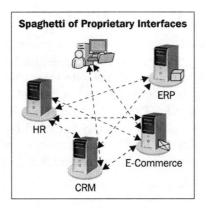

To avoid this problem many organizations use BizTalk as an Integration Broker. This provides the following features:

- Centralized management and administration of integration endpoints and in-flight instances.
- Loose coupling of applications, which means no physical dependencies between applications.
- Durable infrastructure with a scalable model.
- Insight into the message flow and business process through **BizTalk Tracking** and **Business Activity Monitoring**.

The following diagram shows BizTalk in an integration broker role. This is the classic usage of BizTalk and something that has been firmly established in the 10 years since the first version was shipped.

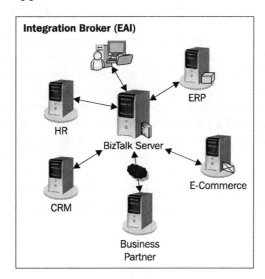

Business-to-Business (B2B)

The second scenario is to use BizTalk as a business-to-business broker to manage all communication across organizational boundaries. BizTalk supports Internet-friendly adapters and can also communicate with legacy and non-Internet friendly system endpoints. It also supports channel and message-based security. BizTalk Server provides native support for EDI and a host of accelerators targeted at specific industry verticals, including a **SWIFT (Society for Worldwide Interbank Financial Telecommunication)**—accelerator for financial services. This significantly decreases the time required to implement durable and robust B2B communication.

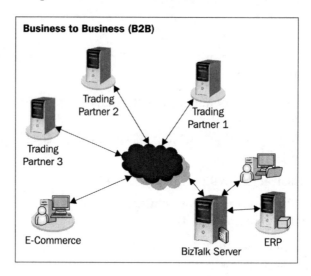

Business Process Automation (BPA)

BizTalk's capabilities can be leveraged to automate current manual processes in organizations. Typically, scenarios that are repetitive have strongly defined rules and those that involve multiple systems are strong cases. One of my first BizTalk Server customers was a financial services organization that received several millions pieces of paper per day. When some financial products mature, there is an option to re-invest (often the default choice) or transfer the funds. In this case, the customer was able to leverage BizTalk to automate the processing of such paper-based applications. A scanning solution translated the paper input into a common XML schema, which was then processed by BizTalk. Human approval was only required in case of an exception or if that particular option selected required it. Therefore by using BizTalk, the customer was able to automate a previously manual, laborious process.

Enterprise Service Bus (ESB)

The final way that people consider BizTalk is as a centralized service bus for the organization, as depicted in the following graphic. By exposing on-ramps to a variety of destinations, which are determined when the message is received, it enables BizTalk to act as a durable message bus that is responsible for coordinating communication across your organization. With *BizTalk Server 2010*, Microsoft released the ESB Toolkit 2.1 which builds on top of the core BizTalk platform to minimize the time needed to implement this scenario.

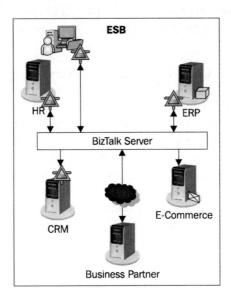

BizTalk architecture

We'll now examine the BizTalk architecture and look at how all the components relate to each other.

BizTalk message flow

The next diagram illustrates a standard message flow through the main components of BizTalk. The BizTalk messaging system has three distinct parts: receive port, MessageBox, and send port.

Messages are received via a **receive port**. A receive port can contain one or more receive locations, which provide the ability to have multiple transport entry points into the application. For example, some customers choose to have a **WCF-Custom receive location** but they also have a file receive location for manual re-submission of messages. A **receive location** is a combination of an adapter and specific pipeline configuration. Certain artifacts can be configured at the **receive location** level, for example the pipeline used and the adapter configuration. Others, such as the map used and enabling failed message routing need to be configured at the port level.

Incoming messages are received from the adapter, and can be transformed via pipelines and maps. If message tracking is turned on, the message is also published to the tracking database.

Once the message arrives at the **MessageBox**, the **Messaging Engine** performs subscription evaluation and delivers it to subscribers whose subscriptions match. Subscription matching is done using predicates based on internal message (context) properties and properties that BizTalk provides. Subscribers can either be instances of orchestrations, where complex workflow is needed, or **send ports** where message transformation and delivery need to be performed. BizTalk fully supports publish-subscription so the same message can go to one or more orchestration and/or send ports. Messages may be delivered to orchestrations for further processing. In messaging scenarios, a message may be delivered to a send port or group. At the send side, the message is again transformed (via pipelines and/or maps), and sent to the final destination via an adapter.

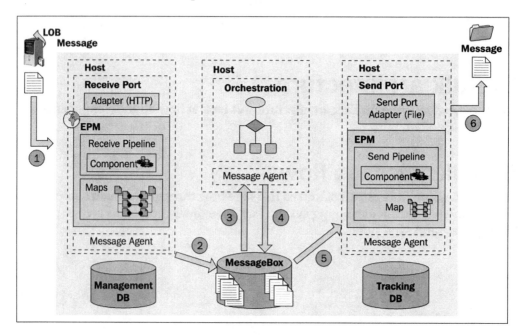

1. A message is received from an entity endpoint. This is handled by a receive port, through one of its receive locations. Once the message has been received by an adapter the **End Point Manager (EPM)** component provides any necessary preprocessing. Message manipulation (debatching, decrypting, and so on) is handled by one or more pipeline components before transformations are applied using the **BizTalk Mapper**.

 BizTalk Server 2010 contains over 25 adapters out of the box. In addition to this, the BizTalk Adapter Pack is available, which provides connectivity for complex applications that require an application-specific context to connect to them. This includes SAP, Siebel, SQL Server, Oracle eBusiness Suite, and Database.

   `http://www.microsoft.com/biztalk/en/us/adapter-pack.aspx`

2. Once a message has been processed by the adapter, pipeline, and map, it needs to be routed to the appropriate subscribers, which can be one or more BizTalk Orchestrations or send ports. The **Message Agent (MA)** is the component responsible for this. It publishes the message to the MessageBox database, which is the centralized queue of BizTalk. The Message Agent is an abstraction layer between the other BizTalk host (BTSNTSVC.EXE) sub-services and is responsible for evaluating subscribers to the message. The abstraction of the MA enables BizTalk to have more than one MessageBox and hence support scaling out of this tier.

3. "Once only" delivery is provided to the MessageBox for transactional systems and "at least once" delivery for non-transactional systems. The **Distributed Transaction Coordinator (DTC)** is used to enforce this. For transactional systems such as MQSeries, their appropriate resource manager will be enlisted in the transaction. For non-transactional adapters, the transaction will occur only between BizTalk and the SQL Resource Manager that hosts the MessageBox. All non-transactional BizTalk adapters are written so that the delete operation on the original endpoint occurs after the message has been published to the MesssageBox.

4. BizTalk enforces loose coupling between inbound messages and subscribers, as part of its publish/subscribe design. On insertion, the Message Agent calls a number of stored procedures to update promoted properties (used for routing), evaluate subscriptions based on the context of the message, and finally make the insertion into the MessageBox spool. If there are multiple subscribers the message is still stored only once to ensure scalability of the system. As part of this operation, a reference is added to the host queue table ready for processing by the subscriber, hosted in the host instance.

5. Each host instance polls the database at regular intervals to look for new work in the queue. In this case, the subscriber is an Orchestration; therefore the MA would have placed a reference for the inbound message into the Orchestration host's queue. The MA is responsible for performing this dequeuing operation and calls a stored procedure `bts_DequeueMesssages_<HostInstanceName>` to perform this. This call will retrieve as many messages as possible up to a configurable limit — the batch size, which by default is 20. The MA hands over the message to an internal queue hosted in the BizTalk process space, from which (in this case) the XLANG/S service will retrieve the message for processing.

6. Once it has finished processing, the MA will publish the message back into the MessageBox using the same process as in step 1 (because there could once more be multiple subscribers). The MA is required to publish a new message to the spool as messages within BizTalk are immutable; for example, they cannot be changed once they are published, and a reference to this message will be added to the send port host's queue.

7. The send host will now de-queue the MessageBox, which again enforces the loose coupling and hands it over to the EPM which will apply any post processing through maps, pipelines, and finally initiate the send adapter to deliver the message over the wire.

8. The EPM hands over the message to the send adapter, which delivers the message to the final endpoint, in this case a file UNC path.

Key BizTalk server terminology

In this section, we will define and describe some of the key terminology that you will need to be familiar with if using BizTalk Server.

BizTalk group

A BizTalk group is a set of BizTalk runtime machines that share a common **BizTalk Management Database**. This enables centralized configuration and administration. The BizTalk Group metadata is stored in a database that is called the BizTalk Management Database. This information includes: servers that are members of the group, database location, host configuration, deployed applications, and artifacts.

Hosts

A BizTalk host is an abstract logical container for BizTalk Server resources including orchestrations and send/receive adapter handlers. Hosts act as the deployment target for processing resources, and provide resource and security partitioning. Hosts are either *in-process*, which means they run within the BizTalk process, or *isolated*, which means they run in a process external to BizTalk such as IIS.

Host instance

Host instances are the physical incarnation of hosts that get physically deployed on a particular machine. A host instance is a physical instance of a logical host on a single machine. We can create an instance of a host on any BizTalk server in the group, but cannot have more than one instance of the same host on any one machine. The following diagram illustrates the relationship between hosts and host instances:

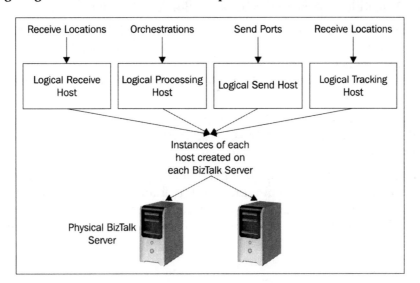

1. A host can contain mixed artifacts (ports and orchestrations).
2. Not all hosts must have instances on all servers. For example, if you have three BizTalk Servers a host could be present as an instance on none, one, two, or all three of these servers.
3. Typically, a host instance is created on at least two servers for high availability reasons so that if a server fails, processing will continue.
4. Enterprise Edition of BizTalk is required to have multiple BizTalk Servers in a Group.

BizTalk databases

BizTalk relies on a number of databases to provide data storage, queuing, and configuration management. Here is a summary of the main ones:

- `BizTalkMgmtDb`: Centralized configuration store for BizTalk used by all servers in the group.

- `BizTalkMsgBoxDb`: Heart of BizTalk Server, provides state management and queuing to support the loose coupling model. It is not directly exposed to the programmer.

- `BizTalkDTADb`: Provides BizTalk Tracking, which provides information on service instances (instances of Send Ports or Orchestrations) and is targeted towards the IT Pro for troubleshooting.

- `BizTalkRuleEngineDb`: This is the policy store for the highly scalable BizTalk Rules Engine that is based on the *Rete algorithm*.

- `SSODB`: This is the metadata store that enables BizTalk to provide Windows to third-party authentication. It is also used to store endpoint information so that adapters that require security details (for example, the Oracle adapter) as part of their connection configuration do not compromise the security of the endpoint.

- `BAMPrimaryImport`: OLTP store that is used by Business Activity Monitoring (BAM). BAM provides a robust, scalable framework that can be used to instrument an application end-to-end.

- `BAMArchive`: To ensure optimal performance of the BAM Primary Import database, this archive is provided to store information that fits outside the "live" operational window. Taking this approach ensures that there is a smaller dataset for the most recent data and, hence when querying this, users get optimal results.

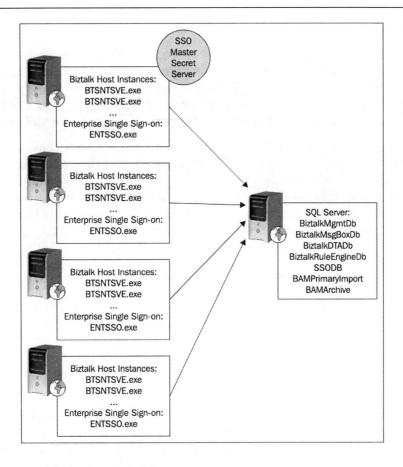

Enterprise Single Sign-On

Enterprise Single Sign-On provides a way to map a Windows user ID to non-Windows user credentials. It is also used to store credentials and configuration information that receive locations and send ports use; this is done to ensure that this sensitive information is stored in a secure manner.

Adapters

Adapters provide wire connectivity to and from BizTalk. All other components have no knowledge of the endpoint they are dealing with, which makes BizTalk truly loosely coupled. There are three classes of adapters:

1. Transport adapters (for example, HTTP, POP3, and so on)

2. Line-of-business adapters (for example, SAP, Siebel, and so on)

3. Data adapters (for example, SQL, DB2, Oracle, and so on)

Message

Messages are the payload that BizTalk Server processes. BizTalk can process XML documents and flat file structures among other formats such as PDF. Messages contain at least one part, which is body; they are immutable and shared, which means that once a message has been published and written to the MessageBox, it cannot be altered. This enables the efficient delivery of messages to multiple subscribers.

The message is defined internally by an XSD schema file. Messages have a set of properties associated with them. If a message is an XML or a flat file message, the schema will specify a *type*, which is typically comprised of the XML namespace and the root node name, for example, `http://MyCompany.Invoice#ApplicationInvoice`. This uniquely identifies the message type to BizTalk Server in the same way that the class name and namespace does in C#.

It is possible to have two schemas with the same root node and target namespace by defining the schema collection used by the XML Disassembler pipeline component. However, in my opinion it is a best practice to have a unique namespace for each document-type and follow a consistent naming and versioning practice.

For more information, see *Chapter 8, Versioning Patterns* from the book "*SOA Patterns with BizTalk Server 2009*", *Richard Seroter*.

A message always has a set of context name/value properties associated with it. This includes details such as the inbound receive port that the message was received through. These properties are attached to the message throughout its processing in BizTalk and are used by the Messaging Engine to evaluate subscriptions. To enable custom property routing, developers can promote their own properties by defining a property schema and marking a particular node as *promoted* in the XSD schema. Custom code can also be used in the pipeline or Orchestration processing can be made to do this.

Pipeline

Used to normalize data into and out of BizTalk, pipelines provide the ability to perform pre and post processing. The typical usage scenario for pipelines is to normalize the inbound payload into an XML message that BizTalk can process. On the outbound side, the XML message is typically transformed into the desired output of the outbound endpoint. Although XML is the preferred payload for BizTalk, it can also manipulate flat files and process binary data. An individual pipeline comprises one or more components such as: decode/encode, decrypt/encrypt, validate, resolve party, and so on. A streaming model is used to provide a flat memory footprint and an integrated pipeline designer is provided in Visual Studio as shown in the following screenshot.

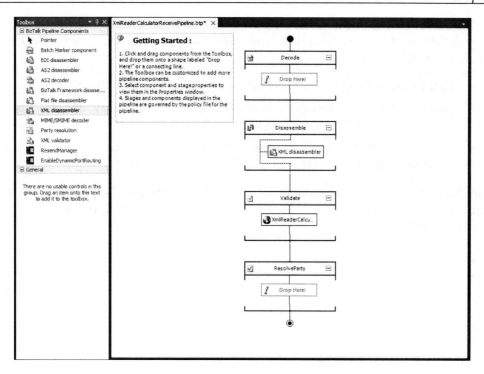

Maps

Maps define one-way transformations between two schemas. An integrated designer is provided in Visual Studio and makes it easier to perform these common transformations than if you were to write your own XSLT. BizTalk Server also provides a set of reusable components called **functoids** and an extensible framework to encode your own complex functionality. The following image shows mapping an Inbound Sales Order information to a destination schema.

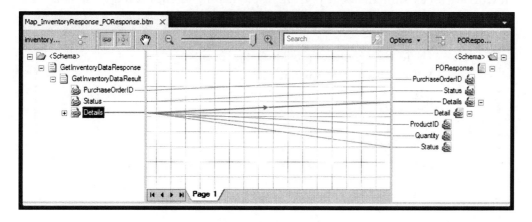

BizTalk Server 2010 introduces the long awaited, **Intelligent Mapper**, which includes many developer productivity updates for those working with large complex maps including the following:

- **Relevance view**: Collapses any non-relevant parts of the schema
- **Auto scrolling of elements**: Automatically highlights the attributes or elements affected by the selected functoid
- **Suggestive match**: Identifies candidates in the destination schema that could be mapped to the current selected element or attribute

In addition, Map Debugging capabilities were added in BizTalk Server 2009; together these improvements significantly reduce the time needed to develop large complex maps.

For more information and an overview of the features that the BizTalk 2010 Intelligent Mapper provides see:

```
http://msdn.microsoft.com/en-us/library/
aa547076(v=BTS.70).aspx
```

Performance of maps

The BizTalk runtime still makes use of the .NET Framework 1.1 `System.Xml.Xsl.XslTransform` class, which was deprecated when the `System.Xml.Xsl.XslCompiledTransform` class was introduced. The `XslCompiledTransform` class provides significant performance benefits over the `XslTransform` because it implements a compile-once cache and re-use model. This means that if the same transformation is performed many times, which is common in an integration scenario, the compilation only occurs once. A colleague in my team made this discovery and has provided two excellent blog articles along with sample code that works with existing maps. If you are implementing complex mapping you can consider using this technique to improve the performance.

The following articles provide further details:

XslCompiledTransform Blog part 1

```
http://blogs.msdn.com/b/paolos/archive/2010/01/29/
how-to-boost-message-transformations-using-the-
xslcompiledtransform-class.aspx
```

XslCompiledTransform Blog part 2

```
http://blogs.msdn.com/paolos/archive/2010/04/08/
how-to-boost-message-transformations-using-the-
xslcompiledtransform-class-extended.aspx
```

Orchestration

Orchestration is the workflow engine that BizTalk provides. It is the original precursor to Windows Workflow Foundation. Interaction with the world is achieved through messages. It provides support for durable, long-running workflows, and uses template shapes to visually represent different activities. The designer provides various shapes: receive, send, parallel, begin, end, decide, loop, construct, transform, and scope. It also provides a **transaction model**, which can model typical atomic DTC-style transactions and long running transactions (for example, a mortgage application process), which cannot use typical locking semantics and involve several systems. An example of this would be ordering an item from a website; the item is typically ordered, payment may be taken and a confirmation e-mail is sent before the item is dispatched. In this scenario, it would not be feasible to hold all systems in a typical ACID-style transaction until the item was dispatched. This would result in a punitive wait for the user and is likely to result in a timeout, locking, or blocking on one or more systems. Therefore if the customer was to cancel the order, a number of actions would need to be taken to ensure that all systems were in a consistent state and the user didn't for example, receive the goods and not be charged for them, or be charged and not receive the goods. Compensation is a robust mechanism provided by BizTalk to enable previously completed work to be rolled back.

The Orchestration engine is version-aware. This is particularly useful for long running business processes that have been modeled. This allows for side-by-side execution with automatic message routing to the correct version of the process. The hosting environment is durable and is tolerant of machine failure, because a DTC transaction is used by a BizTalk Orchestration host every time it makes an immutable change. This means that its state can be resumed on another instance of that host. Orchestrations and Pipelines are automatically instrumented using BizTalk Tracking for basic execution.

Highlights of the BizTalk 2010 release

Some of the key improvements and investments that have been made are as follows:

- Platform realignment and support for the latest generation of Microsoft technology including: Visual Studio 2010, SQL Server 2008 R2, Windows Server 2008 R2, SharePoint 2010, and .NET Framework 4.0

- Intelligent Mapper

- Improved **Trading Partner Management (TPM)**

- Performance dashboard exposes properties, previously only accessible through registry keys

- Support for Backup Compression and Transparent Data Encryption SQL features
- A new System Center Pack
- Updated adapters for Oracle, SAP, SQL 2008 R2, and SharePoint 2010
- Improved FTP adapter and new FTPS adapter

Example solution

In this section, we will walk through creating our very first BizTalk application.

On a machine with the BizTalk Development Tools and Visual Studio 2008 installed, open Visual Studio and select **BizTalk Project | Empty BizTalk Server Project**. The **Solution Name** should be `AppliedArchitecture.Chapter4.BizTalk`. The project name should be `SimpleBizTalkSolution`.

If you are using BizTalk Server 2009 and get "Creating project project name"... "project creation failed" as an error message, there is a solution at:

```
http://blogs.msdn.com/biztalkcrt/
archive/2009/08/21/visual-studio-2008-fails-to-
create-open-biztalk-projects.aspx
```

We will create a `Customer` schema, by adding a new item to the project and selecting **Schema**; name it `Customer.xsd`.

 For a full overview of best practices for schema design, please read the book "*SOA Patterns with BizTalk Server 2009*", *Chapter 5 Schema and Endpoint Patterns*, (Packt Publishing, 2009) by *Richard Seroter*.

Open the BizTalk editor by selecting the schema. You will notice that the schema's target namespace has been populated as follows (if you used the naming structure we provided):

```
targetNamespace= http://AppliedArchitecture.Chapter4.BizTalk.
SimpleBizTalkSolution.Customer
```

We store the following details about our customer: Customer ID, name, address, age, and occupation. Firstly, let's delete the default root node. Right-click on the root node and select **Delete**, then right-click on **Schema** and select **Insert Schema Node | Child Record**. Name the child record **Customer** and leave the default properties for this record.

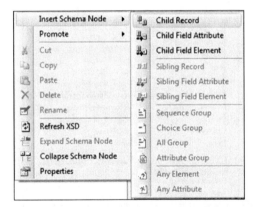

Now we need to insert individual elements that define this customer. Insert a **Child Field Element** called `CustomerID`; this will be used to uniquely identify the message to BizTalk later. Leave the default datatype of `xs:string`.

Now, insert the following child-field elements under `Customer` record. Use the datatypes specified in the following table:

Element name	Datatype
Name	`xs:string`
AddressLine1	`xs:string`
AddressLine2	`xs:string`
City	`xs:string`
State	`xs:string`
Country	`xs:string`
Age	`xs:positiveInteger`
Occupation	`xs:string`

By default, elements are of `String` type; change **Age** to `positiveInteger` by selecting the **Data Type** property in the properties box drop-down list.

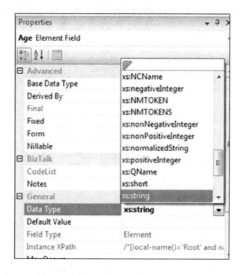

Your schema should now look like the following screenshot:

We are now going to add a `Property` schema, which will be used to separately store a promoted property in the context of the message within the MessageBox. BizTalk separates these two schemas so that we do not need to load the whole message into process space just to make a routing decision. To add a new item to the solution, select the type **Property Schema** and call it `CustomerPropertySchema.xsd`. Rename the default `Property1` to `CustomerID`.

Open your original `Customer` schema now, right-click on `CustomerID`, and select **Promote|Show Promotions**. In the **Promote Properties** window that now appears, select the **Property Fields** tab, then click on the folder icon and select the customer property schema you just created. Now verify that the **Property fields list** has **ns0:CustomerID** selected. You have now done the mapping between your `CustomerID` in the original schema and the corresponding value in the `Property` schema.

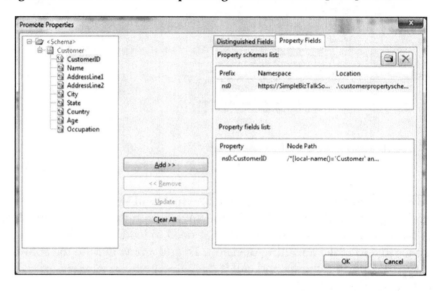

Now that we have a schema to represent our customer, let's imagine that we want to send our customer message to a backend system, which will then respond with the message (a contrived scenario I know, but it will suffice for our purposes). To implement this, we will use an Orchestration.

This scenario can be implemented in a messaging-only fashion and avoid a round trip to the MessageBox. The purpose of this is to demonstrate how the **Orchestration Designer** functions and how it can be used.

Right-click on the project and select **Add|New Item** then select **BizTalk Orchestration** and call it `CustomerRouting.odx`. This will display the **Orchestration Designer** surface. The first step you need to take is to define an Orchestration message. Click on **Orchestration View**, right-click **Messages**, and add a message called `CustomerMsg`. In the **Message Type** property dialog, select the `SimpleBizTalkSolution.Customer` schema you defined earlier.

The **Orchestration Designer** provides a toolbox of shapes that can be used within your Orchestration. For now, we will just use receive and send shapes. I would like you to drag the following shapes, in this order, onto the surface and give them the names in brackets. First a receive shape (`Receive_Initial_Customer`), then a send shape (`Send_Initial_Customer`), then a receive shape (`Receive_Response_Customer`), and finally a send shape (`Send_Response_Customer`). This should look like the following screenshot. For each shape, click on it and in the properties window that appears, set **Message** to `CustomerMsg`.

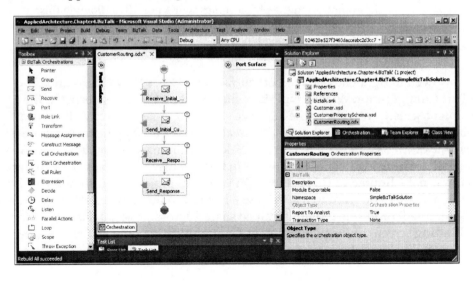

The next screenshot illustrates how the property window looks for the `Receive_Initial_Customer` shape.

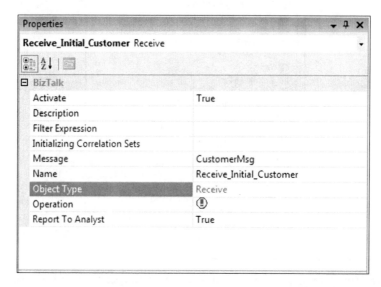

You have now created the send and receive shapes within the Orchestration. For our scenario, we are going to use four file-drop locations, so we need to create four logical one-way ports within the **Orchestration Design** surface. The actual messaging ports that are used will be defined later.

 It is a good practice to separate a logical port configuration in Orchestration from the physical messaging port. By following this, you will enable your solution to run in multiple environments and avoid hard-coded dependencies.

You now need to right-click on the port surface and select **New Configured Port**. The **Port Configuration Wizard** will start; click **Next** on the first screen. On the subsequent screen, enter the name `Receive_Initial_Customer` and click **Next**. On the **Select a Port Type** screen, select **Create a New Port Type**, and enter a port type name of `OneWayCustomerPortType`. Select communication pattern **One-Way** as we will not be using Request-Response in this use case. For **Access Restrictions** select **Internal – limited to this project**. On your real projects, you should consider carefully whether you want to use **Private – limited to this Orchestration**, **Internal** (project limited) or **Public** (no limit; can be shared across projects). Finally on the **Port Binding** screen for **Port Direction of Communication** (and as this is a receive port), select **I'll always be receiving messages on this port**.

As port types don't encapsulate "direction", having a port type that refers to receive or send is usually incorrect. Therefore, we have used the naming convention `<Type|PortType>` and we will reuse the same port type for all our logical ports. This is a useful technique and avoids cluttering of projects with unnecessary port types. The **Type Modifier** property can be set to **Internal**, **Public**, or **Private**, which determines which other projects/solutions can reference the port type and use it.

For port binding, we will leave the default **Specify later**. **Specify now** configures the endpoint properties as part of the project and is *not* the best practice. Direct binding is used for sending only to the MessageBox. Click **Next**, and then **Finish** on the final screen. You should change the `Operation_1` default identifier name on the port to match the receive shape name `Receive_Initial_Customer`. Finally, because this is the first receive shape in the Orchestration, change the **Activate** property to **True**. You have now created the first receive port; join this to the `Receive_Initial_Customer` receive shape by dragging and dropping the receive port operation you just created to the `Receive_Initial_Customer` receive shape on the designer surface as shown.

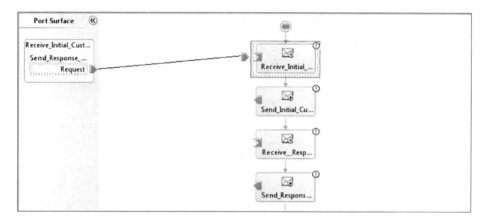

Repeat the wizard a second time to create the first send shape. Join this to the first send port by dragging and dropping on the designer. Use the following values:

- Name: `Send_Initial_Customer`
- Use an existing port type
- Port Type Name: `SimpleBizTalkSolution.OneWayCustomerPortType`
- Port Direction of communications: **I'll always be sending**…
- Port Binding: **Specify later**

Repeat the wizard for a third time to create the second receive port. Use the following values:

- Name: `Receive_Response_Customer`
- Use an existing port type
- Port Type Name: `SimpleBizTalkSolution.OneWayCustomerPortType`
- Port direction of communications: **I'll always be receiving**…
- Port Binding: **Specify later**

Repeat the wizard a fourth time to create the second send port. Use the following values:

- Name: `Send_Response_Customer`
- Use an existing port type
- Port Type Name: `SimpleBizTalkSolution.OneWayCustomerPortType`
- Port Direction of communications: **I'll always be sending**…
- Port Binding: **Specify later**

Join the logical ports you just created with the relevant send and receive shapes. Your Orchestration designer surface should now look something like the following screenshot:

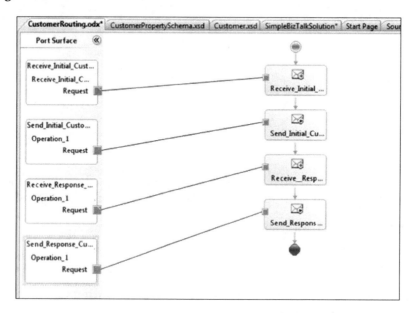

So we now have an Orchestration that receives a message, sends it out somewhere, waits for a response, and delivers the response. In order to make this work fully, we will use a feature that Orchestration provides, called **correlation**. This feature enables BizTalk to match the response with the appropriate instance of an Orchestration, which will ensure that the correct Customer message gets routed back to the right instance of this Orchestration.

Open the **Orchestration View** tab and right-click on **Correlation Set** and select **New Correlation Set**. Change the default name from Correlation_1 to CustomerCorrelation. From the **Correlation Type** drop-down list select **Create New Correlation Type**. A correlation type defines the information that BizTalk will use to correlate the message. In the **Correlation Type** property window that appears, click on the ellipsis (**...**) button. You will see a list of the **Context** properties available. As we defined a **Property** schema earlier, you should also see SimpleBizTalkSolution and under it, a CustomerID element. Select this and click on **Add**, then click **OK**. In the description box type CustomerID_CorrelationType and type the same value in **Identifier**.

For any given correlation set, we generally need to initialize it on the **Send From Orchestration** and then follow it on the receive action. Under the covers, the initialization creates an instance subscription in the BizTalk MessageBox, which enables BizTalk to successfully correlate the response message to the right instance of your Orchestration. This capability enables BizTalk to have multiple instances of the Orchestration process and multiple responses coming in, and it will be able to route each response instance to the relevant process instance. To do this, on the first send port property window (in **Initializing Correlation Sets**) select CustomerCorrelation from the drop-down box. When the CustomerMsg is sent from this send port, a correlation set will be initialized using the value of CustomerID that was in the original message; as long as our customer IDs are unique we will always correlate to the correct instance. On the second receive shape, set the **Following Correlation Sets** property to CustomerCorrelation.

We will now deploy the solution from Visual Studio and configure it in the BizTalk Administration Console. First, you will need to create a Strong Name Key file; this is required for all assemblies that are added to the **Global Assembly Cache** (GAC). The GAC is for .NET what the registry was for COM+; for example, a machine central store. Open a Visual Studio command prompt and navigate using the cd command to the root directory of your solution. Then run the following command:

```
sn -k biztalk.snk
```

Right-click on the BizTalk project and select **Properties**. From the window that appears, select the **Signing** tab. Check the box marked **Sign the assembly**. Then, from the drop-down box select **browse** and select the `biztalk.snk` file you just created. Then select the **Deployment** tab, ensure that the configuration database and server are correct, and enter the application name as `SimpleBizTalkSolution`. Now right-click on the project and select **Deploy**. A message should appear confirming that the deployment succeeded.

Open the BizTalk Administration Console, expand the node for your BizTalk Server group (it should reference your management database) and select **Applications**. If you set the application name correctly, you should see a `SimpleBizTalkSolution` node. Right-click on this and select **Configure** as illustrated in the next screenshot:

This will now bring up a configure application screen, which allows you to configure all BizTalk created artifacts. Under Orchestrations select **CustomerRouting** and select for host **BizTalkServerApplication**. You will now need to configure both the receive and send ports.

For `Receive_Initial_Customer` from the drop-down list select **New Receive Port**. On the screen that appears give it the name `Receive_Initial_Customer`. Then select **Receive Locations** and select **New**. For the name value enter `Receive_Initial_Customer` and then select **File** for the type. For the receive pipeline, and as we are receiving an XML message, select **XMLReceive**. Click the **Configure** button to configure the file drop location. For the receive folder, configure the following location (but leave everything else as default) and click on **OK**:

```
C:\TempStuff\filedrops\receive_initial
```

 The user running the default host instance will be used by the file adapter send and receive handlers to access these locations. Therefore, you should ensure that this account has access to the paths that you specify here.

Repeat the same process for **Receive_Response_Customer** using **Receive_Response_Customer** as receive port and receive location names, **XMLReceive** pipeline and `C:\TempStuff\filedrops\receive_response`.

For the Outbound logical ports, next to `Send_Initial_Customer`, select **New Send Port**. Name the send port `Send_Initial_Customer`. Select type as **File**, and leave the pipeline as `PassThruTransmit` (as no processing is required after the Orchestration). Click on **Configure** and set the destination folder to:

```
C:\TempStuff\filedrops\send_initial
```

Repeat the same process for `Send_Response_Customer` using that as the send port name and set the outbound folder to:

```
C:\TempStuff\filedrops\send_response
```

Your application is now configured; click on **OK**, right-click the application, and select **Start**. We now need to generate a test message to test it. Open up your BizTalk solution in Visual Studio and select your `Customer.xsd` schema. In the properties pane, you will see **Output Instance Filename**. The BizTalk schema editor has a very useful function; it will generate an output message for a defined schema so you can determine whether it fits your criteria. Configure the output location (as shown next) then right-click on the schema in Visual Studio and select **Generate Instance**:

```
C:\TempStuff\filedrops\customer.xml
```

If you browse the previous location, you should see an output file. Open and inspect it. Now drop it into the `Receive_Initial` subfolder. It should disappear almost instantly. If you open the BizTalk administration console and refresh the **Group Hub** page (which is displayed by clicking on the **BizTalk Group** node of the console) you should see an output similar to the following screenshot:

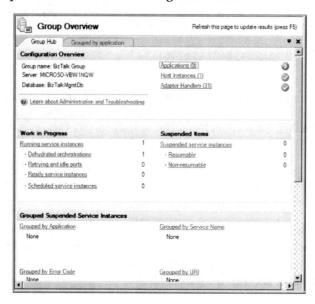

The **Group Hub** page is the dashboard that BizTalk provides to show the current status of service instances within BizTalk. These can be instances of Orchestrations or send ports. As shown in the previous screenshot, I have one running service instance. The following sub-points define the state of the instance:

1. If you open the folder in `C:\TempStuff\filedrops\send_initial` or whichever location you chose for the `Send_Initial_Customer` send port, you will notice that you have an XML file in the folder, which is named as `GUID`. Open it and check if it contains the same contents as the original file. The name of the file in my output folder is: `{E8FCBFC9-E200-48E3-8A35-F6E8A13B3B40}.xml`.

2. Examine the configuration of the `Send_Initial_Customer` send port by right-clicking it in the BizTalk Administration console:
   Applications | SimpleBizTalkSolution | Send Ports.

3. You will see that the URL specified, `%MessageID%`, is a macro that generates a GUID; if you click on **Configure**, the file adapter exposes the `file name` property, which can be modified if you need to adjust it. This can be useful if your backend system only accepts a file with a certain name. Set the URL to:
   `C:\TempStuff\filedrops\send_initial\%MessageID%.xml`

4. Go to the `Send_Initial` folder in your file drop location and cut the message. Place it into the `Receive_Response` folder. The message should disappear and reappear in the `Send_Response` folder, which is the output location specified in your send port configuration.

If you refresh the Group Hub page in the BizTalk Administration Console, you should see that there are no service instances running in your system. What has happened under the covers is that the message conforms to the `Customer` schema type (as specified by the namespace) and the XML receive pipeline promotes the `CustomerID` element. The `CustomerID` element matches the instance subscription that was created when the correlation set was initialized. Therefore, BizTalk knows to return this message to the in-flight orchestration instance. When the message was sent from the first orchestration send port, the correlation set was initialized. This created an instance subscription in the MessageBox, based on the `CustomerID` value as defined in the **Correlation type**. The Message Agent was able to match this instance subscription with the inbound message. Hence, the received message was delivered to the orchestration and it was able to complete its processing.

It's important to note that if 10 orchestrations were waiting on a message with `CustomerID` value `10`, the first message that returned to the MessageBox would be delivered to all 10 dehydrated service instances. The next nine responses would generate a Routing Failure Report, which is BizTalk's internal fault message, used when no subscriber is found. This example illustrates why it is critical that all correlation sets be unique.

Summary

In this chapter, we defined and examined the core use cases for BizTalk, we looked at the core components and tools that BizTalk provides, and we highlighted just a few aspects of BizTalk that make it a compelling tool to use. Please note that we have not even scratched the surface of what BizTalk can do. BizTalk Server provides a scalable messaging engine, robust pub-sub capabilities, and connectivity through over 20 out-of-the-box (plus many more third-party) adapters. Orchestration enables complex workflows to be modeled and the Engine provides persistence and failover to ensure you meet your availability requirements. By building on top of these durable capabilities, many of the world's largest companies have been able to accelerate their development. As such, BizTalk is used by many of the world's largest companies to run mission-critical systems. I have personally worked with customers who have used BizTalk for inter-bank payment and compliance systems, which can affect market liquidity if they fail.

I hope that this chapter gave you some insight into the power of BizTalk, and how it can be used in a service-oriented fashion. In order to assist your evaluation of BizTalk, we have provided a Decision Framework, which shows the methodology that we ourselves have developed and used over time to determine the right technology for a business problem. This will be used to evaluate BizTalk Server against the architectural patterns we present in the rest of this book. For the patterns that BizTalk fits into, we will build sample solutions using best practices that we have used in the real world to architect reusable and maintainable solutions.

5
SQL Server and Data Integration Tools Primer

Way back in the Permian epoch of database technologies, circa 2000 CE to 2005 CE, data integration in the Microsoft stack was accomplished through DTS and MSMQ. Like in the real Permian epoch, huge bugs roamed the landscape, ready to devour the lives of the poor database professional stuck in the La Brea tar pits of system integration support and master data management.

Those of us who look back on those days and shudder were truly grateful for the introduction of **SQL Server Integration Services (SSIS)** and **SQL Server Service Broker (SSSB)** with SQL Server 2005. SQL Server 2008 now supports multiple tools for data integration and master data management, including the following functionalities:

- SSIS new functionality
- SSSB
- Master Data Services
- The Sync Framework, for databases that are only occasionally connected with your networks

With SSIS, SSSB, Master Data Services, and the Sync Framework, database professionals can actually see their children grow up and have an occasional dinner with their loved ones—wonder of wonders! Management will be well pleased as they will no longer need to pay the expenses associated with additional data integration or ETL tools. There could also be less need for support and development of integration for occasionally connected systems, message queuing, and messaging applications because when they purchase SQL Server and Visual Studio 2008/2010 they get the licenses for these powerful tools as well.

What does this technology do?

SQL Server is comprised of multiple components that we will briefly review.

SQL Server Integration Services (SSIS)

SSIS is generally thought of as a tool for **extraction, transformation,** and **loading** (ETL) tasks associated with Business Intelligence (BI) or other reporting applications. Indeed, the classic use of SSIS is for bulk data transfers and large batch data maintenance jobs typically found in the BI world. Most developers consider it "just" an ETL tool.

In fact, SSIS is an extremely powerful tool that you should consider for use in any situation that requires you to move data from one point to another or integrate data across multiple platforms, in or out of the Microsoft stack. SSIS is easily extended with managed code and scales easily to handle everything from a few rows of data to very large data transfers. In addition to data transfers, SSIS can also handle the most common database maintenance tasks with objects available out of the box, and less common tasks through a simple "Execute SQL Task" object that can execute a SQL script or stored procedure on any OLE DB-compliant database. You can even use it to perform maintenance tasks on Oracle or DB2 systems.

The only data integration or data transfer task where SSIS is not a fit would be low latency or very low-volume data transfers. While SSIS can handle these tasks, a better fit might be SQL Server Service Broker.

SQL Server Service Broker (SSSB)

SSSB provides native support for messaging and queuing operations. With SSSB you can build asynchronous, loosely-coupled applications. Unlike traditional message queues, however, the queue is handled through the databases involved and messages can be coordinated, grouped, and prioritized. It requires no additional software. An understanding of **Transact-SQL (T-SQL)** and its basic services is all that you need for SSSB.

Using asynchronous processing can yield big performance gains, particularly when you can prioritize messages. Consider the classic order-entry example that is so often used in books like this one. When an order is placed, certain systems must get data immediately to confirm an order. For example, you need to commit data concerning the customer, the product ordered, and the number of units purchased. On the other hand, the accounts-receivables system and the order-fulfillment system do not need this data to confirm the order. You can send the data that those systems need asynchronously, using SSSB, and even prioritize the messages based on the order priority (rush orders first, for example). In short, you do the minimum work you need to do to—accept the order and complete the rest at your leisure.

The Microsoft Sync Framework

One might normally think of synchronization through the Sync Framework as something to use with small amounts of data and non-critical applications. The most common use of the platform and SDK has been to synchronize handheld devices and MP3 players with data on a personal computer. With the release of SQL Server 2008 and its change tracking utility, Microsoft was able to extend the Sync Framework to databases.

The old-school method of tracking data changes usually involved combinations of timestamps, additional tables and fields, triggers, cleanup processes, and hours of administrative, programming, and break-fix time. There was almost always an adverse impact on system performance, including the resulting I/O overhead needed to write, read, and update the tracking data.

SQL Server 2008 handles these issues for you with the change data capture and change tracking features.

The Sync Framework now allows you to develop applications that will synchronize data across any ADO.NET-enabled database. These databases can also synchronize information with any other source supported by the Sync Framework, such as web services, file systems, and custom data stores.

For integration of applications and data that is only occasionally connected, or connected on some ad hoc basis, the Sync Framework should be seriously considered.

Master Data Services

Master Data Services allows you to easily coordinate data across disparate sources so that all systems, and more importantly, all employees can operate from a single version of truth. With the release of **SQL Server 2008 R2**, Microsoft provided us a tool for dealing with a problem that has been around for a long time; different systems have different data about the same key business entity. The problem arises from a number of sources, including human error in data entry and our own failure as database architects to set up systems to reconcile data discrepancies. The author's personal experience of poor customer service can often be linked to bad, or even non-existent, master data management.

This can be more than a customer service issue; it can also be a human safety issue. Consider the health care industry in the United States. Health care providers seem to have a very large number of small, isolated applications that handle medical specialties; however, these applications are not designed to be integrated with each other. If one department creates a `Patient` record concerning key patient data, there is no guarantee that the data will appear in other "stove piped" specialty applications.

Doctors could therefore, miss key data which might influence their treatment decisions, and might even threaten a patient's life because they did not have the data they needed to make the correct decision.

Master Data Services uses a **hub and spoke model** around key business nouns and their attributes (for example, the noun "customer" and attribute "delivery address"). A central service captures this data and coordinates the resolution of any discrepancies, first using a set of business rules and then relying on human interaction for unanticipated problems or to resolve conflicts in the rules. The resolved data is then sent down the spoke to various systems that require the resolved data.

A very basic and completely insufficient introduction to data integration with SQL Server

There are lots of cool features in SQL Server 2008. Complete books and hundreds of blogs, articles, TechNet, and MSDN pages have been written on each of these subjects. These below sections on SQL Server's suite of tools are focused on data integration problems, with occasional forays into the author's pet peeves around data security. We will, therefore, limit the discussion to key integration technologies and my apologies in advance for merely scratching the surface of these rich and robust environments.

SSIS

SSIS has no core technologies as such; its core is SQL Server itself. One should think of SSIS as a collection of objects that create a powerful visual environment for performing a multitude of tasks associated with master data management, database maintenance, data integration, and ETL projects.

You create SSIS projects in **Business Intelligence Development Studio** in Microsoft Visual Studio. SSIS packages are developed initially with a graphical interface, which handles the more mundane (and boring) tasks associated with project development. The graphical environment is so rich that other developers will frequently accuse SSIS developers of just "drawing pretty pictures". A word of caution: this is a fast way to get yourself punched out by an SSIS developer.

The basic unit of work in SSIS is a **package**. A package contains **tasks**, each of which does a distinct unit of work. Here, for example, we have a package with a script task and a data-flow task, each of which fetches an RSS feed and writes it into different destinations.

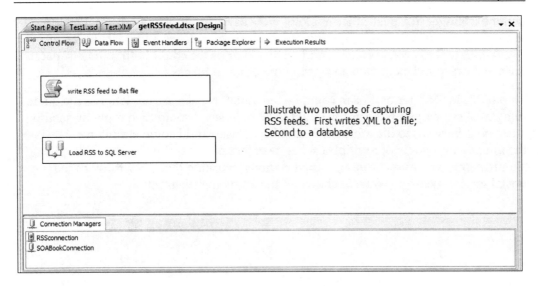

The details of the package are stored as XML. Indeed, a more adventurous reader can use the **View Code** function and directly edit the XML. Those of us who at least attempt to have a life stick to the GUI.

When you install SQL Server you also install the SSIS service that needs to be running for your package to work on a given machine. The service will monitor and control the deployment and execution of packages. Each package can be considered a *script* (we use that term as an analogy only), which is executed by the service.

SSSB

SSSB uses a *post-office* analogy as its model. A user inputs data that must be stored or otherwise handled on multiple systems. The user's application for SSSB purposes, called the **initiator,** initiates a conversation with a target service, builds a message containing the data required to process a task, and sends that message to the target.

Letter exchanges in a post-office analogy were asynchronous operations. For example my cousin Susan, might initiate the correspondence and write to me or I could initiate the correspondence and write to her or we could both initiate separate lines of correspondence, each answering the other in turns.

To put this in SSSB terms, Susan could be the initiator—placing her letter in the queue (the postal system) with me as the **target** in New Jersey. I could then reply by sending a response message to the initiator, Susan. Both Susan and I could simultaneously be the initiator and target of multiple exchange of letters and be involved in multiple, simultaneous, and asynchronous "conversations" working their way through the postal service message queue as shown in the following diagram:

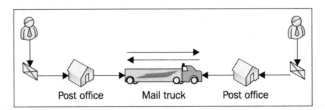

In the SSSB exchange of correspondence, messages are XML-based and are placed in electronic queues, thereby creating a simple asynchronous communication between two systems. Like Susan and me, each system could be both the initiator and the target in any one conversation.

Sync Framework

The Sync Framework is a comprehensive platform that allows for collaboration and coordination across multiple applications or systems. You can use the Sync Framework with any ADO.NET-enabled database system.

The first step is to configure the relevant database. This involves a simple ALTER DATABASE statement, followed by an ALTER TABLE statement to set change tracking on for the database and tables, respectively. SQL Server will store metadata concerning the relevant databases and tables, allowing the system to track changes and coordinate synchronization without the need to do full transfers of entire tables or databases. Only new or changed data is synchronized.

When a synchronization session begins, the source begins the session with a destination. This can be triggered by many events, the most common being the source system detecting that it is connected to the destination system, similar to when your mobile device detects that it is connected to your computer and can synchronize things such as your calendar or your contacts. The metadata is used by the source to send change versions and sources to the destination. Local versions at the destination are then compared to the source system. Business rules are used to resolve conflicts or defer them (for example, from human intervention). The destination system requests the data and applies it, then updates the metadata.

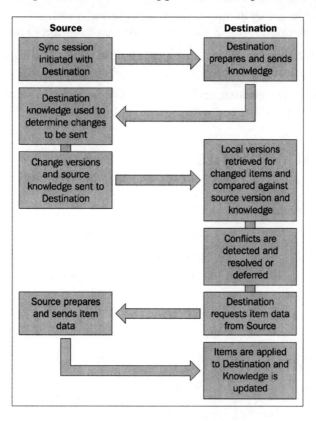

SQL Server 2008 enhancements

The following enhancements are made to SQL Server 2008:

1. The MERGE function. The MERGE function has long been a staple of ETL development for Oracle. It is nice to see Microsoft eliminate the need for writing workaround upsert statements that handle both updates and insertions.

2. New and significantly more powerful encryption functions.

3. **Data-access auditing**, a powerful tool that audits who is accessing what data and when. For certain highly regulated industries, like health care and financial services, this functionality will significantly ease the database administration overhead.

4. **Filtered indexes**, a very useful tool, if one has to select from a field with a significant amount of null values.

5. Parallel query processing on partitioned objects.

6. The ability to associate query plans with actual queries; cuts down on the often significant overhead associated with the creation of a query plan.

7. Security enhancements, including easier data access auditing and transparent data encryption.

8. **Parallel data warehouse**, an integrated SQL Server and storage device with storage optimized for use with SQL Server.

SSIS enhancements

The following enhancements are made to SSIS:

1. Ability to create script tasks that use C#.

2. Improved performance of bulk load operations.

3. The ability to capture changed data.

4. Views of datatype mapping to help prevent annoying datatype mismatch errors.

5. Support for time zone offsets that eliminate the need for messy workarounds.

SSSB enhancements

The following enhancements are made to SSSB:

1. Support for conversation priorities.

2. New diagnostic utilities.

3. Additional object counters to check performance and error states.

Sync Framework enhancements

The Sync Framework version 2.0 was released to leverage the power of change tracking. Almost all of this API's interaction with databases is new with this release.

Typical use cases

The typical use case for each of these tools is rather simple: data is here, it needs to be moved there. The rest is just details. While the classic uses of these technologies are ETL, master data management, and asynchronous processing, they should also be considered for any application that needs to move and transform data in places where simple log shipping or replication will not meet the need or does not provide all the functionality required (for example, diverse data sources).

While each of these tools can be extended to most data-movement scenarios, there are times when one is served better with other tools. The classic case of the need for an Enterprise Service Bus (ESB) application or the need to move data through a workflow, would be good examples of business needs where other technologies might be better suited. There are also industry-specific applications offered by Microsoft that may better fit a need. For example, Microsoft Amalga is designed to handle message queues for the health care industry's HL7 standard formatted data.

Example solution

We can take a look at an example of this technology in action, through a demo application that has some real-world implications beyond "Hello World!". There are numerous RSS feeds available, which expose a wealth of data. In this case, we have chosen a sample feed from Microsoft because it allows us to demonstrate some versatility of SSIS, as well as how data from varying sources can be distributed throughout an enterprise. We take this feed, shred the XML, and write the resulting data to SQL Server. We will then use the Sync Framework to distribute the resulting data.

These feeds also allow us to demonstrate some of the best practices that you should implement with SSIS. They include the following:

- Using the configuration collection of SSIS to store key metadata (for example, the path to the RSS feed)
- Some logging and error-handling best practices

We should note a few things. SSIS defaults to the .NET framework version 2.0, which contained some powerful tools for handling XML. In order to serialize an RSS feed, however, it would be easiest to use the `ServiceModel` class, available in .NET version 3.5. Your projects will need to be reconfigured to use this version and references added to your script objects.

Writing an RSS feed to SQL Server

Here, we will use SSIS to capture data from an RSS feed, load it into a database, then distribute it around the enterprise using the Sync Framework.

Open Visual Studio and create a SQL Server Integration Services project. Rename the package `getRSSFeed.dtsx` to a similar, arbitrary name. Note that you must use the `dtsx` extension. Drag a data flow task into the control flow panel. Open the data flow and drag a script task into the data flow. Next, drag a data conversion task into the flow and connect it to the script task. Finally, drag an OLE DB destination into the flow and connect it to the data conversion task. Define the RSS feed you wish to use as your data source with an HTTP connection manager. Here we used the Microsoft MVP RSS feed. When complete, the data flow should look something like the following screenshot:

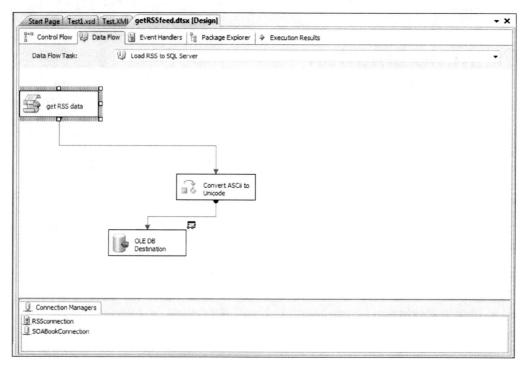

The script task in a data flow is slightly different for those of you who are accustomed to using script tasks in the main package. Here, we start with a pre-execute event and use the `Connectors` collection for our data source.

```
private XmlReader EcoIndicatorData = null;
private System.ServiceModel.Syndication.SyndicationFeed RSS_Data =
                                                                null;

  private string RSS_URL = string.Empty;
  public override void PreExecute()
  {
    base.PreExecute();
    RSS_URL = Connections.RSSConnection.ConnectionString;
  }
```

As we use this script as a data source, we then execute the `CreateNewOutputRows()` method and add rows to the output buffer, defined in the **Script Transformation Editor** interface.

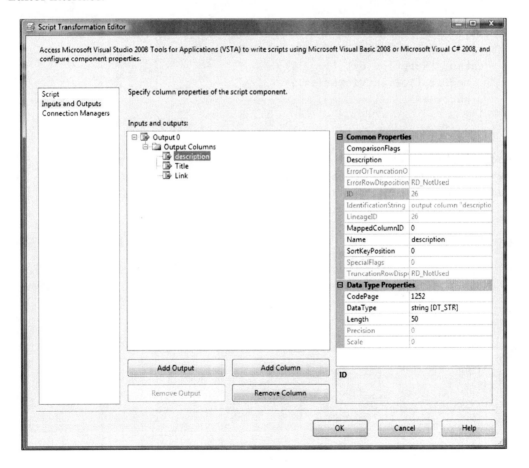

The method itself is a simple loop through the RSS data, writing out the elements we want to load to the database.

```
public override void CreateNewOutputRows()
{
  try
  {
    EcoIndicatorData = XmlReader.Create(RSS_URL);
    RSS_Data = SyndicationFeed.Load(EcoIndicatorData);
    if (RSS_Data != null)
    {
      foreach (var item in RSS_Data.Items)
      {
        Output0Buffer.AddRow();
        Output0Buffer.Title = item.Title.Text;
        Output0Buffer.description = item.Summary.Text;
        Output0Buffer.Link = item.Links[0].Uri.AbsoluteUri;
      }
    }
  }
  catch (Exception ex) {
    LogErrorToEventViewer(ex);
    throw(ex);
  }
}
```

The result of this exercise holds the data as ASCII strings. The relevant table, however, will hold the nvarchar datatype. We therefore need to convert the datatypes in a data conversion task.

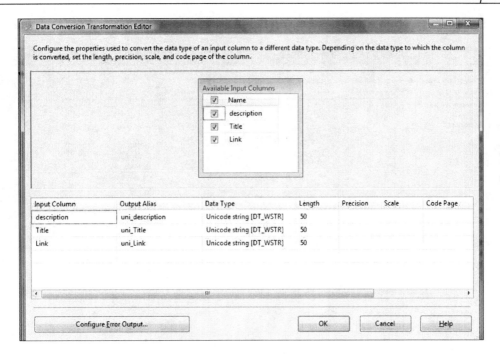

The results are now loaded into SQL Server using an OLE DB destination task.

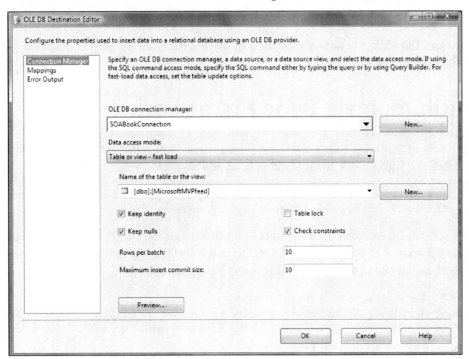

Within this task, source and destination fields are mapped in a visual environment.

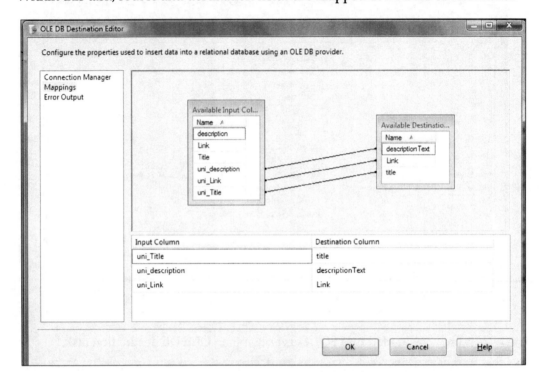

In this case, the Unicode data we created in the transformation step is mapped to the relevant field in the database.

Distribution via Sync Framework

Now that the data is in the database, we will need to distribute it around the enterprise—in this case, using the Sync Framework. You will first need to download and install the framework from Microsoft, available at:

```
http://www.microsoft.com/downloads/details.aspx?FamilyID=89adbb1e-
53ff-41b5-ba17-8e43a2e66254&displaylang=en
```

Drag a script task into the package and open it. We used C# in this exercise, but you can use VB scripts as well. You will need to place certain additional references into the script, as shown in the following code snippet:

```
using Microsoft.Synchronization;
using Microsoft.Synchronization.Data;
using Microsoft.Synchronization.Data.SqlServer;
using Microsoft.SqlServer;
```

```
using System.Data.SqlClient;
using System.Data.Common;
```

The next steps will be to create database connections and add them to
`SqlSyncProvider` objects. `sourceConnString` is a string that contains the
connection data for the database where you stored the RSS feed in the prior section
and `destinationConnString` is a string holding the connection information for
the database where this feed will be sent. You should set these values for your
environment.

```
SqlConnection sourceConn = new SqlConnection(sourceConnString);
  SqlConnection destinationConn = new
                               SqlConnection(destinationConnString);
//set up the source provider
    SqlSyncProvider sourceSqlProv = new SqlSyncProvider();
    sourceSqlProv.ScopeName = "MicrosoftMVPfeed";
    sourceSqlProv.Connection = sourceConn;
```

The scope of the synchronization is then set, the provider is added to a dictionary and
used to create a `RelationalSyncProvider` object that will control the synchronization
between two databases. We would follow the exact same steps for the destination, as it
will also be a SQL Server database. Different steps would be followed if the destination
was a CE database or some other ADO.NET-enabled destination.

```
//provide scope to the source connection
    DbSyncScopeDescription sourceDesc = new
                           DbSyncScopeDescription("MicrosoftMVPfeed");
    SqlSyncScopeProvisioning sourceProvision = new

SqlSyncScopeProvisioning();
    sourceDesc.Tables.Add(SqlSyncDescriptionBuilder.
      GetDescriptionForTable("MicrosoftMVPfeed", (System.Data.
      SqlClient.SqlConnection)sourceSqlProv.Connection));
    sourceProvision.PopulateFromScopeDescription(sourceDesc);
//do not recreate table
    sourceProvision.SetCreateTableDefault(DbSyncCreationOption.Skip);
//all is provided
    sourceProvision.Apply((System.Data.SqlClient.SqlConnection)
                                      sourceSqlProv.Connection);
//add to the provider collection
    providersCollection.Add("Source", sourceSqlProv);
    RelationalSyncProvider source = providersCollection["Source"];
```

Once the setup is done, the actual synchronization occurs with a few simple lines of code. We set up an orchestrator, set a few simple properties—such as the source, destination, and direction—and then execute the synchronization.

```
//actually do the sync
    SyncOrchestrator orchestrator = new SyncOrchestrator();
    orchestrator.LocalProvider = source;
    orchestrator.RemoteProvider = destination;
    orchestrator.Direction = SyncDirectionOrder.UploadAndDownload;
//bidirectional sync
    orchestrator.Synchronize();
```

So we now have a single, easily created C# script. In a single package execution, we fetch the RSS feed and send it out to other servers throughout the enterprise.

SQL Server Service Broker

While synchronization is powerful, it does have certain shortcomings. For example, the source and target tables must be exactly the same for the process to work and there is no way to prioritize what data should be moved first. Often, we will have to synchronize data across systems that have different uses and therefore use significantly different schemas. Also, there often are prioritization rules that must be followed (for example, rush orders versus standard orders). This is where we should be looking at SSSB.

SSSB provides for asynchronous processing of messages. A conversation is initiated by the sending database. A receiving database takes the call, receives the incoming data, validates the data, and acknowledges the receipt. It may then continue the conversation by sending data back.

Open **SQL Server Management Studio** and connect to your development database server. We have created a simple database to illustrate SSSB called SOA_Book.

We start by setting up the database and objects in the database to handle the conversation as follows. First, we enable the service broker with a simple ALTER DATABASE statement.

```
USE master;
GO
ALTER DATABASE SOA_Book
  SET ENABLE_BROKER;
GO
```

We must create message types, contracts, and queues that the service will rely on to actually converse and then create the service. This is done for both the sending and receiving ends of the conversation. Our conversation will consist of well-formed XML. We could validate against a schema as well. You would use the following statement:

```
USE SOA_Book;
GO

CREATE MESSAGE TYPE
   [//SOAbook/SampleQueue/RequestMessage]
   VALIDATION = WELL_FORMED_XML;
CREATE MESSAGE TYPE
   [//SOAbook/SampleQueue/ReplyMessage]
   VALIDATION = WELL_FORMED_XML;
GO
CREATE CONTRACT [//SOAbook/SampleQueue/SampleContract]
   ([//SOAbook/SampleQueue/RequestMessage]
   SENT BY INITIATOR,
   [//SOAbook/SampleQueue/ReplyMessage]
   SENT BY TARGET
   );
GO
CREATE QUEUE SampleTargetQueue;

CREATE SERVICE
   [//SOAbook/SampleQueue/TargetService]
   ON QUEUE SampleTargetQueue
   ([//SOAbook/SampleQueue/SampleContract]);
GO
CREATE QUEUE SampleInitiatorQueue;

CREATE SERVICE
   [//SOAbook/SampleQueue/InitiatorService]
   ON QUEUE SampleInitiatorQueue;
GO
```

Once the objects are set up, we use them for our dialog. We create a dialog from an initiator to a target on a particular contract and send a message of a particular type, all within a transaction.

```
/*
Send the message
*/
DECLARE @InitDlgHandle UNIQUEIDENTIFIER;
DECLARE @RequestMsg NVARCHAR(100);

BEGIN TRANSACTION;
```

```
BEGIN DIALOG @InitDlgHandle
  FROM SERVICE [//SOAbook/SampleQueue/InitiatorService]
  TO SERVICE N'//SOAbook/SampleQueue/TargetService'
  ON CONTRACT [//SOAbook/SampleQueue/SampleContract]
  WITH ENCRYPTION = OFF;
SELECT @RequestMsg =
  N'<RequestMsg>Do not meddle in the affairs of wizards, for they are
                           subtle and quick to anger.</RequestMsg>';

SEND ON CONVERSATION @InitDlgHandle
  MESSAGE TYPE [//SOAbook/SampleQueue/RequestMessage] (@RequestMsg);

SELECT @RequestMsg AS SentRequestMsg, @InitDlgHandle as 'Dialog ID'

COMMIT TRANSACTION;
GO
```

On the receiving end, we receive the message, and in the following sample, send a second message back. We begin with a WAITFOR statement as the receiver does not know when the message will arrive, similar to how a human receiver of a letter does not precisely know when it will arrive via the postal service. Once we receive the message, we open the letter with a SELECT statement and send a reply.

```
DECLARE @RecvReqDlgHandle UNIQUEIDENTIFIER;
DECLARE @RecvReqMsg NVARCHAR(100);
DECLARE @RecvReqMsgName sysname;

BEGIN TRANSACTION;

WAITFOR (
  RECEIVE
    @RecvReqDlgHandle = conversation_handle,
    @RecvReqMsg = message_body,
    @RecvReqMsgName = message_type_name
    FROM SampleTargetQueue
), TIMEOUT 1000;

SELECT @RecvReqMsg AS ReceivedRequestMsg;
SELECT @RecvReqDlgHandle, @RecvReqMsg, @RecvReqMsgName

  IF @RecvReqMsgName = N'//SOAbook/SampleQueue/RequestMessage'
  BEGIN
  DECLARE @ReplyMsg NVARCHAR(100);
SELECT @ReplyMsg = N'<ReplyMsg>And he piled on the whales white hump
all the pain and hate felt by his race from Adam down</ReplyMsg>';
```

```
SEND ON CONVERSATION @RecvReqDlgHandle
  MESSAGE TYPE [//SOAbook/SampleQueue/ReplyMessage]
  (@ReplyMsg);

END CONVERSATION @RecvReqDlgHandle;
END

SELECT @ReplyMsg AS SentReplyMsg;

COMMIT TRANSACTION;
GO
```

The statement `SELECT @ReplyMsg AS SentReplyMsg` simply confirms the successful completion of the conversation.

The initiator must now listen for the reply and take appropriate actions. In this case, it simply ends the conversation. Here again, the initiator will not know when the reply will be delivered or what its content will be, so we follow steps similar to the receiver. We wait for a reply, open it, and then review it once it is received.

```
DECLARE @RecvReplyMsg NVARCHAR(100);
DECLARE @RecvReplyDlgHandle UNIQUEIDENTIFIER;

BEGIN TRANSACTION;

WAITFOR(
  RECEIVE TOP(1)
    @RecvReplyDlgHandle = conversation_handle,
    @RecvReplyMsg = message_body
    FROM dbo.SampleInitiatorQueue
), TIMEOUT 1000;

END CONVERSATION @RecvReplyDlgHandle;

SELECT @RecvReplyMsg AS ReceivedReplyMsg;

COMMIT TRANSACTION;
GO
```

As you can see, SSSB uses a modified set of SQL statements that should be familiar to almost all database developers.

Summary

Here, we have three powerful tools for data movement (SSIS, Sync, and SSSB) that can handle data movement, master data management, and data governance needs of a variety of organizations and in a variety of business circumstances. The tools can be used in a variety of combinations to get data where it needs to be.

6

Windows Azure Platform Primer

With the advent of the Internet, it became possible to access services from just a browser without requiring several hours of setup and configuration time before using a technology. This fast bootstrapping usage of elastic, pay-per-use, internet-accessible services (known as cloud computing), is impacting not just end-consumers, but also businesses of all sizes. Microsoft is trying to cause a disruptive shift in the cloud-computing market and lead the next wave of innovation.

6-12-18 is not a random typo that made it into the book, but these are three numbers discussed by Microsoft executive Oliver Sharp when discussing the deployment patterns of enterprise customers. **Six** represents the percentage of data-center utilization that typically appears in data-center utilization surveys—utilization peaks at around ten percent. **Twelve**, is the twelve million square feet server facilities that Microsoft had bought at the time when Oliver made the note. Finally, **eighteen** is the number of days it took for the existing server capacity to max-out when the traffic increased on a key Microsoft site during the dawn of the web era. This meant that they had to buy and provision new servers every 18 days and the IT manager had to manage this process along with all the capacity, power, and cooling issues associated with it. The net of this is that people are paying significantly more than they need to for infrastructure.

The cost of this excess capacity represents a huge initial **Capital Expenditure (CAPEX)** and ongoing **Operational Expenditure (OPEX)** for capacity that organizations are not using. By paying for only what you use, you can effectively offset a huge amount of both OPEX and CAPEX. In effect, increasing computer power becomes a proportional tax/cost on your increased income. This represents a complete paradigm shift to the way things are done today.

There are many different definitions and applications of cloud. Much of this technology has been developed at Microsoft as a result of the journey and lessons learned from developing and running complex cloud systems such as Bing, Hotmail, and Xbox LIVE.

In fact, many customers are already building "private" clouds using virtualization technology, management tools, and techniques that they have developed over time to run their large distributed systems.

This kind of usage has helped vendors understand customer requirements in areas such as security, scaling, high availability, and offline scenarios. In the last three to five years, the first generation of these generic platform resources based on over a decade of learning have been moved to the cloud — Amazon Web Services, Google App Engine, and Windows Azure platform.

For the purposes of this chapter, we will define the following three cloud requirements. The cloud must fulfill the following tasks:

- Protect and secure my data
- Manage my distributed computing environment at the lowest possible cost
- Provide an agile computing environment which can change quickly to respond to business environment changes and scale incrementally

Throughout each solution implementation, the common requirement is to be successful in an ever changing, geographically dispersed world; cloud resources need to be elastic in nature — it needs to make computing resources commoditized and simple to use. The ultimate vision is for cloud computing to transform in the same way that utility electricity replaced on-premise power generation. They should be easy to use, with a shorter setup and maintenance time. This removes the requirement for companies to purchase infrastructure upfront assuming that they would need these resources at some point down the road. With the cloud, they simply leverage the cloud computing resources and throttle usage as and when required. For example, if you are a beginner working on an innovative idea, you don't have to immediately invest in procuring hardware resources, software licenses, and staffing IT operations; instead, you can start focusing on your innovation by leveraging things in the cloud. This is huge! Finally, these resources should be accessible from almost anywhere and be enterprise-ready. IT administrators must be able to button-down security provisioning for a set of user accounts as well as restrict usage, if necessary, from "public" clouds. One of the core advantages of cloud-based systems is that users do not have to roll out the updates themselves, they simply utilize the service which is upgraded seamlessly; this is a key advantage for many companies that spend significant amounts rolling out new versions of traditional thick-client, on-premise software.

Microsoft's approach to cloud computing has been a *Software plus Services* strategy. This model allows a combination of on-premise resources and on-cloud resources with a seamless usage of development tools. This approach makes sense from a customer standpoint, where they can leverage existing hardware and software infrastructure in addition to developer skills and tools. So, there is a seamless, integrated approach with the choice and decision controlled by the customer.

The following are three key pivots to this strategy, which is central across all the Microsoft offerings:

1. Provide the ability to store and access data in the cloud.

2. Enable services that run in the cloud to be accessed.

3. Run custom code—compute power—in the cloud.

The Windows Azure platform supports all these requirements. The components it provides are as follows:

1. **Windows Azure**: The underlying Windows cloud-based operating system environment which provides compute and data storage capabilities.

2. **Windows Azure AppFabric**: Provides the Service Bus and Access Control components which enable complex, hybrid, service-based applications to be hosted in the cloud or connected (relayed) through the cloud.

3. **SQL Azure**: Extends SQL Server capabilities to the cloud. It is a cloud-based relational database—the database resource in the cloud—which provides TDS and T-SQL-based access and programmability, enabling customers to take leverage and run their existing applications in the cloud.

The following diagram illustrates these components:

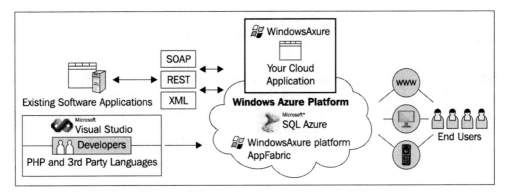

In this chapter, we provide an overview of the platform with a simple solution and walkthrough instructions to host the solution in the Windows Azure platform.

What does this technology do?

In this section, we will drill down deeper into three key aspects of the Windows Azure platform—Windows Azure, SQL Azure, and Windows Azure AppFabric.

Windows Azure

Windows Azure is the operating system in the cloud. It supports hosting a piece of application code in disparate Microsoft data centers, while automatically making it highly available, scalable, on-demand, and accessible from a set of clients over the Internet. This application does not have to be web-centric as it could be any piece of code that can be hosted in Windows Azure—for example, it can be a piece of unmanaged code that uses a computation-intensive algorithm and operates without an HTTP face. The platform allows non-Microsoft languages and supports popular standards, languages, and protocols such as SOAP, REST, XML, and PHP.

Usage

Windows Azure provides a familiar development and deployment environment to build and scale-out applications. Essentially, the platform builds on a set of three key tenets which are applicable to all of the cloud technologies—easier manageability, elastic scalability, and developer agility.

When an administrator uses Windows Azure, only a set of logical entities are exposed—no direct access to the actual virtual machines or complicated, physical deployment topology is required. The administrator controls a set of application behaviors. For instance, the administrator can control the deployment topology by indicating the locality of application access such as the entire US, North Central, or South Central. In addition, the administrator can create an affinity group which can call out the dependency of this service/application with other deployed applications. From here on, the application will be automatically provisioned for use and deployed in the data center.

Elastic scaling is exposed in Windows Azure via configuration knobs. When an application is deployed, the number of "entry points" or the amount of background computation can be specified. This will be used to automatically provision a number of virtual machine nodes for the application to run. This knob can be tweaked anytime to increase or decrease scaling, based on the scaling requirements.

One important differentiator from competing offerings is the developer experience on top of this platform. Visual Studio developers can easily build solutions using existing knowledge instead of having to adopt a new development paradigm. For example, developers can use the Visual Studio cloud project template and build new cloud services using popular programming languages and patterns. The new cloud deployment and application packaging model are natural extensions that are easy to adopt. The cloud application can use either the Windows Azure storage or SQL Azure.

Architecture

Windows Azure architecture can be broken down into the following three main layers:

- Fabric controller.
- Compute.
- Storage.

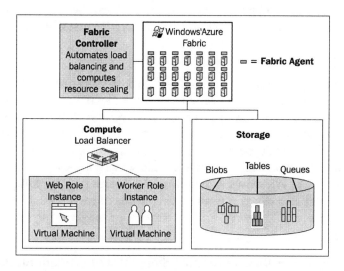

Fabric controller

When applications are deployed across Microsoft data centers, the fabric controller is the layer that provisions the application, detects failures, and automatically spins up new instances. It also manages updates to maintain zero downtime for your application code. When an application is deployed, in addition to the code, metadata or application configuration (also known as service model) is included in the deployment package. The fabric uses this information to deploy the application on a set of nodes (compute resources), sets up the network settings, configures the load balancer, and maintain the life cycle of the application. The usage of the fabric controller is part of the Windows Azure technology and is not directly exposed to the end-user.

Compute

The compute layer represents the set of processing resources exposed as configurable roles to run portions of the applications. All of the machines in the Microsoft data center are configured to host a set of virtual machines using a **Hyper-V** environment running a customized 64 bit Windows Server 2008 OS. As Microsoft releases future versions of Windows Server, these VMs will be upgraded, giving customers the benefit of new OS capabilities without having to perform upgrade cycles themselves. A service or application hosted in Windows Azure can be configured to consist of one or more web roles and worker roles.

Web role

A web role is used to host any frontend of an application requiring the UI to accept and respond to user HTTP requests. Typically, one can expose an ASP.NET, ASP.NET MVC, WCF service, or even PHP applications as a web role. When an application is configured to have a set of web roles, then the fabric controller deploys the application on a set of virtual machines that have IIS installed on them.

Worker role

Typically, applications also require "headless" background processing to perform computations or interactions with backend systems. Such a model is exposed through the worker role. For example, consider an airline website that searches for tickets. The frontend exposed as a web role will accept the user criteria. Then a service might need to match the user request with the airline tickets' inventory and price, and generate a set of valid responses. This service logic could be configured to run as a worker role. Windows Azure-hosted services may be comprised of one or both types of roles and can run multiple instances of each type. One could host a generic WCF service, a TCP server, an FTP service, or maybe even an Apache service in a worker role.

Virtual machine instances that are running these roles can communicate among themselves synchronously or use the asynchronous model through the Windows Azure storage services. For example, a web application hosted in a web role can directly call into a calendar service, hosted in a worker role. If the web application wants to queue messages then it can write to the Windows Azure storage (more on this topic in the next section) and another worker-role instance can read-off the queue and perform background processing.

Role instances can be added or removed based on demand, and allow applications to quickly and economically scale-up or down when the need arises.

More compute roles are being planned to be available in the future. One popular one is the VM role that will provide administrators with more control to install, configure, and manage the virtual machine running the applications.

Storage

There are three durable storage options that can be used by a Windows Azure-hosted application or by a set of desktop applications accessing the storage in the cloud. For example, a web application may need to store images in a photo album or queue some transient requests for processing a user request. Applications can leverage this highly available and scalable storage that is replicated across a set of windows server machines in Microsoft data centers.

Windows Azure storage services includes blob services for storing text and binary data, table services for semi-structured storage that can be queried, and queue services for reliable and persistent messaging between services.

Blobs

Blob storage is comparable to the typical hard disk storage available on machines. It can be used to store any kind of data such as images, documents, media, and the like. Each blob object is replicated and three copies are maintained to make it highly available and to guarantee persistence across data crashes. The storage is highly optimized to store several pieces of a large file and supports uploading and reading the required portions. There are two different types of blobs—block and page. A block blob is used for storing streaming content like video files, while page blob is useful for random reads and writes.

Table

Table storage is a misnomer—it does not represent a database table nor does it replace SQL Azure functionality. It merely represents a C# hashtable or list-like construct that can be used to store semi-structured data without enforcing a schema. An application can store any key-value pair in the table service.

Queue

Queues are typically used as a light-weight messaging system between different compute roles. They provide a reliable mechanism to do asynchronous processing and build loosely coupled systems. When a user inputs data, a web role can store data in a queue and instantly return to the caller for a snappy user experience. Another worker role that typically runs for a longer duration of time, can read-off the queue and perform additional processing such as writing or looking-up against a set of tables in SQL Azure, for example. If the worker role instance were to crash for some reason, the queue storage has ways to guarantee durability; whereby, the message will re-appear in the queue for another worker role instance to start processing again.

Drive

Windows Azure Drive is a type of storage that lets applications use NTFS API to access and store data in the cloud. This type of storage is useful for applications that use data from a directory structure. An administrator can create and mount a drive for usage by an application. The drive guarantees durability across hardware and application failures. Underneath, the drive implementation actually uses the Windows Azure page blob, which performs well for random reads and writes.

Provisioning model

In order to provision an application on Windows Azure, you will need to create a Windows Azure account and buy a subscription from `http://www.microsoft.com/windowsazure/account/`. While signing up, the Windows Azure platform has a set of subscription offers which vary depending on several factors—the number of compute hours, the number of transactions, network bandwidth, duration of commitment, and so on. Once you sign up for the suitable selection using your Windows Live ID, the subscription can be managed from `https://mocp.microsoftonline.com/Site/Manage.aspx`. Once the system activates the account, details will be sent to the e-mail address linked with your Windows Live ID.

You can then visit the portal `https://windows.azure.com/Cloud/Provisioning/Default.aspx` to get started. Using this portal, you can create a new service which allows two options—to create a storage account or a hosted service. When creating a storage account, you are essentially provisioning a globally accessible endpoint, registered as a URL to access the supported storage options—queues, tables, or blobs. For example, after this process, you will see a set of endpoints similar to the following ones:

```
http://appliedarchstorage.blob.core.windows.net/
```

```
http://appliedarchstorage.queue.core.windows.net/
```

```
http://appliedarchstorage.table.core.windows.net/
```

For each storage account, there are a set of access keys for security purposes. When an application needs to use a particular storage account, it needs to specify the correct access key before it is published from Visual Studio. These settings can be specified in the **Properties** tab for the web and worker role from Visual Studio.

Another unique feature is the availability of a **Content Delivery Network (CDN)** option for the storage account. Windows Azure CDN has several locations around the world to cache the storage closer to the end-users accessing it. For example, if the storage is set up in a US data center and enabled to use CDN, then a user from Australia could access a cached version from a CDN location closer to their geographic location, giving a better performance and end-user experience.

When one chooses the hosted service option (the other option while creating a new service), a compute node (64 bit virtual machine) is provisioned to run your application. The provisioning process is similar when one must choose a globally unique public name, accessible as a URL for the service. At the end of this step, a cloud-host environment is set up to run your application.

During this process for setting up a storage account or a hosted service, administrators can also define an affinity group which decides the closest Microsoft data center where the resource must be physically located. This is especially useful when there is a need to co-locate the compute and storage for better performance. In such cases, one would create an affinity group with a friendly name such as "US_Region" and tie it to a physical location such as North Central US or South Central US. While creating a service or storage account, it can be associated with the affinity group "US_Region", and thus be co-located. Modifying the mapping of the friendly name to the physical location will affect all the associated services. In scenarios where there is no need to use affinity groups, the actual physical location can be directly specified while creating the service.

Diagnostics and monitoring

A key aspect of any application deployment is to get diagnostics and monitoring data for analysis. With Windows Azure Diagnostics, it is possible to collect diagnostic data for performance-tuning analysis, capacity planning, and general resource-usage monitoring, in addition to common tasks such as debugging and troubleshooting. The diagnostics can be enabled within your service code or from outside of it. As part of diagnostics, it is possible to collect data from the following sources for web and worker roles — Windows Azure logs, IIS 7.0 logs, Windows diagnostic infrastructure logs, failed request logs, Windows event logs, performance counters, crash dumps, and custom error logs. The DiagnosticMonitor class provides a set of APIs to configure your required set of data sources and this can be used from within your code, as well as hosted and run on Windows Azure. With the new release, the platform supports a TraceListener, which allows applications to write to the standard **Event Tracing for Windows (ETW)** or use Trace Debug statements as part of the application code.

```
DiagnosticMonitorConfiguration diagConfig =
            DiagnosticMonitor.GetDefaultInitialConfiguration();
// Add performance counter monitoring for % processor time
// Run typeperf.exe /q to query the counter list
PerformanceCounterConfiguration procTimeConfig = new
                            PerformanceCounterConfiguration();
procTimeConfig.CounterSpecifier = @"\Processor(*)\% Processor Time";
procTimeConfig.SampleRate = System.TimeSpan.FromSeconds(1.0);
diagConfig.PerformanceCounters.DataSources.Add(procTimeConfig);
// Start the diagnostic monitor with this custom configuration
DiagnosticMonitor.Start("DiagnosticsConnectionString", diagConfig);
// Capture complete crash dumps
Microsoft.WindowsAzure.Diagnostics.CrashDumps.EnableCollection(true);
```

When you need to set this up from outside the actual code running, the diagnostics can also be enabled from a remote location by using the DeploymentDiagnosticsManager and RoleInstanceDiagnosticManager classes. For certain data sources, modifying the configuration file before deploying the solution will take effect. This diagnostic data can then be transferred to the storage account as part of a scheduled job or on-demand for analysis. There is also a monitoring agent that can be used to gather the collected diagnostic data. This data can then be transferred for analysis of the application behavior and to enforce action.

For example, by gathering data from a "Photos R Us" application, you can understand that the application actually needs an additional worker role to optimize the performance. The action to increase the worker roles can be done using the portal or programmatically, using the Service Management API. The action can be done using a custom script or a PowerShell commandlet to auto scale the application. All the Service Management APIs are based on **Representational State Order** (**REST**) and expose all functionality other than creation, deletion of accounts, and billing data.

How do I get started?

The Windows Azure SDK presents a set of APIs, tools, samples, and Visual Studio project templates to help bootstrap the development experience. It also offers a development experience that simulates the cloud infrastructure (fabric and storage services) on a developer machine. Using the project templates and the development fabric, it is easy to understand the various APIs and deployment model without procuring or getting an online account.

After you have ramped up on the development fabric, you can visit `http://www.microsoft.com/windowsazure/account/` and follow the instructions from the **Provisioning Model** section for moving the solution to the cloud. The sample lab exercise at the end of this chapter has a walkthrough of steps to get a solution up and running on Windows Azure.

SQL Azure

SQL Azure Database is a cloud database service from Microsoft. SQL Azure offers a scalable and secure cloud-based relational database built on SQL Server technology. SQL Azure provides the familiar T-SQL programming model and TDS connectivity support, which from a development perspective, provides the ability to seamlessly use these databases in the cloud even though the data sits in Microsoft-owned data centers. These key factors allow an organization to take advantage of their existing SQL Server skills and capabilities while leveraging new usage paradigms.

Usage

SQL Azure is built on three key tenets: manageability, scalability, and developer agility. We will quickly examine each of these.

SQL Azure provides the high availability of an enterprise data center for only a fraction of the associated costs. The logical administration is an abstract ion of the physical; the latter being handled by Microsoft. This means that regular database administration, logins, users, and roles must be administered by the DBA, but all physical deployment details are handled by Microsoft. At present, to deploy a new application on-premise typically requires coordination among multiple groups in order to purchase servers, provision them, open ports on the firewall, and numerous other tasks. SQL Azure enables customers to provision new servers and databases within minutes, which means that you no longer have to worry about hardware acquisition and setup. This reduces costs by allowing companies to provision just what they need upfront. The data that you store on SQL Azure is automatically made redundant, including automatic failover capabilities in the event of a disaster.

Scalability is a key advantage of the cloud model; SQL Azure can meet the needs of small departmental and large global applications alike. The "pay as you grow" pricing model enables extra capacity to be spun up for seasonal demand or as the usage steadily increases. Because SQL Azure runs in global data centers, new markets can be reached immediately without the typical management and operations costs. SQL Azure provides the ability to implement multitenancy, which may be of interest to ISVs providing hosted solutions.

The third point we will address is developer agility. By building SQL Azure on the T-SQL language, Microsoft allows developers to use their existing knowledge and skills, and quickly leverage the cloud as an alternative to an on-premise database. SQL Azure supports **Tabular Data Stream (TDS)**, which is a protocol used for communication between a client and an on-premise SQL Server. Therefore, a desktop client application can connect to SQL Azure Database in the same way it connects to an on-premise SQL Server instance. This means that your code that was built using ADO.NET, ODBC, or any other technology you chose to work with, can be easily migrated to the cloud. **Secure Sockets Layer (SSL)** is required when a client application connects to the SQL Azure Database TDS endpoint to ensure security.

SQL Azure provides a relational database experience in the cloud, which is familiar to developers and administrators. Building on existing, proven, scalable, on-premise technology has minimized the deployment burden. The units of deployment in SQL Azure are servers and databases which are familiar concepts to DBAs and administrators.

Architecture

SQL Azure provides the following four main layers of abstraction.

1. **Client layer**: This is the layer responsible for communicating with SQL Azure, and can reside on-premise or be hosted in Windows Azure. We will discuss deployment options later in this chapter.

2. **Services layer**: This layer is responsible for several critical functions including billing, metering, and provisioning new servers to meet client demand. The final responsibility is for routing connections between the application and physical servers where the data resides. This layer hides the complexity of numerous physical servers.

3. **Platform layer**: This layer addresses the physical servers and services required to provide the services of SQL Azure. This consists of many instances of SQL Server, which are managed and controlled by the SQL Azure fabric to enable automatic failover, health monitoring of servers, data replication, and more necessary supporting operational services. Essentially, this layer is responsible for the management of the SQL Azure software stack.

4. **Infrastructure layer**: Responsibility lies here for the management and operational support of the physical hardware infrastructure that provides the SQL Azure computing power.

These layers are illustrated in the following diagram:

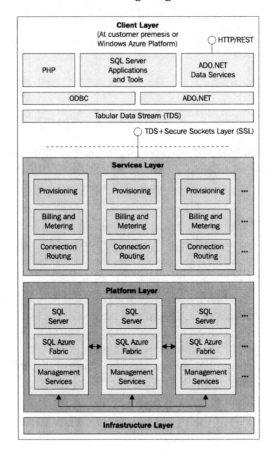

Provisioning model

SQL Azure possesses a logical hierarchy to enable you to manage your data effectively. Before using the service, you must register for a Windows Azure platform account at http://www.microsoft.com/windowsazure/offers. Each account can be associated with multiple SQL Azure Servers, each of which can contain multiple databases; this mirrors the on-premise options that enable one company to have multiple SQL Server instances across multiple servers, each containing multiple databases.

The SQL Azure Server is a logical container and an administration point for a group of databases. This allows you to specify logins, similar to those in SQL instances. Each server is given a fully-qualified domain name (FQDN), which can be accessed across the Internet. The geographic hosting region is also chosen at this level. The SQL Azure Server is similar in many ways to the on-premise product that provides a familiar security model based on logins and each server has a master database.

As with a traditional SQL Server instance, a SQL Azure Server may include multiple databases. They can be created by either the CREATE TABLE T-SQL statement or through the online portal. SQL Azure implements identical security principals as the on-premise product, based on SQL Server logins, database users, and role permissions. This enables DBAs to use familiar concepts and proven security models to protect access to their organization's cloud data. These principals can be modified by running appropriate T-SQL statements or using the functionality that the SQL Azure portal provides.

SQL Azure can store terabytes of information. Currently each individual database is limited to 50 GB in size. Therefore, a scale-out technique such as **Data sharding** can be used to scale your application data across multiple independent SQL Azure servers.

Data access and usage patterns

There are two broad approaches for SQL Azure that I have seen with regard to deployment. The first approach is to deploy only the database-tier within the cloud and then have the application-tier access the data in the cloud from a remote location over the Internet. The second approach is to host both the application and the data-tier within Windows Azure. The second approach enables you to minimize the network latency between application-tier and data-tier. The first approach enables an organization's desktop-based application to be migrated to SQL Azure with minimal disruption. This strategy may be also be useful for services which are primarily used by workers who constantly require remote access to the system. For example, consider an expense report system for travelling sales people, which would allow access to the system's data over the Internet even if the client application was sitting on the employee's computer desktop. The second approach enables web applications written in PHP, ASP.NET, or Silverlight to be hosted in Windows Azure, and utilizes the underlying SQL Azure service with minimum possible latency.

The following diagram illustrates this model:

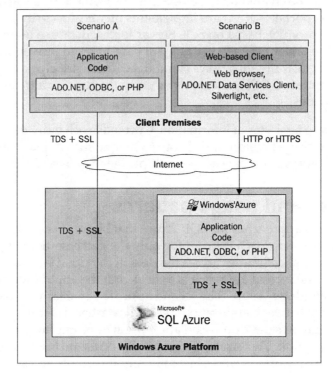

SQL Azure–what is supported and what is not

Not all of the features from SQL Server 2008 R2 are currently supported in SQL Azure.

Features included at the time of writing are as follows:

- Tables, indexes, and views.
- Stored procedures.
- Triggers.
- Constraints.
- Table variables, session temp tables (#t).
- OLTP.
- T-SQL DML statements.
- T-SQL DDL statements that do not attempt to modify physical resources.
- T-SQL statements that do not attempt to modify physical resources. For example, file placement on physical drives.
- SQL 2008 datatypes that were not deprecated.

Features that are not present in this version are as follows:

- Distributed transactions
- Distributed query
- Common Language Runtime (CLR)
- Service broker, analysis services, and reporting services
- Spatial
- Physical server or catalog DDL and views
- Any statements or options that manage physical resource usage; for example, T-SQL commands and resource governor
- Server options or trace flags
- Datatypes that were deprecated in SQL 2008 release

How do I get started?

Log into the SQL Azure Portal with your Windows Azure platform account `https://sql.azure.com`. Then create a test database using the instructions provided on the portal. In this example, I have completed these steps already and the database name I have used is `SQLAzurePrimer`. I will walk you through how to connect to the server using SQL Management Studio and then how to run an existing T-SQL `CREATE TABLE` command in a database that we have created.

To get started, we will use SQL Server Management Studio. Open the application and change the authentication mode to **SQL Server Authentication**. **Object Explorer** does not function correctly when pointing to the SQL Azure endpoint; so first click on **Cancel** on the initial connection screen. Click on **New Query** to connect from this connection screen. Then enter the cloud server name which was specified at creation time. You will need to select **Connection Properties** and explicitly enter the name of the database that you wish to connect to; for example, in this case `SQLAzurePrimer`.

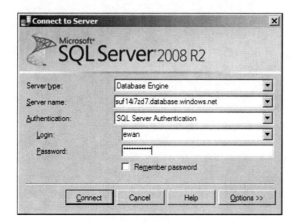

You should now be connected to your SQL Azure Server. To create a table you can use traditional T-SQL syntax as shown in the following screenshot. One important caveat is that any table you create on SQL Azure must have a clustered index.

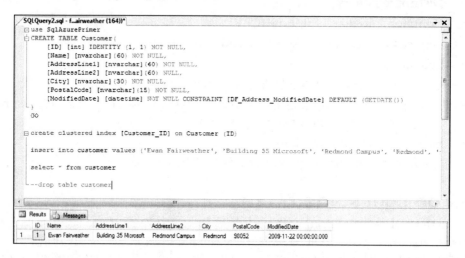

As shown in the previous screenshot, SQL Azure provides familiar management tools (SQL Management Studio) and traditional T-SQL programming language to enable you to quickly create and migrate existing on-premise applications and take advantage of the scalability that the cloud provides.

Windows Azure Platform AppFabric

Azure AppFabric includes the Service Bus and Access Control components of Windows Azure platform which enable complex, hybrid, service-based applications to be hosted in the cloud or connected through the cloud.

Usage

When you want two applications running on different machines (deployed across firewalls, security domains, and maybe even across enterprises) to communicate, there are interesting challenges to make this happen. With the advent of cloud applications, our applications can also span deployments on-premise and across the cloud. Typically, to access services outside an enterprise deployment, you might choose to either open a firewall port or use a VPN. Both these infrastructure-related options have cumbersome challenges for configuration and for ongoing maintenance. The problem also tends to compound when there are several such applications that require firewall or VPN changes.

The second problem is authorizing users for certain applications based on their identity claims. This is simplified in an enterprise using the same Active Directory (AD), but becomes very challenging when this is across enterprises where each one has its own identity systems, possibly on different platforms.

Windows Azure Platform AppFabric is a set of services that make it simpler to securely interoperate applications and services running on different networks that use different authorization systems. This is done by exposing the on-premise services through a cloud endpoint that acts as a secure communication relay. This web-based service helps solve both network infrastructure complexities and authorization of users across different claims systems.

Architecture

There are two following key pieces to the Windows Azure AppFabric:

1. Service Bus.
2. Access Control Service.

 Windows Server AppFabric consists of hosting and caching capabilities for on-premise applications, while Windows Azure AppFabric provides cloud Service Bus and Access Control Services.

Service Bus

The Azure Platform AppFabric Service Bus provides secure connectivity between loosely-coupled services and applications, enabling them to navigate firewalls or network boundaries.

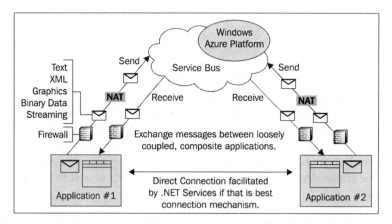

Consider a customer who has deployed a three-tier solution in the Windows Azure Platform where web-tier logic is hosted in ASP.NET, business logic is hosted as WCF services, and relational data is in a SQL Azure database. All of these architecture components are deployed and run in the Microsoft data center. In most cases, there is context, business logic, and data communication that needs to flow between the customer's on-premise systems and the Windows Azure Platform. In addition, clients (mobile and desktop) running within on-premise deployment also may need to receive events or process data from the cloud. In order to wire all this together there is a lot of custom effort required. The Azure AppFabric Service Bus provides an easy mechanism that customers can leverage to solve this problem.

The Service Bus exposes a cloud-based communication fabric, which ensures that different systems spanning on-premise applications and the cloud can plug-in and communicate in a secure manner. It abstracts the various listeners and services into a unified namespace asset which makes it easy for services to be accessed using an Internet-accessible URL irrespective of the location. The global hierarchical namespaces are DNS and transport-independent entities.

The Service Bus can be used to fulfill the following tasks:

- Connect disparate applications across firewalls
- Connect Windows Azure applications and SQL Azure databases with existing applications and databases
- Bridge on and off-premise applications
- Create composite applications

Access Control Service

The Access Control Service helps build federated authorization into your applications and services that extend beyond organizational boundaries.

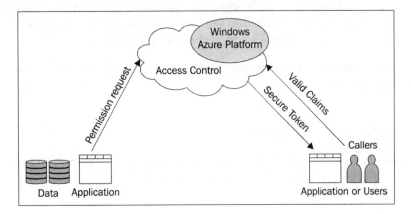

In the same scenario as above, consider providing application and service access to a set of partners. Each partner-identity system could be different and possibly running on a different platform. There might be a need to provide access to each partner for a set of applications or services.

The Access Control Service help solve the problem by allowing user accounts to federate the customer's existing identity management system whether based on the Active Directory service or other standard directory systems, and integrate with the authorization model defined for your application or service in the cloud. It exposes a simple declarative model of rules and claims that enable applications to respond as if the user accounts were managed locally.

The service is a flexible, standards-based service that supports web protocols such as REST. It also supports multiple credentials, including X.509 certificates. It is a developer-friendly programming model based on the Microsoft .NET Framework and Windows Communication Foundation.

Provisioning model

You can provision the Azure AppFabric account and access more information from `https://appfabric.azure.com/`.

You can then create a services namespace that represents the namespace for the Service Bus and Access Control. For example, Contoso Corp might have a services namespace called `contoso-prod` and the following Service Bus connection string: `sb://contoso-prod.servicebus.windows.net`.

Project "Dallas"

Microsoft Codename "Dallas" is a new information marketplace allowing developers and information workers to easily discover, purchase, and manage premium data subscriptions in the Windows Azure Platform. Additionally, Dallas APIs allow developers and information workers to consume this premium content with virtually any platform, application, or business workflow.

You can get more details on this portal from `http://www.microsoft.com/windowsazure/dallas/`.

Example solution

A simple example solution of Azure components may go a long way in helping you grasp the benefits of using the Microsoft cloud to host your application.

Scenario

Consider a training company that delivers tutorials for students using the web. The training company is moving to the Windows Azure Platform in order to scale the solution for a larger customer base across the globe. The frontend application is built using ASP.NET and leverages SQL Azure to store the tutorial sessions and results. All the tutorials and quizzes can be taken by students via a web browser. In this lab, we will build a small portion of the lab and focus on the building blocks of hosting the solution on Windows Azure.

Setup

A project solution `AppliedArchitecture.Chapter6.WinAzure` has been created in `<Installation Directory>\Chapter6\WindowAzure\Begin` folder. You will start building the solution using the following set of instructions. A completed solution is also provided in the `End` folder.

 Before beginning the lab, you must have the latest Windows Azure SDK installed on your development machine. Please visit `http://www.microsoft.com/windowsazure/windowsazuresdk/` to download the required tools and SDK for your environment. Also, make sure all the system requirements and instructions to install any latest hot-fixes have been followed.

These labs have been developed using Visual Studio 2010 and the Windows Azure Tools for Microsoft Visual Studio 1.2 (June 2010).

As part of the installation, you should get the **Windows Azure Cloud Services** project template, the development fabric, and the development storage fabric on your machine. The development fabric simulates the cloud environment by simulating a hosting environment for the web and worker roles part of the project. From the task bar, you can start or shut down the development fabric.

If you need to host the solution on Windows Azure then you need to register on the Windows Azure portal and have an account setup. For this lab, this is not a necessity and you can run it on the local development fabric until step 13 as follows:

Steps

1. Launch Visual Studio.NET 2010 and create a new project. Choose the **Windows Azure Cloud Service** project template installed under **Cloud**.

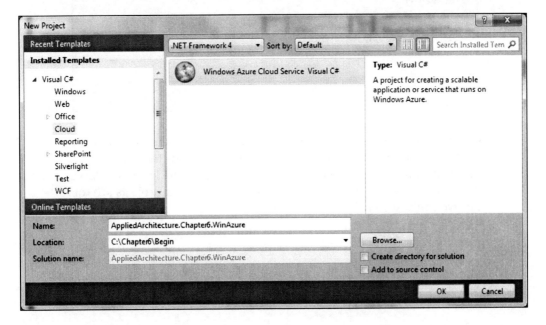

2. You will then see a pop up that asks for the various .NET roles that are a part of your project. For this lab, we will use one ASP.NET web role and one worker role. Make the selections as shown in the following screenshot and hit **OK**.

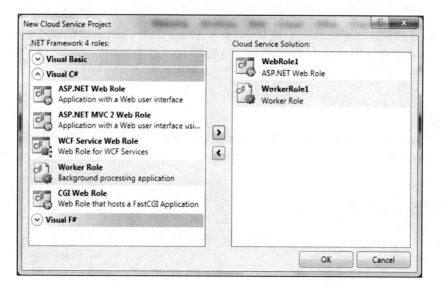

3. You will see three projects as part of your solution—the first project is used to generate the deployment package. It contains the configuration and definition that will be used by development fabric and Windows Azure to correctly deploy the solution. The other two projects are for the two roles (web role and worker role).

4. Open the designer for `default.aspx` and create a page as shown in the next screenshot:

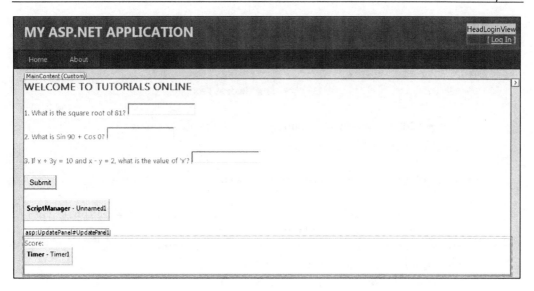

5. Open `Default.aspx.cs` and at the beginning, add the following set of `using` statements:

```
using Microsoft.WindowsAzure;
using Microsoft.WindowsAzure.ServiceRuntime;
using Microsoft.WindowsAzure.StorageClient;
```

6. In the same file, add the following code:

```
static string connectionString;
private CloudStorageAccount csa;
private CloudQueueClient qclient;
protected void Page_Load(object sender, EventArgs e)
{
  connectionString =
RoleEnvironment.GetConfigurationSettingValue(
                      "DiagnosticsConnectionString");
  // create a handle to the cloud storage or the developer
        fabric based on the connectionString
  csa = CloudStorageAccount.Parse(connectionString);
  //get a handle to using the queue storage
  qclient = csa.CreateCloudQueueClient();
}
protected void Button1_Click(object sender, EventArgs e)
{
  // create a queue for user answers and add the response as a
        message
```

```
CloudQueue q = qclient.GetQueueReference("userquizinput");
bool q_exists = q.CreateIfNotExist();
string quizanswers = "Q1:" + TextBox1.Text
                  + ":Q2:" + TextBox2.Text
                  + ":Q3:" + TextBox3.Text;

    q.AddMessage(new CloudQueueMessage(quizanswers));
  Label1.Text = "";
}
protected void Timer1_Tick(object sender, EventArgs e)
{
  //Check if the worker role processed results are available in
      the user output queue
  CloudQueue q = qclient.GetQueueReference("userquizoutput");
  bool q_exists = q.CreateIfNotExist();
  CloudQueueMessage msg = q.GetMessage();
  if (msg != null)
  {
    q.DeleteMessage(msg);
    Label1.Text = "Score: " + msg.AsString + " / 3";
  }
}
```

7. Now click on the `WorkerRole1` project and open `WorkerRole.cs`. At the beginning add the following set of `using` statements:

```
using Microsoft.WindowsAzure;
using Microsoft.WindowsAzure.ServiceRuntime;
using Microsoft.WindowsAzure.StorageClient;
public Hashtable evalHT = new Hashtable(4);
```

8. Modify the `OnStart()` method to set up the contents for the hashtable.

```
evalHT.Add("Q1", "9");
evalHT.Add("Q2", "2");
evalHT.Add("Q3", "4");
```

9. In the `Run()` method, add the following code:

```
public override void Run()
{
  string connectionString =
RoleEnvironment.GetConfigurationSettingValue(
                          "DiagnosticsConnectionString");
```

```
CloudStorageAccount csa =
            CloudStorageAccount.Parse(connectionString);
CloudQueueClient qclient = csa.CreateCloudQueueClient();
// queue where the user responses are stored
CloudQueue q_in = qclient.GetQueueReference("userquizinput");
q_in.CreateIfNotExist();
// queue to store the user results after evaluation
CloudQueue q_out =
    qclient.GetQueueReference("userquizoutput");
q_out.CreateIfNotExist();
// will upload the user responses as a blob since the queue
    messages are deleted after processing
CloudBlobClient bclient = csa.CreateCloudBlobClient();
CloudBlobContainer container =
        bclient.GetContainerReference("quizcontainer");
container.CreateIfNotExist();
CloudBlob blob =
    container.GetBlobReference("userresults.txt");
while (true)
{
  CloudQueueMessage msg = q_in.GetMessage();
  if (msg != null)
  {
    // process the results. Eval method will use a HashTable
        which has the questions
    // and the right answers.
    string results = Eval(msg.AsString);
    if (results != null)
    {
      q_out.AddMessage(new CloudQueueMessage(results));
      blob.UploadText(String.Format("Received {0} at {1}",
            msg.AsString, DateTime.Now.ToLongTimeString()));
      q_in.DeleteMessage(msg);
    }
  }
  Thread.Sleep(1000);
}
}
```

10. Add the logic in `Eval()` method to handle the user response and compute the score.

11. Build the project.

12. From the first project, if you double-click on the `WebRole1` and `WorkerRole1` under **Roles | Settings** you will see that **useDevelopmentStorage** is set to **True**. First, we will test the application on the development fabric.

13. Run the application and enter values in the browser window. To confirm that the application is writing to the storage, click on the Visual Studio **Server Explorer** and browse the **Windows Azure Storage** node. Under the **(Development)** node, there should be the container that was created in this lab. If you click on it, you should then see the `userresults.txt` file that was created.

14. Next, let's create storage on Windows Azure and run the solution. In this case, the application will run on your development machine and store the results in the cloud database. Note that if you don't have a Windows Azure account, you should skip the next set of steps.

15. Create the storage account from `https://windows.azure.com/Cloud/Provisioning/Default.aspx`. Prior to this, you should have signed up for a Windows Azure account. Create a new project or choose an existing one. Then click on **Create a new service**. Choose the option to create a storage account. In the end, your account will look something like the following screenshot:

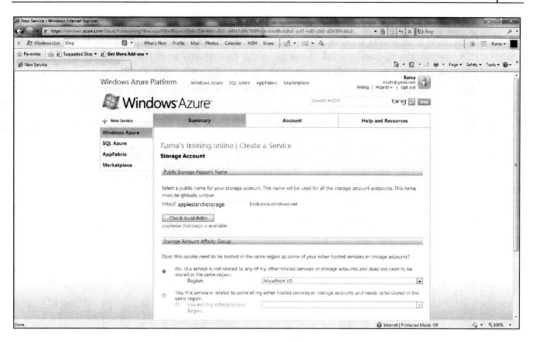

16. Copy the storage account name and the key. You will need to modify the diagnostics connection string setting in Visual Studio using these values. Refer to the instructions from step 12 onwards to modify it.

17. Build and run the application. To confirm that the application is writing to the Windows Azure storage, click on **Server Explorer** and now look under the cloud storage account. Refer to the instructions from step 13.

18. We then modify the solution to host it on Windows Azure. Go to `https://windows.azure.com/Cloud/Provisioning/Default.aspx`, click on your project and then click on **Create a new service**. Choose **Hosting service** and give a friendly name to your service, with the publically accessible URL.

19. Now, you are ready to publish the solution to Windows Azure. Before doing this, you will need to associate your solution with a certificate and upload the certificate to the portal. This is done to ensure that the right security is in place to access your online account. If you don't have a certificate already, this is how it needs to be created. Right-click on the `AppliedArchitecture.Chapter6.WinAzure` project and select **Publish**. From **Credentials**, select **Add**. This will bring a pop up which will look like the following screenshot:

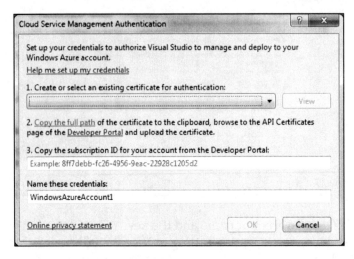

20. From the first drop down shown in the previous screenshot click on **Create**, which creates a new certificate on your machine.

21. Next, click on **Copy the full path** of the certificate and then click on **Developer Portal**, which will open a browser window. You might need to run the browser in administrator mode.

22. From the developer portal, choose your project name, the correct hosted service that was created, and then choose the **Account** tab on the top. Click on **Manage My API certificates**. You should see an option to upload the certificate file from local storage. Click on **Browse** and paste the certificate path that was copied in the earlier step. Upload the certificate to the portal. Then from the Account page, copy the **Subscription ID** to the clipboard.

23. Go back to the Visual Studio window and paste the subscription ID in step three as shown in the previous screenshot and continue with the publish process. At the end of this process, your window should look similar to the next screenshot:

24. This will ensure that the solution gets to the staging area on your Windows Azure portal. Test the staging link and see if it works fine. You can then promote the solution from staging to production and access the friendly URL from a browser. You should see something like the following output:

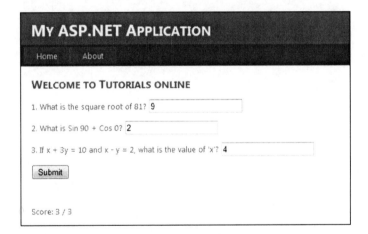

Summary

At the time of writing, it was four years since Ray Ozzie first outlined the "services transformation" occurring within our industry how it would impact users, developers, and IT. Ray outlined how software-plus-services would enable customers to protect existing on-premise investments while transitioning to more cloud-oriented architectures where it made sense.

Since then, Microsoft has had great success with Xbox LIVE and launched a suite of online business productivity messaging and collaboration solutions. It has also released a public version of Office Web Apps. Now with the Windows Azure Platform, it enables customers to take existing applications on the Microsoft stack on-premise and deploy portions of them onto the cloud.

When deciding on the suitability of Windows Azure platform for your problem domain, we encourage you to make use of the book's decision framework and benefits explained in this chapter. Here is a brief summary of some of the factors you should consider:

- Potential cost savings (CAPEX and OPEX). For a short to medium term, cost saving varies from customer to customer, depending on whether they have spare capacity or not. Over the long term the majority of customers can save both.

- Supportability of preferred development platform in the cloud. For example, MySQL is not supported, but PHP is.

- Visual Studio usage within current environment. If the customer already uses this, then they will benefit from the integrated .NET, Windows Azure, and Visual Studio templates which are provided as a web download.

7
Simple Workflow

We have provided an overview of each of the core technologies that this book will focus on. We will now evaluate the possible technology solutions for our first pattern using the decision framework we defined in *Chapter 1, Solution Decision Framework*.

Use case

Sam Maccoll Financial is a financial services organization based in Perth, Scotland. They are focused on providing quality individuals and corporate financial services with a special focus on individual retirement planning. They employ over 3,000 employees in Scotland. The majority of their branches are in Scotland, but they are slowly expanding into England and parts of Ireland and Wales.

The company's focus on long term buy-and-hold investments has meant that their retirement and investment products fared comparatively well in the sub-prime downturn due to limited exposure. This has meant that they have grown rapidly over the last 18 months and anticipate further growth. They found that many customers take multiple products from the Sam Maccoll portfolio; they want to encourage this as it increases "stickiness".

They have had online banking available for checking and savings account products since their inception, but they now want to add their other products to enable self-service. Users increasingly expect an available, self-service portal that provides a consolidated view across all products. Their current Internet Bank application is coded in ASP and calls ASMX web services from the application tier to access savings and checking account information. The current portal does not provide a summary view for checking, savings, and retirement account information as users have to log into a separate portal to access this information.

Recently, customer complaints have risen and the company wants to take actions to provide the best possible customer experience. They want to expand and provide a consistent dashboard for their checking, savings, and retirement account information. They would like a platform that provides extensibility; specifically, this requirement is the ability to add new products and accounts to the dashboard with minimal code changes. A flexible solution will enable the company to provide a better portal, which in turn will enable customers to get a fast and real-time view of their financial products, thereby improving customer satisfaction.

Sam Maccoll's major systems run on the Windows platform and have a web service facade to which they can connect. As a part of this project, they will be upgrading these to WCF. They do have a sizeable number of .NET developers and own some of Microsoft's major server platforms like SharePoint server and Exchange Server. The downstream systems that hold financial information are standardized on SQL Server backend databases and have the same identical security model; for example, restrict each customer to have access only to their own data and provide internal employees with minimum possible information necessary to perform their job.

Sam Maccoll has adopted a "buy versus build" strategy where they prefer using existing, well-tested frameworks and products with extensibility points instead of custom-building their own solutions from the ground up. They try to build their solutions in a very loosely coupled way, using a common open standard wherever possible to minimize development effort and the ongoing supportability burden that comes from maintaining custom code. This is relevant in this case as it is expected that the Internet Bank will need to expand and add additional systems integration as the number of self-service products increases. As a first step, the Sam Maccoll architecture team has asked to see a critical comparison of different architectures against their requirements. In the recommended approach, they would like to see a proof of concept, which demonstrates a sample dashboard with an end-to-end implementation.

Key requirements

The following are key requirements for a new software solution:

- A single dashboard view for all financial service products that customers have.
- An online banking application that is easier to maintain and requires less custom code.

Additional facts

There are some additional details gathered after the initial use case was shared with the technical team. The requirements derived from this include:

1. The frontend does not have to know where the information comes from; it should only contact a single point.

2. All calls should be made in a service-oriented fashion.

3. The system needs to be able to scale to more than one million users over a 24 hour period, which equates to approximately 12 users per second.

4. During peak usage, which occurs at the beginning of a day and during the evening, the maximum number of users is 25 per second.

5. Response time is critical for the dashboard page as this is the page used by 90 percent of customers every day. They would like 95 percent of users to receive a response within three seconds and 99 percent to receive a response within five seconds.

6. The bank would like to have a consistent workflow platform that supports synchronous, asynchronous, short, and long running workflows.

7. The system must provide tracking and monitoring capabilities.

8. The system must provide exception management at every stage.

9. Initially, the system must address the dashboard requirement, but must provide the capabilities necessary to add additional services to the Internet Bank including the following services:

    °   Handling transactional workflows. This is a requirement for Maccoll Bank to implement workflows requiring guaranteed once-only delivery (for example, payment workflows).

    °   Long-running asynchronous workflows. The bank is considering implementing an end-to-end mortgage application; in the future, many of the transactions required in this type of process can be long running and may require human intervention/approval. The system should be able to support these capabilities.

    °   The system must be capable of providing real-time updates if payments are implemented on the system.

Pattern description

In this scenario, we need to receive a single inbound request and then, based on the content in that request call, several backend services gather information about the customer and then correlate the responses, aggregate them, and finally send them in a single response message. The web application will then display their personalized information to them. The logical choice is to use an aggregator, which is responsible for the collection of requests, performing transformations (if they are required), and returning the response. All of this also needs to be done in the shortest possible time, as users are not willing to wait more than three to five seconds for this type of information. This pattern is commonly referred to as a **Scatter-Gather pattern**.

In the Scatter-Gather pattern, information is broadcast to multiple recipients then the responses are re-aggregated back into a single message. An aggregator component is responsible for receiving the initial request message, broadcasting in an appropriate format to all the target systems, and finally, combining the results of these individual but related messages and returning them as a single response so they can be processed as a whole. Typically in this pattern, the aggregator is implemented as a separate tier so it can abstract the logic necessary to maintain the overall message flow and handle any exceptions from any of the systems queried.

This pattern is particularly successful if you follow service-oriented concepts and require a loosely-coupled, scalable aggregator which can be reused by different applications across your organization. As the calling application only calls a single method on the aggregator, the source of the information and how it is extracted is abstracted from that tier. This enables additional targets or sources of information to be added with no update required on the client side. The following image depicts a high-level representation of what this could look like for Maccoll bank. As is evident from the diagram, separating the aggregator from the consumer of the aggregator (the Internet Bank) creates a layer of abstraction between them and the endpoints, if properly designed. It also means that the consumer need not worry about implementing any logic that is specific to the interface that the backend systems provide. The aggregator in this example makes calls to the three target systems in parallel.

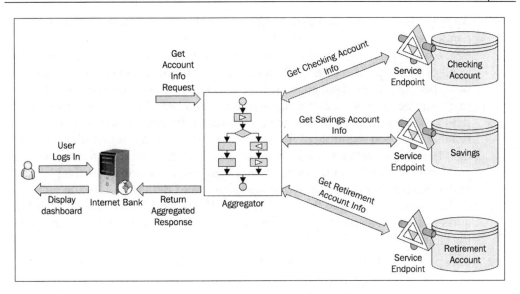

Factors affecting implementation details

As we have alluded to so far in this chapter, there are many key factors that need to be taken into consideration when implementing this pattern. Here I am going to outline the ones that I consider when evaluating solutions for this type of problem with customers. The factors that I consider are as follows:

1. **Completeness**: This determines when are we ready to publish the aggregated response message. Whether returning of partial data is useful or not is perhaps the most important factor to consider when implementing this pattern. This will depend on the scenario and the client's requirements. For example, in a price-comparison engine that queries hundreds of sources, partial data is likely to be valuable and relevant. In cases where results from multiple sources need to be merged to one coherent response, partial data may not be useful.

2. **Aggregation strategy**: The strategy you use depends primarily on the completeness criteria and SLAs that the aggregator needs to meet. The two most common scenarios I have seen are: **Timeout**, where the aggregator waits for a specified length of time for responses and then either returns the response or an exception to the client: and **Wait for all**, which is used when an incomplete order is not meaningful. Typically, it is important that the aggregator knows the expected number of responses and has appropriate exception handling capabilities. An exception to this is where the aggregation concludes based on some external event; for example, the end of a trading day may conclude the aggregation of the value of all stock trades in that period.

3. **Aggregation algorithm**: Typically, there will be a requirement to sort or condense the data in some way. Factors affecting this include the size of the aggregated response that is to be returned and whether the user is interested in all of the responses or a small subset of the responses. One extreme would be if there is a single best answer; for example, in an auction site the seller may only be interested in the highest confirmed bid. If a larger amount of data is being returned, it may need to be sorted by one or more criteria; hotels are a good example of this. Factors for consideration include price, facilities, and distance from local amenities. Whether the data should be condensed depends on the type of data being returned, numeric data is best suited for this; for example, when analyzing sales data it is often the volume and average order value that is of interest. If you decide to condense the data and only return a subset, you should consider whether you wish to archive the complete selected data for later evaluation.

4. **Exception handling and appropriate timeout**: How this is implemented depends on the aggregation strategy algorithm and completeness criteria for your system. Even in a "wait for all" aggregation strategy, it is unlikely that waiting indefinitely is the desired behavior, especially in a synchronous request-response scenario. A timeout and exception handlers should be implemented so that the aggregator can handle all possible scenarios including one of the endpoints being unavailable; for example, due to system outage. If an exception occurs, it must return an appropriate response message to the client and you should also log this in the appropriate log.

5. **Monitoring and tracing**: This is distinct from exception handling, providing the ability to monitor and trace the aggregator. If implemented correctly, this can be used in a number of ways, such as providing average processing times for the aggregator over a 24 hour period, or to enable system administrators to determine the progress of in-process operations. This can be provided by the following platforms — Windows Server AppFabric provides monitoring capabilities, so does BizTalk Server, which enhances this further with the option of implementing **Business Activity Monitoring (BAM)**.

6. **Type of response to return (data format)**: How you represent the data to consumers is an important consideration. Using WCF ensures that you make appropriate use of message contracts, data contracts, and the bindings it provides so that you get the right trade-off between performance, client-side operations that are available on the data set, and interoperability.

7. **Number of calls versus expected usage**: Returning smaller data sets typically places less load on the backend systems that are queried, requires smaller payload size, less CPU overhead, and can provide better performance as measured by response time. However, if implementing this approach requires that each user now needs to make multiple calls to the aggregator component's operations, this may actually place more overhead on the system and provide a poorer perceived performance. Consider the scenario where someone logs into their online bank, views their summary page of all account balances, and then looks at the detailed statement of one account, for example, their credit card account. There are two succinct operations that are performed here. Whether all this information should be returned by the aggregator in a single response or requires two calls, is an important design decision to make. Typically, this depends on the normal usage of the system and the customer requirements. In this case, I would typically ask you to see historical usage or trending data if it was available. One large Internet Bank that I worked with had a majority of their logged-in customers who would examine only the dashboard view and then log out. By only returning the condensed summary data, we were able to minimize the load on the backend systems and improve response time.

8. **Correlation**: This is handled implicitly in the platform; for example, if you are calling synchronous two-way services using a request-response port in BizTalk, you will need to define this yourself based on Message ID or some other unique value.

9. **Processing—parallel or sequential**: Unless sequential processing is a typical requirement, an aggregator should perform all the back end calls in parallel to minimize processing time and latency.

10. **Durability of in-flight data**: You should determine whether the data is transient or transactional. Normally in a Scatter-Gather pattern, data is transient; for example, if the user does not receive a response they will simply retry. This pattern is intended to service, primarily, read requests from multiple systems. If you are performing a transaction such as a payment, you might want to consider implementing this as a separate component and requiring the client to call this. The Internet Bank I mentioned previously opted to take this approach. They implemented a single orchestration as their Scatter-Gather aggregator, and then had separate messaging components if any stock trade or funds transfer was initialized. If transactional processing semantics are required, you should determine whether the platform supports this; for example, the BizTalk orchestration engine which guarantees no loss of messages.

Candidate architectures

We have two viable choices when looking to implement a Scatter-Gather pattern using an aggregator. One of them is the new Windows Server AppFabric release and the other is the BizTalk orchestration engine.

Candidate architecture #1–BizTalk Server

BizTalk is Microsoft's Enterprise Integration tool and has a robust messaging and workflow (orchestration) engine. Maccoll Bank is already, largely a Microsoft-based technology firm. BizTalk provides full and complete integration with Microsoft and other heterogeneous technology through its adapter framework. For the purpose of this analysis, the assumption will be that BizTalk is not already in use within the organization.

We can take a look at the decision framework as it relates to BizTalk to see if a BizTalk-based solution is a fit for this use case.

Solution design aspects

The system needs to be capable of processing one million messages over a 24 hour period. The peak load represents 25 messages per second. When dealing with requirements like this, it is always good to have a margin of safety in terms of throughput ceiling. Therefore, this system will require a robust and proven host, which can scale to meet these throughput requirements and beyond. To implement this pattern, we would require use of the BizTalk orchestration Engine, which can easily be used for service aggregation and provide support for correlation. BizTalk also has the ability to expose an orchestration through a SOAP or WCF endpoint. Each call to the backend services could be implemented in an inline fashion using a .NET helper class to instantiate a WCF channel factory or call the service and retrieve the response. The more traditional approach is to use the logical request/response ports that BizTalk server provides to do this. Making the calls in an inline fashion may be beneficial in this scenario as it reduces the number of persistence points required, and also the round trips via the MessageBox.

From a performance perspective, recent benchmarks by the *BizTalk Customer Advisory* Team demonstrated that BizTalk can scale to process tens of millions of messages per day well-tuned mid-tier hardware. Specifically, for two-way calls they have obtained over 60 messages per second, for a Scatter-Gather pattern that made five backend calls. These tests were performed on mid-tier Enterprise hardware, which is available to the customer. This gives us sufficient margin of safety as it is more than double our peak requirements. BizTalk Server also provides a comprehensive monitoring infrastructure with out-of-the-box built-in capabilities and the Business Activity Monitoring framework, which can be used to provide a customized business-centric monitoring solution.

Solution delivery aspects

Sam Maccoll Financial is predominantly a Microsoft technology based organization. The assumption here is that they do not already have BizTalk running, therefore if the decision was made to use this particular product, they would also have to bear the additional infrastructure and solution support necessary to support a system like this.

Given that they have already made extensive use of other Microsoft technologies, they have some of the platform skills required. However, BizTalk is quite a complicated product to understand and maintain, therefore they would need to invest in training some key staff to establish one or more subject matter experts (SMEs) within their architect, development, and operations teams. Given that they currently do not have the in-house expertise and the amount of money that would be required for training, unless they have planned broader needs and uses of BizTalk, it would be a negative factor in this use case.

Solution operations aspects

As stated, Sam Maccoll Financial does not have an existing BizTalk implementation. Therefore, they would need to invest in training their operational team, putting processes in place to support BizTalk as well as the necessary infrastructure. Supporting BizTalk requires a rather unique set of skills.

Solution operations are a negative factor in using BizTalk for this use case.

Organizational aspects

Sam Maccoll Financial does not already have an existing BizTalk platform that they can leverage and they do not have the experience in running and maintaining this system. Therefore this is a negative factor in using BizTalk for this use case.

Solution evaluation

Design	Delivery	Operations	Organization

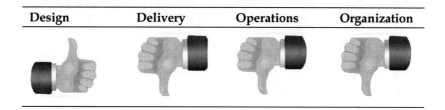

Candidate architecture #2–Windows Server AppFabric

Windows Server AppFabric provides a rich host for WCF and WF applications. The AppFabric host provides supporting services, tools, and diagnostics to make hosting and managing services simpler. An AppFabric solution would leverage the existing capabilities that Sam Maccoll has in .NET. WCF is something they are already planning to use for their backend services; WF is capable of providing the durable workflow tier that they need in order to implement the aggregator.

The aggregator could be implemented as a workflow service. In .NET 4.0, workflow services have been expanded to provide more features and easier integration with WCF endpoints. WCF supports several out-of-the-box bindings and additional bindings are available through several sources, including the BizTalk adapter pack. Standardizing on WCF would therefore allow them to communicate with their existing backend services (which will move to a WCF interface) and also add connectivity to other systems that they want to aggregate in the future. Adding additional services would be done in a visual drag-and-drop design environment, minimizing the development time. Any required message transformation could be done in custom activities. The **Parallel Actions** shape provides the capabilities to call systems in a synchronous manner and a timeout can be implemented within the shape to enforce SLAs for maximum client-wait duration. In addition to this, persistence is provided in the .NET 4.0 Framework through the SQL Workflow Instance Store. This allows durability requirements to be met if required at a later date, for example, if transactional data such as payments is to be processed by AppFabric.

Now, we will look at the decision framework and evaluate AppFabric as an implementation fit for this use case.

Solution design aspects

As stated previously, the throughput requirements equate to a peak load of 25 messages per second. Implementing this pattern would require a single aggregator workflow service that must fulfill the following tasks:

- Expose a request-response endpoint to the client
- Call the backend systems, aggregate the responses
- Perform any necessary translation
- Implement timeouts to ensure that client SLAs were met
- Send the aggregated responses back to the original client

The backend services that need to be integrated are WCF-based; by adding service references to these endpoints the logic is automatically encapsulated into a WF activity, which can be used within the aggregator workflow. Adding service references is a straightforward process and means that if additional WCF endpoints need to be added, it can be done quickly and easily. WF also provides the ability to write code-based activities that can also be used to encapsulate any specific code, such as code transformation. Any code-based activities can be defined in a separate assembly, which would allow this functionality to be reused across different workflows and applications.

By utilizing AppFabric as a host, one can take advantage of the scale-out capabilities that it provides. This would enable Sam Maccoll Financial to scale-out their aggregator tier if it became necessary due to the throughput requirements.

Solution delivery aspects

Sam Maccoll Financial develops complex solutions on .NET and they will be moving their backend services to WCF as a part of their new Internet Bank project. They already have a large installed base of Windows Server 2008 and have gradually, over the last six months, begun rolling out Windows Server 2008 R2. AppFabric, available as a free download, is an extension on top of IIS/WAS and the development team already has extensive experience in developing web solutions on the .NET platform.

Workflow services will reduce the coding effort required to build this application as the aggregator can be implemented without lots of custom code. This will speed up development and reduce testing time compared to what it would be if they were to fully customize all this logic and hosting capability in C#.

Solution operations aspects

Sam Maccoll Financial already has an existing Windows Server 2008 and R2 infrastructure on which they can deploy AppFabric. Supporting workflow systems like AppFabric and BizTalk are paradigm shifts for many operations staff so training will be required.

Organizational aspects

As stated, Sam Maccoll Financial already has an existing Windows infrastructure that can support AppFabric. While this is a new technology and will require some training, it is not expected that this will be a significant burden. Therefore, AppFabric represents a good fit for the organization.

Solution evaluation

Design	Delivery	Operations	Organization

Architecture selection

Let us look at how these candidate architecture technologies stack up against each other. We can break down the primary benefits and risks of each choice in the following manner:

BizTalk Server

Benefits	Risks
<ul><li>Many out-of-box adapters, which means connecting to the majority of systems is only a configuration task</li><li>Provides durability throughout with the MessageBox</li><li>Enterprise-class hosting infrastructure</li></ul>	<ul><li>Perceived large server footprint</li><li>Requirements can be met for free with AppFabric; therefore, cost is prohibitive as the customer will not exploit all the capabilities that the product provides</li></ul>

AppFabric

Benefits	Risks
<ul><li>Lightweight, high throughput feature, rich host for .NET 4 Windows Workflow</li><li>Debugging, monitoring, and exception handling capabilities</li><li>Provides load balancing capabilities</li><li>Implicit and explicit correlation capabilities</li><li>Provides persistence through workflow persistence provider</li></ul>	<ul><li>New product, which means accepting inevitable immaturity and likely changes in tooling and capabilities in subsequent versions</li></ul>

There are a number of key benefits of AppFabric in this scenario. It meets all the requirements with no additional cost over and above Windows license fees. It provides support for the latest version of .NET 4.0 Windows Workflow, which is not provided today in the current BizTalk Server 2010 release. BizTalk provides a lot of additional features, which are not necessarily required in this scenario, where the priority is on processing transient data. These include BAM, the Business Rules Engine, and the host of adapters it provides. These are valuable features, but at present this scenario does not require them.

Therefore, in evaluating these options against the problem scenario, Windows Server AppFabric is the most appropriate choice. Although both BizTalk Server and AppFabric meet the necessary solution and design aspects, the organization already has the infrastructure necessary to support AppFabric with no additional licensing costs. As they have no firm plans to use BizTalk and do not require any of the additional functionality, such as BAM or complex mapping, AppFabric becomes the prominent and chosen candidate.

Building the solution

For this solution demonstration, we will implement three WCF backend services representing the checking, payment, and retirement account systems; these services will have data contracts, but will be "stubbed out". We will then implement a workflow service, which will be our aggregator, and also a sample ASP.NET page which will represent our web tier. A key aspect of this solution architecture is to follow service-oriented principles and keep our design as loosely coupled as possible. Within the organization, passing data by a data contract is acceptable; if we were interfacing with external systems we would implement message transformation.

- Internet Bank–ASP.NET page
- Aggregator–Windows Server AppFabric workflow
- Checking Account–WCF service
- Savings Account–WCF service
- Retirement Account–WCF service

The following diagram outlines the main components of the solution:

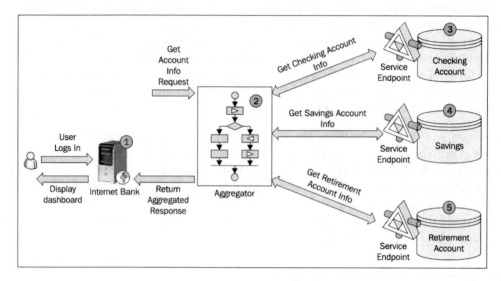

Implementing this solution demonstration will allow us to evaluate AppFabric's capabilities to implement the Scatter-Gather pattern.

 For simplicity purposes, we will not implement a timeout in this workflow. Chapter 17, *Low Latency Request-Reply*, covers how to implement this.

Setup

Initial setup is needed to simulate the backend services. For demo purposes, the backend checking, saving, and retirement account services will be implemented as separate projects, each containing a single WCF service contract with an arbitrary operation implementation to return an object representing the account. A separate data contracts project has been used to define the `Customer` and `Account` classes that we will use to exchange data between different parts of the application. The `DataContract` attribute of these classes allows WCF to serialize the objects and pass them efficiently between different tiers. It is a good practice to deploy common data contracts and types to separate assemblies so that they can be reused within different applications in an organization.

This project also contains an empty aggregator project, which will host our workflow service, and a web-tier project, which will host our ASP.NET page. In this solution demonstration, you will deploy the backend WCF services that have been provided and then implement a Workflow service that serves as our aggregator. Finally, we will create an ASP.NET page which will consume our aggregator service.

First, let's begin with the setup. Before starting, you will need to ensure you have the following software on your machine:

1. Visual Studio 2010 (the code that I am writing was created on the RTM version of this software). For a list of Visual Studio prerequisites see: `http://msdn.microsoft.com/en-us/library/77z6b8tz(VS.100).aspx`.

2. Windows Server AppFabric and required components:
    ○   SQL Server 2008/R2—any edition including Express is supported (at time of writing)
    ○   Microsoft .NET Framework

3. Review the release notes provided. If you have previously installed a beta version of the framework or AppFabric, there are specific steps that need to be followed.

4. Compatible operating system for Windows Server AppFabric and Visual Studio 2010.

5. The Visual Studio IIS deployment tools require that the IIS 6.0 Manager Compatibility feature is enabled. Specifically, the IIS 6.0 Management consoles, IIS metabase, and IIS 6.0 configuration compatibility sub-features need to be enabled. You will also need to run Visual Studio 2010 as an administrator for this feature to work.

6. Launch Visual Studio .NET 2010 and open the `Chapter7.SamMaccollBank.sln` in the `<Installation Directory>\Chapter7\Begin\Chapter7.SamMaccollBank\` folder. This contains the projects to help get started with building the solution. You should see the following project structure :

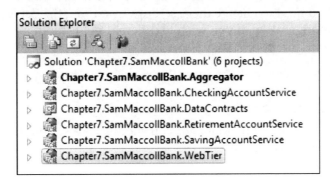

7. Now you will build and publish each of the following projects:

    ○ Chapter7.SamMaccollBank.CheckingAccountService

    ○ Chapter7.SamMaccollBank.RetirementAccountService

    ○ Chapter7.SamMaccollBank.SavingAccountService

8. Let's start with the SamMaccollBank.CheckingAccountService project first and select **Publish**. You will see a screen similar to the following screenshot:

9. Note that the publishing settings that are set up are as follows:

    ○ Target location is a virtual directory http://localhost/<SubProjectName>. So for this project it is http://localhost/CheckingAccountService.

    ○ The default physical location of the virtual directory is configured to C:\inetpub\wwwroot\<SubProjectName>. You need to change these settings by editing the deployment configuration, if you wish to different publishing configuration.

10. Click on **Publish** and then repeat this process for the Chapter7.SamMaccollBank.RetirementAccountService and Chapter7.SamMaccollBank.SavingAccountService projects.

11. When you now open IIS Manager you should see a screen similar to the following screenshot:

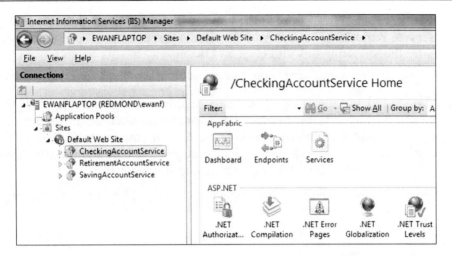

12. To verify that all services have been installed correctly using the appropriate **Application Pools** and are running the right version of the framework (should be 4.0), click on **Default Web Site**. Then in the main window under AppFabric, double-click on **Services**. This is shown in the following screenshot:

13. In the screen that is displayed, you should see three services as shown in the following screenshot:

Service Name	Application Name	Service Virtual Path	Site Name	Application Pool	Managed Runtime...
Chapter7.SamMaccollBank.SavingAccountServi...	SavingAccountSer...	/SavingAccountSe...	Default Web Site	ASP.NET v4.0	v4.0.30319
Chapter7.SamMaccollBank.RetirementAccount...	RetirementAccou...	/RetirementAccou...	Default Web Site	ASP.NET v4.0	v4.0.30319
Chapter7.SamMaccollBank.CheckingAccountSe...	CheckingAccount...	/CheckingAccoun...	Default Web Site	ASP.NET v4.0	v4.0.30319

14. We will now use the `WCFTestClient.exe` tool to test `RetirementAccount`. `WCFTestClient.exe`; by default, is included in the following directory with Visual Studio 2010:

```
C:\Program Files (x86)\Microsoft Visual Studio 10.0\
Common7\IDE\
```

15. Start `WCFTestClient.exe`. In the window that appears, right-click on **My Service Projects** and select **Add Service**. When prompted for the endpoint, enter the following link and click on **OK**:

    ```
    http://localhost/RetirementAccountService/RetirementAccount.svc
    ```

16. This should add the `RetirementAccountService` (the tool references the interface which is implemented). Click on the `GetRetirementAccount()` operation and then enter a customer's details. If you enter `New York` as the city name, the `CurrentBalance` that is returned will be significantly higher (as per our stub). The following screenshot illustrates this:

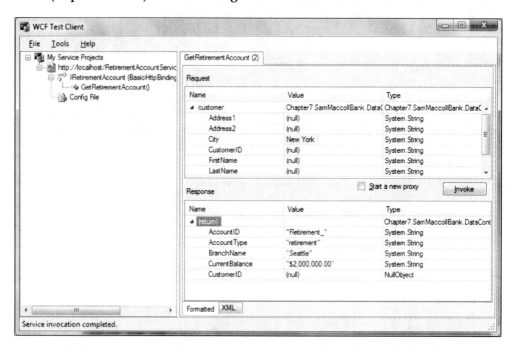

17. If the operation of the retirement account service is successful, verify the checking and savings services using the same techniques. Here are the endpoints you'll need to add as references in the **WCF Test Client** (assuming default configuration):

    ```
    http://localhost/CheckingAccountService/CheckingAccount.svc
    http://localhost/SavingAccountService/SavingAccount.svc
    ```

18. One thing to note if you view the **Endpoints** for these services (one of the AppFabric extensions available in IIS Manager)—you will see that the endpoints that are exposed (basicHttpBinding, serviceMetadataHttpGetBinding, and netNamedPipeBinding) are all default bindings. This is a new feature of WCF 4.0; in previous versions, an endpoint must be specified in the web.config file on any deployment with the new framework. If there are no endpoints present, defaults are created. In a production scenario, we would certainly specify our own, but the defaults will satisfy our demonstration purposes.

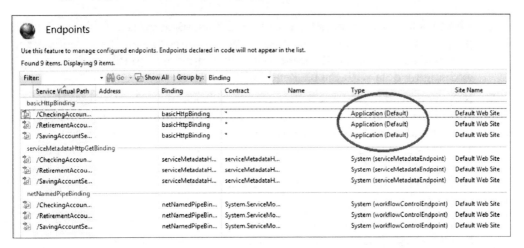

Building the service aggregator workflow service

So you have successfully deployed the backend WCF services and utilized the WCF Test Client tool to test and verify the functionality of each of these. We will now implement the service aggregator workflow service.

1. Launch Visual Studio.NET 2010 and open the Chapter7.SamMaccollBank.sln solution in the <Installation Directory>\Chapter7\Begin\Chapter7.SamMaccollBank\ directory.

2. Expand and open the Chapter7.SamMaccollBank.Aggregator project. You will see there is a placeholder workflow service Service1.xamlx. Right-click and rename it to AccountAggregator.xamlx.

3. Now right-click on `AccountAggregator.xamlx`, select **View Code,** and update the class name from `Service1` to `AccountAggregator` as shown in the following screenshot:

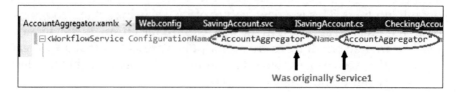

4. Right-click on **References** for the `Chapter7.SamMaccollBank.Aggregator` project and add a reference to `Chapter7.SamMaccollBank.DataContracts`. This will allow you use the data contracts defined within this project when exchanging data with the backend WCF services.

5. Now you need to add a service reference to each of our backend WCF services. Right-click on the `Chapter7.SamMaccollBank.Aggregator` project and select **Add Service Reference**. The address should be `http://localhost/CheckingAccountService/CheckingAccount.svc` and the namespace should be `CheckingAccountService`. Your screen should look similar to the following screenshot. Click on **OK** to add the reference.

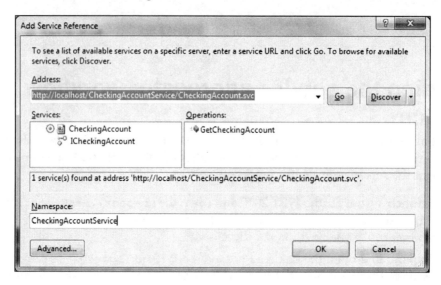

6. Repeat the previous process, adding service references for the retirement and savings account services using the following details:

Service	Address	Namespace
Retirement	`http://localhost/` `retirementaccountservice/` `retirementaccount.svc`	`RetirementAccountService`
Savings	`http://localhost/` `SavingAccountService/` `SavingAccount.svc`	`SavingAccountService`

7. Once you have added these service references and you have rebuilt the project, open the `AccountAggregator.xamlx` workflow. In the toolbox, you should see three new custom activities, which have been generated and can be used to call the backend services.

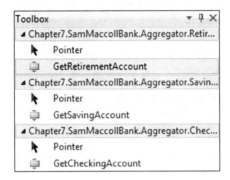

8. Now we will implement the required logic for the `AccountAggregator.xamlx` workflow. Within the workflow, click on the **Imports** tab and enter the `Chapter7.SamMaccollBank.DataContracts` namespace.

9. Now drag-and-drop a **Sequence** shape onto the empty workflow space. Change the display name from `Sequence` to `AccountAggregatorScope`.

10. Our service will receive an object of type `Customer` and will return a sorted dictionary of type `<String, Account >`. Because all objects are modeled using our common base class `Account`, we will use a single instance of the `Systen.Collections.Generic.SortedDictionary` class to return the aggregated account information to the consumer of the service. To create these two objects, click on the `AccountAggregatorScope` and then click on the **Variables** tab and create the following two objects. Note that to create both of these objects, you will need to select **Browse for type...** when selecting the variable type.

Name	Variable Type	Scope	Default
`currentCustomer`	`Customer` (Browse `Chapter7.SamMaccollBank.DataContracts` to select).	`AccountAggregator Scope`	
`accountDictionary`	`Dictionary <String, Account>` (Type `Dictionary` in the **Type Name** to select the `System.Collections.Generic.Dictionary` class).	`AccountAggregator Scope`	`New Dictionary (Of String, Account)`

11. We will also need variables for the request and response messages to the three backend services that the account aggregator is consuming. The types were already created for us when we added the service reference. By clicking on **Browse for type ...**, you can see them under:

    `Chapter7.SamMaccollBank.Aggregator.CheckingAccountService`
    `Chapter7.SamMaccollBank.Aggregator.RetirementAccountService`
    `Chapter7.SamMaccollBank.Aggregator.SavingAccountService`

12. For each of these, there is a request message type which is of the format `<OperationName>Request` and a response message type with the format `<OperationName>Response`. A sub-set of them is shown in the following screenshot:

13. As we have a project reference and access to the data contracts assembly, our generated classes use these types. This enables us to pass the `currentCustomer` object to each of the backend service-request operations as an input variable. This is one of the advantages of having a shared data contracts assembly. We can also create some variables of type `Account` to represent the responses. Now create the following variables, by clicking on the `AccountAggregatorScope` first:

Name	Variable Type	Scope	Default
checkingResponse	Account	AccountAggregatorScope	
savingResponse	Account	AccountAggregatorScope	
retirementResponse	Account	AccountAggregatorScope	

14. Your screen should now look like the following screenshot:

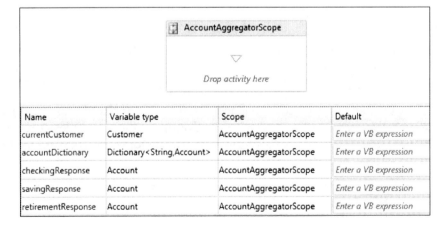

15. Now add a **Parallel** shape inside the `AccountAggregatorScope` and change its display name to **Aggregate Call**.

16. Within the **Aggregate Call** shape, add three sequence shapes, which should be side-by-side. From left to right, call them `Checking Account`, `Saving Account`, and `Retirement Account` respectively.

17. Within the `Checking Account` shape, add a `GetCheckingAccount` activity from the toolbox.

18. You now need to define the input parameters. Click on the `GetCheckingAccount` activity you just added. In the **Properties** window you will see a couple of parameters that need to be configured including `Customer`, which allows you to specify the input object for this parameter. `GetCheckingAccountResult` allows you to specify where the result of this service operation call will be stored. We will use the variables that we defined earlier. Configure them as shown in the following table:

Name	Variable Type
`Customer`	`currentCustomer`
`GetCheckingAccountResults`	`checkingResponse`

19. This should look like the next screenshot:

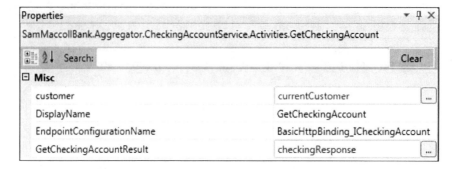

20. Below the `GetCheckingAccount` activity, add an **InvokeMethod** activity and name it `Add Checking to Dictionary`. Configure the properties as shown in the next table. Note that to configure the parameters you will need to click on the ellipsis button.

Property	Value
TargetObject	`accountDictionary`
MethodName	`Add`
Parameters	

Direction	Type	Value
In	String	checking
In	Account	checkingResponse

21. Within the **Saving Account** shape add a GetSavingAccount activity from the toolbox.

22. You now need to define the input parameters. Click on the GetSavingAccount activity you just added. In the **Properties** window, you will see a couple of parameters that need to be configured. Customer allows you to specify the input object for this parameter. GetSavingAccountResult allows you to specify where the result of this service operation call will be stored. We will use the variables that we defined earlier. Configure them as shown in the table:

Name	Variable Type
Customer	currentCustomer
GetSavingAccountResults	savingResponse

23. Below the GetSavingAccount activity add an **InvokeMethod** activity and name it as Add Saving to Dictionary. Configure the properties as shown in the table. Note that to configure the parameters you will need to click on the ellipsis button.

Property	Value
TargetObject	accountDictionary
MethodName	Add
Parameters	

Direction	Type	Value
In	String	saving
In	Account	savingResponse

24. Within the **Retirement Account** shape add a GetRetirementAccount activity from the toolbox.

25. You now need to define the input parameters. Click on the `GetRetirementAccount` activity you just added. In the **Properties** window you will see a couple of parameters that need to be configured including `Customer`, which allows you to specify the input object for this parameter. `GetRetirementAccountResult` allows you to specify where the result of this service operation call will be stored. We will use the variables that we defined earlier. Configure them as shown in the following table:

Name	Variable Type
`Customer`	`currentCustomer`
`GetRetirementAccountResults`	`retirementResponse`

26. Below the `GetRetirementAccount` activity add an **InvokeMethod** activity and name it as **Add Retirement to Dictionary**. Configure the properties as shown in the following table. Note that to configure the parameters you will need to click on the ellipsis button.

Property	Value
TargetObject	`accountDictionary`
MethodName	`Add`
Parameters	

Direction	Type	Value
In	`String`	`retirement`
In	`Account`	`retirementResponse`

27. Your workflow should now look like the following screenshot:

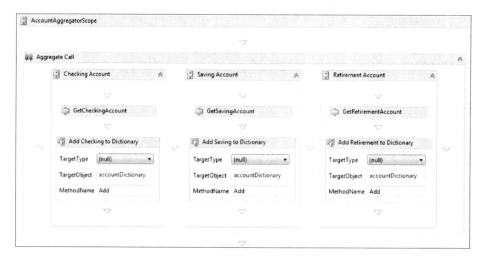

28. Now drag and drop a `ReceiveAndSendReply` activity at the top of your workflow just inside the `AccountAggregatorScope`. This will add a new **Sequence** activity, which contains a `Receive` and a `SendReplyToReceive` activity.

29. Create a new variable called `handle` with the following property:

Name	Variable Type	Scope	Default
handle	CorrelationHandle	AccountAggregatorScope	

30. Drag the `Receive` and `SendReplyToReceive` activity above the **Sequence** activity (but still within the `AccountAggregatorScope`). Now delete the empty **Sequence** activity.

31. Drag the `SendReplyToReceive` activity to the bottom of the workflow and place it just outside the **Aggregate Call** parallel activity. Your workflow should now look like the following screenshot. Note that some of the sections have been collapsed for visibility.

32. Click on the `Receive` activity and change **DisplayName** to `Receive Customer Request`. Set the following properties, which represent the WCF service, operation, and parameter information for consumers of this workflow service. You should follow sensible naming conventions as you would when defining properties for code-based WCF services:

Property	Value
ServiceContractName	`http://tempuri.org/` `IAccountAggregator`
OperationName	`GetCustomerAccounts`

33. To define the parameter information that the consumer will see, click on the ellipsis button of the **Content** property of the `Receive Customer Request` activity. Then click the **Parameters** radio button. Set the following parameter:

Name	Type	Assign to
`Customer`	`Chapter7.SamMaccollBank.` `DataContracts.Customer`	`currentCustomer`

34. On the `Receive Customer Request` activity you also need to make sure that the **CanCreateInstance** property is checked true. If this is not selected, this `Receive` activity will not be able to instantiate the workflow service. Then click on the ellipsis button for the **CorrelationInitializers** property. Make sure that the initializer is set to the `handle` variable that we defined earlier.

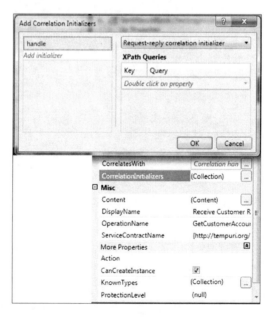

35. Click on the `SendReplyToReceive` activity and click on the ellipsis button of the **Content** property. Here select the **Message** radio button and define the following properties. This defines the return type that consumers of the workflow service will receive for the operation we defined with the earlier `Receive` activity.

Property	Value
Message Data	`accountDictionary`

Message Type	`System.Collections.Generic.Dictionary`
	`<System.String, Chapter7.SamMaccollBank.`
	`DataContracts.Account>`

36. Your workflow is now complete and should look like the following screenshot:

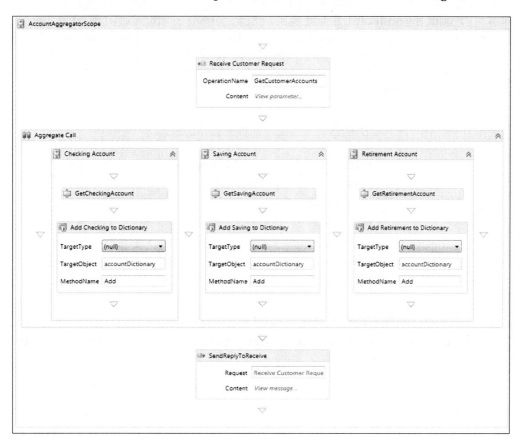

Testing the service aggregator workflow service

We will now use the WCF Test Client Tool to test our aggregator service.

1. Right-click on the `SamMaccollBank.Aggregator` project and select **Publish** to deploy this to your local IIS server with the following settings:

   Virtual directory: `http://localhost/Aggregator`

   Folder location: `C:\inetpub\wwwroot\Aggregator`

2. Open the WCF Test Client tool. Right-click on **My Service Projects** and select **Add Service**. Enter the endpoint as follows:

   `http://localhost/aggregator/AccountAggregator.xamlx`

3. Expand the endpoint. Select `IAccountAggregator` (the `Service Contract` name, which is as you configured it in the `Receive` workflow activity). Select the `GetCustomerAccounts()` operation. The WCF Test Client Tool will allow you to define the `Customer` input parameter. Define it with the following values:

Property	Value
Address1	Avenue Q
Address2	Somewhere On
City	New York
CustomerID	1234
FirstName	It Is Great
LastName	To Be Me
State	New York
Zip	98765

4. Click the **Invoke** button; ignoring all warnings.

5. All the three accounts should be returned as a `Dictionary` object as per the following screenshot:

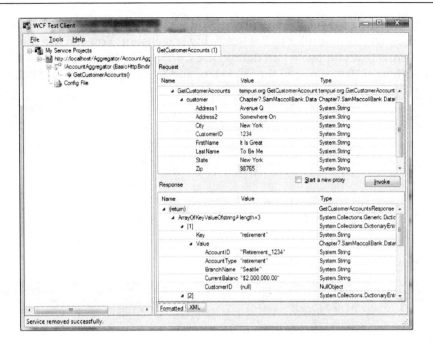

6. To debug the workflow, open the `Chapter7.SamMaccollBank.Aggregator` project and open the `AccountAggregator.xamlx` workflow. Right-click on the `Receive Customer Request` activity and select **Breakpoint | Insert Breakpoint**. In the **Solution Explorer** window, right-click on the `AccountAggregator.xamlx` file and select **Set As Start Page**.

7. Now that you have set the start page, right-click on the `Chapter7. SamMaccollBank.Aggregator` project and select **Debug | Start New Instance**. This will automatically open an instance of the WCF Test Client and will host the `AccountAggregator.xamlx` workflow in the ASP.NET development web server that Visual Studio provides.

8. Fill in the required customer details for the `GetCustomerAccounts()` operation as you did previously in the WCF Test Client Tool then select **Invoke**.

9. You should now hit the breakpoint you set previously in the workflow. The screen will look similar to the following screenshot. You can use the standard controls that you use when debugging C# .NET code; for example, *F5* to continue, *F10* to move to the next step, and *F11* to move one step backwards.

10. Hit *F11* repeatedly to walk through the workflow. If you want to spend a long time debugging, you may wish to increase the timeout values, which are stored in the `web.config` file in the project.

Now that you have successfully created the aggregator component and deployed the backend services, we will make an ASP.NET page to present this data to the users.

Consuming the service aggregator workflow service with ASP.NET

We will now finish the implementation of the ASP.NET page which will take entry of customer details, consume our service, and then from the returned `Dictionary` object, will display those results to the end user.

1. You should now open the `Chapter7.SamMaccollBank.WebTier` project. This contains a stub implementation of the page we will implement.

2. Right-click on `Default.aspx` and select **View in Browser**. You should see a page similar to the following screenshot:

3. The page has implemented a number of `<asp:TextBox>`, `<asp:Button>`, and `<asp:Label>` objects. The `<asp:>` tag prefix indicates that there is either local script or server-based dynamic content that needs to be processed; for example, the user will see the output of this dynamic ASP.NET call in their browser as standard HTML. You can see this by right-clicking on the `Default.aspx` page and selecting **View Markup**. This is shown in the following screenshot:

4. The **getAccountInfo** button has an `OnClick()` method call with `getCustomer_Click` specified. If you right-click on the `Default.aspx` page and select **View Code** you can see the empty implementation of this method. If you view the page in the browser again and click on the **Get Account Details** button, you will notice that nothing changes.

5. Add a reference in this project to `Chapter7.SamMaccollBank. DataContracts`. This will allow us to access the `Customer` and `Account` objects that we will need.

6. Also, add a service reference to the Account aggregator workflow service you just deployed and tested. The following are the settings:

Property	Value
Address	`http://localhost/aggregator/accountaggregator. xamlx`
Namespace	`AccountAggregator`

7. In the `Default.aspx.cs` file add the following `using` statement:

```
using Chapter7.SamMaccollBank.DataContracts;
```

8. In the `Default.aspx.cs` file add the following implementation of `getCustomer_Click`:

```
public void getCustomer_Click(object sender, EventArgs e)
{
    //Create the customer object
    Customer customer = new Customer();
    //Get the values from the text boxes and assign them to the
        customer object properties
    customer.FirstName = FirstName.Text;
    customer.LastName = LastName.Text;
    customer.CustomerID = CustomerID.Text;
    customer.Address1 = Address1.Text;
    customer.Address2 = Address2.Text;
    customer.City = City.Text;
    customer.State = State.Text;
    customer.Zip = ZIP.Text;
    //Create the client using the classes generated
        by our Service Reference
    AccountAggregator.AccountAggregatorClient svcClient = new
                    AccountAggregator.AccountAggregatorClient();
    AccountAggregator.GetCustomerAccounts request = new
                        AccountAggregator.GetCustomerAccounts();
    request.customer = customer;
    //Create dictionary object to store results
    Dictionary<string, DataContracts.Account>
        accountDictionary = svcClient.GetCustomerAccounts(request);
    //Update Text boxes for each of the accounts
```

```
CheckingBalance.Text =
                 accountDictionary["checking"].CurrentBalance;
CheckingID.Text = accountDictionary["checking"].AccountID;
RetirementID.Text =
                 accountDictionary["retirement"].AccountID;
RetirementBalance.Text =
              accountDictionary["retirement"].CurrentBalance;
SavingBalance.Text =
                 accountDictionary["saving"].CurrentBalance;
SavingID.Text = accountDictionary["saving"].AccountID;
}
```

9. Right-click again on `Default.aspx` and select **View in Browser**. Enter customer details as was done previously and then click the **Get Account Details** button. You should see a page similar to the following:

Summary

This solution, using Windows Server AppFabric, WCF, and WF from .NET 4.0, demonstrated how Workflow services can be used to orchestrate communication between backend service endpoints with minimal code. There was no need to tightly couple any of the components and any of them could be reused by other applications. By utilizing well-defined data contracts, we can follow service-oriented practices and deploy loosely-coupled applications. The Scatter-Gather pattern is a powerful pattern to implement if you want to provide a dashboard view for users from multiple sources. As well as for financial services, this can also be used to provide a single view about an individual across corporate systems; payroll, vacation, and so on. AppFabric is a very powerful host and with some of its additional features such as persistence, it is something you should consider for use within your organization.

8
Content-based Routing

Communication between enterprise systems is an essential part of an organization's architecture. How you decide to link these systems and by which criteria you distribute data, is something that you will be faced with time and again. In this chapter, we will look at how to send data messages to the correct target system.

Use case

McKeever Technologies is a medium-sized business, which manufactures latex products. They have recently grown in size through a series of small acquisitions of competitor companies. As a result, the organization has a mix of both home-grown applications and packaged line-of-business systems. They have not standardized their order management software and still rely on multiple systems, each of which houses details about a specific set of products. Their developers are primarily oriented towards .NET, but there are some parts of the organization that have deep Java expertise.

Up until now, orders placed with McKeever Technologies were faxed to a call center and manually entered into the order system associated with the particular product. Also, when customers want to discover the state of their submitted order, they are forced to contact McKeever Technologies' call center and ask an agent to look up their order. The company realizes that in order to increase efficiency, reduce data entry error, and improve customer service they must introduce some automation to their order intake and query processes.

McKeever Technologies receives less than one thousand orders per day and does not expect this number to increase exponentially in the coming years. Their current order management systems have either Oracle or SQL Server database backends and some of them offer SOAP service interfaces for basic operations. These systems do not all maintain identical service-level agreements; so the solution must be capable of handling expected or unexpected downtime of the target system gracefully.

The company is looking to stand up a solution in less than four months while not introducing too much additional management overhead to an already over-worked IT maintenance organization. The solution is expected to live in production for quite some time and may only be revisited once a long-term order management consolidation strategy can be agreed upon.

Key requirements

The following are key requirements for a new software solution:

- Accept inbound purchase requests and determine which system to add them to based on which product has been ordered
- Support a moderate transaction volume and reliable delivery to target systems
- Enable communication with diverse systems through either web or database protocols.

Additional facts

The technology team has acquired the following additional facts that will shape their proposed solution:

1. The number of order management systems may change over time as consolidation occurs and new acquisitions are made.
2. A single customer may have orders on multiple systems. For example, a paint manufacturer may need different types of latex for different products. The customers will want a single view of all orders notwithstanding which order entry system they reside on.
3. The lag between entry of an order and its appearance on a customer-facing website should be minimal (less than one hour).
4. All order entry systems are on the same network. There are no occasionally connected systems (for example, remote locations that may potentially lose their network connectivity).
5. Strategic direction is to convert Oracle systems to Microsoft SQL Server and Java to C#.
6. The new order tracking system does not need to integrate with order fulfillment or other systems at launch.
7. There are priorities for orders (for example, "I need it tomorrow" requires immediate processing and overnight shipment versus "I need it next week").
8. Legacy SQL Servers are SQL Server 2005 or 2008. No SQL Server 2000 systems.

Pattern description

The organization is trying to streamline data entry into multiple systems that perform similar functions. They wish to take in the same data (an order), but depending on attributes of the order, it should be loaded into one system or another. This looks like a content-based routing scenario.

What is **content-based routing**? In essence, it is distributing data based on the values it contains. You would typically use this sort of pattern when you have a single capability (for example, ADD ORDER, LOOKUP EMPLOYEE, DELETE RESERVATION) spread across multiple systems. Unlike a publish/subscribe pattern where multiple downstream systems may all want the same message (that is, one-to-many), a content-based routing solution typically helps you steer a message to the system that can best handle the request.

What is an alternative to implementing this routing pattern? You could define distinct channels for each downstream system and force the caller to pick the service they wish to consume. That is, for McKeever Technologies, the customer would call one service if they were ordering products A, B, or C, and use another service for products D, E, or F. This clearly fails the SOA rules of abstraction or encapsulation and forces the clients to maintain knowledge of the backend processing.

The biggest remaining question is what is the best way to implement this pattern. We would want to make sure that the routing rules were easily maintained and could be modified without expensive redeployments or refactoring. Our routing criteria should be rich enough so that we can make decisions based on the content itself, header information, or metadata about the transmission.

Candidate architectures

A team of technologists have reviewed the use case and drafted three candidate solutions. Each candidate has its own strengths and weaknesses, but one of them will prove to be the best choice.

Candidate architecture #1–BizTalk Server

A BizTalk Server-based solution seems to be a good fit for this customer scenario. McKeever Technologies is primarily looking to automate existing processes and communicate with existing systems, which are both things that BizTalk does well.

Solution design aspects

We are dealing with a fairly low volume of data (1000 orders per day, and at most, 5000 queries of order status) and small individual message size. A particular order or status query should be no larger than 5KB in size, meaning that this falls right into the sweet spot of BizTalk data processing.

This proposed system is responsible for accepting and processing new orders, which means that reliable delivery is critical. BizTalk can provide built-in quality of service, guaranteed through its store-and-forward engine, which only discards a message after it has successfully reached its target endpoint. Our solution also needs to be able to communicate with multiple line-of-business systems through a mix of web service and database interfaces. BizTalk Server offers a wide range of database adapters and natively communicates with SOAP-based endpoints. We are building a new solution which automates a formerly manual process, so we should be able to design a single external interface for publishing new orders and querying order status. But, in the case that we have to support multiple external-facing contracts, BizTalk Server makes it very easy to transform data to canonical messages at the point of entry into the BizTalk engine. This means that the internal processing of BizTalk can be built to support a single data format, while we can still enable slight variations of the message format to be transmitted by clients. Similarly, each target system will have a distinct data format that its interface accepts. Our solution will apply all of its business logic on the canonical data format and transform the data to the target system format at the last possible moment. This will make it easier to add new downstream systems without unsettling the existing endpoints and business logic.

From a security standpoint, BizTalk allows us to secure the inbound transport channel and message payload on its way into the BizTalk engine. If transport security is adequate for this customer, then an SSL channel can be set up on the external facing interface.

To assuage any fears of the customer that system or data errors can cause messages to get lost or "stuck", it is critical to include a proactive exception handling aspect. BizTalk Server surfaces exceptions through an administrator console. However, this does not provide a business-friendly way to discover and act upon errors. Fortunately for us, BizTalk enables us to listen for error messages and either re-route those messages or spin up an error-specific business process. For this customer, we could recommend either logging errors to a database where business users leverage a website interface to view exceptions, or, we can publish messages to a SharePoint site and build a process around fixing and resubmitting any bad orders. For errors that require immediate attention, we can also leverage BizTalk's native capability to send e-mail messages.

We know that McKeever Technologies will eventually move to a single order processing system, so this solution will undergo changes at some point in the future. Besides this avenue of change, we could also experience changes to the inbound interfaces, existing downstream systems, or even the contents of the messages themselves. BizTalk has a strong "versioning" history that allows us to build our solution in a modular fashion and isolate points of change.

Solution delivery aspects

McKeever Technologies is not currently a BizTalk shop, so they will need to both acquire and train resources to effectively build their upcoming solution. Their existing developers, who are already familiar with Microsoft's .NET Framework, can learn how to construct BizTalk solutions in a fairly short amount of time. The tools to build BizTalk artifacts are hosted within Visual Studio.NET and BizTalk projects can reside alongside other .NET project types.

Because the BizTalk-based messaging solution has a design paradigm (for example, publish/subscribe, distributed components to chain together) different from that of a typical custom .NET solution, understanding the toolset alone will not ensure delivery success. If McKeever Technologies decides to bring in a product like BizTalk Server, it will be vital for them to engage an outside expert to act as a solution architect and leverage their existing BizTalk experience when building this solution.

Solution operation aspects

Operationally, BizTalk Server provides a mature, rich interface for monitoring solution health and configuring runtime behavior. There is also a strong underlying set of APIs that can be leveraged using scripting technologies so that automation of routine tasks can be performed.

While BizTalk Server has tools that will feel familiar to a Windows Administrator, the BizTalk architecture is unique in the Microsoft ecosystem and will require explicit staff training.

Organizational aspects

BizTalk Server would be a new technology for McKeever technologies so definitely there is risk involved. It becomes necessary to purchase licenses, provision environments, train users, and hire experts. While these are all responsible things to do when new technology is introduced, this does mean a fairly high startup cost to implement this solution.

That said, McKeever technologies will need a long term integration solution as they attempt to modernize their IT landscape and be in better shape to absorb new organizations and quickly integrate with new systems. An investment in an enterprise service bus like BizTalk Server will pay long term dividends even if initial costs are high.

Solution evaluation

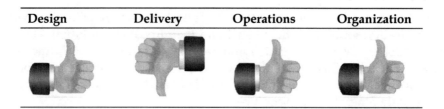

Design	Delivery	Operations	Organization

Candidate architecture #2–SQL Server 2008 R2

It is possible to build a solution that meets our needs based on SQL Server tools.

Solution design aspects

The basis of this solution is a master repository that stores order information. Orders arrive into McKeever Technologies and get placed in the new `Orders` database. Each order is then routed to the appropriate target system based on routing rules.

If the target system is SQL Server-based then we can use SQL Server Service Broker (SSSB) to transmit data and return acknowledgements to the master repository. When the target system has an underlying Oracle database store, then we will leverage SQL Server Integration Services (SSIS) to move data between the systems.

There is a lot of value in establishing this master data repository. This will allow a single customer to enter an order for multiple products delivered from multiple legacy systems and remove the potential for improper routing of orders based on human error. Also, this makes it possible for orders to be queried from a single location instead of federating the query across multiple order management systems.

The major issue is that there will be significant data lag using SSIS and master data management tools. These systems work as batch processes, not as real-time systems. While you can make SSIS run in near real time, it requires extensive customization.

Solution delivery aspects

This solution would make heavy use of McKeever's existing SQL Server expertise. The team is well-versed in building bulk data movement jobs in SSIS, but has only limited experience authoring SSSB conversations.

Solution operation aspects

The main advantage SSIS and SSSB offer is that they are provided with McKeever's existing SQL Server licenses, avoiding the additional cost of BizTalk licenses. McKeever does have staff with on-hand experience in using SQL Server and working with SQL statements.

Organizational aspects

While McKeever Technologies hopes to move to a centralized order management system at some point in the future, they are currently more focused on extracting value from existing systems. Creating a master order management repository now moves the organization in the right direction, but there are significantly more hurdles to overcome when gaining the consensus needed to make this happen. In a federated model, each order management system can still receive and process orders using existing procedures. We may be creating more work by trying to define and synchronize a master data store. Also, this solution requires more effort when the company inevitably absorbs new companies and tries to integrate their processing systems.

Solution evaluation

Design	Delivery	Operations	Organization

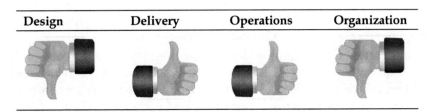

Candidate architecture #3–WCF and Windows Server AppFabric

One of the key new features of WCF in .NET 4.0 is the ability to do content-based routing. This means that data inside the message can be used by the WCF framework at runtime to determine what service endpoint needs to be called. Furthermore, if nothing matches the content pattern for routing, a default endpoint can be selected to handle these requests. Routing in .NET 4.0 is accomplished using the **Routing service**, which can be configured and hosted inside IIS. Using Windows Server AppFabric for hosting this service will ensure the best possible execution with all the AppFabric benefits (See Chapter 3, *Windows Server AppFabric Primer,* for more specific details).

Let us walk though the decision framework to see if .NET 4.0 and Windows Server AppFabric would work for this scenario.

Solution design aspects

Solving this problem with .NET 4.0 and Windows Server AppFabric would have two parts. The first part would handle the order messages and the second part would handle order status messages. Both parts would follow similar patterns.

- **Order Messages**: Order messages will be routed to one of the backend systems using .NET 4.0 content-based routing. Each backend system will be fronted by a workflow service. This service will ensure guaranteed delivery of the message to the backend system and allow for various communication protocols between the frontend and various backend systems. Routing occurs based on the product being ordered, and product identifiers below a certain value go to one system, while product identifiers above a certain value go to the other. This means we can use the routing service to inspect the message content and choose which Workflow service to invoke.

- **Order Status**: Order status query messages will be routed to one of the backend systems using .NET 4.0 content-based routing. Each backend system will be fronted by a WCF service to allow for various communication protocols to these systems. If one of the backend systems is down, the WCF service will return a "not available" message to the client.

Solution delivery aspects

McKeever Technologies currently has a staff of .NET developers and has experience in developing complex solutions with .NET technologies and managing them in production. While learning some of the new features of .NET 4.0 and Windows Server AppFabric would take a little bit of time, this is something the existing resources should be able to handle.

The timeline is less than four months and given the preceding solution outline, this should be easily accomplished in that timeline.

Solution operation aspects

McKeever Technologies currently has a large block of .NET developers and hence has Information Technology support resources in this area. Further solutions based on .NET, should be easily supported by the existing operations staff. Windows Server AppFabric is a new technology for the McKeever administrators, but the integration with IIS 7 makes Windows Server AppFabric fairly easy to understand.

Given the relatively low load of the system — 1,000 orders a day — performance of the system is not a huge concern. That said, a Windows Server AppFabric-based solution has extensive control on persistence points and tracking, to allow or only a minimal amount of performance impact.

As the solution is based on dealing with orders, it must be able to receive orders and to retry in the event that the backend system is down. Windows Server AppFabric would need a frontend **network load balancer** to ensure a highly available service endpoint, in addition to a clustered SQL data store for the persistence information. Both of these would be available for a client with existing .NET applications in production.

Organizational aspects

Organizationally, McKeever Technologies will be taking a slight risk by using Windows Server AppFabric simply because it is a new technology and employees will need to learn it. But to that point, investing now in the new technology will ensure a solution that will be around for years to come. This drives towards a key point related to maintainability and the need for this solution to survive many years.

Solution evaluation

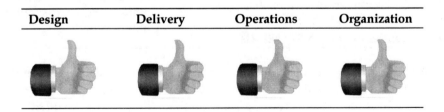

Design	Delivery	Operations	Organization

Architecture selection

Each solution has benefits and risks that we can use to make a final decision.

BizTalk Server	
Benefits	**Risks**
• Out-of-the-box adapters to multiple target formats, including SQL Server and Oracle database • Reliable messaging infrastructure which can guarantee message delivery • Architecture built to support routing messages based on content	• Lack of in-house expertise will require extensive training of both the developer and operations staff • Would take longer to build and deploy solutions that are purely code-based

SQL Server	
Benefits	**Risks**
• Leverages in-house expertise with SQL Server tools • Encourages master data approach which provides a unified frontend to clients • Can natively communicate with our target database formats	• Incapable of processing real-time data requests • Different implementation techniques based on the type of target database

WCF and Windows Server AppFabric	
Benefits	**Risks**
• Rapid, lightweight way to build service-oriented solutions • Built-in capability to do content-based routing in real time • Includes durable messaging to promote guaranteed delivery • Leverages existing .NET skill sets	• New technologies at the development (.NET 4.0) and operations tier (Windows Server AppFabric) • Routing rules are relatively primitive and won't support complex conditions

With all that said, the best choice for this scenario is the Windows Server AppFabric solution. This provides us a lightweight means to rapidly deploy a flexible and easy-to-maintain content-based routing solution that still gives us the quality of service that an enterprise solution such as BizTalk Server provides. In the long term, this organization will seriously consider investing in an enterprise service bus, but for this scenario, a Windows Server AppFabric host can meet the current and future needs of the company.

Building the solution

In this section, we will actually construct a working version of the proposed solution, which will leverage core components of .NET 4.0 (WCF and Windows Workflow Services) as well as the AppFabric extensions to IIS. Note that for this demonstration, we are only building the first aspect, which accepts orders, not the second piece which supports querying the status of a given order. The flow of the solution looks like the following:

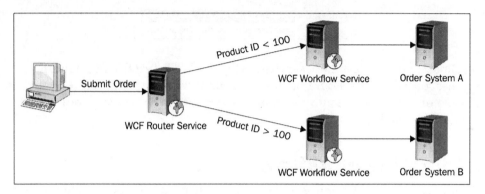

An order comes from a customer to a single endpoint at McKeever Technologies. This single endpoint then routes the order based on the content of the order (that is, the value of the `Product ID` element). The router sends requests to WCF Workflow Services, which can provide us durability and persistence when talking to the backend order management systems. If an order system is down, then the workflow gets suspended and will be capable of resuming once the system comes back online.

Setup

First, create a new database named `Chapter8Db` in your local SQL Server 2008 instance. Then locate the database script named `Chapter8Db.sql` in the folder `<Installation Directory>\Chapter8\Begin` and install the tables into your new database. When completed, your configuration should look like the following screenshot:

```
□ 📁 Databases
   ⊞ 📁 System Databases
   ⊞ 📁 Database Snapshots
   ⊞ 📦 ApplicationServerExtensions
   □ 📦 Chapter8Db
      ⊞ 📁 Database Diagrams
      □ 📁 Tables
         ⊞ 📁 System Tables
         ⊞ 📄 dbo.OrderManagement_SystemA
         ⊞ 📄 dbo.OrderManagement_SystemB
```

Next, open `Chapter8.sln` in the `<Installation Directory>\Chapter8\Begin` folder. In this base solution you will find two WCF services that represent the interfaces in front of the two order management systems at McKeever Technologies. Build the services and then add both of them as applications in IIS. Make sure you select the .NET 4.0 application pool.

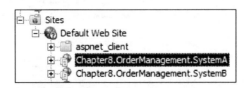

If you choose, you can test these services using the WCF Test Client application that comes with the .NET 4.0 framework. If your service is configured correctly, an invocation of the service should result in a new record in the corresponding SQL Server database table.

Building the workflow

Now that our base infrastructure is in place, we can construct the workflows that will execute these order system services.

1. Launch Visual Studio.NET 2010 and open `Chapter8.sln` in the `<Installation Directory>\Chapter8\Begin` folder. You should see two WCF services.

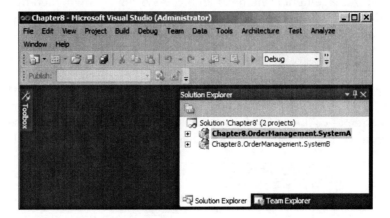

2. We now must add a new workflow project to the solution. Recall that this workflow will sit in front of our order service and give us a stronger quality of service, thanks to the persistence capability of AppFabric. In Visual Studio .NET 2010, go to **File** and select **New Project**.

3. Select the **WCF Workflow Service** project type under the **Workflow** category and add the project named `Chapter8.SystemA.WorkflowService` to our existing solution.

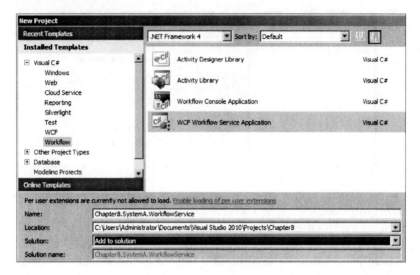

4. This project is now part of the solution and has a default workflow named `Service1.xamlx`.

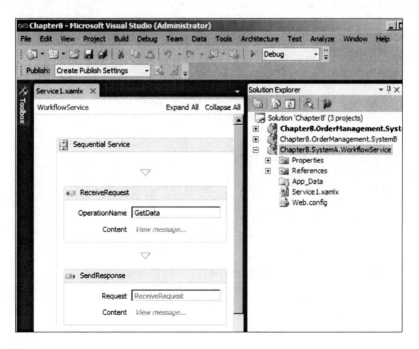

5. Rename the `Service1.xamlx` file to `SystemAOrderService.xamlx` from within the **Solution Explorer**. Also click the whitespace within the workflow to change both the **ConfigurationName** and **Name** properties.

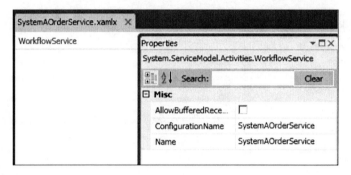

6. We want all our service-fronting workflows to have the same external-facing contract interface so that we can effectively abstract the underlying service contracts or implementation nuances. Hence, we add a new class file named `OrderDataContract.cs` to this workflow project. This class will hold the data contracts defining the input and output for all workflows that sit in front of order systems.

7. Make sure the project itself has a reference to `System.Runtime.Serialization`, and then add a `using` statement for `System.Runtime.Serialization` to the top of the `OrderDataContract.cs` class. Add the following code to the class:

```
namespace Chapter8.WorkflowService
{
  [DataContract(
      Namespace = "http://Chapter8/OrderManagement/DataContract")]
  public class NewOrderRequest
  {
    [DataMember]
    public string OrderId { get; set; }
    [DataMember]
    public string ProductId { get; set; }
    [DataMember]
    public string CustomerId { get; set; }
    [DataMember]
    public int Quantity { get; set; }
    [DataMember]
    public DateTime DateOrdered { get; set; }
    [DataMember]
    public string ContractId { get; set; }
    [DataMember]
    public string Status { get; set; }
  }
```

```
[DataContract(
    Namespace = "http://Chapter8/OrderManagement/DataContract")]
public class OrderAckResponse
{
    [DataMember]
    public string OrderId { get; set; }
}
}
```

8. Open the `SystemAOrderService.xamlx` workflow, click on the top
   ReceiveRequest shape, and set the following property values. Note that we
   will use the same values for all workflows so that the external-facing contract
   of each workflow appears the same.

Property	Value
DisplayName	**ReceiveOrderRequest**
OperationName	**SubmitOrder**
ServiceContractName	{http://Chapter8/OrderManagement} ServiceContract
Action	http://Chapter8/OrderManagement/SubmitOrder
CanCreateInstance	**True**

9. Click the **Variables** tab at the bottom of the workflow designer to show the
   default variables added to the workflow.

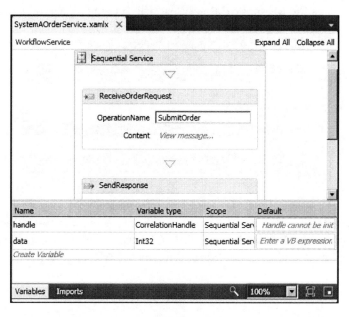

10. Delete the `data` variable.

11. Create a new variable named `OrderReq`. For the variable type, choose **Browse for Types** and choose the **NewOrderRequest** type we defined earlier in the `OrderDataContract.cs` class.

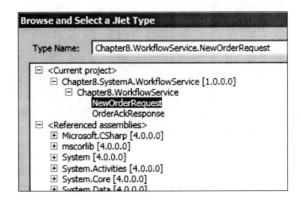

12. Add another variable named `OrderResp` and choose the previously defined `OrderAckResponse` .NET type.

13. The `OrderReq` variable gets instantiated by the initial request, but we need to explicitly set the `OrderResp` variable. In the **Default** column within the **Variables** window, set the value to `New OrderAckResponse()`.

14. Set a proper variable for the initial receive shape by clicking on the **ReceiveOrderRequest** shape and click on the **View Message** link. Choose `OrderReq` as the **Message data** and set the type as `NewOrderRequest`.

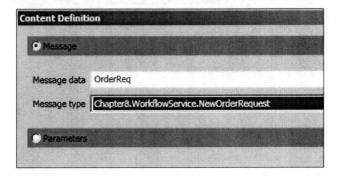

15. Now we do the same for the response shape. Select the **SendResponse** shape and click on the **View Message** link. Choose the `OrderResp` variable as the **Message data** and `OrderAckResponse` as the **Message type**.

16. Keep the **SendResponse** shape selected and set its **PersistBeforeSend** property to **On**. This forces a persistence point into our workflow and ensures that any errors that occur later in the workflow will lead to a suspended/resumable instance.

17. We can test our workflow service prior to completing it. We want to populate our service response object, so go to the **Workflow** toolbox, view the **Primitives** tab, and drag an **Assign** shape in between the existing receive and send shapes.

18. In the **Assign** shape, set the **To** value to `OrderResp.OrderID` and the right side of the equation to `System.GUID.NewGUID().ToString()`. This sets the single attribute of our response node to a unique tracking value.

19. Build the workflow and if no errors exist, right-click the `SystemAOrderSystem.xamlx` workflow in the **Solution Explorer** and choose **View in Browser**.

20. Open the **WCF Test Client** application and point it to our Workflow Service endpoint. Double-click the **Submit Order** operation, select the datatype in the **Value** column, and enter test input data. Click on the **Invoke** button and observe the response object coming back with a GUID value returned in the `OrderId` attribute.

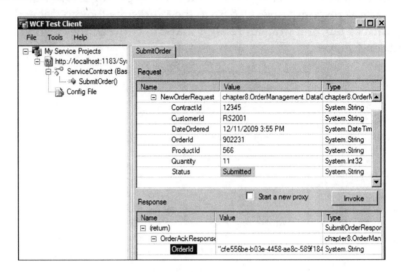

21. Now we're ready to complete our workflow by actually calling our target WCF service that adds a record to the database table. Return to Visual Studio. NET, right-click the `Chapter8.SystemA.WorkflowService` project, and choose **Add Service Reference**.

22. Point to the service located at `http://localhost/Chapter8.OrderManagement.SystemA/OrderIntakeService.svc` and type `SystemASvcRef` as the namespace.

23. If the reference is successfully added and the project is rebuilt, then a new custom workflow activity should be added to the workflow toolbox. This activity encapsulates everything needed to invoke our system service.

24. Add variables to the workflow that represent the input and output of our system service. Create a variable named `ServiceRequest` and browse for the type `Order`, which can be found under the service reference. Set the default value of this variable to `New Order()`.

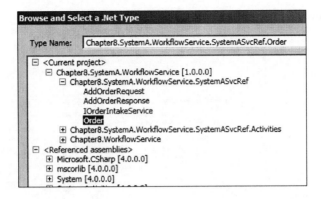

25. Create another variable named `ServiceResponse` and pick the same order object but do not set a default value.

26. Drag the custom **AddOrder** activity from the workflow toolbox and place it *after* the **SendResponse** shape. This sits after the workflow service response is sent, so that if errors occur the caller will not be impacted.

27. Click the **AddOrder** shape and set its **NewOrder** property to the `ServiceRequest` variable and its **AddOrderResult** property to `ServiceResponse`.

28. Now we have to populate the service request object. Drag a **Sequence** workflow activity from the **Control Flow** tab and drop it immediately before the **AddOrder** shape.

29. Add six **Assign** shapes to the Sequence and set each activity's left and right fields as follows:

Left Side	Right Side
ServiceRequest.ContractId	OrderReq.ContractId
ServiceRequest.CustomerId	OrderReq.CustomerId
ServiceRequest.DateOrdered	OrderReq.DateOrdered
ServiceRequest.OrderNumber	OrderResp.OrderId
ServiceRequest.ProductId	OrderReq.ProductId
ServiceRequest.Quantity	OrderReq.Quantity

Note that the `OrderNumber` value of the request is set using the `OrderResp` object as that is the one to which we added the GUID value.

30. Our final workflow should look like the following:

31. Open the web.config file for the Workflow Service and add the following configuration entry within the System.ServiceModel node. This makes our Workflow Service leverage the WsHttpBinding by default and eliminates issues that arise when using the BasicHttpBinding with the WCF Routing Service.

```
<protocolMapping>
    <add scheme="http" binding="wsHttpBinding"/>
</protocolMapping>
```

32. Build the workflow and switch to IIS. Add a new application named `Chapter8.SystemA.WorkflowService` to the **Default Web Site**. Choose a .NET 4.0 application pool and set the path to the location of your service project.

33. Right-click the **Default Web Site**, choose **Edit Bindings**, and ensure that `net.pipe` is listed there.

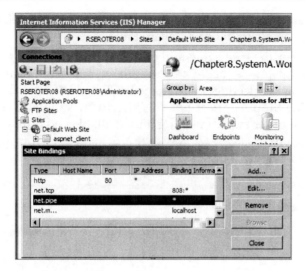

34. Visit the **Advanced Settings** of the default website and make sure that
net.pipe is part of the **Enabled Protocols**. This is needed to support the
AppFabric persistence functionality.

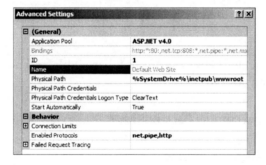

35. Right-click the new WF service application and choose **Manage WCF and
WF Services** and select **Configure**. On the **Workflow Persistence** tab, make
sure that **SQL Server Workflow Persistence** is selected. On the **Workflow
Host Management** tab, confirm that the **Action on Unhandled Exception** is
set to **Abandon and suspend**.

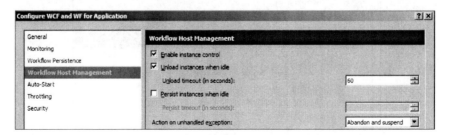

36. Now we can employ the WCF Test Client to call our workflow service and see a record show up in our database table.

37. In order to flex the true value-add of the AppFabric hosting environment, turn off the `Chapter8.OrderManagement.SystemA` application by right-clicking it, selecting the **Manage WCF and WF Services** menu item, and choosing **Stop Application**. This effectively simulates failure of our downstream order system making it unavailable and offline.

38. Call the workflow service again and if you view the AppFabric dashboard, you should see a **Suspended** message.

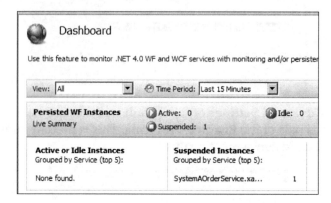

39. Confirm this fact by viewing your database table and noticing that no new record has been added.

40. Restart the `Chapter8.OrderManagement.SystemA` application to simulate our order system coming back online.

41. Click on the suspended message in the AppFabric console and choose to resume the suspended instance.

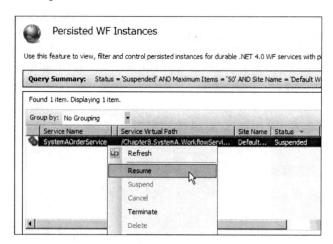

42. The instance is resumed and a new record should be added to the `OrderManagement_SystemA` database table.

43. Build one more workflow that is nearly identical to this first one, except that it consumes the system B order system service.

44. Create a new WCF Workflow Service application named `Chapter8.SystemB.WorkflowService` and add it to the existing Visual Studio.NET solution.

45. Rename the physical xamlx file to `SystemBOrderService.xamlx` and set both the **Configuration Name** and **Name** property of the workflow to `SystemBOrderService`.

46. Copy the `OrderDataContract.cs` file from the `Chapter8.SystemA.WorkflowService` project to the `Chapter8.SystemB.WorkflowService` project. Recall that we want all workflows of the front order systems to have the same external-facing data contract.

47. On the **ReceiveRequest** shape, change the name to `ReceiveOrderRequest`, **Operation Name** to `SubmitOrder`, **ServiceContractName** to `{http://Chapter8/OrderManagement}ServiceContract`, and **Action** to `http://Chapter8/OrderManagement/SubmitOrder`. These values are identical to our previous workflow and help us have the same external-facing contract definition for both services.

48. Add a service reference to `http://localhost/Chapter8.OrderManagement.SystemB/OrderService.svc` and set the namespace to `SystemBSvcRef`.

49. Create the variables for the workflow service request and response as well as the system B service request and response.

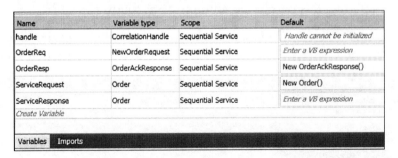

Name	Variable type	Scope	Default
handle	CorrelationHandle	Sequential Service	*Handle cannot be initialized*
OrderReq	NewOrderRequest	Sequential Service	*Enter a VB expression*
OrderResp	OrderAckResponse	Sequential Service	New OrderAckResponse()
ServiceRequest	Order	Sequential Service	New Order()
ServiceResponse	Order	Sequential Service	*Enter a VB expression*
Create Variable			

50. Add an **Assign** shape between the workflow service request and response and set the response's `OrderId` value equal to `System.GUID.NewGUID().ToString()`.

51. After building the project, drag the new custom **AddNewOrder** workflow activity below the service response shape, set its input and output attributes to the previously defined variables, and finally set its six properties using a sequence of **Assign** shapes.

52. Exactly like the earlier Workflow Service, add the following configuration block to the web.config file:

```
<protocolMapping>
    <add scheme="http" binding="wsHttpBinding"/>
</protocolMapping>
```

53. Compile the service and create an IIS web application named `Chapter8.SystemB.WorkflowService` and configure it identically to the `Chapter8.SystemA.WorkflowService` application.

54. Test the service by calling it via the WCF test client and confirming that your data is added to the `OrderManagement_SystemB` database table.

Adding a router service

Now we have two independent workflow services that sit in front of our order systems. We don't want our customers to know which service to call, but rather, we want them to send all their orders to one place and expect that McKeever Technologies will figure out a way to enter data accurately into appropriate systems.

WCF 4.0 introduces a pre-built routing service that uses configuration values to direct messages to endpoints, based on a variety of criteria. We can route messages based on their content, SOAP action, custom headers, and more. There's a great amount of flexibility we can add to our solution architecture when rich capabilities like message routing are simply baked into a framework.

The steps for building this part of the solution are as follows:

1. In Visual Studio.NET, add a new website of type **WCF Service** to our existing solution and name it `Chapter8.OrderManagement.RoutingService`.

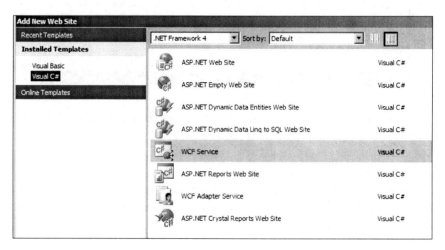

2. Delete the code files (interface and service implementation). We are leveraging the native WCF 4.0 Routing Service and therefore don't need any code files.

3. Add a project reference to `System.ServiceModel.Routing`.

4. Rename the `.svc` file to `OrderRouter.svc`.

5. Open the service file (`.svc`) and change its `Service` attribute reference to `System.ServiceModel.Routing.RoutingService, System.ServiceModel.Routing, version=4.0.0.0, Culture=neutral, PublicKeyToken=31bf3856ad364e35`. This tells the WCF service to use the built-in router service for its implementation.

6. We need to set up the `web.config` file to implement the routing capability. within the `System.Configuration` tags, add the `<client>` node. This holds the endpoint definition for both of our order system workflow services. Note that we don't identify the contract definition because this project technically has no idea about our service or its contract implementation.

```
<client>
  <endpoint
    address="http://localhost/Chapter8.SystemA.WorkflowService/
        SystemAOrderService.xamlx" binding="wsHttpBinding"
        bindingConfiguration="" contract="*" name="OrderSystemA" />
  <endpoint
    address="http://localhost/Chapter8.SystemB.WorkflowService/
        SystemBOrderService.xamlx" binding="wsHttpBinding"
        bindingConfiguration="" contract="*" name="OrderSystemB" />
</client>
```

7. We create the new WCF 4.0 `routing` section. We first have a namespace table, which allows us to create an alias to the namespace of our data message. Next, we have a `filters` collection where we have XPath filters for each order system and which sends messages with `ProductId < 100` to system A and `ProductId > 100` to system B. Finally, we have a filter table, which links the filters and determines which endpoint to use when the filter is satisfied.

```
<routing>
  <namespaceTable>
    <add prefix="custom"
      namespace="http://Chapter8/OrderManagement/DataContract"/>
  </namespaceTable>
  <filters>
    <filter name="SystemAFilter" filterType="XPath"
          filterData="//custom:ProductId &lt; '100'"/>
```

```
        <filter name="SystemBFilter" filterType="XPath"
               filterData="//custom:ProductId &gt; '100'"/>
    </filters>

    <filterTables>
        <filterTable name="filterTable1">
        <add filterName="SystemAFilter" endpointName="OrderSystemA"
         priority="0"/>
        <add filterName="SystemBFilter" endpointName="OrderSystemB"
         priority="0"/>
        </filterTable>
    </filterTables>
</routing>
```

8. We add a service and behavior entry. The behavior refers to the new routing capability, and the service points to the framework-provided routing service.

```
<services>
    <service behaviorConfiguration="RoutingBehavior" name="System.
ServiceModel.Routing.RoutingService">
        <endpoint address="" binding="wsHttpBinding"
bindingConfiguration=""
        name="RouterEndpoint1" contract="System.ServiceModel.
Routing.IRequestReplyRouter" />
    </service>
    </services>
    <behaviors>
    <serviceBehaviors>
        <behavior name="RoutingBehavior">
        <routing routeOnHeadersOnly="false"
filterTableName="filterTable1" />
        <serviceDebug includeExceptionDetailInFaults="true"/>
        <serviceMetadata httpGetEnabled="true" />
        </behavior>
    </serviceBehaviors>
    </behaviors>
```

9. Build the application and create a new IIS application named `Chapter8. OrderManagement.RoutingService`, which runs in the .NET 4.0 application pool.

10. We can browse directly to the service address to see if our service is online: `http://localhost/Chapter8.OrderManagement.RoutingService/ OrderRouter.svc`.

11. If you browse the WSDL of this service, you will notice that it has a generic request-reply message exchange pattern. Clients of this service should point to a well-defined WSDL that outlines the specific service and data contracts.

12. To test this service, create a new console application and add a service reference to either of our previously built workflow services. Add the following code to the `Main` operation:

```
static void Main(string[] args)
{
    Console.WriteLine("Starting Up Service Client ...");
    Console.WriteLine("Enter a product to order");
    string prodId = Console.ReadLine();

    OrderSvcRef.ServiceContractClient c = new
                        OrderSvcRef.ServiceContractClient
                        ("wsHttpBinding_
                                    ServiceContract");

    OrderSvcRef.NewOrderRequest request = new
                                OrderSvcRef.
NewOrderRequest();
        request.ContractId = "001";
        request.CustomerId = "333";
        request.DateOrdered = DateTime.Now;
        request.ProductId = prodId;
        request.Quantity = 10;
        request.Status = "Submitted";
    OrderSvcRef.OrderAckResponse response = c.SubmitOrder(request);
    Console.WriteLine("Response is " + response.OrderId);
    Console.ReadLine();
}
```

13. Open the `app.config` file for the project and find the endpoint added by the service reference. Remove the URL to the specific workflow service and replace it with the generic router address. `http://localhost/Chapter8.OrderManagement.RoutingService/OrderRouter.svc`.

14. Build and run the console application and if you enter a product ID below 100, you should see a record added to the `SystemA` database table, and conversely, if you enter a product ID greater than 100, you should find a new record in the `SystemB` database table.

Summary

In this chapter, we saw how to route messages to specific backend systems. If this fictitious organization already had an in-house BizTalk Server and a staff of highly trained developers, then we would have chosen to go down a different path. Moreover, the .NET 4.0 Routing Service offers a compelling way to hide downstream endpoints and apply simple content-distribution filters.

9

Publish-Subscribe

In this chapter, we will look at how to broadcast information to a variety of parties using the Microsoft technology best suited for this task.

Use case

LarHans Pharmaceuticals is a multinational health sciences company with a special focus on the human immune system. Because of the nature of their work, the company is subject to regulations set by governmental agencies around the world (for example, the Food and Drug Administration in the United States, or the National Institute for Health and Clinical Excellence in Great Britain). As a result, LarHans Pharmaceuticals has strict guidelines to which it adheres regarding product safety and alerting the public to changes in a product's safety profile.

When there is a product recall or change to the product's label, the LarHans team must send immediate communication to at least the following three distinct locations:

1. **Federal agencies**: A notice of product recall or label change must be distributed to governmental bodies within a very short period of time. This interval may differ by country, but companies face harsh fines if they delay communication of this information.

2. **Internal sales teams**: The LarHans sales force must be notified in a timely fashion to make sure they provide physicians with the latest and most accurate information regarding product safety.

3. **Public website news feed**: LarHans conveys product changes to the consumer population through their public-facing website.

Today, when such an event occurs, the LarHans organization fills out a series of paper forms for faxing to each governmental body, crafts and sends out e-mail messages to various sales organizations, and creates a work order with the website ownership team. This process has proved to be arduous and LarHans has nearly missed several filing deadlines because of the frantic coordination of resources and document preparation.

Moving forward, LarHans Pharmaceuticals wants to establish an automated process which allows a single label change or product recall event to trigger notification to all interested parties. Each of the three communication targets outlined before has some sort of technology interfaces which can be leveraged by this solution. Each governmental body has either a secure web service interface or FTP drop-spot which can receive these safety notifications. The directors of the company sales teams are willing to create e-mail templates that get populated by an automated solution instead of hand-crafting these customized notices. Finally, the team that runs the public website is willing to open a channel to the news feed database so that entries can be added without requiring website administrator interaction.

Because of the sensitivity and impact of this solution, the LarHans team has placed high importance on quality of service and guaranteed delivery. They want to make sure that they do not lose or skip notices to government agencies, or open themselves up to fines or penalties for failure to notify the public.

LarHans Pharmaceuticals is primarily a Microsoft shop with existing investments in SQL Server, SharePoint Server, BizTalk Server, and .NET development. While LarHans has entered early-adopter programs for some Microsoft applications, they typically wait until a service pack is released prior to deploying new software into the environment.

Key requirements

The following are key requirements for a new software solution:

- Automated distribution of the same message to multiple interested parties.
- Guaranteed delivery of messages or at minimum, notice of failed delivery.
- Flexibility to support future data recipients without reengineering the process.

Additional facts

There are some additional details gathered after the initial use case was shared with the technical team. These include the following facts:

1. This is a low volume solution that puts a higher priority on reliable delivery than raw throughput or load.

2. The solution must initially address the three known types of notification targets (government agencies, sales team, and public website), but there may be future internal and external parties interested in acting upon product recall or label change events.

3. There are multiple sales teams and not all teams receive e-mails for all events. Product recalls or label changes may be specific to a particular country (or set of countries), so we need the flexibility to notify only the teams that are directly impacted.

4. Similarly, not all governmental agencies need all notifications. Based on the scale of the recall or label change (and at whose request that change was made), only some agencies require notification.

5. While there is an industry-standard data format for these notifications, not all countries currently accept data in this format. This means that a transformation strategy is needed.

6. If a transmission to a governmental agency fails, the LarHans team must proactively be notified so that they can perform manual publication within the legally required time window.

Pattern description

Unlike the content-based routing scenario which targets a single destination system, this scenario calls for the broadcast of an event to a variable number of interested consumers. Similar to the content-based routing pattern where the publisher of a request does not know who is consuming the information, the publish/subscribe pattern relies on decoupling the sender from the receiver(s). In a publish/subscribe scenario, a set of subscribers asynchronously receive a message in parallel to each other and independently act upon it. This pattern is very successful if you need a very loosely coupled, scalable way to funnel data to multiple recipients.

Ideally, a message broker in a publish/subscribe solution can provide a robust quality of service to the subscribers. This typically means that the broker can notify subscribers in parallel (versus sequentially), perform in a store-and-forward fashion so that downstream unavailability does not result in lost messages, and filter out messages that are not of any interest to a particular subscriber.

There are a few things to look out for when building a publish/subscribe solution. First, the ability to tap into the data stream is a blessing and a curse as well. On one hand, this is good as it allows for easy troubleshooting by adding another subscriber who does not impact any other part of the solution. On the negative side, this means that someone (with proper access) could siphon-off very sensitive information. Hence, thorough design and governance is needed to make sure that sensitive data is not freely stored and accessible by curious third parties. Another downside of this pattern is the inability for the publisher of the message to have any real assurance that its message was consumed properly. Loose coupling can be great for scalability and maintainability, but you sacrifice the capacity for publishers to receive accurate acknowledgements. The publish/subscribe broker needs to take ownership of the delivery guarantees that make up a service-level agreement because the publisher has no knowledge about the subscribers and their system availability.

Candidate architectures

There are three ways that we decided to tackle this problem. Each possible solution brings with it some benefits and risks.

Candidate architecture #1–Azure Platform AppFabric Service Bus

Although going with a Windows Azure solution may be a bit aggressive for a more traditional IT shop, there are strategic benefits to seriously considering a publish/subscribe solution hosted in the cloud.

Solution design aspects

While not dealing with an enormous load, the solution does require us to deal with a varied usage profile and bursts of changes. A cloud-based infrastructure is an asset when we have inconsistent load and wish to design a solution that scales up or down based on our needs. Likewise, our clients need to pay only for their data usage (in the Azure Platform AppFabric case, we pay per connection and for the data transfer per GB) instead of setting up hardware sized for the peaks, but idle during the valleys.

One of the unique aspects of the Azure Platform AppFabric candidate proposal is the ability to decentralize the attachment of listeners from the router administrator. The `NetEventRelayBinding`, special to Azure Platform AppFabric, provides a way to do a one-way multicast to multiple applications listening on a single endpoint. Each listener attaches itself to the endpoint by starting up their listener service and providing proper authentication to the Azure Platform AppFabric Service Bus. This technique provides a very loosely-coupled routing infrastructure where data consumers can be rapidly provisioned and decommissioned without the intervention of a central administrator. The downside of this mechanism is that it becomes difficult to do impact analysis and have a central console which manages the data flow.

So how do we achieve reliable delivery and automatic retries in the cloud? The Azure Platform AppFabric Service Bus has the concept of *buffers*, which act as temporary queues with limited lifetime and message storage. However, these buffers are not meant to be a durable store that sits between cloud routers and service listeners. Instead, we need to build reliability into our listener service which fronts the backend systems. This means using a durable queue/repository that can store messages in the event that the target system is unavailable or overloaded.

The Azure Platform AppFabric Service Bus is a light-weight router and thus does not have a rich set of services for data quality or error handling. However, it can leverage the Access Control Service to cleanly and efficiently allow both internal and external parties to authenticate to our service. Exception handling and auditing will need to be managed at the individual service layer.

Solution delivery aspects

Windows Azure solutions are built using a mix of Visual Studio.NET components and Azure administration interfaces. Developers who are comfortable building WCF projects in Visual Studio can easily extend their toolbox to new Azure WCF bindings and configuration options.

Solution operations aspects

A cloud-based solution means that we have fewer physical infrastructure concerns and can establish confidence in the ability of the shared cloud platform to perform predictably under load and properly failover in the event of a node malfunction.

The tooling for Azure administrators is still relatively immature, so solution administrators will have to establish their own best practices and governance for monitoring our active router and performing effective troubleshooting.

Organizational aspects

LarHans Pharmaceuticals prefers to invest in existing products and minimize their exposure to fully custom-built solutions. While components of the Windows Azure AppFabric solution would require custom code, the core routing infrastructure, security, and usage patterns are already well defined and ready-to-use.

The organization can use their existing .NET resources to build AppFabric projects and they can be confident that such a solution can be very rapidly provisioned and deployed. However, there is clearly a risk involved in going with a new offering and LarHans would have to deem the strategic value in moving to the cloud and whether it is worth accepting newfound operational and solution risk.

Solution evaluation

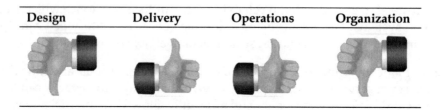

| Design | Delivery | Operations | Organization |

Candidate architecture #2–BizTalk Server

A loosely-coupled service bus like BizTalk Server can offer unique quality-of-service capabilities that closely match the needs of this customer.

Solution design aspects

A BizTalk solution offers us a few key benefits during the design of this solution. First and foremost, we get an enterprise-scale infrastructure built around reliable delivery. When we send a product recall message to the Food and Drug Administration (FDA) in the United States, we can configure our solution to retry the message in the case of failure, and proactively alert an administrator if a defined set of retries is exhausted. The BizTalk architecture assures us that messages get queued in the case of downstream unavailability. If this customer could tolerate a solution where a message may get missed (for example, a stock ticker message where another will be coming along later), then non-durable solutions could be a fit. However, for "can't miss" solutions that demand delivery guarantees, BizTalk is the leading choice.

We have a need to talk to existing web services, databases, and e-mail systems. BizTalk has a series of adapters that make connectivity to these protocols a code-generation and configuration task, instead of a custom coding or scripting task. Each message target may accept a different data format for product recalls and label changes, so here we would want to leverage BizTalk's mapping capability to transform data at the point of delivery.

Extensibility and loose coupling is also important to this solution. We may have new or changed endpoints in the future and want to be able to isolate those changes. BizTalk's publish and subscribe architecture means that a single publisher can stay decoupled from all the independent consumers of a message. There will be zero impact on other subscribers if an existing subscriber needs to be modified (for example, URI address change, alteration to the endpoint's message format) or a completely new subscriber is added. If this solution needs a very fluid, dynamic set of subscribers that change with regularity, then the Azure cloud offering might be a prime choice. However, if you have a static set of endpoints and find central management and impact analysis to be critical, then BizTalk is the right fit.

Finally, we see that our customer has a very time-sensitive transmission schedule so failures need to be captured and handled in a consistent, actionable manner. Our BizTalk solution could actually subscribe on any exceptions thrown by the delivery service and initiate an additional process or simply notify a group or a person where manual delivery of a message may be needed to beat the required deadlines. BizTalk has a number of options for handling exceptions and after a reasonable number of automated attempts (through configurable retry intervals), alternative options (for example, fax) are required.

Solution delivery aspects

The LarHans IT organization has existing skill in working with BizTalk Server, so they have a pool of available developers who can design and implement this solution. These developers currently store their BizTalk artifacts in an open-source Subversion source control repository. While BizTalk Server is not installed on all developer workstations, the organization invests in project-specific virtual machines that are accessed by developers through remote access.

Solution operations aspects

The time-sensitive nature of the data being distributed by this solution means that a robust and rich monitoring environment is needed. Also, we need to have confidence in the infrastructure being able to support this new application on top of all the existing solutions deployed into the BizTalk environment. Our solution has a small load requirement, but the project stakeholders want to make sure that bursts of data from other applications do not block the server from processing our mission-critical messages. BizTalk provides built-in load balancing and we can even segment our solution into its own processing space to help ensure that it maintains a high priority for processing.

BizTalk Server comes with a dashboard for monitoring and interacting with failed messages. This allows us to proactively resume failed transmissions or delete them if the data ends up being submitted manually to its targets.

Organizational aspects

The BizTalk-based proposal can serve as a long term solution that meets the needs of LarHans Pharmaceuticals for years to come. It has built-in extensibility points which allow us to add, change, or remove endpoints without impacting the rest of the solution. This solution leverages the existing organizational investment in BizTalk and the developers who are trained in the tool. It also complies with their preference to configure applications, instead of building them, and gives them the assurance of reliability necessary to transition a critical manual process to an automated one.

Solution evaluation

Design	Delivery	Operations	Organization

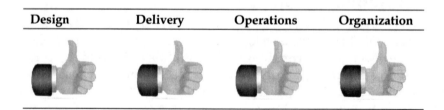

Candidate architecture #3–SQL Service Broker

This scenario requires a shift of perspective for most database professionals as we tend to think of publish-subscribe scenarios as replication issues. Here we are pushing data to diverse routes. These routes are controlled by folks outside of the control of LarHans Pharmaceuticals. It is difficult enough to maintain route definitions when the enterprise controls the start and end points. The loss of end-point control and diversity of potential protocols and message formats will create administrative issues that we will need to account for in any application.

SQL Server Service Broker is, at first glance, a potentially useful technology match nonetheless. We are faced with a situation where specific data must be sent with guaranteed delivery in a specific format, to a specific service. That is a sweet spot for Service Broker.

Solution design aspects

It is rare that one has a "pure-play" solution in any SQL Server-based technology. This pattern is particularly illustrative of that fact. We require to set up the following:

1. User interfaces to allow input of data (for example, input of details around product recalls).

2. Some form of notification to relevant sales staff (for example, SQL Mail to pre-defined relevant teams stored in tables).

3. Service Broker conversations with multiple end points, each of which requires different data, in different formats, and potentially different languages. These would include:
    ° Transmissions to regulatory agencies
    ° External publication to the consumer and medical communities

All of this would require a fairly complex and custom solution and is not something easily achieved in SQL Server tooling.

Solution delivery aspects

One of the key requirements of this application will be to handle CYA (Call Your Attorney) situations. Failure to notify can give rise to expensive regulatory and, at least in the United States, tort liabilities. We need to track precisely when, where, and how each message was sent and when (or whether) it was delivered. Moreover, if the message is not delivered within some pre-determined time frame, it must allow for human intervention. For example, we may want to account for a central FTP server being unavailable to receive messages for some time period. Beyond that time period, we may want someone to call the regulatory agency in question or fall back to alternative methods of delivery.

A second key consideration will be the long term evolution of data that must be sent. We are dealing with multiple regulatory authorities in multiple countries, each of which will have their own required format for the data. Of course, each will want the data in their own national language. As a part of this solution; therefore, we will need a user interface and database schema that will provide the flexibility for doing the following tasks:

1. Capturing the data that is required at present.
2. Sending the data in an appropriate format.
3. Allowing edits to that format; hopefully, with minimal IT involvement.
4. Storing that data in a way that allows someone to reconstruct what was sent, the format used, and when it was sent.

Using SSSB presents advantages for these requirements. First, both physical and logical access to this data is always under the control of the enterprise. It is also very easy to relate the data that we leverage in this application with data stored in other enterprise databases. For example, recall data can be linked to quality control, order fulfillment, and manufacturing systems to make it easier to obtain a complete view of the recall process or to respond to any request for further information sent in by regulatory agencies. We can even place this ability into the hands of power users using PowerPivot technologies available in Office 2010.

The LarHans team has extensive SQL Server development experience and could build this solution, but they are relatively new with SQL Server Broker and typically do not construct SQL solutions that communicate with non-database endpoints.

Solution operations aspects

For this application, IT can never be a bottleneck for getting data out the door. It is not only regulatory and liability issues dictating this requirement, sufficient though they may be. Real harm, even death can come to real people from ingesting potentially defective medications. As architects, we should be very well aware of the real world consequences our designs may impose on people.

Once in operation, this application must allow business users to get appropriate data, at the appropriate place, in correct format, and in a timely manner. Formats, data, and potentially even the definition of "timely" can change rapidly over time and according to a given situation. The application must be flexible enough to handle such requirements and allow for easy updates to formats, business rules, and the data stored in the application to meet these requirements. So in addition to the creation of an SSSB application, we would also need to provide user frontends to handle these requirements or an IT staff person whose primary role would be to create and send these messages via SSSB.

Organizational aspects

As noted earlier, LarHans Pharmaceuticals prefers to invest in existing products and minimize their exposure to completely custom-built solutions. An SSSB solution will require significant investment in custom code or a DBA dedicated primarily to operating this system.

Solution evaluation

Design	Delivery	Operations	Organization

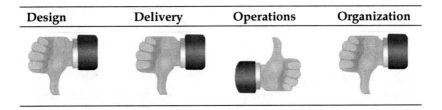

Architecture selection

Let us look at how these candidate architecture technologies stack up when evaluating the risks and benefits of each.

Azure Platform AppFabric Service Bus

Benefits	Risks
• Rapid provisioning of endpoint listeners	• No durable component to store failed messages
• No new hardware needed to host message routing function	• No centralized management of data subscribers
• Internet-based host allows for secure access for internal and external endpoints	• Requires endpoints to be able to integrate with Service Bus

BizTalk Server

Benefits	Risks
• Reliable messaging engine that can ensure delivery of critical data	• BizTalk Server does have an out-of-the-box business dashboard for monitoring and resubmitting failed messages
• Diverse set of adapters that can natively communicate with all the protocols our client demands	
• Loosely-coupled infrastructure that allows us to add/remove/change endpoints in a non-disruptive fashion	• Requires additional modules or code

SQL Server

Benefits	Risks
• Reliable delivery of data between database systems	• Requires significant coding effort to communicate with diverse endpoints
• In-house staff to develop and maintain the solution	• Solution would have to be made up of multiple components weaved together
	• Non-trivial effort to modify or create new endpoints

In evaluating these options against the problem scenario, BizTalk Server is the most appropriate choice. BizTalk provides us a quality-of-service guarantee through persistent storage, automatic retry, and flexible exception handling mechanisms. We also have a static set of endpoints so the powerful, distributed Azure model is not needed here.

Building the solution

For this solution demonstration, we will publish to two of the desired endpoints: the FDA web service endpoint and the LarHans website database endpoint. This gives us a chance to evaluate BizTalk's capabilities to communicate with standard web services as well as database platforms.

One key aspect of our solution architecture is to keep our design as loosely coupled as possible. In our case, that means embracing canonical formats when performing routing operations instead of polluting our message processing rules with endpoint-specific formats. Also, we want our endpoints to be as distinct and separate from each other as possible, so that changes to one endpoint have little to no impact on existing message consumers.

Setup

We start off by creating a new database named `Chapter9` on a SQL Server 2008 instance. After the database is created, execute the database script `Chapter9.sql` in the folder `<Installation Directory>\Chapter9\Begin` and install the tables into your new database. This is the database which holds the public website's company news feed entries.

Now open the `Chapter9.sln` Visual Studio.NET solution located in the `<Installation Directory>\Chapter9\Begin` folder. In this solution, you will find a single WCF service which represents the destination endpoint of the FDA. Build the solution and add this to IIS 7.0 as a new web application named `Chapter9.FDA.SafetySubmissionService`. Testing this service via the WCF Test Client application should yield a result consisting of a tracking number and timestamp.

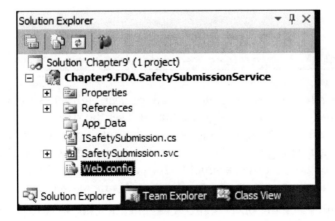

Building the canonical solution artifacts

Now that our foundational database and services are in place, we are ready to develop the canonical solution components which are independent of any particular downstream system.

1. Launch Visual Studio.NET 2010 and open the `Chapter9.sln` in the `<Installation Directory>\Chapter9\Begin` folder. You will find a single WCF service already in place.

2. The first BizTalk project is needed to hold enterprise canonical schemas. Specifically, these are the standard schemas representing a product recall notice, label change, and government agency response. Regardless of the data formats required by various subscribers, our core messaging solution only routes canonical formats.

3. Right-click the solution in Visual Studio.NET and choose **Add | New Project**. Choose the **BizTalk Projects** category and select **Empty BizTalk Server Project**. Name the project `Chapter9.LarHans.SafetySchemas`.

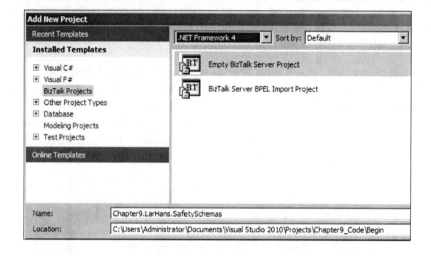

4. Immediately after creating the BizTalk project, right-click the project, select **Properties**, highlight the **Signing** tab, and set the strong name key. If you do not have an existing strong name key to reference, select **New...** from the **Choosing a strong name key** drop down box. In the **Create Strong Name Key** dialog box, set the parameters for your new key. Finally, switch to the **Deployment** tab and set the **Application Name** to `Chapter9`.

5. Now, right-click the BizTalk project again and choose **Add | New Item**. Under the **Schema Files** category, select **Schema** and name it `ProductRecall_XML.xsd`.

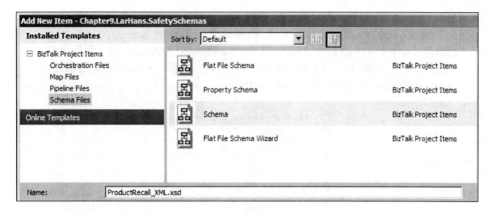

6. Click on the topmost node in the schema named **<Schema>** and look in the Visual Studio.NET **Properties** window for the **Target Namespace** property. Change this value to `http://Chapter9.LarHans.SafetySchemas`. Use this value as the target namespace for all canonical schemas in this project.

7. Define the schema so that it looks like the following screenshot. Note that all elements are of a `string` data type, and the **Lot** and **Incident** nodes are marked with an unbounded maximum occurrence in their Visual Studio properties window. This is because our recall notice may impact multiple lots of the product, and we can have any number of reported incidents associated with a recall.

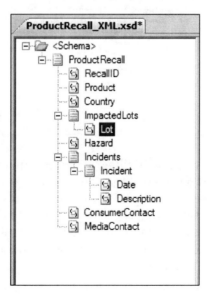

8. Next, right-click the BizTalk project and add another schema named `ProductLabelChange_XML.xsd`. Rename its target namespace to the same value designated in step 6. This schema should look like the following screenshot. Note that all elements are of type `string` and there are no changes to the default node properties.

9. Now we need a schema to hold the acknowledgements that we receive from each government agency. Right-click the BizTalk project and add an XML schema named `AgencySubmissionAcknowledgement_XML.xsd`. Once again, alter its target namespace as per the value we identified earlier. This schema has a simple structure that looks like the following screenshot:

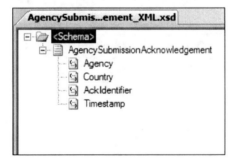

10. We want to have the option to filter our subscriptions for product recalls and label changes based on some of the values in the messages. Specifically, a particular subscriber may only wish to receive notifications for a particular product or for those affecting a specific country. To do content-based routing in BizTalk solutions, we need to promote message nodes via property schemas. Right-click the BizTalk project and add a new **Property Schema** named `SafetyRouting_PropSchema.xsd`.

11. This schema has two nodes for country and product.

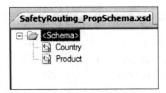

12. We now need to get our product recall and label change schemas to point to this property schema, so that we can perform content-based routing on each message type. Open the `ProductRecall_XML.xsd` schema, right-click the root **<Schema>** node, select **Promotions | Show Promotions**. On the **Property Fields** tab, choose to **Add a Property Schema** to the list by pointing to our previously built property schema. Then create the relationship between the **Country** and **Product** nodes, and their corresponding property schema nodes.

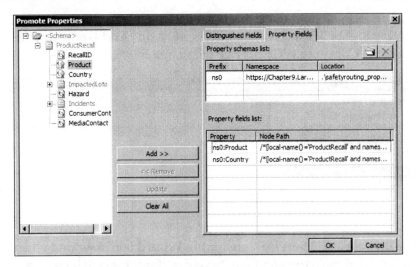

13. Save the schema and then repeat this same process on the `ProductLabelChange_XML.xsd` schema. At this point, you should have a BizTalk project with four complete schemas in it.

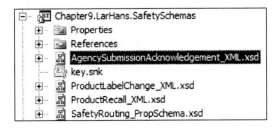

Building the FDA subscriber solution artifacts

With our canonical objects in place, we can now define subscriber-specific artifacts. Each subscriber will have its own BizTalk project to hold any schemas and maps associated with that particular endpoint. Why not bunch them together in a single project? We want a clear separation of concern and allow isolation of change. If one subscriber changes their endpoint schema, why should it impact all the other unchanged endpoints as well? By separating the projects, we establish a very modular solution with a clear extension pattern.

1. In Visual Studio.NET, right-click the solution and choose to add a new project. Select the **Empty BizTalk Project** type and name the project `Chapter9.LarHans.FDA.SafetySubscriber`. Upon project creation, right-click the project, select **Properties**, and set the strong name key and **Application Name** to `Chapter9`.

2. This project will hold the artifacts needed to communicate with the FDA service. Right-click the project and choose **Add | Add Generated Items**. Select the **Consume WCF Service** menu option.

3. The **BizTalk WCF Service Consuming Wizard** launches, and when prompted, choose the **Metadata Exchange Endpoint** as the service source.

4. For the metadata URL, use the URL of the service you installed into IIS during the earlier solution setup (for example, `http://localhost/Chapter9.FDA.SafetySubmissionService/SafetySubmission.svc`).

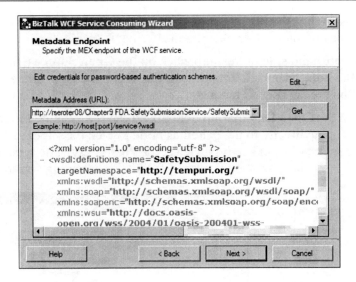

5. Keep the default namespace on the next wizard page and click on the **Import** button.

6. This wizard creates a host of artifacts in our BizTalk project including an orchestration, multiple schemas, and two send port binding files.

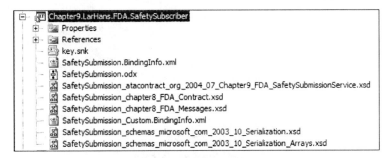

7. Now we need to add three maps to this project:

    ° Canonical product recall format to FDA input format

    ° Canonical label change format to FDA input format

    ° FDA acknowledgement format to canonical government agency response format

8. Right-click the BizTalk project and choose to add a reference. Point to the `SafetySchemas` project so that we can access the canonical schemas defined there.

9. Then right-click the BizTalk project and choose **Add | New Item**. Select the **Map** type and name it `ProductRecall_To_FDASafetyIssue.btm`.

10. On the left-hand side of the map, click on the **Open Source Schema** link and go to the **References** folder and open the `SafetySchemas` project. Find and select the **ProductRecall** message.

11. Click on the **Open Destination Schema** on the right-hand side of the map and navigate directly to the **Schemas** node to pick the `SafetySubmission_chapter8_FDA_Contract` type. Select the **PostSafetyIssue** type from the pop-up box. The map should now look like the following screenshot:

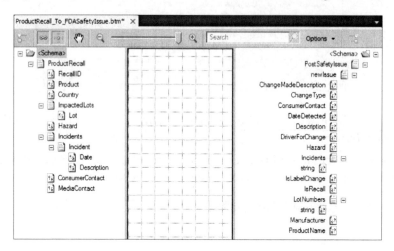

12. Create the mapping as follows:

Source	Destination	Comments
Product	ProductName	
ImpactedLots/Lot	LotNumbers/string	
Hazard	Hazard	
Incidents/Incident/Date	Incidents/string	Use Concatenate functoid to combine source nodes
Incidents/Incident/Description		
ConsumerContact	ConsumerContact	
	isLabelChange = `false`	Hard code Value property
	isProductRecall = `true`	Hard code Value property
	Manufacturer = `LarHans`	Hard code Value property

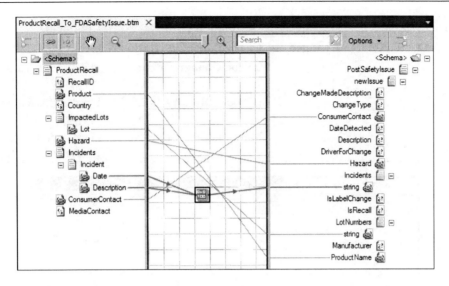

13. It is a good practice to test the map when you complete it, so create an instance file of the source schema (by right-clicking the **ProductRecall** schema in the `SafetySchemas` project and choosing **Generate Instance**) and set it as an input to this map via the **Properties** window. Then right-click the map and select **Test Map**. Your output should show all the relevant source data values in the destination schema.

14. Next, we need the map from the label change to the FDA safety issue. Right-click the BizTalk project and select **Add | New Item**. Select the **Map** type and name the map `LabelChange_To_FDASafetyIssue.btm`.

15. For the source schema, navigate to the **References** node and select the **ProductLabelChange** type in the `SafetySchemas` project.

16. The destination schema should be the same `SafetySubmission_chapter8_ FDA_Contract` type as before. Select the **PostSafetyIssue** type from the pop up box.

17. Create the mapping as follows:

Source	Destination	Comments
Product	**ProductName**	
ContactDetails	**ConsumerContact**	
ChangeDetails/Change Type	**ChangeType**	
ChangeDetails/ReasonForChange	**DriverForChange**	

Source	Destination	Comments
ChangeDetails/ContentChanged	**ChangeMadeDescription**	
	isLabelChange = `true`	Hard coded Value property
	isProductRecall = `false`	Hard coded Value property
	Manufacturer = `LarHans`	Hard coded Value property

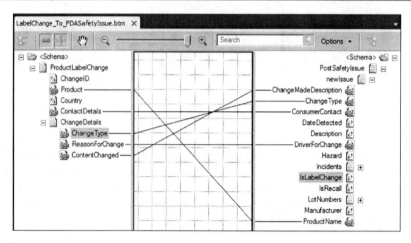

18. Create an instance of the LabelChange message and confirm that the map functions as expected.

19. Our final map for this subscriber is for the acknowledgement message. Add a new item to the BizTalk project, choose the **Map** type, and name it `FDAResponse_To_AgencySubmissionAcknowledgement.btm`.

20. Select the `SafetySubmission_chapter8_FDA_Contract` type for the **Schema Source** and choose the `PostSafetyIssueResponse` from the pop-up window. For the destinations schema, navigate to the **References** node and choose the `AgencySubmissionAcknowledgement` schema.

21. Create the mapping as follows:

Source	Destination	Comments
AckID	**AckIdentifier**	
Timestamp	**Timestamp**	
	Agency = `FDA`	Hard code **Value** property
	Country = `USA`	Hard code **Value** property

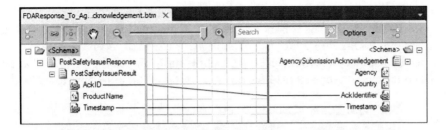

22. Build all the projects currently in the Visual Studio.NET solution.

23. Right-click `Chapter9.LarHans.SafetySchemas` and select **Deploy**. This will load this project's assembly into the GAC and register the relevant artifacts with the BizTalk Server.

24. Once that operation succeeds, right-click and deploy the `Chapter9.LarHans.FDA.SafetySubscriber` project.

25. Open the BizTalk Administration Console and navigate to the `Chapter9` application. You can confirm the deployment by opening a node such as **Maps** to confirm that our recently built maps appear.

Configuring the data publisher and FDA subscriber

Now that we have the schemas and maps necessary for exchanging information with the FDA, we can construct the actual endpoint which transmits data. Before we can build the endpoints that consume the data, we have to set up the publisher which pulls data into the BizTalk Server. To do that, we configure a BizTalk receive port and location that publish the product recall and label change messages into the bus. In this scenario, we are picking up the canonical message via a BizTalk FILE adapter. Note that we could very well use any adapter to send messages into the BizTalk bus.

1. Within the BizTalk Administration Console, navigate to the `Chapter9` application and create a new, one-way receive port named `Chapter9.LarHans.ReceiveProductRecall`.

2. Add a receive location named `Chapter9.LarHans.ReceiveProductRecall.FILE` to our new receive port.

3. Select the FILE adapter and set the **Receive Pipeline** to the **XMLReceive** pipeline. Choose to configure the FILE adapter and set the polling location to `<Installation Directory>\Chapter9\Filedrop\PickupRecall` folder.

4. Create another one-way receive port named `Chapter9.LarHans.`
   `ReceiveProductLabelChange` with a FILE receive location named `Chapter9.`
   `LarHans.ReceiveProductLabelChange.FILE`. That receive location
   should also use the **XMLReceive** pipeline and point to the `<Installation`
   `Directory>\Chapter9\Filedrop\PickupLabelChange` directory.

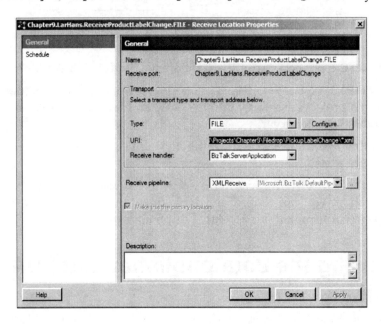

5. Note that there are no maps here as we receive the canonical format and
   do not want to translate to subscriber formats until the latest point
   possible (send ports).

Now that our publisher is built, we can move on and create the FDA subscriber. We
do this by building BizTalk send ports and pointing them to our destination
web service.

1. We could create the FDA send port manually, but when we referenced
   the WCF service in our Visual Studio.NET project, the BizTalk wizard
   auto-generated the binding files for the send port. Right-click the BizTalk
   application in the Administration Console and choose **Import** and
   then **Bindings**.

2. Navigate to the `Chapter9.LarHans.FDA.SafetySubscriber` project and
   choose the `SafetySubmission_Custom.BindingInfo.xml` file.

3. When the import is complete, you can go to the **Send Ports** folder in the
   Administration Console and see our new send port pointing to
   our WCF service.

4. Remember that this single send port accepts data for either recalls or label changes. So, we need to apply both maps here so that regardless of which message comes in, the correct message goes out. Go to the **Outbound Maps** tab and select both the maps that result in a FDASafetyIssue format.

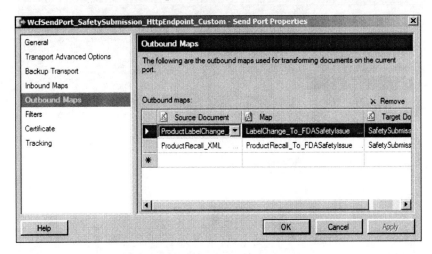

5. Next, we have to add the **Inbound Map** so that the acknowledgement that comes back from the FDA maps to our canonical format. Recall that "inbound" in this context refers to messages coming back into BizTalk from this send port (that is, the response value from the service call).

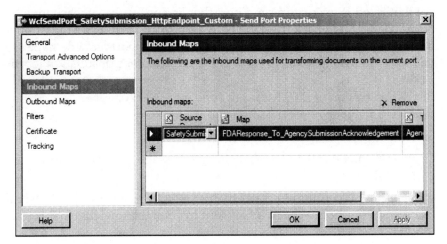

6. Finally, we have to create our subscriptions so that this port picks up the correct messages from the BizTalk MessageBox. Specifically, we want an OR condition where the **BTS.MessageType** is equal to either `http://Chapter9.LarHans.SafetySchemas#ProductRecall` or `http://Chapter9.LarHans.SafetySchemas#ProductLabelChange`. However, as this is a United States agency, we want to make sure to send notices that relate only to US recalls or label changes. So, here we also add a filter based on country as well.

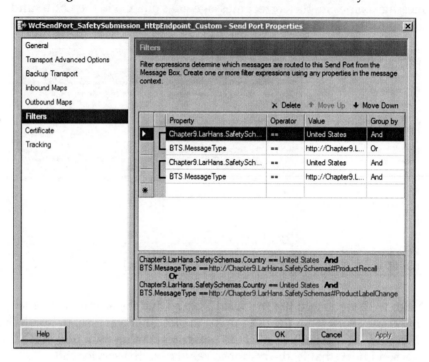

7. All that is left is to create a send port that listens for the synchronous acknowledgement back from the FDA service and publishes the canonical format to disk. Create a new one-way, static send port named `Chapter9.LarHans.SendAgencyAck.FILE`. Set the file adapter's destination location to `<Installation Directory>\Chapter9\Filedrop\DropOffAck\` and use a filter subscription of **BTS.MessageType** = `http://Chapter9.LarHans.SafetySchemas#AgencySubmissionAcknowledgement`.

8. Start both the receive locations and send ports.

9. Drop a product recall and a label change message into their respective pickup folders.

10. If everything is configured correctly, then the FDA service should be called twice and you should see two files sent to your acknowledgements folder.

```
- <ns0:AgencySubmissionAcknowledgement
    xmlns:ns0="http://Chapter9.LarHans.SafetySchemas">
    <Agency>FDA</Agency>
    <Country>USA</Country>
    <AckIdentifier>9bfc6d8f-a6d1-41b8-970b-f44256b343ed</AckIdentifier>
    <Timestamp>2010-01-15T14:02:56.4981344-08:00</Timestamp>
  </ns0:AgencySubmissionAcknowledgement>
```

Building the website database subscriber solution artifacts

With our first subscriber working, we can now build the pieces necessary to share data with our second subscriber—the LarHans website database.

1. Return to Visual Studio.NET and right-click the solution and add a new **Empty BizTalk Project** named `Chapter9.LarHans.WebsiteDb.SafetySubscriber`.

2. Right-click the project and choose **Properties** to set its strong name key and **Application Name** parameters.

3. Right-click the new project and choose **Add | Add Generated Items**. Select the **Consume Adapter Service** menu option.

4. When the **Consume Adapter Service** window opens choose **sqlBinding** from the bindings menu. Note that the next screenshot shows only a portion of the large wizard window that pops up.

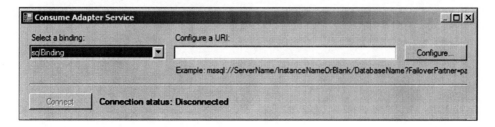

5. Click the **Configure** button next to the **Configure a URI** text box.

6. Select **Windows** as the **Client Credential** type on the **Security** tab.

7. On the **URI Properties** tab, set the **Initial Catalog** to Chapter9 and the **Server** to " . ".

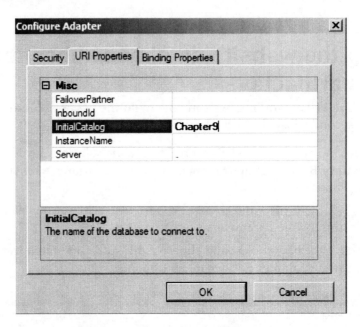

8. Click **OK** to exit the URI configuration window and click on the **Connect** button on the **Consume Adapter Service** wizard page to establish a connection to our database.

9. We are adding records to a table, so after choosing **RecallNews** under the **Tables** node, select the Insert operation and add it to the list of operations to generate.

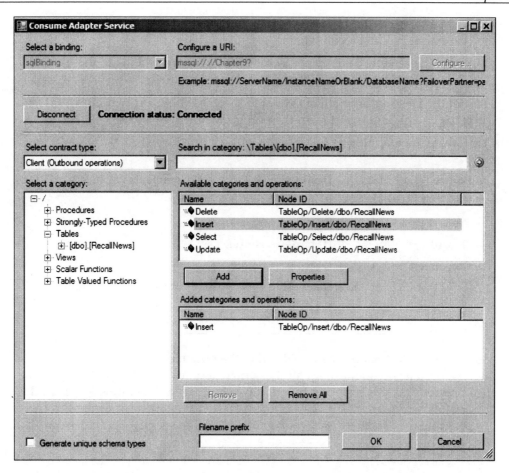

10. After clicking on **OK**, the wizard generates the artifacts necessary for BizTalk to communicate with this database table. The BizTalk project in Visual Studio.NET should now have schemas and a send port binding file.

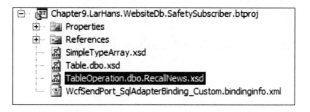

11. A single map is needed from the canonical product recall schema to the database specific format. Right-click the BizTalk project and select **Add | New Item**. Choose the **Map** type and name the map `ProductRecall_To_InsertRecallNews.btm`.

12. Add a reference to the `SafetySchemas` project so that we can point to our canonical product recall schema.

13. Once the reference is in place, set the map's source schema to the **ProductRecall** type found in the **References** node.

14. Set the **Destination Schema** equal to the `TableOperation.dbo.RecallNews` type and choose **Insert** from the pop up window.

15. Create the mapping as follows:

Source	Destination	Comments
RecallID	**ItemID**	
Product	**Product**	
Hazard	**HazardDescription**	
ConsumerContact	**ConsumerContact**	
	DatePosted	Date and time functoid
	Lots	Scripting functoid leveraging Inline XSLT

16. The **Lots** destination field holds all of the possible lots listed in the recall, so we need a way to mash up all the source node values. As mentioned in the previous table, a scripting functoid was leveraged. The Inline XSLT used is as follows:

```
<Lots
xmlns="http://schemas.microsoft.com/Sql/2008/05/Types/Tables/dbo">
    <xsl:for-each select=" /*[local-name()='ProductRecall' and
        namespace-uri()='http://Chapter9.LarHans.SafetySchemas']
        /*[local-name()='ImpactedLots' and namespace-uri()='']
        /*[local-name()='Lot' and namespace-uri()=''] ">
      [<xsl:value-of select="." />]
    </xsl:for-each>
</Lots>
```

17. The completed map looks like the following screenshot:

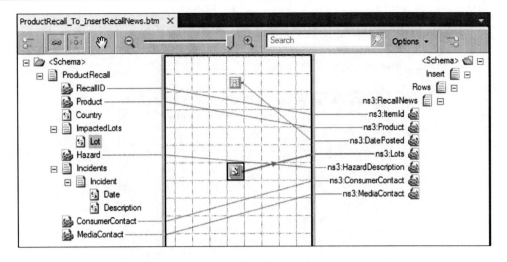

18. This BizTalk project can now be deployed to the BizTalk Server by right-clicking the project and choosing **Deploy**.

19. Confirm that the deployment was successful by locating our new assembly and components in the `Chapter9` application found in the BizTalk Administration Console.

Configuring the website database subscriber

Our final activity is to configure the necessary messaging components to distribute product recall messages to the LarHans website database. Because of the way we have architected our solution, we can achieve this simply by adding a single new send port to the application. There is no need to change anything about our publisher, and there is no impact on our existing FDA service subscriber.

1. While the Consume Adapter Service did produce a binding file (much like when we consumed a WCF service), we do not want to use it. The binding file generated was for a two-way send port, but we are not interested in the result of the database insert operation. So, create a new, one-way static send port named `Chapter9.LarHans.WebsiteDb.SendRecall.Sql`.

2. Choose the `WCF-Custom` adapter type and click **Configure**.

3. Switch immediately to the **Binding** tab and choose the **sqlBinding**.

4. Move back to the **General** tab and enter an address value of `mssql://.//Chapter9?`

5. For the SOAP Action header, use the following XML configuration:

```
<BtsActionMapping xmlns:xsi="http://www.w3.org/2001/
    XMLSchema-instance"
```

```
    xmlns:xsd="http://www.w3.org/2001/XMLSchema">
<Operation Name="Insert" Action=
                            "TableOp/Insert/dbo/RecallNews" />
</BtsActionMapping>
```

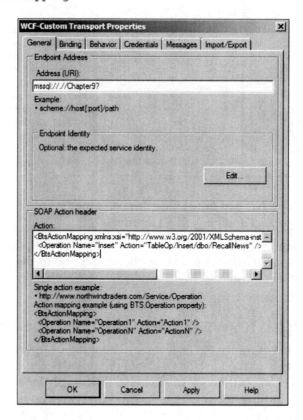

6. Click on **OK** to save the adapter configuration settings.

7. Next, we need to set the single outbound map that takes the canonical product recall format and transforms it into the data structure expected by the database adapter. View the send port's **Outbound Maps** tab and set the map to ProductRecall_To_InsertRecallNews.

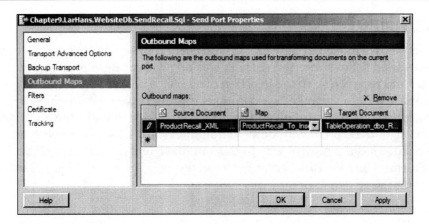

8. Now go to the **Filters** tab so that we can set the subscription for this send port. The filter should look for any **BTS.MessageType** equal to `http://Chapter9.LarHans.SafetySchemas#ProductRecall`.

9. After saving and starting the send port, drop a new product recall message into BizTalk and you should observe both an acknowledgement file on disk (from the FDA subscriber) and a database record (from the website database subscriber).

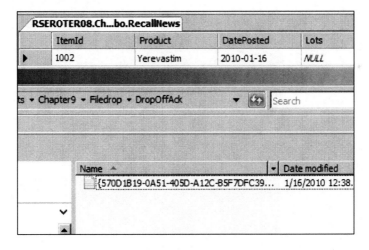

10. If you publish a product recall message that targets a country besides the United States, than you'll find that the FDA subscriber does not pick it up, but the website database subscriber does. This is because our FDA subscriber is only interested in recalls targeted at the United States while the website subscriber is grabbing any recall message that it encounters.

Summary

In this chapter, we looked at a customer who needed the ability to send a single event to a varied list of subscribers. There was no need for tight coupling of the sender and receiver(s), so the injection of a service broker in the middle was a sensible way to leverage asynchronous routing between endpoints. By clearly isolating our subscription endpoints we were able to make the addition, modification, or deletion of endpoints a straightforward task. The publish and subscribe pattern is a powerful way to transmit data, and the use of canonical message formats and BizTalk Server gave us enterprise-grade quality-of-service attributes that were demanded by this scenario.

10
Repair/Resubmit with Human Workflow

Workflows can take many forms, such as sequential, a flow chart, and state machine to name a few. Most workflows model system interactions that operate without direct human intervention. At times, however, direct human interaction is needed inside a workflow to correct errors or make judgment-based decisions.

Use case

Bowl For Buddies is a non-profit organization that sets up bowling parties to raise money for charity. As part of this effort, people raise money by going house-to-house and asking for donations. The donations are based on the number of pins the participants knock down during the bowling party (for example, $0.05 for each pin knocked down). During the house visit, donors give an e-mail address to which a donation request can be sent after the bowling event is over. In this e-mail, the donors receive the amount they need to pay and a link to the secure payment processor. Once payment is made, Bowl For Buddies is notified.

Currently, much of this process is done manually. Data is collected on paper forms and entered into an Excel spreadsheet. Once the bowling event is over, a volunteer calculates the amount owed by each person and sends them an e-mail requesting payment. If no response is received from the donor, it may be weeks before it is identified through the Excel sheet. Sometimes, delays arise due to an invalid e-mail and as a result, the donor needs to be contacted over the phone. Finding the total amount still to be collected and from whom is also difficult, as many different Excel sheets are used for tracking donor data for various events. The existing Excel solution is being replaced by an internal SharePoint 2010 implementation.

Bowl For Buddies currently has a co-located website running on an ISP-supported Windows instance. Eventually, they want to be able to collect donations on the website. This will be a separate system similar to the way payments are currently collected and tracked. Donations through the website should follow the same process as donations though the house-to-house method, in terms of collection.

The end-to-end payment collection process needs an overhaul. Bowl For Buddies is looking at developing e-mail and payment services to add automation to the collection process. As part of this process, they would like to develop a defined set of guidelines for the payment collection process with a goal of automating whatever is possible. The solution will need to work with the new SharePoint 2010 site and should allow easy modification later to work with the website.

Bowl For Buddies does not have a large IT department or IT budget. The website they currently have is ASPX-based and the e-mail and payment services they are building will be done through WCF services. They are willing to make investments in areas that aid in the donation collection process and that could be expanded to other branches if the company expands.

Key requirements

The following are key requirements for a new software solution:

- Automate the process for processing donation pledges.
- Include proactive notifications to staff for delinquent payments or data errors.
- Work with an organization's future strategy around SharePoint and .NET solutions.

Additional facts

We've identified some additional solution aspects that may help us decide upon the right solution:

1. SharePoint 2010 is used to maintain lists of customers including their e-mail addresses and donation amounts.
2. When an e-mail is invalid, returned, or a donor does not pay within a set amount of time, a person will call to verify the intent of the donor.
3. When the website is able to accept donations, it will use SQL Server to store user information.
4. A general process for donation collection will include sending the user an e-mail, evaluating the results of sending the e-mail, waiting for payment, notification by a human if data needs to be corrected, updating the data for resubmission, and updating the system once payment is received.

Pattern description

Workflows, by definition, are a series of steps that are related to each other. These steps may require interaction with outside resources. Typically, these resources are other systems and the interaction can complete in an automated fashion without any human intervention. In some cases, the workflows require human intervention to fix and correct data, or the workflows are totally related to human processes like a document approval process. When a workflow is related to human activity, it is known as a **Human Workflow**.

Human workflows can interact with people in several ways. Some of these include SharePoint, e-mail, text messaging, instant messenger, and web forms. What makes human workflows different from non-human workflows is the variability introduced by the human factor. People can be slow to respond, out of town, unwell, or have other factors that prevent them from interacting with the workflow as expected. This adds a degree of uncertainty to all human workflows and ensures that they are typically long-running.

Using automated workflows to model a business process allows for that process to be applied in the exact same way, time and again. This is something difficult in a manual, people-driven progression of data collection and processing. In addition to repeatability, using a central environment for processing these workflows provides a way to monitor many types of workflows. This allows you to analyze the collective results of all the workflows and increase efficiency by removing bottlenecks or streamlining unnecessary steps.

Modeling the Bowl For Buddies payment process in a workflow will help them apply the same business activity over and over in the same manner. This workflow can be exposed as a service to allow many different outside entities to interact with it. The service layer hosting the e-mail and notification service will provide the abstraction from specific destination systems.

The logical architecture of the solution is as follows:

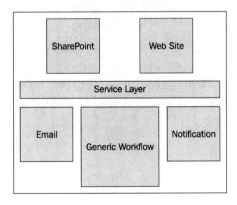

Candidate architectures

We will look at two candidate architectures which can be used to solve the problems faced by Bowl For Buddies.

Candidate architecture #1–BizTalk Server

BizTalk is Microsoft's enterprise integration tool, which could be used to help Bowl For Buddies coordinate the payment collection process. The previous releases of BizTalk Server had basic built-in human workflow support. This was not widely adopted nor used in the marketplace and hence is no longer part of the latest version of the product.

Even without the specific human workflow components, BizTalk does have a robust orchestration engine that can be easily used to model a business process like the payment collection process. BizTalk has built-in adapters for SharePoint and SQL, making it an ideal candidate for consideration.

The following is a detailed review of BizTalk's role in this scenario.

Solution design aspects

A BizTalk Orchestration can model the payment collection process. BizTalk can expose this orchestration to outside consumers through a WCF service adapter, SQL Server adapter, or SharePoint adapter. Any or all of these adapters can be used to activate a new instance of the payment collection process.

Once started, the orchestration makes external calls to the e-mail service to send the e-mail to the donor. If an invalid response is received, the notification service will be used to update SharePoint and wait for corrected data to be sent back to the long-running orchestration. If the response from the e-mail transmission is successful, the orchestration will wait for the response for payment service and update SharePoint with the results. If the payment result is not received, the process will wait for updated information from SharePoint and try again.

The SharePoint adapter will be used to read and write information to SharePoint. When the SQL Server-based solution is added later, the SQL Server Adapter can easily be added. BizTalk's extensive routing ability will be used as needed, to route messages between SQL Server, SharePoint, and external services.

Solution delivery aspects

Bowl For Buddies does not have a large IT staff. Using a full-blown enterprise integration tool like BizTalk Server might be a large undertaking for a small IT organization. In addition, learning to develop BizTalk-based solutions requires additional training and effort. This is probably something Bowl For Buddies cannot undertake given the small staff.

Solution operation aspects

Bowl For Buddies does not have BizTalk running nor do they have servers for BizTalk to run on. In addition to BizTalk, they would require SQL Server. Both of these carry heavy licensing costs and require extensive operation monitoring in order to have a successful implementation. Also, monitoring BizTalk requires training on how to handle suspended messages and how to reprocess them. This is something likely to be outside the scope of what the existing IT staff can handle.

Organizational aspects

Bowl For Buddies is not a large organization. Using an enterprise server tool like BizTalk would not be a good fit for them. Even though they have expansion plans that could add additional offices, the need for BizTalk in areas other than payment collection is unknown.

Solution evaluation

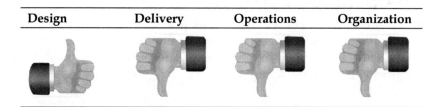

| Design | Delivery | Operations | Organization |

Candidate architecture #2–Windows Server AppFabric

A Windows Server AppFabric-based solution would leverage .NET 4.0 technologies to support this use case. We would use a .NET 4.0 Workflow service to expose endpoints to a SharePoint Workflow. SharePoint 2010 does not support the latest 4.0 version of Windows Workflow, but rather, supports the .NET 3.5 version. In order to meet the scenario and provide reuse outside a pure SharePoint-hosted process workflow, putting core logic inside a service-exposed .NET 4.0 Workflow allows for reuse by other systems.

Solution design aspects

SharePoint has a built-in workflow engine. This uses .NET 3.5 Workflow technologies to provide out-of-the-box workflow templates for common scenarios and to support extensive customization. This could provide a complete solution if the solution would be totally contained in SharePoint. Given the addition of a future web-based solution, moving the core workflow logic out of SharePoint is a better answer.

Moving the business process out of SharePoint allows for the use of .NET 4.0 and Windows Server AppFabric to host the solution. This provides a single point of tracking and monitoring with the new features of .NET 4.0 Workflow.

Our solution would use a simple SharePoint Workflow to call into a .NET 4.0 Workflow service. The .NET 4.0 Workflow would be a workflow service—a workflow exposed as a WCF service. This workflow would have the payment collection process modeled to include sending an e-mail, waiting for a payment response, and sending notifications. Custom service calls would be needed for interaction with external systems for email, payment processing, and notifications.

Solution delivery aspects

Bowl For Buddies does not have a tight timeline. The adoption of workflow technology and workflow services through WCF will speed the delivery process, reducing the amount of testing needed versus a custom-coded solution.

Solution operation aspects

Using .NET 4.0 and Windows Server AppFabric provides a lot of features out-of-the-box including logging, monitoring, and troubleshooting support. This is done through a plugin into IIS—something that many IT resources know well. As Bowl For Buddies already has an ASPX-based website, its IT staff is already accustomed to this interface.

Organizational aspects

Adoption of .NET 4.0 and Windows Server AppFabric would not require significant investment in software licenses as these technologies are all included with the price of Microsoft Windows. The existing intranet-based server running the SharePoint site could be used for this solution. Adoption of this technology is a low risk endeavor, given the fact that it is built into Windows framework.

Solution evaluation

Design	Delivery	Operations	Organization

Architecture selection

Let's look at how these candidate architecture technologies stack up against each other. We can break down the primary benefits and risks of each choice as follows:

BizTalk Server

Benefits	Risks
• Out-of-box adapters for SQL Server and SharePoint • Robust enterprise-class hosting infrastructure for processes exposed as WCF Services • Built-in admin tool with extensive monitoring information	• Additional licensing costs • Large learning curve for development, monitoring, and operations • Large infrastructure requirements

Windows Server AppFabric

Benefits	Risks
• Robust hosting environment • Easy configuration-based tracking and monitoring options including detailed message bodies • Low cost of ownership • Leverage existing hardware	• New technology could face some breaking-in issues • Learning curve for development, monitoring, and operations

---

A key benefit of using .NET 4.0 and Windows Server AppFabric is its light-weight solution without extensive additional software expenditures. This release of the .NET Framework has significant changes compared to past .NET releases and it supports Windows Server AppFabric as a rich hosting environment. While this new technology introduces a level of risk into the solution, this is acceptable, given the overall benefits gained from this technology. While BizTalk can do exactly what is needed for this scenario, it would be an overkill. Given the small size of Bowl For Buddies and the lack of need for BizTalk in other areas of the company, it is not a right fit in this case.

For this scenario, Windows Server AppFabric is the best choice.

Building the solution

This solution has two key areas—Windows Server AppFabric solution and SharePoint solution. An ideal layout of the physical architecture is shown in the following image:

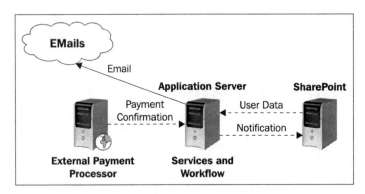

While it would be possible to run all the applications on a single server, separation of the application server running Windows Server AppFabric and SharePoint components is ideal.

SharePoint 2010 runs with .NET 3.5 Workflow and Windows Server AppFabric uses .NET 4.0. While these can co-exist on the same server, the solution is cleaner when separated.

Setup

This sample is broken down into two sections. The first section walks through the creation and testing of a .NET 4.0 Workflow solution to process payments. The second section creates a SharePoint customer list. SharePoint is not needed for the first section and a testing tool is provided to test the workflow. To run the solution end-to-end, SharePoint 2010 needs to be installed.

This solution has several parts. The key areas are as follows:

1. Various existing services for sending e-mail, processing credit card payments, and updating the SharePoint list.
2. Windows Server AppFabric hosted workflow—called from the SharePoint Workflow or test application—to manage the flow of payment processing and data correction.
3. SharePoint site for hosting the Bowl For Buddies list of customers.

4. SharePoint workflow triggered from additions and changes to the customer list.

Some initial setup is required. These steps assume that SharePoint 2010, InfoPath 2010, and Windows Server AppFabric are all installed on the same server. Even if you are just running the workflow section, you are required to complete the following steps because the solution is built around the website names used in them.

Prepare your environment by following these steps:

1. When installed, SharePoint 2010 takes over both port 80 and the default website as an ASP.NET 2.0-based site. Create a new website inside IIS running on port 1234. This will host the external services and core workflow. Ensure the default application pool is running .NET 4.0—this is likely to default to .NET 2.0 so it must be changed. Name the website `HumanWorkflow` and point it to the `C:\HumanWorkflow` folder.

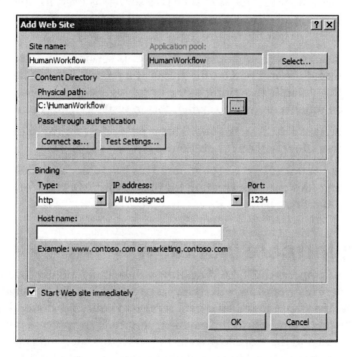

2. Launch Visual Studio .NET 2010 and open the `Chapter10.HumanWorkflow.sln` in the `<Installation Directory>\Chapter10\Begin` folder. When prompted to create the virtual directories click on **OK**.

3. Once the virtual directories are created, the `HumanWorkflow.Notification` service must run in an application pool with access to the SharePoint site. For this demo, create an application pool running .NET 4.0, as an administrator, and name it as `WF4-SPAccess`. Change the application pool for this service to use the one we have just created.

4. Depending on the operating system, you may need to create event log sources used by this code. Add the following sources inside the server's application log: `ProcessPayments`, `EmailService`, and `NotificationService`.

5. The following projects are included in the `Begin` solution:

   ○ `HumanWorkflow.CoreWorkflow`: This is the main project that will contain the process payments workflow called by external systems.

   ○ `HumanWorkflow.EmailSvc`: This service is used to simulate sending an e-mail. Pass in an e-mail address that starts with an "F" to test the failure logic.

   ○ `HumanWorkflow.Notification`: This service is used to update SharePoint on the status of a record. For this demo, this defaults to writing to the event log. See the service comments on how to switch this to write to SharePoint.

   ○ `HumanWorkflow.Tester`: This is a Windows form to test the workflow without SharePoint.

   ○ `HumanWorkflow.HelperDocs`: This is a folder with helper text files used for creating the SharePoint workflow and SharePoint list.

Building the core workflow

First, the Process Payments .NET 4.0 Workflow will be built and deployed to Windows Server AppFabric. This workflow will receive a payment request message that starts the process. The first step is to call an e-mail service to notify the donor. If the response is successful, the process moves to the payment service. If the process returns an error, a notification is sent and the workflow waits to receive updated information. Once updated information is received (note that only e-mail address updation is shown in the demo), the e-mail is sent again. Once moved into the **Receive Payment Notice** flow, the workflow waits to receive payment information. This must be done using the supplied testing application and the user ID must match with that of the submitted record. Once payment is received, a success notification is made. If payment errors, the process sends a notice and waits for updated user information.

In this section, the following tasks will be accomplished:

- Adding a new .NET 4.0 Workflow service to an existing project
- Building request-response contracts for SharePoint integration
- Building a flowchart workflow logic for the process payment procedure
- Calling several external services and evaluating the response
- Setting up content correlation for payment and updated data to be sent back into the same running workflow instance
- Deploying the solution to Windows Server AppFabric

This solution starts with a workflow service project already created and includes existing service references for e-mail (called **Send Email**) and notification (called **Send Notification**) external services. The project has been set up to run on port 1234 at the following address: `http://localhost:1234/HumanWorkflow.CoreWorkflow/ProcessPayment`. This solution also includes a helper custom activity for writing information to the event log. This will be used for some basic process-flow tracking. The tracking features of Windows Server AppFabric could be used for this, but for simplicity, the event log will work for this demo.

1. Launch Visual Studio.NET 2010 and open `Chapter10.HumanWorkflow.sln` in the `<Installation Directory>\HumanWorkflow\Begin` folder.

2. A project called `HumanWorkflow.CoreWorkflow` already exists.

3. Right-click on **Project** and select **Properties**. Select the **Web** tab. Ensure the **Use Local IIS Web Server** radio button is selected. Click on **Create Virtual Directory** to ensure the directory exists in IIS.

4. Rick-click on the project and select **Add New Item**. Select the workflow templates under **Visual C#** and add a new **WCF Workflow Service** called `ProcessPayment.xamlx`.

5. Click on the top-level **Sequential Service** and click on the **Variables** tab at the bottom left. Delete the `data` variable (this is created by default and not used).

6. Add the following variables to the workflow:

   ○ Name: `ListHandle`, type: `CorrelationHandle` (this is the correlation variable used to receive payment confirmation and updated user data if needed, located under `System.ServiceModel.Activities`)

   ○ Name: `listID`, type: `Int32`

   ○ Name: `listName`, type: `String`

- ○ Name: `listEmail`, type: `String`
- ○ Name: `listBowlingScore`, type: `Double`
- ○ Name: `listDonationAmount`, type: `Double`
- ○ Name: `listTotalDonation`, type: `Double`

7. Click on the **ReceiveRequest** activity. Under **Content**, click on **Viewparameter**.

8. Select the **Parameters** radio button and enter the following parameters:

- ○ Name: `ID`, type: `Int32`, assign to: `listID`
- ○ Name: `Name`, type: `String`, assign to: `listName`
- ○ Name: `BowlingScore`, type: `Double`, assign to: `listBowlingScore`
- ○ Name: `DonationAmount`, type: `Double`, assign to: `listDonationAmount`
- ○ Name: `EmailAddress`, type: `String`, assign to: `listEmail`

9. With **ReceiveRequest** selected, click on the **CorrelationInitializes** property (if the properties window is not visible press *F4*). Select **Add initialize**. Add the **ListHandle**. Select **Query correlation initializer** from the drop down list. In the **XPath Queries** dropdown list, select **ID: Int32**. Click on **OK**. This will set up a correlation value that can be used by other receive activities to get information back into this same workflow instance.

10. With **ReceiveRequest** selected, ensure the **Can Create Instances** checkbox is checked. This is located under the properties of the activity. Press *F4* if they are not visible.

11. Click on the **SendResponse** activity. Under **Content**, click on **Define**. Select the **Parameters** radio button and enter the following parameters:

- ○ Name: `Result`, type: `Boolean`, value: `True`

12. With **SendResponse** selected, ensure the **PersistBeforeSend** checkbox is checked. This is located under **Properties**.

13. Drag the custom activity called **EventLogHelper**, located under `HumanWorkflow.CoreWorkflow`. Place it between the **ReceiveRequest** and **SendResponse** activities. Set the **TextEventLog** property to `Received GETDATA Message`. If this activity is not available, build the solution and it should be seen in the toolbox.

14. Drag an **Assign** shape from the **Primitives** section of the toolbox and place it under the **EventLogHelper** activity. Set the **To** value to listTotalDonation. Set the **Value** to listDonationAmount * listBowlingScore. IntelliSense should recognize these values.

15. Drag a flowchart shape from the **Flowchart** section of the toolbox. Place it under **SendResponse**. The workflow should look like the following screenshot:

16. Double-click on the **Flowchart** activity to drill down to the flowchart surface.

17. The end result of the next few steps will be a flowchart for the payment collection process. The final result will look like the following screenshot:

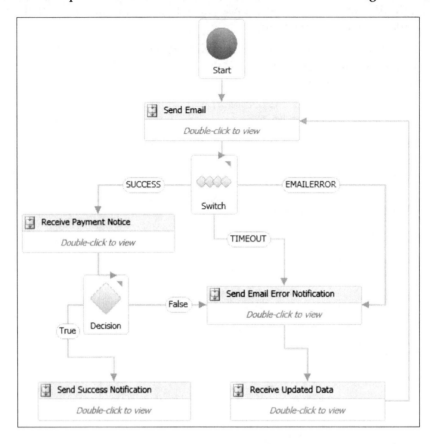

18. Click on the top-level flowchart and click on the **Variables** tab at the bottom left. Add the following variables. These will be within the flowchart scope:

    ° Name: `EmailResult`, type: `String`

    ° Name: `paymentReceived`, type: `Boolean`

    ° Name: `errorMessage`, type: `String`

19. Drag a **Sequence** activity from the **Control Flow** section of the toolbox onto the flowchart surface under the **Start** arrow. Rename this to **Send Email**. This activity will call the external e-mail service to send the user an e-mail. The result of this call will determine the next step in the flow.

20. Draw a line from the **Start** shape to the **Send Email** sequence activity.

21. Under the **Send Email** activity, add a **Switch** activity from the flowchart section of the toolbox. Select type to be `String` when adding the shape to the surface. Set the **Expression** property to **Email Result**.

22. Draw a line from the **Send Email** sequence activity to the **Switch** activity.

23. Drag a **Sequence** activity from the control flow section of the toolbox onto the flowchart surface, left from the **Switch** activity. Rename this to **Receive Payment Notice**. This activity will wait for a payment message from an external source for a fixed amount of time. Sending the payment notice can be done using the provided Tester Windows forms tool located under the tester project.

24. Draw a line from the left of the **Switch** activity to the **Receive Payment Notice** sequence. Uncheck the **IsDefaultCase** checkbox. Set the **Case** value to `SUCCESS`.

25. Drag a **Sequence** activity from the control flow section of the toolbox onto the flowchart surface to the bottom right from the **FlowSwitch** activity. Rename this to **Send Email Error Notification**. This activity will send error message information back out of the workflow — in this case back to SharePoint.

26. Draw a line from the bottom of the **Switch** activity to **Send Email Error Notification** sequence. Uncheck the **IsDefaultCase** checkbox. Set the **Case** value to `TIMEOUT`.

27. Draw a line from the right of the **Switch** activity to the **Send Email Error Notification** sequence. Uncheck the **IsDefaultCase** checkbox. Set the **Case** value to `EMAILERROR`.

28. Drag a **Sequence** activity from the control flow section of the toolbox onto the flowchart surface under the **Send Email Error Notification** sequence activity. Rename this to **Receive Updated Data**. This activity will wait for updated user data from the external data provider — in this case SharePoint.

29. Draw a line from the bottom of the **Send Email Error Notification** sequence activity to the **Receive Updated Data** sequence.

30. Draw a line from the right-side of the **Receive Updated Data** sequence activity to the **Send Email** sequence activity.

31. Moving to the left-side of the flowchart, under the **Receive Payment Notice** activity, add a **FlowDecision** activity from the flowchart section of the toolbox. Set the **Condition** property to `paymentReceived`.

32. Draw a line from the bottom of the **Receive Payment Notice** sequence activity to the top of the **Decision** activity.

33. Drag a **Sequence** activity from the control flow section of the toolbox onto the flowchart surface, under the **Decision** activity. Rename this to **Send Success Notification**. This activity will update the external data provider with a success message—in this case SharePoint.

34. Draw a line from the left side of the **Decision** activity to the top of the **Send Success Notification** sequence activity. This represents the true result.

35. Draw a line from the right-side of the **Decision** activity to the left-side of the **Receive Updated Data** sequence activity. This represents the false result. Notice how once an activity is defined for an event, like **Receive Updated Response**, it is easy to reuse that logic.

36. Now the basic flow of the flowchart is complete. The solution should now build with no errors. Verify this by right-clicking on the project and selecting **Build**. The next steps will add logic to the five sequence shapes that were added to the flowchart.

37. On the main flowchart surface, double-click on the **Send Email** activity. This set of activities will compose the request and response messages to the external e-mail service, evaluate the response message, and generate error messages if needed. At the end, the process will look like the following screenshot:

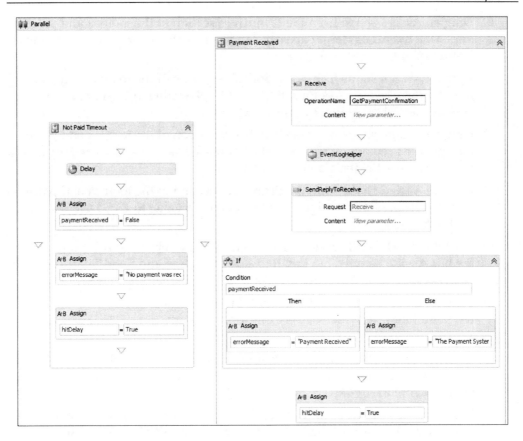

38. Click on the top-level **Send Email** sequence activity and click on the
    Variables tab on the bottom left. Add the following variables:

    ° Name: `emailRequest`, type: `EmailRequest` (from **Send
      Email** add service reference), default: `New HumanWorkflow.
      CoreWorkflow.SendE-mail.E-mailRequest()`

    ° Name: `emailResponse`, type: `EmailResponse` (from **Send
      Email** add service reference)

    ° Name: `emailCount`, type: `Int32`

    ° Name: `emailResultLocal`, type: `String`

39. Drag the custom activity called **EventLogHelper** located under
    `HumanWorkflow.CoreWorkflow`. Place it as the first activity in the sequence.
    Set the **TextEventLog** property to **Started Send Email**.

40. Drag an **Assign** shape from the **Primitives** section of the toolbox and place it under the **EventLogHelper** activity. Set the **To** value to `emailCount`. Set the **Value** equal to `emailCount + 1`.

41. Drag an **Assign** shape from the **Primitives** section of the toolbox and place it under the previous **Assign** activity. Set the **To** value to `emailRequest.AmountDue`. Set the **Value** to `listTotalDonation`.

42. Drag an **Assign** shape from the **Primitives** section of the toolbox and place it under the previous **Assign** activity. Set the **To** value to `emailRequest.EmailAddress`. Set the **Value** to `listEmail`.

43. Drag an **Assign** shape from the **Primitives** section of the toolbox and place it under the previous **Assign** activity. Set the **To** value to `emailRequest.ID`. Set the **Value** to `listID`.

44. Drag the **Send Email** service reference from the toolbar and place it under the last **Assign** activity. Set **Email** to `emailRequest` and **SendEmailResult** to `emailResponse`. If this is not present in the toolbar, rebuild the solution.

45. Drag an **If** activity from the **Control Flow** section of the toolbar under the **Send Email** activity. Set the **Condition** property to `emailResponse.Response`.

46. Drag an **Assign** shape from the **Primitives** section of the toolbox and place it inside the **Then** side of the **If** activity. Set the **To** value to `emailResultLocal`. Set the **Value** to `SUCCESS`.

47. Drag an **If** activity from the control flow section of the toolbar and place it inside the **Else** side of the **If** activity. Set the **Condition** property to `emailCount =< 3`.

48. Drag a **Sequence** activity from control flow section of the toolbox into the **Then** side of the **If** activity. Set the **DisplayName** property to **Email Error**.

49. Drag an **Assign** shape from the **Primitives** section of the toolbox and place it inside the **Email Error** sequential activity. Set the **To** value to `errorMessage`. Set the **Value** to `"The email process returned an error sending the message"`.

50. Drag an **Assign** shape from the **Primitives** section of the toolbox and place it below the previous **Assign** activity. Set the **To** value to `emailResultLocal`. Set the **Value** to `EMAILERROR`.

51. Drag a **Sequence** activity from control flow section of the toolbox into the **Then** side of the **If** activity. Set the **DisplayName** property to **Timeout**.

52. Drag an **Assign** shape from the **Primitives** section of the toolbox and place it inside the **Timeout** sequential activity. Set the **To** value equal `errorMessage`. Set the **Value** to `"The e-mail process has hit more than 3 errors"`.

53. Drag an **Assign** shape from the **Primitives** section of the toolbox and place it below the previous **Assign** activity. Set the **To** value to `emailResultLocal`. Set the **Value** to `"TIMEOUT"`.

54. Drag an **Assign** shape from the **Primitives** section of the toolbox and place it outside of the **If** activities as the last activity of the workflow. Set the **To** value equal `emailResult`. Set the **Value** to `emailResultLocal`.

55. Return to the main flowchart surface by using the bread crumbs on the top of the workflow surface. Double-click on the **Receive Payment Notice** activity. This set of activities will wait for a response from the payment service, evaluate the response message, and generate an error message based on the response or a timeout. This set of activities is only reached if SUCCESS is returned from the **Send Email** sequence. At the end, the process will look like the following screenshot. Note that the following screenshot does not show the top and bottom event log activity.

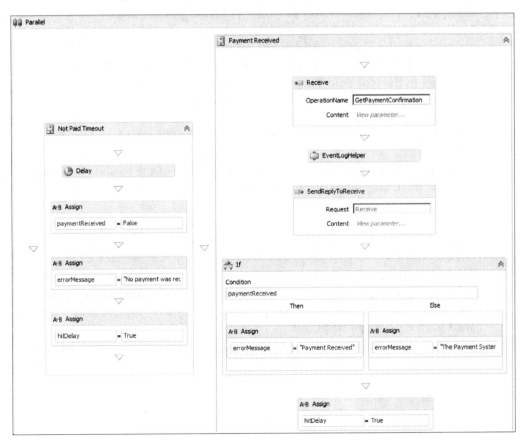

56. Drag the custom activity called **EventLogHelper** located under `HumanWorkflow.CoreWorkflow`. Place it as the first activity in the sequence. Set the **TextEventLog** property to `Started Receive Payment Notice`.

57. Drag a **Parallel** activity from control flow section of the toolbox right under the **EventLogHelper** activity.

58. With the **Parallel** activity selected, click on the **Variables** tab on the bottom left. Add the following variable at the **Parallel** scope:

59. Name: `hitDelay`, type: `Boolean`, default: `False`

60. With the **Parallel** activity selected, set the **CompletionCondition** to `hitDelay`. This will allow the parallel shape to complete even when all the branches have not finished.

61. Drag a **Sequence** activity from the control flow section of the toolbox onto the flowchart surface inside the **Parallel** activity. Set the **DisplayName** to **Not Paid Timeout**.

62. Drag a **ReceiveAndSendReply** from the **Messaging** section of the toolbox and place it to the right of the last sequence activity inside the parallel activity. This will add a new sequence activity to the flow. Set the **DisplayName** of the new right **Sequence** activity to **Payment Received**.

63. Working in the **Not Paid Timeout** sequence, drag a **Delay** activity from **Primitives** section of the toolbox. Set the **Duration** property to `New TimeSpan(0, 2, 0)`. This will set a delay of two minutes. While in real life this would be longer, we do not want to have to wait for a few days to run the demo.

64. Drag an **Assign** shape from the **Primitives** section of the toolbox and place it below the **Delay** activity. Set the **To** value to `paymentReceived`. Set the **Value** to `False`.

65. Drag an **Assign** shape from the **Primitives** section of the toolbox and place it below the previous **Assign** activity. Set the **To** value equal `errorMessage`. Set the **Value** to `"No payment was received in the set amount of time"`.

66. Drag an **Assign** shape from the **Primitives** section of the toolbox and place it below the previous **Assign** activity. Set the **To** value equal `hitDelay`. Set the **Value** to `True`. This will cause the parallel activity to complete rather than wait for the payment response.

67. Working in the **Payment Received** sequence activity, click on the **Receive** activity. Rename **Operation** to **GetPaymentConfirmation**. Under **Content**, click on **View parameter...**. Select the **Parameters** radio button and enter the following parameters:

    ° Name: `paymentID`, type: `Int32`

    ° Name: `paymentResult`, type: `Boolean`, assign to: `paymentReceived`

68. With **Receive** selected, click on the **CorrelatesWith** property. Set this to **ListHandle**. Click on **CorrelatesOn**. Select `paymentID` from the drop down and click **OK**. This will set the receive activity to follow the correlation based on the ID of the donor record.

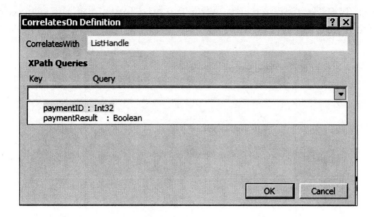

69. Click on the **SendReplyToReceive** activity. Under **Content** click on **Define...** and select the **Parameters** radio button. Enter the following parameters:

    ° Name: `Result`, type: `Boolean`, value: `True`

70. With **SendReplyToReceive** selected, ensure the **PersistBeforeSend** checkbox is checked.

71. Drag the custom activity called **EventLogHelper** located under `HumanWorkflow.CoreWorkflow`. Place it between the receive and send activities. Set the **TextEventLog** property to `Received Payment Message`.

72. Drag an **If** activity from the control flow section of the toolbar and place it under the **SendReplyToReceive** activity. Set the **Condition** property to `paymentReceived`.

73. Drag an **Assign** shape from the **Primitives** section of the toolbox and place it inside the **Then** side of the **If** activity. Set the **To** value equal to `errorMessage`. Set the **Value** equal to `Payment Received`.

74. Drag an **Assign** shape from the **Primitives** section of the toolbox and place it inside the **Else** side of the **If** activity. Set the **To** value equal to `errorMessage`. Set the **Value** equal to `"The Payment System returned an error in the payment"`.

75. Drag an **Assign** shape from the **Primitives** section of the toolbox and place it below the previous **If** activity, ensure it is outside the **If** block. Set the **To** value equal to `hitDelay`. Set the **Value** equal to `True`. This will cause the parallel activity to complete rather than wait for the delay.

76. Drag the custom activity called **EventLogHelper** located under
    `HumanWorkflow.CoreWorkflow`. Place it outside of the parallel shape. Set the
    TextEventLog property to the `errorMessage` variable.

77. Navigate back to the main flowchart surface; double-click on the **Send
    Success Notification** activity. After the next few steps, the process will look
    like the following screenshot:

78. With the **Send Success Notification** sequence activity selected, click on the
    Variables tab on the bottom left. Add the following variables:

    ○ **Name:** `notificationRequest`, **type:** `NotificationRequest`
      (under the **Send Notification** reference type), **type:** `New`
      `HumanWorkflow.CoreWorkflow.SendNotification.`
      `NotificationRequest()`

    ○ **Name:** `notificationResponse`, **type:**
      `NotificationResponse` (under the **Send Notification**
      reference type)

79. Drag the custom activity called **EventLogHelper**, located under
    `HumanWorkflow.CoreWorkflow`. Place it as the first activity in the sequence.
    Set the **TextEventLog** property to `"Started Send Success Notice"`.

80. Drag an **Assign** shape from the **Primitives** section of the toolbox and place it below the **TextEventLog** activity. Set the **To** value equal to `notificationRequest.ID`. Set the **Value** equal to `listID`.

81. Drag an **Assign** shape from the **Primitives** section of the toolbox and place it below the previous **Assign** activity. Set the **To** value to `notificationRequest.NotificationType`. Set the **Value** to SUCCESS.

82. Drag the custom activity called **SendNotification**, located under `HumanWorkflow.CoreWorkflow.SendNotification`. Place it under the **Assign** activity. Set the **Notification** property to `notificationRequest`. Set the **SendNotificationResponse** property to `notificationResponse`.

83. Navigate back to the main flowchart surface; double-click on the **Send Email Error Notification** activity. After the next few steps, the process will look like the following screenshot:

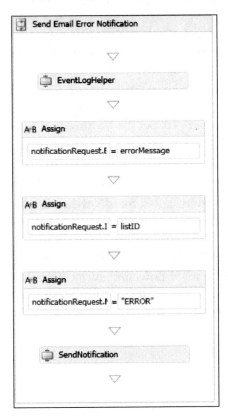

84. With the **Send Email Error Notification** sequence activity selected, click on the **Variables** tab on the bottom left. Add the following variables at the **Parallel** scope:
    - Name: `notificationRequest`, type: `NotificationRequest` (under the **Send Notification** reference type), default: `New HumanWorkflow.CoreWorkflow.SendNotification.NotificationRequest()`
    - Name: `notificationResponse`, type: `NotificationResponse` (under the **Send Notification** reference type)

85. Drag the custom activity called **EventLogHelper** located under `HumanWorkflow.CoreWorkflow`. Place it as the first activity in the sequence. Set the **TextEventLog** property to `"Started Send Email Error Notification"`.

86. Drag an **Assign** shape from the **Primitives** section of the toolbox and place it below the **TextEventLog** activity. Set the **To** value to `notificationRequest.ErrorMessage`. Set the **Value** to `errorMessage`.

87. Drag an **Assign** shape from the **Primitives** section of the toolbox and place it below the previous **Assign** activity. Set the **To** value equal to `notificationRequest.ID`. Set the **Value** equal to `listID`.

88. Drag an **Assign** shape from the **Primitives** section of the toolbox and place it below the previous **Assign** activity. Set the **To** value equal to `notificationRequest.NotificationType`. Set the **Value** equal `ERROR`.

89. Drag the custom activity called **SendNotification** located under `HumanWorkflow.CoreWorkflow.SendNotification`. Place it under the **Assign** activity. Set the **Notification** property to `notificationRequest`. Set the **SendNotificationResponse** property to `notificationResponse`.

90. Navigate back to the main flowchart surface; double-click on the **Receive Updated Data** activity. After the next few steps, the process will look like the following screenshot:

91. Drag the custom activity called **EventLogHelper**, located under
    HumanWorkflow.CoreWorkflow. Place it as the first activity in the sequence.
    Set the **TextEventLog** property to Started Receive Updated Data.

92. Drag a **ReceiveAndSendReply** from the **Messaging** section of the toolbox
    and place it under the **EventLogHelper** activity. This will add a new
    sequence activity to the flow. Set the **DisplayName** of the new **Sequence**
    activity to **Update Data**.

93. Working in the **Update Data** sequence activity, click on the **Receive activity**. Rename **Operation** to **GetUpdatedData**. Under **Content** click on **View parameter....** Select the **Parameters** radio button and enter the following parameters:

    ° Name: `ID`, type: `Int32`, **assign to:** `listID`

    ° Name: `Email`, type: `String`, **assign to:** `listEmail`

94. With **Receive** selected, click on the **CorrelatesWith** property. Set this to `ListHandle`. Click on **CorrelatesOn**. Select **ID** from the drop down. Click on **OK**. This will set up this receive activity to follow the correlation based on the ID of the donor record.

95. Click on the **SendReplyToReceive** activity. Under **Content**, click on **Define....** Select the **Parameters** radio button and enter the following parameters:

    ° Name: `Result`, type: `Boolean`, value: `True`

96. With **SendReplyToReceive** selected, ensure the **PersistBeforeSend** checkbox is checked.

97. Drag the custom activity called **EventLogHelper**, located under `HumanWorkflow.CoreWorkflow`. Place it between the receive and send activities. Set the **TextEventLog** property to `Received GETUPDATEDDATA Message`.

98. Save the workflow. Right-click on the project and select **Build**. The workflow service will now be available to be called from within IIS.

Testing the workflow without SharePoint

The preceding tasks can be tested using the supplied Windows Application in the `Begin` or `End` folder:

1. Open IIS and view the **AppFabric Dashboard** for the `HumanWorkflow. CoreWorkflow` application. This will show the status of requests and workflows being processed.

2. Launch `Tester.exe` located inside the `Bin\Debug` folder.

3. Click on the **New User** button. This will create a new user ID and call the Process Payment workflow. The result of this WCF call should be **True**.

4. Click on the **Process Payment** button. Make sure to enter the same user ID as before. This will send a payment message for this user.

5. This completes the workflow. Check the event log to follow the flow of the workflow.

6. Change the e-mail address to Fdemo@demo.com. Click on the **New User** button. This will create a new user ID and call the Process Payment workflow. The result of this WCF call should be **True**.

7. This time a message in the event log will highlight an error condition. The workflow is now waiting for updated information. Change the e-mail address on the form to demo@demo.com. Click on **Update User**.

8. Click on the **Process Payment** button. Make sure to set the user ID value to the same value as before. This will send a payment message for this user.

9. This completes the workflow. Check the event log to follow the flow of the workflow.

10. Continue to try various combinations while following messages in the event log and inside the IIS Dashboard.

Building the SharePoint site and SharePoint workflow

In this section, we build the SharePoint site and SharePoint workflow used for this solution. The SharePoint site will contain a single list used to store customer information. The SharePoint workflow will monitor new and updated records and send the list information to the core workflow created in the first step based on two flag values.

When the core workflow detects an e-mail issue or the user takes a long time to pay, the SharePoint list will be updated with an error message. A human will need to research the issue and may have to contact the person about the donation. Once this happens, the employee will update the information in SharePoint. When the data needs to be resubmitted into the core workflow, the reprocess flag should be set. In this section, the following tasks will be accomplished:

1. Create a new SharePoint site for Bowl For Buddies

2. Create a new customer list

3. Modify the customer list to include fields specific to Bowl For Buddies donation and bowling needs

4. Create a new SharePoint workflow project in Visual Studio that will respond to new customers and changes to the customer list

5. Create a .NET 3.5-based workflow to send list information from SharePoint into a .NET 4.0 Windows Server AppFabric hosted workflow

These steps assume that InfoPath is installed on the SharePoint server. If InfoPath is not available, the form columns can be created inside SharePoint using the **Create Column** button. Ensure the columns are named the same as in Step 20 of the section below.

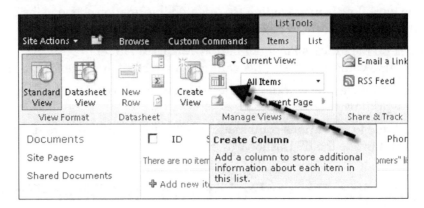

Creating the SharePoint site and customer list

1. Change the hard-coded `useSharePoint` boolean variable in the provided notification service code to update SharePoint rather than the event log. See the comments of the service for more details.

2. Launch **SharePoint 2010 Central Administration** application from the Windows start menu.

3. Click on **Manage web applications** under **Application Management**.

4. Click on **New** on the top left of the screen.

5. Keep all the default values but ensure the **Port** is 44130. The port value is used in the **IIS Name**, the **IIS Port** field, the **IIS Path**, **Public URL**, and **Application Pool Name**.

6. Under **Application Pool**, go to **Select a Security Account**. Select **Preferred** and **Network Service** from the dropdown list.

7. Click **OK**.

8. Click on **Create site collection** under **Application Management**.

9. Make sure the **Web Application** is set to the default site on port 44130 created in the previous steps.

10. Set the **Title** to **Bowl For Buddies**.

11. Make no changes to the **Website Address**. This will make the address for the Bowl For Buddies site `http://<MachineName:44130>/`. It is essential to access the website using the machine name and not the localhost.

12. Set the **Primary Site Collection Administrator** to a user on the server. In this case, the virtual machine's administrator account was used.

13. Click **OK** to crease the site.

14. Navigate to `http://<MachineName:44130>/`. Ensure the site loads with no issues.

15. Click on **List** at the middle left.

16. Click on **Create** near the top of the page.

17. Select **Custom List** as the template type and name the list **DonationCustomers**. If you do not see the template icons in the selection window, ensure that you are accessing the site using the machine name and not localhost.

18. Click on **Create**.

19. Ensure the **List** tab is selected under **List Tools**. Click on **Customize Form**. This will open an InfoPath forms editor.

20. Create the following **Fields** by clicking on **Add Field** under **Actions** on the right. Ensure the case of the fields below is the same as listed here:

    ° Display name: **Sent**, data type: **Yes/No**

    ° Display name: **Name**, data type: **Single line of Text**, check: **Cannot be blank**

    ° Display name: **Email** Data Type: **Single line of text** Check: **Cannot be blank**

    ° Display name: **Phone** Data Type: **Single line of text** Check: **Cannot be blank**

    ° Display name: **Donation Amount** Data Type: **Currency** Check: **Cannot be blank**

    ° Display name: **Bowling Score** Data Type: **Number** Check: **Cannot be blank**

    ° Display name: **Paid** Data Type: **Yes/No**

    ° Display name: **Reprocess** Data Type: **Yes/No**

    ° Display name: **Error** Data Type: **Multiple lines of text (plain text)**

21. Edit the **Title** field by right-clicking on it and selecting **Field Properties**. Ensure the **Cannot be blank** check box is unchecked.

22. Arrange the fields on the form to make it look something like the following picture. You can add new rows to the form by right-clicking and selecting **Insert–Rows Below**. Remove the two existing fields for **Title** and **Attachment**.

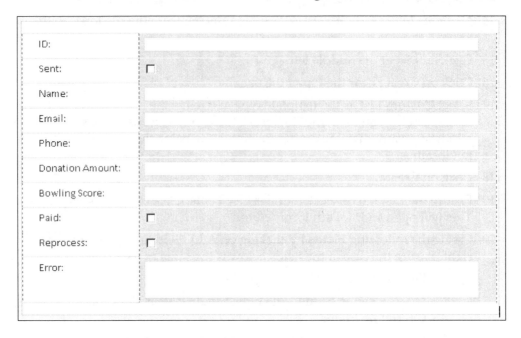

23. Once complete, click on **File**. Click on **Quick Publish** to publish this list to SharePoint. Close InfoPath.

24. The form is saved as `DonationCustomerList.xsn` in the `<Installation Directory>\HumanWorkflow\HumanWorkflow.HelperDocs` folder. Note that the form in the directory will be data bound to a hard-coded machine name so use this form as reference only.

25. Navigate back to the list view at `http://<MachineName>:44130/Lists/DonationCustomers/AllItems.aspx`

26. Click on the **Modify View** button (dropdown off the **All Items** link) and make the following changes:

    ◦ Uncheck **Attachments** and **Title** check boxes
    ◦ Check the **ID** check box and set the position to 1
    ◦ Click **OK** at the bottom of the form

Create the SharePoint workflow

1. Open the **HumanWorkflow** solution from the `Begin` folder if it is not already open.

2. Create a new SharePoint Sequential Workflow project (located under **Visual C# | SharePoint | 2010**) named `HumanWorkflow.DonationListWorkflow`. Make sure you create the project inside the `HumanWorkflow` folder. Note that even if the .NET version 4.0 is selected, the project will be created using version 3.5 as SharePoint does not support .NET version 4.0 at this time.

3. The next steps walk you though the wizard that opens as part of the project template.

4. On the **Specify the site and security level for debugging** window, ensure the correct site is selected in the drop down. It should be `http://<MachineName>:44130/`. Ensure the **Deploy as a farm solution** is selected. Click on **Next**.

5. On the **Specify the workflow name for debugging** window, set the name to `HumanWorkflow.DonationListWorkflow-ProcessPayments`. Ensure the **List Workflow** radio is selected. Click on **Next**.

6. On the **Select the lists you will use when debugging** window, select **DonationCustomers** in the dropdown list for the library or list to associate your workflow with. Ensure the **Yes, associate...** checkbox is checked. Click on **Next**.

7. On the **Specify the conditions for how your workflow is started** ensure that only the **The workflow starts automatically when an item is created** and **The workflow starts automatically when an item is changed** checkboxes are checked. Click on **Finish**. This will create the project inside the solution with a default workflow named `Workflow1`.

8. In order to rename the workflow, it is easier to delete the default and create a new one. Delete the `Workflow1` workflow created by-default.

9. Right-click on the project and add a new item. Add a new **Sequential Workflow** named **ProcessDonationCustomers**.

10. Keep the defaults on the **Specify the workflow name for debugging** window.

11. On the **Select the lists you will use when debugging** window, select **DonationCustomers** in the dropdown list for **The library or list to associate your workflow with**. Ensure the **Yes, associate...** checkbox is checked. Click on **Next**.

12. By default, the sequential workflow has an **onWorkflowActivated1** activity. Keep this shape.

13. The flow of the workflow will be created using the following activities. Drag each activity from the **Toolbox**.

14. Drop a **logToHistoryListActivity** (under SharePoint Workflow) under the **onWorkflowActivated** activity.

15. Drop an **ifElse** (under Window Workflow v3.0) under the **logToHistoryListActivity**.

16. Drop a **SendActivity** (under Windows Workflow v3.5) inside the left branch of **ifElse**.

17. Drop a **logToHistoryListActivity** (under SharePoint Workflow) under the **SendActivity** inside the left branch of the **ifElse**.

18. Drop another send activity (under Windows Workflow v3.5) inside the right branch of the **ifElse**.

19. Drop a **logToHistoryListActivity** (under SharePoint Workflow) under the **SendActivity** inside the right branch of the **ifElse**. The overall workflow is shown in the following screenshot:

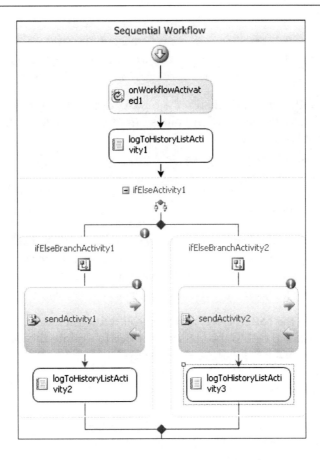

20. Set the **HistoryDescription** property value on the three **logToHistoryListActivity** activities. No need for quotes in the strings.

    ° Top Activity: **Workflow Started**
    ° Left IfElse Activity: **New Record Completed**
    ° Right IfElse Activity: **Update Record Completed**

21. Right-click on the **onWorkflowActivated1** activity and select **Generate Handlers**. This will create a class to be called when this activity is completed.

22. Above the onWorkflowActivates1_Invoked() method add the following code to declare workflow-level variables. All code is in the WorkflowCode. txt file located under the <Installation Directory>\HumanWorkflow\ HumanWorkflow.HelperDocs folder.

```
public Int32 listID = default(System.Int32);
public Double listBowlingScore = default(System.Double);
public Double listDonationAmount = default(System.Double);
```

```
public String listE-mail = default(System.String);
public String listName = default(System.String);
public bool listReprocess = default(System.Boolean);
public bool listSent = default(System.Boolean);
```

23. Copy the following code inside the `onWorkflowActivates1_Invoked()` method. This will read the list values out of the workflow properties and set them to the local variable.

```
listID = workflowProperties.ItemId;
listBowlingScore =
                (double)workflowProperties.Item["BowlingScore"];
listDonationAmount =
                (double)workflowProperties.Item["DonationAmount"];
listE-mail = (string)workflowProperties.Item["E-mail"];
listName = (string)workflowProperties.Item["Name"];
listReprocess = (Boolean)workflowProperties.Item["Reprocess"];
listSent = (Boolean)workflowProperties.Item["Sent"];
```

24. While inside the code view, create the following method. They will be called after a successful call to the external service to update the list properties to know if a record is new or needs to be updated.

```
private void ServiceCall_AfterResponse(object sender,
SendActivityEventArgs e)
{
  workflowProperties.Item["Sent"] = true;
  workflowProperties.Item["Reprocess"] = false;
  workflowProperties.Item["Error"] = "";
  workflowProperties.Item.Update();
  workflowProperties.List.Update();
}
```

25. Save the workflow and return to the workflow designer. Select the **ifElseBranchActivity1**. This should be on the left side of the **ifElse** activity. Rename this to `NewRecord` using the properties window.

26. Select **Declarative Rule Condition** under the **Condition** property. Expand the condition by clicking on the plus sign on the left. Select the **...** on the **ConditionName**.

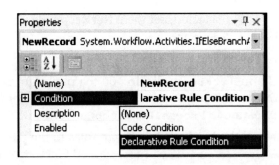

27. On the **Select Condition** window select **New**. This will open the **Rule Condition Editor**. Set the rule to `!this.listSent`.

28. Click on **OK**.

29. Click on **Rename** on the **Select Condition** window. Name the condition **IfNewRecord**.

30. Click on **OK** to close the window.

31. Select the **ifElseBranchActivity2**. This should be on the right-side of the **ifElse** activity. Rename this to **UpdateRecord** using the properties window.

32. Select **Declarative Rule Condition** under the **Condition** property. Expand the condition by clicking on the plus sign on the left. Select the **...** on the **ConditionName**.

33. On the **Select Condition** window select **New**. This will open the **Rule Condition Editor**. Set the rule to `this.listReprocess`.

34. Click on **OK**.

35. Click on **Rename** on the **Select Condition** window. Name the condition **IfUpdateRecord**.

36. Click on **OK** to close the window.

37. Add a service reference to the Windows Server AppFabric workflow created earlier. Right-click on the SharePoint project. Select **Add Service Reference**. The address of the service should be `http://localhost:1234/HumanWorkflow.CoreWorkflow/ProcessPayment.xamlx` and name the reference as **ProcessUserData**.

38. Inside the designer, select `sendActivity1`. Click the **...** on **ServiceOperationInfo**.

39. On **Chose Operation**, click on **Import** on the top right.

40. Select the **IService** from the **Current Project**. Click on **OK**.

41. Select **GetDate** and click on **OK**.

42. With `sendActivity1` selected, set the **AfterResponse** property to `ServiceCall_AfterResponse`.

43. Select **ChannelToken** and name it `myChannel`.

44. Expand the **ChannelToken** by clicking on the plus sign. Set the **EndpointName** to `BasicHttpBinding_IService`. Set the **OwnerActivityName** to `ProcessDonationCustomers`.

45. This step will bind the local workflow variables to the parameters for the service call. With `sendActivity1` (now named **GetData** on the surface) still selected, set the following properties by clicking on the **...** and selecting the workflow property. These are located under the **Parameters** section of the properties.

    ○ **(Parameter)Name** bind to `listName`
    ○ **BowlingScore** bind to `listBowlingScore`
    ○ **DonationAmount** bind to `listDonationAmount`
    ○ **EmailAddress** bind to `listEmail`
    ○ **ID** bind to `listID`

46. The end result should look like the following screenshot:

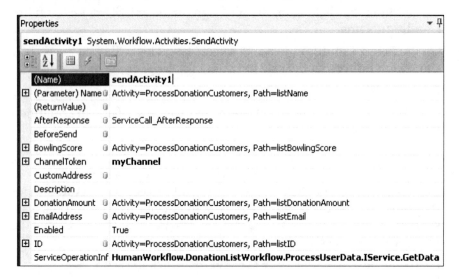

47. Inside the designer, select **sendActivity2**. Click on the **...** on **ServiceOperationInfo**.

48. Select **GetUpdateDate** and click on **OK**.

49. With `sendActivity2` selected, set the **AfterResponse** property to `ServiceCall_AfterResponse`.

50. Select **ChannelToken** and select `myChannel` from the dropdown.

51. This step will bind the local workflow variables to the parameters for the service call. With `sendActivity2` (now named **GetUpdatedData** on the surface) still selected, set the following properties by clicking on the ... and selecting the workflow property. This has fewer properties as it is an update call into an existing workflow.

    ◦ **EmailAddress** bind to `listE-mail`

    ◦ **ID** bind to `listID`

52. Next, we want to add some basic exception logging. On the top workflow green arrow, click on the dropdown. Select **View Fault Handlers**.

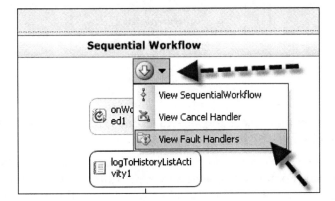

53. Drag a **FaultHandler** activity from the Windows Workflow v3.0 toolbox and place it inside the **Drop FaultHandlerActivity Here** section.

54. On `faultHandlerActivity1` set the **FaultType** property by clicking on ... and type in `System.Exception`. Click on **OK**.

55. Drag a **logToHistoryListActivity** activity from the SharePoint workflow toolbox inside the `faultHandlerActivity1`.

56. Bind the **HistoryDescription** to `faultHandlerActivity1.`
    `faultHandlerActivity1.Fault.StackTrace` and **HistoryOutcome** to
    `faultHandlerActivity1. faultHandlerActivity1.Fault.Message`. At the
    end, the exception workflow will look like the following screenshot:

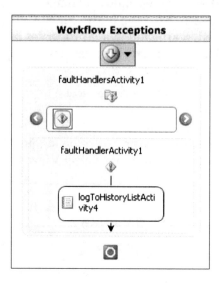

57. Right-click on the project and select **Deploy**. This will publish the workflow
    to SharePoint.

58. The last piece is to copy the WCF endpoint information from the local project
    into the SharePoint site so the deployed workflow can call the service. Open
    the `App.config` file inside the local project. Copy all the information inside
    the `<system.serviceModel>` tags. Do not copy the tags and make sure you
    remove the Net Named Pipes endpoint.

59. Open the `web.config` file for the default SharePoint site located at `C:\`
    `inetpub\wwwroot\wss\VirtualDirectories\44130\`. Paste the data
    inside the `<system.serviceModel>` right after the following line:
    `<serviceHostingEnvironment aspNetCompatibilityEnabled="true" />`.

60. Edit the WCF timeout values from the default value of one minute and
    set them to two minutes each. The values are **closeTimeout**=`"00:02:00"`,
    openTimeout=`"00:02:00"`, and **sendTimeout**=`"00:02:00"`.

Testing the solution using SharePoint

The following steps outline how to test the solution:

1. Open SharePoint and navigate to `http://<MachineName>/`
   `BowlForBuddies/Lists/DonationCustomers/AllItems.aspx`.

2. Click on **Add New Items**. Fill in the form with the following information:
   - ID: `<Read Only>`, **sent**: `<Default>`
   - Name: `Some Donor`, **e-mail address**: `SomeDonor@SomeDonorE-mail.com`
   - Phone Number: `555-555-5555`, donation amount: `1.50`, bowling score: `300`
   - Paid: `<Default>`
   - Reprocess: `<Default>`
   - Error: `<Default-Blank>`

3. This will start a new workflow instance of the `ProcessPayments` workflow. Do a refresh on the SharePoint list to check the results of the workflow. Click on the **completed** link to see the details of the workflow.

4. Once a record is submitted using SharePoint, note the ID of the user and open the test application. Set the **user ID** field to the SharePoint ID and click on the **Process Payment** button. This will complete the workflow. Check the event log for details on the process.

5. Create another user with an e-mail starting with the letter "F". See the error message show up in the SharePoint list. Edit the e-mail address to not start with an "F" and set the **reprocess** flag. The workflow should continue.

Summary

In this chapter, we looked at how to use SharePoint to call a Windows Server AppFabric hosted workflow service. Using a workflow external to SharePoint allows for reuse of the business process by other systems. Using Windows Server AppFabric gives us a single processing environment which reduces the complexity of monitoring and administration.

11
Remote Message Broadcasting

The ability to communicate with a large number of remote systems is a unique programming and network challenge. Today, nearly every piece of installed software checks for updates either on a set schedule or upon application startup. Typically, these are polling-based service calls to a central location. This approach works well for items that are not event-driven or that have infrequent updates.

As the frequency and urgency of the updates increase, the traditional means of updating systems through polling operations gets more and more inefficient. At some point, replacement of the polling-based system must be considered in favor of a push-based approach allowing updates to be sent immediately to remote systems. With a push-based system, connectivity to the backend could become an issue due to network and firewall complexity. In general, it is more acceptable to let connections out of a network than back in, thus causing problems with the push approach.

Use case

Virtual Cow Media is a small, Midwestern-based media company offering cable television and related services. They have an existing subscriber base of about 50,000 customers, of which, about half subscribe to the digital video recording (DVR) service. One major customer complaint is about the digital video recording service is the impact of schedule changes to recorded events. If a baseball game runs late or the U.S. President decides to speak, customers may lose out on parts of recorded events. In addition, other companies offer end-users the ability to schedule recording events from a remote location through either a company website or mobile applications. In these cases, the user will receive real-time confirmation of the recording event after the site has confirmed the update to the home system. Virtual Cow Media has a superior pricing package, but they are losing customers to other providers that offer a richer set of offerings.

As part of a larger premium offering, Virtual Cow Media plans to offer customers near real-time updates to programming changes that could be affected by live events running late or other program interruptions. In addition, they are also offering customers the ability to create and update recorded events online with instant notification that the event has been confirmed on the customer's DVR system.

They expect around 2000 customers to subscribe to this service. The number of customer subscriptions will change daily with users continuously adding and removing their premium service. While this offering is expected to drive new customers and stop attrition, the long term success of the offering is unknown. If customer demand slows down or better options come up, this service could stop at any time.

Virtual Cow Media currently uses a polling-based updated system for sending daily downloads of data to customer devices. This approach needs to be reviewed based on the proposed new service offering. Virtual Cow Media does not want to invest in new infrastructure at this time given that the extended long-term validity of this offering is unknown.

Virtual Cow Media is an old company with deep roots in the community. They have been keeping current with technology trends and have invested in skilled resources to deliver value-added offerings to customers in order to compete in this intense market space.

Key requirements

The following are key requirements for a new software solution:

- The ability for users to easily subscribe and unsubscribe to the service.
- Remote systems should receive scheduling updates frequently and ad hoc.
- For synchronous ad hoc requests, remote systems need to return a response confirmation.

Additional facts

There are some additional details gathered after the initial use case was shared with the technical team. These include the following facts:

1. Virtual Cow Media has a small IT operation competing with many large national media providers.

2. Service offerings tend to have a short life span so investing in new hardware and software must be well justified.

Pattern description

A connection to the Internet is a critical component to many devices at home and the office. Home computers, televisions, and even disk players require ready access to the Internet to open a new range of features for the end-user to enjoy.

Typically, in-home devices make outbound calls to download and return requested information. This could be done via a web service call when the device starts up or is scheduled through a built-in polling system to check new content. This mechanism is efficient when updates are infrequent.

A new range of possibilities arise when connections outside home and office can be made back to the devices. This would allow for remote users to make adjustments, as needed, to in-home devices in order to view pictures or access data. Technical users can use a combination of home-router adjustments and a dynamic DNS service to keep a pathway open for external access—with of course the risk of opening these ports to the outside world. Professional devices could use a dedicated **virtual private network (VPN)** connection to register backend connections or would need to make sure of similar dynamic DNS systems for communication with remote devices. The complexity of this backend connection limits the true potential.

The efficiency of a polling or VPN-based solution is affected by the frequency of updates, the speed at which updates must be applied, latency between updates, and the variety of networks the systems must support. Polling or VPN solutions require having a reliable, secure, continuous connection to the Internet for external applications across many different networks.

This use case introduces two core problems: how to accomplish both message broadcasting and point-to-point communication to remote systems. We want the message broadcasting capability to support mass updates to all target systems and the point-to-point communication to address individual DVR updates. The following diagram outlines the two scenarios:

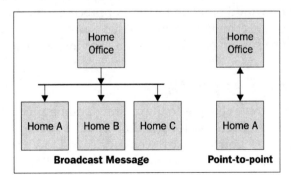

The problem can be solved in one of three ways:

1. **Polling**: Remote system goes out and gets the data it needs.
2. **Pushing**: Remote system in the home receives data via a web call or file drop by the Virtual Cow Media office.
3. **Continuous**: Remote system is always connected to the network through a VPN.

Some key factors that affect the solution include:

1. **Network**: What type of connection exists between the Virtual Cow Media office and the customer's home?
2. **Distance**: How far from the Virtual Cow Media office are the remote hosts?
3. **Security**: How sensitive is the data and is encryption needed?
4. **Message Size**: What is the size of the message payload?
5. **Volume**: How many messages are expected per day?
6. **Reliability**: What happens if a remote home or home office is offline?

The following candidate architecture section outlines three different potential solutions to this problem.

Candidate architectures

The following are three different architecture options to solve this problem. Let's take a look at the details of each option to determine the best fit for this scenario.

Candidate architecture #1–.NET-based polling

Currently, the existing home units use infrequent polling to check for updates. A polling-based solution would build on top of that process to increase the frequency to meet requirements. This solution would not have any network connectivity issues as the customer's home system has already been carrying out this process.

Solution design aspects

This solution would involve changes to the existing polling process for scheduled updates. The current system checks for schedule updates nightly, using the customer's Internet connection to make a web-service call to Virtual Cow Media's office. If updates are found, they are downloaded and installed.

As scheduling changes to live events can happen with little notice and customers have the ability to set up remote recordings, the polling interval would need to be increased. We assume the interval would need to be for a little less than a minute in order to meet the goals of the system. When the customer makes a real-time recording update externally through the website, they would need to wait for the next polling interval to confirm that their DVR was updated.

The overhead of this constant polling will introduce noticeable strain on Virtual Cow Media's infrastructure and may even negatively impact the customer's home network.

Solution delivery aspects

This solution would require very little time to implement as the existing process is polling-based. This process would require some changes to the frontend website code to handle waiting longer for the response message when a user makes an off-site recording request. It is possible that some additional hardware may be required to handle the new load, resulting in an additional cost.

Solution operation aspects

Virtual Cow Media and the home users would be negatively affected by this approach. It would use up a large amount of bandwidth on both sides to have thousands of customers' home systems polling the Virtual Cow Media office for downloads.

Organizational aspects

Given that this approach is consistent with the existing process for schedule updates, this is a proven and reliable process that would be easy for the existing staff to deliver and support.

Solution evaluation

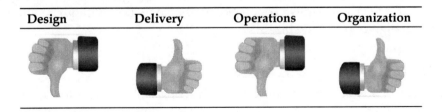

Design	Delivery	Operations	Organization

Candidate architecture #2–BizTalk Server

BizTalk Server is Microsoft's premiere integration server. It has a strong message distribution engine that could be used by Virtual Cow Media to communicate with remote devices in customers' homes.

Solution design aspects

A BizTalk-based solution would involve two key pieces: connectivity back to the end-customer's digital video recorders through a virtual private network (VPN) and the BizTalk component to route messages to those systems.

The VPN is needed to ensure that the remote address of the customer's system can be easily and securely found on the network. This VPN solution could already exist on the system and would only be activated when a user subscribes to the premium service. This VPN solution would work in a majority of the situations, but it may not be possible to ensure VPN connectivity on all Internet service providers and network topologies. This would end up being a limitation of the offering if a customer chose to purchase it.

BizTalk Server can be used to route messages to many destinations through a **send port group** and to single destinations using a **send port**. In the case of Virtual Cow Media, two send ports would be needed for each end-customer to route both the one-way broadcast messages for television schedule updates and the request-response point-to-point messages for ad hoc remote recording events. The send ports would either need to already exist and be enabled, or created when a user purchases the premium service. The first send port would need to be placed into a send port group in order to receive the broadcast messages. The second send port would have filters that could be used to ensure point-to-point communication with a response for a single user using the service to request a recording event.

BizTalk Server has a built-in persistence store to ensure that no messages are lost. Communication failures can be retried until they reach the final destination. When using BizTalk Server for this solution, we would have to figure out how to ensure a secure, continuous, and known connection to the home unit without creating a maintenance nightmare inside BizTalk.

Solution delivery aspects

The timelines of this project are quick, given the consistent changes to the residential entertainment market. Building out a BizTalk-based solution would take some time to set up the new hardware. Additional time would be needed to train team members on how to build, support, and manage a BizTalk environment.

Solution operation aspects

Virtual Cow Media is offering the premium service on a trial basis. While time and money have been spent on the initial solution built out, they do not want to spend money on additional software and hardware for a solution that might get retired in six to twelve months. Plus, operationally they would need a way to programmatically create and destroy ports so that they do not have operators constantly fiddling with send ports. This could result in additional integration work with customer management systems.

Organizational aspects

Given the young and skilled IT staff, Virtual Cow Media would be able to handle a BizTalk-based solution organizationally. One concern is the monitoring and administration involved with BizTalk Server given the small team.

Solution evaluation

Design	Delivery	Operations	Organization
👍	👎	👎	👍

Candidate architecture #3–Windows Azure Platform AppFabric

Windows Azure Platform AppFabric is Microsoft's cloud-based solution for secure remote system connections. AppFabric consists of two key offerings. The first product is the Service Bus—Microsoft's cloud-based service broker, which provides a secure Internet-addressable endpoint for services. This is used for systems of all types to communicate with each other across many network boundaries by everyone connecting to the central service bus. The second product is the Access Control Service. This controls who can connect to the Service Bus and communicate with applications.

Solution design aspects

A solution using the Microsoft Platform AppFabric Service Bus would be a total replacement for the existing daily polling done by the home units today. The new approach would be to expose two endpoints on the Service Bus for each customer who purchased the premium service. The first endpoint would support mass updates based on a schedule change. This would use a client application at Virtual Cow Media's home office to publish a message on the Service Bus for this type of notification. The second endpoint would be for a specific point-to-point update via a remote device, either a website or mobile device. While the point-to-point interface could have retry logic built into the website and mobile application, message broadcasting would not. Broadcast messages may need to be sent more than once to ensure they are received by all endpoints.

To ensure a secure connection, the endpoint would be secured using the built-in Access Control Service integration with the Service Bus. This would ensure that only authenticated systems can connect to the Service Bus.

Solution delivery aspects

It only takes a few moments to sign up for an account with Windows Azure Platform AppFabric. Once the WCF services are built, it is a simple configuration change to update the endpoints to use the Service Bus and support the correct access control tokens. While pricing can change at any time, the current offering charges a set amount for a connection to the Service Bus. Depending on the number of users, connection charges could start to rack up although the number of users can scale up or down drastically without any other hardware or software costs.

This solution would fit into the quick timeline of this solution delivery.

Solution operation aspects

As the Service Bus is hosted in the cloud and supported by Microsoft, very little support and maintenance is needed by the Virtual Cow Media staff. They would need to develop a solution to enable the endpoints in home units. This could be added as part of the nightly polling process to trigger the move to real-time endpoints.

As the cloud can flex the connections nearly instantly from few to thousands, adding and removing new customers would not require any additional hardware or bandwidth on the Virtual Cow Media's home office.

Organizational aspects

Given the skilled IT staff at Virtual Cow Media, the supported Microsoft cloud, and the simplicity of the solution, the staff would have no problems supporting this solution. While using the cloud is still a forward thinking approach, the benefits in this case far outweigh the risks.

Solution evaluation

Design	Delivery	Operations	Organization
👍	👍	👍	👍

Architecture selection

Let's look at how these candidate architecture technologies stack up against each other.

We can break down the primary benefits and risks of each choice as follows:

.NET polling	
Benefits	**Risks**
• Extends on the existing approach used today	• Extensive use of customer and home office network resources
• Short production time as the hardware and services are already in place	• Latency in remote user recording events via the website

BizTalk Server	
Benefits	**Risks**
• Extensive routing ability using publish and subscribe	• Required new software and hardware
• Reliable messaging	• Endpoint maintenance
• Variety of endpoint choices if needed for future offerings	• Using a VPN could tie up customer network traffic
	• Ramp-up time is needed to be effective with BizTalk Server

AppFabric	
Benefits	**Risks**
• No additional software licenses or hardware costs — pay as you grow model	• New, unproven technology in the cloud
• Elastic so customers can be added and be removed easily	• Costs could be high over a long term
• Hosted solution meaning less support for onsite staff	• Broadcasting could be unreliable resulting in missed messages

While reviewing the use case and the previous table, we can call out a clear winner. The driving factors are: no investment in additional hardware and software, the flexibility of the cloud, and ability to easily cross network boundaries.

For this scenario, AppFabric is the best choice.

The solution would look as shown in the following figure:

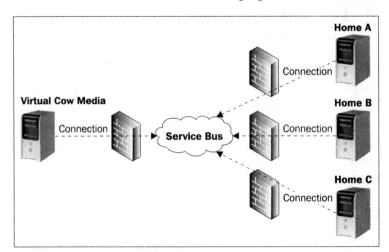

This outlines the use of the Service Bus as the message broker for all communication between the endpoints. As each of the endpoints connect to the Service Bus, a secured, tunneled connection is established. This is all accomplished in the cloud with few changes to existing code. Let us take a closer look at this solution in the next section.

Building the solution

This solution will take an existing WCF service and a client application and update them to use the Windows Azure Platform AppFabric Service Bus. The Service Bus will allow for asynchronous message broadcasting to all clients or synchronous point-to-point communication to the same endpoint. This is all done using Microsoft's highly available, scalable infrastructure.

The WCF binding configurations are made available after installing the AppFabric SDK. The SDK provides a collection of six bindings used for communication with the Service Bus. The corresponding WCF binding is listed as well (if applicable).

Service Bus WCF bindings are as follows:

- `BasicHttpRelayBinding` (`BasicHttpBinding`): General purpose, SOAP 1.1
- `WebHttpRelayBinding` (`WebHttpBinding`): Non-SOAP, REST-ful
- `WS2007HttpRelayBinding` (`WS2007HttpBinding`): Provides support for WS-*
- `NetTcpRelayBinding` (`NetTcpBinding`): TCP, Service Bus-to-Service Bus communication
- `NetOnewayRelayBinding` (Service Bus specific): One-way only
- `NetEventRelayBinding` (Service Bus specific): Message broadcasting

The two bindings used in the following solution are `NetOnewayRelayBinding` and `NetEventRelayBinding`. These are specific to the Service Bus. Be aware that the maximum payload size for Service Bus messages is around 60 KB each and message delivery to all endpoints in the `NetEventRelayBinding` is not guaranteed.

In this section the following tasks will be accomplished:

1. Signing-up for a Microsoft Windows Azure Platform AppFabric Account.
2. Creating a WCF service to listen for a broadcast message securely on the Service Bus.
3. Creating a WCF service to listen for a unique update message and return a response securely on the Service Bus.

The solution assumes the following software is already installed:

- Visual Studio 2008 with Service Pack 1
- Windows Azure platform AppFabric SDK V1.0 — April update

Signing up for an Azure AppFabric account

1. Go to `http://www.microsoft.com/windowsazure/appfabric/`.

2. Look for the **Sign Up Now** link on the right side.

3. Review the packages and specials available and select the package that is best for you.

4. Enter your Windows Live credentials.

5. Enter your profile information including your address and phone number on the next few screens.

6. Review your purchase options. In this case, Microsoft has a special offer for my region. Select **Buy Now**.

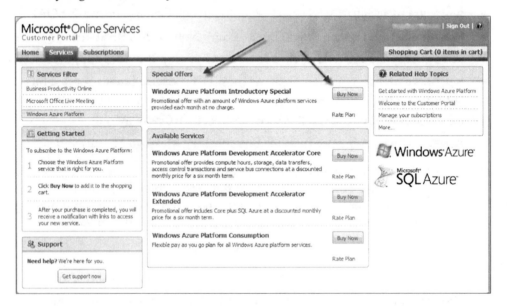

7. Read the terms and conditions, check the checkbox, and select **Check Out**.

8. If you have an existing credit card on file, you can use that. Otherwise, enter a new credit card. Click on **Next**.

9. Review and agree to the service agreement. Click on **I Accept**.

10. Review your purchase one last time. Click on **Complete Order**.

11. Note your confirmation number on the next page. Proceed with the activation.

12. Give your subscription a meaningful name. In this case, the name `AppliedArchitecture.Chapter11.ServiceBus` is used to identify this subscription.

13. Confirm the service administrator details and review the next few screens.

14. An e-mail confirmation will be sent to the administrator once the service is available for use. This can take up to 24 hours.

15. Click on the AppFabric link in the e-mail or navigate to `https://appfabric.azure.com`. This page will list the available projects for AppFabric.

16. Click on the created project, `AppliedArchitecture.Chapter11.ServiceBus`, unless you named it otherwise.

17. Click on the **Add Service Namespace**. A service namespace is a globally unique name to represent a Service Bus and access control solution.

18. Enter a **Service Namespace**. Something like: `AppliedArchitecture-Chapter11-<Initials or ZipCode or PhoneNumber>`. This sample uses `AppliedArchitecture-Chapter11`.

19. Set the **Region** closest to you. This sample uses **United States (North/Central)**.

20. Set the **ServiceBus Connection Packs**. This sample uses **0**. If your application will use a known number of connections, it is best to purchase a connection pack. Rates are about 50 percent less through the connection pack.

21. The end result should look like the following screenshot:

Create New Service Namespace

A Service Namespace represents a namespace for Service Bus and Access Control.

For example Contoso Corp might have a Service Namespace called 'contoso-prod':
sb://**contoso-prod**.servicebus.windows.net

Service Namespace
This is a globally unique string which is used in your code and configuration. A Service Namespace must be 6-50 characters long and may only contain alphanumeric characters (a-z,0-9) or dashes (-). Additionally the first and last characters may not be dashes (-).

AppliedArchitecture-Chapter   Validate Name ⬅
The Service Namespace is valid and available.

Region
Please select a region for your Service Namespace to run in.

United States (North/Central)   ▼

ServiceBus Connection Packs
Please indicate the size of the Connection Pack for this service namespace:

0 Connections   ▼

You will be charged for these connections even if you don't use them, but the charge is substantially lower than the charge for Individual Connections! You can use more connections than the size of the Connection Pack, but you will be charged for the additional connections at the higher rate for Individual Connections. Please refer to the AppFabric pricing information for details.

22. In a moment, the page will refresh and an **Active** status will be shown next to the newly created project. Click on the service namespace.

23. This displays all the connection information for this account. The **Registry URL**—in this case it is `https://appliedarchitecture-chapter11.servicebus.windows.net/`—and the default issuer name and key. This information will be needed to have services listen and send messages to the Service Bus.

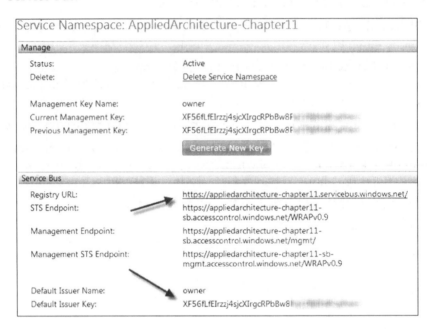

Create the WCF services to listen on the Service Bus

1. Launch Visual Studio.NET 2008 and open the `AppliedArchitecture.Chapter11.ServiceBus.sln` in the `<Installation Directory>\Chapter11\Begin` folder.

2. This solution contains the following projects:
    ° `Chapter11.ServiceBus.HomeA`: Service application to simulate a home DVR device. This code needs to be updated to listen to the Service Bus.

    ° `Chapter11.ServiceBus.HomeB`: Service application to simulate a home DVR device. This code is complete but needs to be updated to listen to the Service Bus.

    ◦   `Chapter11.ServiceBus.HomeC`: Service application to simulate a home DVR device. This code is complete but needs to be updated to listen to the Service Bus.

    ◦   `Chapter11.ServiceBus.Tester`: Client application to send broadcast and point-to-point messages to the Service Bus. This needs to be updated to connect to the Service Bus.

3. Open the `Program.cs` file in the `Chapter11.ServiceBus.HomeA` project.

4. Review the two existing contracts and service implementations. The `QuickScheduleUpdate` implements a one-way service to receive a broadcast message and `RecordingScheduleUpdate` is a request-response service to receive a point-to-point message and return a response.

5. The code to host the console services is missing. Add the following code to the `Main` method:

```
Console.WriteLine("Starting Home A");
// Create the Host for the QuickScheduleUpdate and
RecordingScheduleUpdate
ServiceHost hostQuickScheduleUpdate = new
ServiceHost(typeof(ScheduleUpdate));
ServiceHost hostRecordingScheduleUpdate = new
ServiceHost(typeof(SyncScheduleUpdate));
// Open Each Host on the Service
BushostQuickScheduleUpdate.Open();
hostRecordingScheduleUpdate.Open();
Console.WriteLine("Listening on the Service Bus for Home A");
Console.WriteLine("Press ENTER to exit");
Console.ReadLine();
// Close the HostshostQuickScheduleUpdate.Close();
hostRecordingScheduleUpdate.Close();
```

6. As it stands now, this is just a basic WCF service with service contracts, implantation logic, and a host. An `App.config` file is needed to outline the communication details for these services. The existing `App.config` has missing key information.

7. Inside the `App.config` file, each service and endpoint needs to be defined. Create a `Service` node for each service. Inside the service, create an endpoint and set the address, behavior configuration, binding, and contract.

8. The address is the Service Bus project name created in the first section. Ensure you use the `sb://` address prefix rather than the `https://`. Add namespace components after the assigned namespace to differentiate the two service endpoints as shown in the code:

   ○ The Schedule Update service should use the `netEventRelayBinding` and `QuickScheduleUpdate` as the added namespace.

   ○ The Sync Schedule Update service should use the `netTcpRelayBinding` and `ScheduleUpdate/HomeA` as the added namespace.

9. Both services should use the same binding configuration. For now, just call it `serviceBusCredentials`.

10. The following is how the setting should look in the `App.config` file:

```
<service
      name="AppliedArchitecture.Chapter11.
          ServiceBus.HomeA.ScheduleUpdate">
  <endpoint address="sb://appliedarchitecture-chapter11-<Your
        Info Here>.servicebus.windows.net/QuickScheduleUpdate"
        behaviorConfiguration="serviceBusCredentials"
        binding="netEventRelayBinding"
        contract="AppliedArchitecture.Chapter11
            ServiceBus.HomeA.IScheduleUpdate"/>
</service>
<service
      name="AppliedArchitecture.Chapter11.
          ServiceBus.HomeA.SyncScheduleUpdate">
  <endpoint address="sb://appliedarchitecture-chapter11-<Your Info
      Here>.servicebus.windows.net/ScheduleUpdate/HomeA"
      behaviorConfiguration="serviceBusCredentials"
      binding="netTcpRelayBinding"
      contract="AppliedArchitecture.Chapter11.
          ServiceBus.HomeA.ISyncScheduleUpdate"/>
</service>
```

11. One of the key benefits of the Service Bus is the ability to securely connect to the bus. In order to do so, an issuer name and issuer secret key are needed. This is found on the namespace details page of the Azure portal from the first section.

12. Create the behavior with your credentials as shown:

```
<behavior name="serviceBusCredentials">
  <transportClientEndpointBehavior
      credentialType="SharedSecret">
```

```
<clientCredentials>
  <sharedSecret issuerName="owner" issuerSecret="<Your Key
                                             Here>"/>
</clientCredentials>
</transportClientEndpointBehavior>
</behavior>
```

13. This completes HomeA. The App.config files for HomeB and HomeC need to be updated with your Service Bus namespace and secret key.

14. Once the individual services are complete, the **Tester** application needs to be updated. All the service names and endpoints are already set up. Update the endpoint address and the behavior secret key just like in the previous steps.

15. We are ready to test the solution. Make sure you review the Microsoft Platform AppFabric Billing to understand the impact of connecting to the Service Bus. Currently, the default package includes two connections. This solution uses four. To avoid additional charges, only use the **Client** and a single **Home** test application.

16. By default, the solution is set up to start all three services and the client. Simply press *F5*. Three console application windows will open along with the test client as shown in the following screenshot:

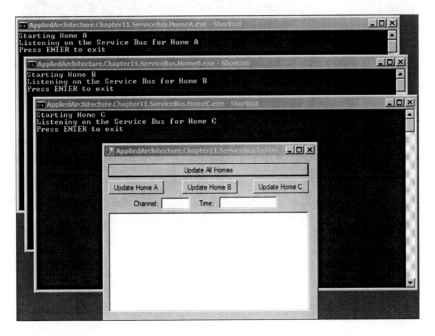

17. Set a **Channel** and **Time**. Click on **Update All Homes** button at the top. Notice each console windows get an update message.

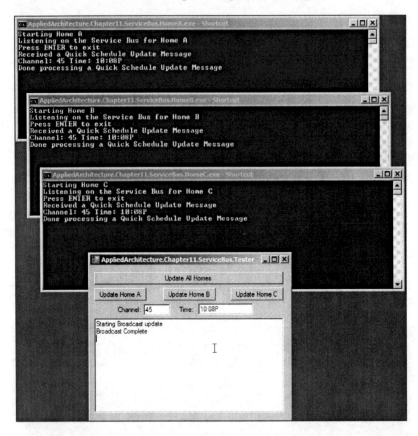

18. Set a **Channel** and **Time**. Click on **Update Home C**. Notice only the console window for Home C gets the update and a response is returned to the client.

Summary

In this chapter, we took a look at various ways to update remote systems using .NET Polling, BizTalk, or the Windows Azure Platform AppFabric Service Bus. For this use case, using the Service Bus was the right decision, having been given the requirements of Virtual Cow Media. The Service Bus is elastic, flexible, and has all the features required by a company like Virtual Cow Media.

12
Debatching Bulk Data

Debatching data is the process of turning one huge pile of data into many small piles of data.

Why is it better to shovel one ton of data using two thousand, one pound shovels instead of one big load from a huge power shovel? After all, large commercial databases and the attendant bulk loader or SQL Loader programs are designed to do just that: insert huge loads of data in a single shot.

The bulk load approach works under certain tightly constrained circumstances. They are as follows:

1. The "bulk" data comes to you already matching the table structure of the destination system. Of course, this may mean that it was debatched before it gets to your system.
2. The destination system can accept some, potentially significant, error rate when individual rows fail to load.
3. There are no updates or deletes, just inserts.
4. Your destination system can handle bulk loads. Certain systems (for example, some legacy medical systems or other proprietary systems) cannot handle bulk operations.

As the vast majority of data transfer situations will not meet these criteria, we must consider various options. First, one must consider which side of the database event horizon one should perform these tasks. One could, for example, simply dump an entire large file into a staging table on SQL Server, and then debatch using SQL to move the data to the "permanent" tables. There are, of course, multiple tools for debatching large bulk data loads including BizTalk Server and SQL Server Integration Services (SSIS). One can use such tools to break up large batches of data, manipulate it as needed, and send it on to its next reincarnation (for example, into an API, a relational database, or a text file). In this chapter, we will take a look at options for processing large data sets.

Use case

Big Box Stores owns and operates retail chains that include huge Big Box warehouse stores, large retail operations in groceries and general department stores and small convenience stores that sell gasoline, beverages, and fast food. The company has added brands and stores over the past few years through a series of mergers. Each brand has its own unique point of sale system. The stores operate in the United States, Canada, Mexico, and Western Europe.

The loss prevention department has noticed that a number of store sales and clerical staff are helping themselves to "five-finger bonuses." The staff members use various ruses to take money from cash registers, obtain goods without paying for them, or otherwise embezzle money or steal goods from Big Box. These patterns typically unfold over periods of several days or weeks. For example, employees will make purchases using their employee discount at the store where they work, then return the product for full price at another store where they are not known or they have an accomplice return the goods to the employee for a full refund.

The various methods used to steal from Big Box fall into these recognized patterns and a good deal of this theft can be uncovered by analyzing patterns of sales transactions. Standard ETL techniques will be used to import data concerning the stores, products, and employees to a database where we can analyze these patterns and detect employee theft.

We have been tasked with designing a system that will import comma-delimited files exported by the point of sales (POS) systems into a SQL Server database that will then perform the analysis. Data concerning each sale will be sent from each of the point of sale systems. The files will hold all or part of the prior day's sales and will range from 30,000 to over 2.5 million rows of data per file. For stores that have "regular" business hours, files will become available approximately one hour after the stores close. This time will vary based on the day of the week and the time of year. During "normal" operations, stores typically close at 9:00 PM local time. During certain peak shopping periods (for example, Christmas or local holiday periods) stores remain open until midnight, local time. Convenience stores are opened 24 hours per day, 7 days per week. Data will be sent for these stores after the POS system has closed the books on the prior day, typically at 1:00 AM local time.

The POS systems can be extended to periodically expose "final" sales to the system throughout the business day via a web service. The impact of using this method during a peak sales period is unknown, and performance of the POS may degrade. A full day's data may also be extracted from the POS system in the comma-delimited format discussed as follows. The web service would expose the data using the natural hierarchy of "sales header" and "sales detail."

All data must be loaded and available to the loss prevention department by 9 AM CET for European stores and 9 AM EST for North American stores. It should be noted that the different POS use different data types to identify stores, employees, products, and sales transactions. The load job must account for this and properly relate the data from the store to the master data loaded in a separate application.

The data will be sent in two comma-delimited files, one containing the "Sales Header" data and one containing the sales details. The data will be in the following format:

Sales Header

```
SalesID, StoreID, EmployeeID, EmployeeFirstName, EmployeeLastName,
RegisterID, RegisterLocation, storeAddress, StoreCity, StoreProvince,
StorePostalCode, CustomerID, CustomerFirstName, CustomerLastName,
CustomerPostalCode, Date, Time, Method of Payment, CreditCardNumber,
TotalSales, Amount Tendered, Change, PriorSalesID, Return
```

Sales Detail

```
SalesID, ProductID, Quantity, markedPrice, ActualPrice, ReturnItem,
DiscountCode, DiscountPercent, DiscountDescription, OriginalPurchaseDate,
OriginalPurchaseStore, OriginalPurchaseSalesID, originalCustomerID,
OriginalFirstName, OriginalLastName, OriginalStoreID, OriginalRegisterID,
OriginalEmployeeID
```

Key requirements

Our mission is to move this data into a data mart that will use a standard star schema for this analysis. Big Box intended to prosecute employees for larceny or theft offences based on evidence this system gathers. Given the legal requirements that evidence gathered through this process must stand up in court, it is vital that this data be correct and loaded with a minimal number of errors or issues.

Additional facts

As is fairly typical, the use case above does not contain information on all of the facts we would need to consider when designing a solution. Every company has operating assumptions that the enterprise takes as a "given" and others we learn through our own involvement with the enterprise. These "facts" are so ingrained into an organization's culture that people may not even recognize the need to explicitly state these requirements.

For example, if a consultant arrives at a company in Denver, CO that only does business in the United States, then he or she can expect that the business language will be English with US spelling. The exact same company in Calgary, doing business in Canada will need both English with British spelling and French. It is doubtful one would ever see such "requirements" stated explicitly, but anyone designing a solution would do well to keep them in mind.

Other facts may be extrapolated or derived from the given requirements. When you are designing a solution you must take these criteria into account as well. It would be at best unwise to design a solution that was beyond the skill set for the IT staff, for example. In this case, it is probably safe to say the following:

Fact or Extrapolation	Reason
Big Box has a very sophisticated IT staff that can handle any advanced and sophisticated technologies.	They are currently handling multiple POS systems on 2 continents and already do sophisticated ETL work from these systems to existing BI systems.
Getting the deliverable "right" is more important than getting it done "fast".	Legal requirements for using data as evidence.
Data must be secure during movement to avoid allegations of evidence tampering.	Legal requirements for using data as evidence.
Some level of operational control and monitoring must be built into the application we will design.	Common courtesy to the Network Operations Center (NOC) staff who will deal with this, if nothing else.

Candidate architectures

We can tackle this problem from multiple angles, so let us take a look at the available options.

Candidate architecture #1–SSIS

First, we will explore the pros and cons of using SSIS for our solution platform.

Solution design aspects

This scenario is the sweet spot for SSIS. SSIS is, first and foremost, an ETL and batch data processing tool. SSIS can easily read multiple files from a network drive and has the tools out of the box that can debatch, either before or after loading to a database.

Nonetheless, we are faced with certain hurdles that will need to be accounted for in our design. We do not control precisely when the POS data will be made available.

There are a number of variables that influence that timing, not the least of which is the potential need for human intervention in closing books for the day and variable times throughout the year and across the globe when a particular store's books will be closed. We need to expect that files will be delivered over a time range.

In some ways this is helpful, as it spreads some of the load over time.

One of the great things about SSIS in this situation is the flexibility it provides. We can load all of the data in a single batch to a staging table then move it (debatch) to its final destinations using SQL, or we can debatch on the application side and load directly to the final tables, or any combination that suits us and the strengths of the development team. SSIS can also be extended to monitor directories and load data when it becomes available. Finally, SSIS integrates easily into NOC monitoring systems and provides the ability to guarantee data security and integrity as required for this application. Moreover, SSIS does not incur any additional licensing costs, as it ships with SQL Server out of the box.

Solution delivery aspects

It is not clear from our use case what depth of experience Big Box staff has with SSIS. However, they certainly have experience with database technologies, SQL queries, and with other advance technologies associated with data transfer and integration, given the size of the enterprise operations. We can reasonably expect them to pick up any unfamiliar technologies quickly and easily.

This application will require some extensions to the typical ETL paradigm. Here data must go through some amount of human intervention through the daily "closing" before it is made available. This will involve tasks such as physically counting cash to make sure it matches the records in the POS system. Any number of factors can accelerate or delay the completion of this task. SSIS will therefore need to monitor the directories where data are delivered to ensure the data is available. Also, we will need to design the system so that it does not attempt to load partially completed files. This is a classic ETL problem with many potential solutions and certainly does not present insurmountable issues.

Solution operations aspects

In this case, we have one vitally important operational requirement; the solution must guarantee data integrity and security so that the data can be used to prosecute thieves or otherwise stand up to evidentiary rules. SSIS and SQL Server 2008 Enterprise Edition can handle these requirements. SQL Server 2008 security and data access auditing features will meet chain of custody requirements and ensure that no data tampering occurred. SSIS can enforce business rules programmatically to ensure the precise and accurate transfer of the data sent by the POS systems.

Many of these requirements will be filled with the design of the database itself. We would use, for example, the data access auditing now available with SQL Server 2008 to monitor who has been working with data. The database would use only Windows-based security, not SQL Server based security. Other steps to harden SQL Server against attack should be taken.

All the previously mentioned features secure the data while at rest. We will need to focus on how to ensure data integrity during the transfer of the data—while the data is in motion. SSIS has logging tools that will be used to monitor unsuccessful data transfers. Moreover, we can extend these tools to ensure either a complete data load or that we will have an explanation for any failure to load. It should be noted that the loss prevention staff is interested in outliers, so they will want to carefully examine data that fails to meet business requirements (and therefore fails to load to our target system) to look for patterns of theft.

Organizational aspects

We understand that Big Box staff has the technical wherewithal to handle this relatively simple extension to existing SQL Server technologies. This is a group of database professionals who deal with multiple stores performing over 2 million transactions per day. They support the POS, financial, inventory, and other systems required to handle this volume on two continents. This is a small step for them in terms of their ability to live with this solution.

Solution evaluation

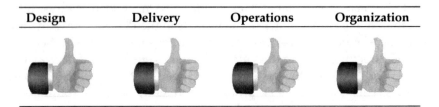

Design	Delivery	Operations	Organization

Candidate architecture #2–BizTalk Server

While not primarily targeted at bulk data solutions, BizTalk Server can parse large inbound data sets, debatch the individual records, and insert them into a target system.

Solution design aspects

The POS systems that provide sales data to the Big Box data hub typically produce comma-delimited files. Using BizTalk Server, we can define the document structure of delimited files and natively accept and parse them. The requirements earlier also stated that the POS systems could be extended to publish a more real-time feed via web services as opposed to the daily file drop of data. This is more in tune with how BizTalk does standard processing (real-time data feeds) and would be a preferred means to distribute data through the BizTalk bus.

BizTalk Server's SQL Server adapter is built to insert a record at a time into a database. This means that the BizTalk solution needs to break apart these large inbound data sets and insert each record individually into the final repository. Messages are debatched automatically in BizTalk via pipeline components and specially defined schemas, but this is a CPU-intensive process. We would want to isolate the servers that receive and parse these data sets so that the high CPU utilization doesn't impede other BizTalk-based solutions from running.

Solution delivery aspects

Big Box leverages SQL Server all across the organization, but does not currently have a BizTalk footprint. This means that they'll need to set up a small infrastructure to host this software platform. They do have developers well-versed in .NET development and have typically shown a penchant for utilizing external consultants to design and implement large enterprise solutions. It would be critical for them to build up a small center of excellence in BizTalk to ensure that maintenance of this application and the creation of new ones can progress seamlessly.

Solution operations aspects

BizTalk Server provides strong operational support through tooling, scripting, and monitoring. If the downstream database becomes unavailable, BizTalk will queue up the messages that have yet to be delivered. This ensures that no sales information gets lost in transit and provides a level of guarantee that the data mart is always accurate.

Given the relatively large sets of data, the operations team will need to configure a fairly robust BizTalk environment, which can handle the CPU-intensive debatching and perform the database inserts in a timely fashion.

Organizational aspects

Big Box would be well served by moving to a more real-time processing solution in the near future. This way, they can do more live analysis and not have to wait until daily intervals to acquire the latest actionable data. A messaging-based solution that relies on BizTalk Server is more in tune with that vision.

However, this is a critical program and speed to market is a necessity. Big Box accepts a high level of risk in procuring a new enterprise software product and getting the environments and resources in place to design, develop, and support solutions built upon it.

Solution evaluation

Design	Delivery	Operations	Organization

Architecture selection

SQL Server and SSIS	
Benefits	**Risks**
• Easily deployed and extensible ETL tool	• Need to build sophisticated error handling systems
• Designed to handle batch processing of large files, exactly the task at hand	
• No additional licensing costs – comes with SQL Server	
• Can be built and maintained by current staff	

BizTalk Server	
Benefits	**Risks**
• Provides for live, real-time analysis	• CPU-intensive processes
• Can leverage BizTalk capability to send events to downstream transactional systems	• High database process overhead
	• Additional licensing and capital costs
• Enterprise-class hosting infrastructure	• Not clear if staff has the skills to support product

When all is said and done, this is exactly the scenario that SSIS was designed to handle, a batch load to a data mart. Moreover, the selection of SSIS entails no additional licensing costs, as might be the case with BizTalk.

Building the solution

This section outlines the construction of a proof-of-concept application that will implement the functionality required for this application. The details of data warehousing, OLAP, and data security each would require large, detailed books in and of themselves. At a minimum, we would suggest you consider studying the following topics:

- Partitioning strategies for data storage and loading
- Compression strategies
- Transparent data encryption
- Data access auditing for PID
- Multi-dimensional data structures
- Encryption strategies for data in motion
- SAN and physical infrastructure design

From a very high level (and shown below), we will be taking data already encrypted on the source system using agreed upon encryption algorithms, decrypting it, debatching it, and loading it into our database, or, as an alternative, loading it into a staging table then debatching it using SQL:

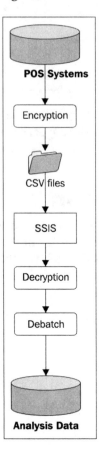

Encryption

We are dealing with people's credit card numbers so we must encrypt this data, particularly if we plan on sending it to a potentially open folder in a .csv format. There are numerous methods for handling encryption, and the determination of which methods to use will depend largely on both data sources and data targets. In this case, we will use simple symmetric key encryption available with SQL Server, mostly because it is easy for purposes of illustration. Moreover, the data will be transferred using internal Big Box networks so we can also rely on network-level security to protect the data. Asymmetrical keys should also be considered here for real-world scenarios.

In order to generate our simple .csv files we created a mock point of sale (POS) database named SourceOfWisdom with two tables for our sales header and sales detail data. To encrypt the data, we first create a master key, then a certificate, and finally a symmetric key.

```
use SourceOfWisdom
go
IF EXISTS(
  SELECT *
    FROM sys.certificates
    WHERE name = N'AppPatternCert'
)
DROP CERTIFICATE AppPatternCert
GO

CREATE MASTER KEY ENCRYPTION BY PASSWORD = 'InY0urDre@ms'; /* Note
Password complexity */
GO
CREATE CERTIFICATE AppPatternCert WITH SUBJECT = 'Key Protection';
GO
CREATE SYMMETRIC KEY DebatchPatternKey WITH
    KEY_SOURCE = 'KeepMeSecret',
    ALGORITHM = AES_256,
    IDENTITY_VALUE = 'ThisIsSecret2'
    ENCRYPTION BY CERTIFICATE AppPatternCert;
GO

-- a simple test for the certificate
OPEN SYMMETRIC KEY DebatchPatternKey
    DECRYPTION BY CERTIFICATE AppPatternCert;
GO
SELECT 'CreditCardNumber',
  encryptbykey(key_guid('DebatchPatternKey'), 'CreditCardNumber' )

GO
```

Target system

As one would expect, we have a target system that does not match our sources. Moreover, we can expect the iron law of BI systems will be strictly enforced here. That law is "no one ever tells the BI staff anything." Psychic abilities are part of the job description. We can expect that there will be changes made to our source systems, or that data will be entered in one system but not in another. We must design our systems accordingly.

Our target schema is shown as follows. You can create this sample database with the accompanying project.

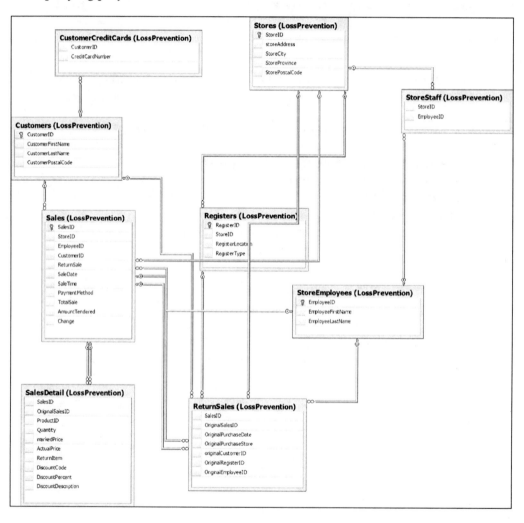

Debatching with SSIS and SQL Server

With our sources and targets defined, we now must decide how we will debatch the data so that it is properly loaded into the target tables. While using SSIS we can decide to leverage the objects that come with SSIS out of the box, or simply load the data into staging tables and use SQL set operations to move the data to target tables.

There is no "right" answer to this issue any more than there is a "right" answer to "which is better, a hammer or a screwdriver?" We have a box full of very useful tools and we use them for their most appropriate tasks. There are some general rules that should be followed.

Set operations should be done with SQL. A set operation is the operation any relational database uses to match data by common characteristics across data sets. Databases are based on set or relational algebra and therefore handle these operations very efficiently.

"Non-set" operations should be handled within the SSIS package, using the objects available or with custom scripts.

If there is a specific object on either system that makes your life easier, use that.

Always default to the system that allows you to write the most efficient code. Generally, this will be where you are most comfortable.

In this case, we have used the SQL Server symmetric key encryption to secure PID. This data is held in the `SalesHeader.csv` file, so we will need to work with this data on the SQL side of things. For purposes of illustration, we will demonstrate debatching the sales detail data on the application side.

We will also make certain assumptions for this illustration that would be risky in real-world applications. First, we will assume that all of data we will be loading is fresh and there are no updates to previously loaded records. Second, we will assume that the source files will not be locked and will be a complete data set when we begin our loading process. There are numerous ways to control for this in the real world, including the use of empty trigger files.

We will create a single SSIS package for extracting the data from the flat files, transforming it, and finally loading it into the appropriate tables in the destination database. The appropriate code is in two separate sequence containers. We will assume a certain amount of familiarity with SSIS here, including the primer information, and not outline every step in the detail one would see in a book dedicated to the product.

Debatching with SQL

"Debatching" in this context can fit into the "transform" or the "load" phases of any ETL job. Here we will take one of our source batches of data, load it as a single batch into a staging table, then "debatch" using SQL statements.

You will need a staging table on your target database for this solution. We will be doing a significant amount of our transformation and loading using SQL, and this is a fast way to get the data where we can use SQL. Note that we also create a storage schema. Long term, this schema will allow storage flexibility by allowing us to manipulate which physical storage devices hold a particular schema. The table can be created with the following script:

```
CREATE SCHEMA staging AUTHORIZATION dbo
GO

CREATE TABLE staging.SalesHeaderSource(
    SalesID int  NULL,
    StoreID int NULL,
    storeAddress nvarchar(75) NULL,
    StoreCity nvarchar(50) NULL,
    StoreProvince nvarchar(2) NULL,
    StorePostalCode nvarchar(5) NULL,
    EmployeeID int NULL,
    EmployeeFirstName nvarchar(25) NULL,
    EmployeeLastName nvarchar(25) NULL,
    RegisterID int NULL,
    RegisterLocation nvarchar(10) NULL,
    RegisterType nvarchar(30) NULL,
    DateOfSale nvarchar(50) NULL,
    TimeofSale nvarchar(25) NULL,
    Method_of_Payment nvarchar(25) NULL,
    CreditCardNumber nvarchar(max) NULL,
    CustomerID nvarchar(max) NULL,
    CustomerFirstName nvarchar(max) NULL,
    CustomerLastName nvarchar(max) NULL,
    CustomerPostalCode nvarchar(max) NULL,
    TotalSales numeric(9, 2) NULL,
    AmountTendered numeric(9, 2) NULL,
    Change numeric(9, 2) NULL,
    PriorSalesID nvarchar(76) NULL,
    ReturnTrans NVARCHAR(2) NULL
)
GO
```

Start an SSIS project in Visual Studio, rename the default package to debatch.dtsx, then drag a sequence container from the tool box to the package. Rename the sequence container "Load Header" or any similar descriptive term that floats your boat. Place an execute SQL Task (named "prep staging table" for our example), a data flow task (named "Load Staging Table" for our example), and a second execute SQL task (named "Cleanse Return Data"). These three steps will handle our staging table load.

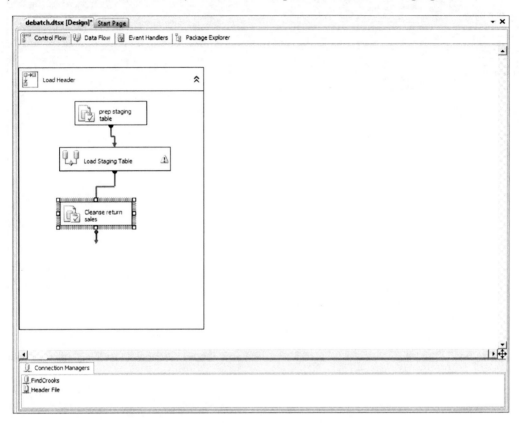

You should also note the creation of connection managers for both our source CSV file and our target database.

Our data flow task will take data from our `.csv` file—which will, of course, be in ASCII—convert the data to the appropriate data type, and load it into the staging table.

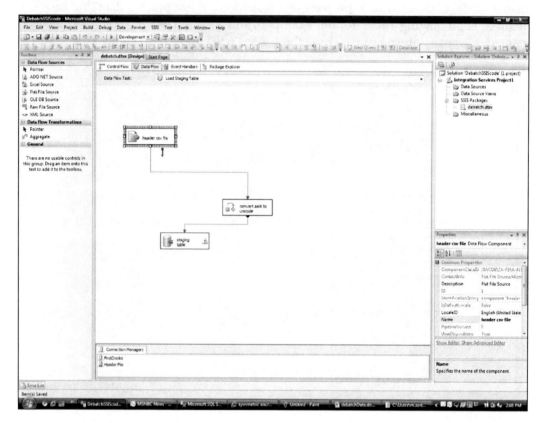

The .csv file does not have column names in the first row. For ease of coding and because we mere mortals cannot remember the names of fields by a numeric designation, we will need to go into the source connection manager and rename our columns.

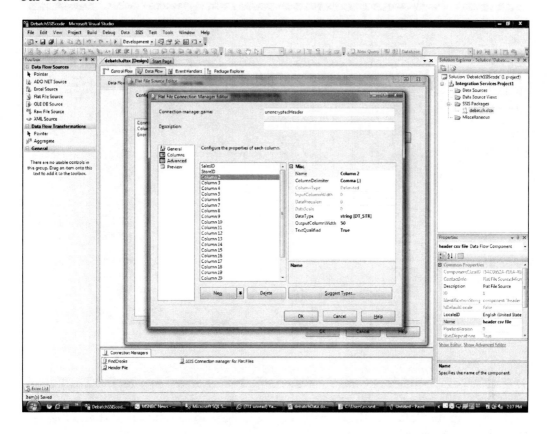

Mapping these column names to the target field in the database will make your life easier in the long term.

Next, we will need to convert our ASCII data to the appropriate data types. Many of us got spoiled by earlier versions of SQL Server doing ASCII to Unicode conversions for us under the covers. You must make this explicit with SSIS.

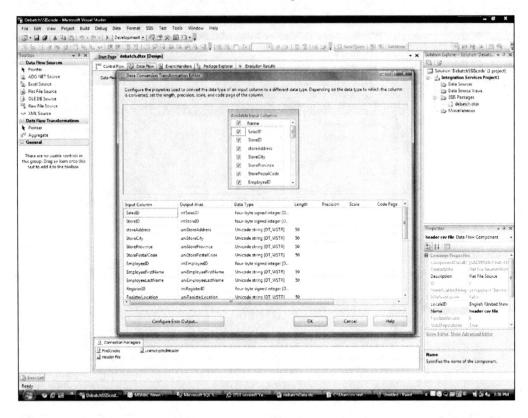

Next, we map the data into the correct staging table fields as shown next and the data will load to staging.

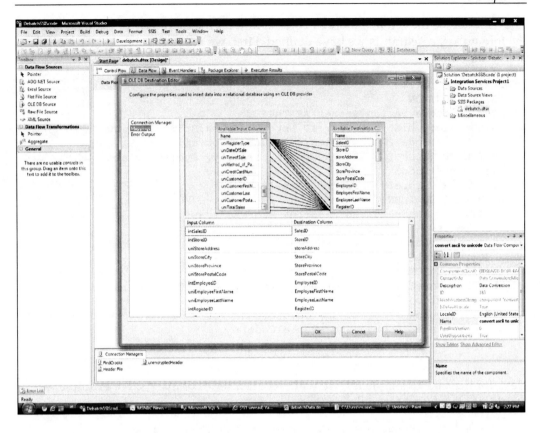

We want to make sure we have the correct values, particularly for data that comes from the source as a null. Often SSIS will treat this as a string and load the word "null" instead of a null value. We therefore perform an execute SQL task that simply executes the following:

```
UPDATE staging.SalesHeaderSource SET PriorSalesID = null WHERE
ISNUMERIC(PriorSalesID) = 0
GO
UPDATE staging.SalesHeaderSource SET ReturnTrans = 0
WHERE ISNUMERIC(ReturnTrans) = 0
GO
```

Now that our data is properly staged, we will move it to the final tables using a series of SQL statements. Recall that we made an admittedly dangerous assumption that applies to this step—all of our data is new. We will illustrate a merge statement, new with SQL Server 2008 and a very convenient alternative to the hoops that we previously jumped through to "upsert" data.

The data will be moved in a manner consistent with the hierarchy of the data and the foreign key constraints we have defined. First, we move the stores data with a merge statement.

```
BEGIN
SET NOCOUNT ON
MERGE LossPrevention.Stores AS TARGET
USING(select distinct StoreID, storeAddress,StoreCity, StoreProvince,
StorePostalCode FROM staging.SalesHeaderSource)
AS SOURCE (StoreID, storeAddress,StoreCity, StoreProvince,
StorePostalCode)
ON (TARGET.StoreID = source.StoreID)
WHEN MATCHED THEN
UPDATE SET storeAddress = source.storeAddress,
  StoreCity = source.StoreCity,
  StoreProvince = source.StoreProvince,
  StorePostalCode = source.StorePostalCode
WHEN NOT MATCHED THEN
INSERT (StoreID, storeAddress,StoreCity, StoreProvince,
StorePostalCode)
VALUES (source.StoreID, source.storeAddress, source.StoreCity, source.
StoreProvince, source.StorePostalCode);
END;
GO
```

Next, for the sake of simplicity, we will execute a series of inserts. For example, we would use this insert for registers:

```
INSERT INTO [FindCrooks].[LossPrevention].[Registers]
            ([RegisterID]
            ,[StoreID]
            ,[RegisterLocation]
            ,[RegisterType])
    (
     select distinct
    RegisterID, StoreID, RegisterLocation, RegisterType
    FROM
    staging.SalesHeaderSource
    )
  GO
```

The balance of the inserts may be found in the accompanying code.

Of course, all of the merge and insert statements can be placed within stored procedures and executed there.

Here, we have taken a large "batch" of data and broken it apart (debatched) using SQL statements.

Debatch with SSIS

Here, we will start once again with a data flow task; however, after bringing the data into the SSIS process we will debatch within that process, rather than on the database. Once again, drag a sequence container onto the package and label it "Load Details". Next, drag a data flow task into the sequence container and label it "get details".

As in the earlier data flow, drag a flat file source into the data flow. You will need a new connection object to the details CSV file and, as before, you should rename the columns to make them human readable.

We will illustrate the loading of two tables, the "SalesDetail" and "ReturnSales" tables, using an SSIS multicast object.

The first issue we encounter is that our source system has used the word "Null" for null values. SSIS interprets this value as a string holding the word "null" so we will need to deal with this issue, particularly on the numeric and integer value columns. Add a derived columns object and connect it to the flat-file source. For illustration, we will add a new column for the "Original Customer ID" value by substituting an empty string for the word "Null" and we will replace the "Null" in the "DiscountPercent" field with "0" as illustrated next. Note that this is a simple "REPLACE" function.

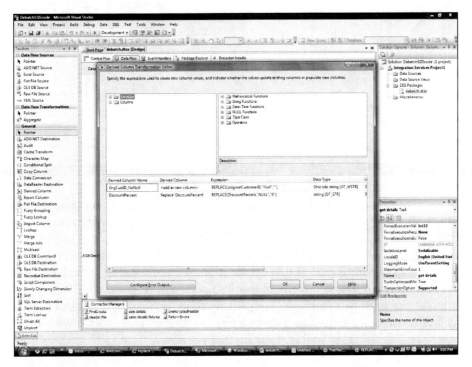

We must then perform our data type conversions, as we did earlier, converting ASCII to Unicode and strings to the appropriate numeric or integer types, as required. In order to preserve relational integrity, we will need to get the store identifier, along with other specific data that was provided in the sales header file. For this, drag a lookup transformation onto the data flow. In the data transformation stage, we will have already converted the sales ID to a four byte signed integer data type. This will allow us to relate the sales header data to the sales detail data in an accurate manner.

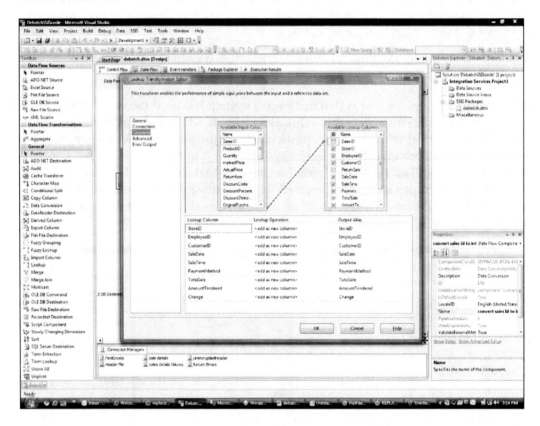

We will be sending our data to two separate tables. Drag a multicast task onto the flow. This will allow you to send duplicate datasets to multiple destinations. For you *Matrix* fans, think of multicasts as the agent Smith of ETL. As you can see from the illustration shown next, we simply send this to the OLEDB destinations using fast loads for the tables. Recall that in this application, we are looking for sales that do not meet certain rules. These require closer inspection as they may indicate employee theft or customer theft (for example, shoplifting then "returning" the item for a full refund). In this case, we send this data to a flat file. In the "real world" we would send this to an "alerts" table to flag it for further review.

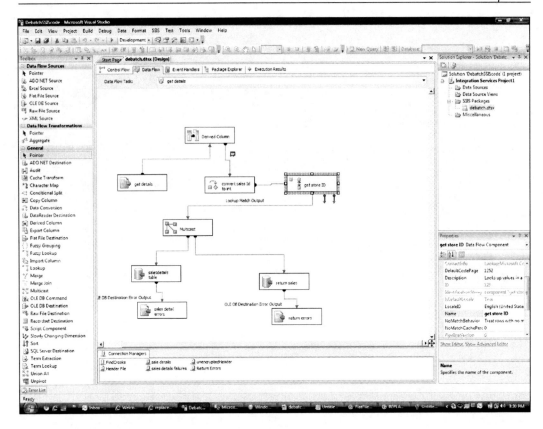

Summary

Here we have three powerful tools for data movement, SSIS, Microsoft Sync Framework, and SQL Server Service Broker that can handle the data movement, master data management, and data governance needs of a variety of organizations and in a variety of business circumstances. The tools can be used in a variety of combinations to get data where it needs to be.

13
Complex Event Processing

Every day, business users and IT professionals acquire information by running reports against their business data. However, as organizations require more agility and crave the ability to make more timely decisions, we find that traditional analytical methods are insufficient. In this chapter, we will discuss how to correlate different high-volume streams of data and uncover previously undetected business insight in real time.

Use case

Watson Media Properties is a rapidly expanding network of websites, which sell objects (such as attire, key chains, and so on) under the "Screaming" brand. Their initial website, "Screaming Pets" was a viral sensation as hundreds, then thousands, and then tens of thousands of users flocked to the site to pick up irreverent bandanas, bumper stickers, and toys for their pet animals. Thereafter, "Screaming Geeks" was launched and now the company has plans to unleash their most anticipated property yet— "Screaming Fans".

As Watson Media grows, they have become hyper-sensitive to customer experience and establishing deep loyalty and affection to the brand. However, their rapid growth has meant that they are constantly adding hardware to their existing data centers, and occasionally experience performance slowdowns on the site. A series of month-end reports has shown a rise in the percentage of site visitors who populate a shopping cart with items and eventually abandon their cart. The marketing director is concerned that customers who experience performance problems on the website during their shopping experience eventually get frustrated and decide to leave the site before completing their purchase. This deprives Watson Media of revenue, but more importantly, hurts the brand and impacts long-term customer perception.

While some analytics have been run on the correlation between site performance and cart abandonment, the Watson team is more concerned with how to quickly re-engage customers who have just left the site after experiencing hiccups. Running reports at the end of the month, or even the end of the day, is too late to discover problems and try to win back the customer's business. Watson Media is looking for a way to immediately reach out to customers who abandoned the site in the midst of an ongoing performance problem. Ideally, if there are more than four timed-out requests in any one minute period throughout the day (which indicates that there may be a growing problem in the data center), then any customer who abandons their cart during that particular time window should be notified that they will receive a 15 percent discount on their cart if they return and complete their purchase.

Watson Media has grown organically as a company and therefore has a fairly homogenous set of core technologies. Their websites are built on ASP.NET, and they have numerous .NET developers on staff. Their primary database platform is SQL Server, but they have a number of commercial line-of-business applications that leverage Oracle databases. As a result of rapid growth of the organization, software purchases are often done in a best-of-breed manner, instead of building or buying technology that is cohesively integrated. Thus, early on, the IT director made an investment in BizTalk Server to ensure that they had a central integration bus that could tie their disparate technologies and external partners together.

Key requirements

The key requirements are as follows:

- Analyze user actions in near real time to discover behavior and re-engage users who face interruptions during the purchase process.
- Identify short-term trends in server performance.
- Connect to multiple sources of data events and correlate events across sources.

Additional facts

There are some additional details gathered after the initial use case was shared with the technical team. These include the following:

1. The original website, Screaming Pets, receives nearly 245,000 unique visitors per day. The follow-up site, Screaming Geeks, averages about 39,000 unique visitors per day. Each site has proved to be fairly sticky with web sessions typically lasting for over 15 minutes and producing dozens of click activities for users.

2. This solution is not meant to be the primary processor of transactional data; rather, it should pull observational events for the purpose of inspecting and responding to customer behavior. Therefore, the output of this event processing solution is a notification to a Watson Media customer service representative (or more preferably, an automated e-mail) and no communication with back-office processing systems is expected.

3. The client is looking for a flexible solution that can talk to a variety of source systems so that they can extract events from transactional systems, logs, and other sources of business events.

4. Time windows are important to this solution because Watson Media does not want to be randomly handing out discounts, or misreading temporary glitches as broad system instability. However, this is a nice-to-have as the most important thing is to re-engage customers, even if this means sending out discounts to casual users who simply left the site for other reasons.

5. Speed is arguably more important than reliability, in the sense that Watson Media wants to quickly re-acquire these departed visitors, and would be willing to let a few visitors slip through the cracks if it meant a leaner solution.

Pattern description

This solution calls for an **event-driven architecture (EDA)** and complex event processing across independent sets of data. When you leverage an event-driven interaction (versus time/batch-oriented interactions, or request-driven interactions), you expect systems to produce events as they occur and distribute them in an asynchronous fashion. An EDA lets an organization respond quickly to opportunities or threats to the business, reduces latency of business processes, and improves the overall availability of strategic information.

A well-built event processing engine will act as an efficient intermediary that filters out noise and amplifies events that demand attention. Such an engine also may transform the raw events into more canonical formats, enrich events with reference or lookup data, or even create entirely new events based on detected patterns. Ideally, the engine can also reorder out-of-sequence events, perform aggregations (for example, count, produce averages, and so on) and receive events from a variety of source systems and devices.

One can do simple event stream processing where conditions are evaluated against the data in a particular stream, or one can invest in **complex event processing** (**CEP**). CEP is a way of extracting insight from a number of distinct business events through correlation across data streams and then emitting complex events that can be acted upon. The queries leveraged by a CEP engine are where institutional knowledge is turned into rich pattern definitions. However, do not mistake CEP for a data mining activity. With the CEP model, you establish up front what you are looking for by defining queries that match, aggregate, or filter data across streams. In this case, the data comes to the questions rather than the questions coming to the data.

What Watson Media is looking to do is a close fit for CEP. They have what are typically independent sets of data (server logs/administrative events and user interaction events) with an intersection established between them so that they can achieve a business objective: establishing brand loyalty and demonstrating superior customer service during a period of growth. A key point of what they need is the ability to immediately act upon detection of the complex event so that they can rapidly woo back their disheartened customer. An EDA with complex pattern matching can help them quickly identify and respond to customer behavior by improving the availability of information.

Candidate architectures

We have two viable choices when looking to extract and process business events as they occur. One of them is the new Microsoft StreamInsight engine and the other is the BizTalk integration bus.

Candidate architecture #1-StreamInsight

SQL Server 2008 R2 includes StreamInsight as a new product for low latency processing of high-volume data streams. Watson Media is looking for a way to parse high volumes of data, perform data analysis in seconds, and join traditionally disconnected data sources. StreamInsight offers an efficient, high performing way to latch onto stream producers and handle a rich set of queries across streams.

Solution design aspects

One of the key requirements of this solution is the ability to quickly and reliably process large volumes of data. We are dealing with very small bits of information (log events, click events, and so on) that need to be rapidly consumed. StreamInsight is built to provide efficient, in-memory data stream processing against standing queries. Given that StreamInsight can handle hundreds of thousands of simultaneous events, we are confident that this solution can scale with our customer's needs.

We also need the ability to plug into a wide variety of sources in order to produce event streams. StreamInsight leverages an adapter model where developers are free to build adapters in a few different styles. Adapters can poll for data or be recipients of pushed data. For this solution, we can build a push-oriented adapter that responds immediately to events produced in the source systems. The fact that StreamInsight does not limit the types of source systems that you can communicate with is a huge plus for our client. Basically, if you can communicate with it through .NET, then you can use its data in StreamInsight.

The StreamInsight architecture enables a clean separation of concerns where you have adapters independent from the queries and the source and target systems. StreamInsight works in a very asynchronous manner, which means that our high-volume stream producers do not have to worry about waiting for the downstream CEP engine to process their events.

Solution delivery aspects

StreamInsight solutions are built using the .NET framework, so Watson Media can easily leverage their existing .NET developers when building CEP solutions. Also, the standing queries in StreamInsight are built using LINQ, which is a relatively new way in the .NET Framework to query a wide variety of data sources in a consistent fashion. Watson Media developers who have written LINQ queries for other applications, will find it very natural to build StreamInsight queries. StreamInsight is more of a toolkit than a packaged product. Therefore, developers can easily install and operate the engine locally before deploying the finished product to a more robust environment. Also, because everything in a StreamInsight solution is contained within .NET projects, we can manage our code using the prescribed Watson Media source control repository.

This is a new product from Microsoft. The community ecosystem is still maturing and developers will have to rely more on the provided documentation and samples than on hoping that internet searches will return relevant answers to problems.

Solution operations aspects

This is an area where the StreamInsight product still has room to grow. While there are no concerns over its ability to handle load and gracefully manage excessive bursts of data, the story around high availability and support tooling remains relatively weak. That is not to say that we cannot peek into how our engine is running. StreamInsight comes with a Management Service API, which returns diagnostic results on queries, adapters, schedulers, and more. You can build an interface that leverages this API or use PowerShell to return diagnostic information. There is also a fairly elegant visual debugging tool where we can monitor events and see how events are processed and aggregated. However, at this point, we do not have a robust administration user interface for managing our StreamInsight environment.

Organizational aspects

The company is looking for something that can fill this immediate need while serving as a viable long-term solution. StreamInsight is a new product so we can only expect it to improve as it matures in the marketplace. It leverages existing developer skill sets and adds no net new licensing cost to the business. StreamInsight also provides a well-thought-out stream processing framework that utilizes a rich multi-threaded design. This would be difficult for Watson Media developers to produce on their own. Instead, they can use their expertise at writing queries and leave the server processing to the StreamInsight engine. That said, developers are required to build their adapters, so we are still asking Watson Media to accept some level of risk and may require outside assistance to build the most robust solution possible.

Solution evaluation

The following table shows the factors to derive a solution:

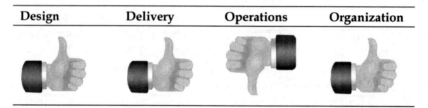

Design	Delivery	Operations	Organization

Candidate architecture #2–BizTalk Server

Watson Media has an existing investment in BizTalk Server, which could be leveraged here to build a solution with mature out-of-the-box components for designing and maintaining a data processing solution.

Solution design aspects

While BizTalk is not widely known for its low latency and high throughput, recent benchmark numbers have shown that a single BizTalk Server machine can process millions of messages per day. Therefore, even though this particular solution has a relatively high volume of event traffic, this should not be prohibitive for BizTalk to handle. Now, one big question is how would BizTalk handle time-window oriented processing? One solution would be to leverage a singleton orchestration that listens for timeout events and only runs for a specific amount of time. However, this would end up being fairly complicated and would cause "zombie message" scenarios in a high throughput situation. So, we would probably have to leverage custom code and temporary database storage to aggregate events over sliding windows. Alternatively, because "windowing" is desired but not a crucial feature, we could build out a simpler solution that filters out unwanted click events and notifies customers via e-mail about their discounts.

BizTalk's rich adapter model makes the receipt of system events quite simple. BizTalk adapters come in "push" or "pull" styles, so we could accommodate systems that either do not naturally publish their events, or systems that are built to natively produce events for interested listeners. In this scenario, we could either leverage a WCF TCP adapter, or build a more loosely-coupled model based upon MSMQ.

The other benefit of using BizTalk and its messaging backbone is that events received from upstream systems could go through other processing within the bus. This might include insertion into other systems, or triggering of rich business processes that should respond to specific events or patterns.

Solution delivery aspects

BizTalk solutions are built primarily in Visual Studio.NET. Watson Media developers are already familiar with constructing these projects and keeping the code in source control systems. Also, given BizTalk's maturity, there are numerous community tools and written descriptions of how to best implement certain patterns. As there is a need to build some fairly robust custom code to handle the window-oriented aggregation requirements, we will expect a longer development cycle than if this were a traditional messaging solution.

Solution operations aspects

Application operations are a strong suit of BizTalk solutions. The product has a clear model for associating application components into a single manageable entity. Packaging and deployment of solutions is relatively straightforward, and the operations dashboard provides a clear view into the state-of-the-server environment. Debugging BizTalk solutions can be challenging, especially as the solution gets more distributed and loosely coupled. However, the BizTalk tooling is usually sufficient for identifying the source of any system or business error.

BizTalk also provides a straightforward way for scaling up and out to grow its ability to handle an increased workload and provide redundancy. Given that this solution is more about rapid data processing than guaranteed delivery or enterprise infrastructure, the rich BizTalk administrative capabilities are useful, but not of paramount importance.

Organizational aspects

Watson Media has already made a strategic move to leverage BizTalk as their integration hub. Building this solution in BizTalk Server would let Watson Media use their existing software, developer, and infrastructure resources and rely on a mature, scalable product. BizTalk solutions are typically fast to market, but given the customized nature of some of the event processing that this solution requires, the company would be facing an extended development time and will have to maintain a fair bit of custom code.

Solution evaluation

The following table shows the technique for solution evaluation:

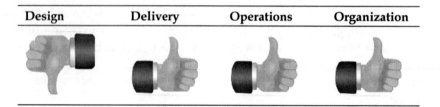

Design	Delivery	Operations	Organization

Architecture selection

Let us look at how these candidate architecture technologies stack up against each other. We can break down the primary benefits and risks of each choice as follows:

StreamInsight	
Benefits:	**Risks:**
• Lightweight, high-throughput product	• Lack of community code/ resources
• Advanced stream processing capabilities including windowing	• Relatively immature hosting model with limited load balancing and failover
• Rich query language	• New product, which means accepting inevitable gaps and likely changes in tooling and capabilities

BizTalk Server	
Benefits:	**Risks:**
• Many out-of-box adapters means connecting to event producers is only a configuration task	• Complicated design needed to accommodate windowing.
• Can leverage BizTalk capability to send events to downstream transactional systems	• BizTalk solutions are made up of multiple components so slight pattern algorithm changes are not easily deployed.
• Enterprise-class hosting infrastructure	• While BizTalk can handle large loads of data, processing tens, if not hundreds of thousands of events per hour could strain the environment.

A key benefit of complex event processing is its ability to reduce data overload by filtering out less important events and highlighting the difference-makers. In a BizTalk-oriented solution, each event message would still have to proceed through the BizTalk infrastructure, potentially introducing significant performance degradation even though much of the traffic is unwanted. StreamInsight is built for doing in-memory processing of events with the LINQ query language. It makes crafting queries a straightforward task. While BizTalk could be bent to try to fit this solution, it would be a less-than-ideal use of the product. We would spend excessive amounts of time customizing and scaling BizTalk, when we could instead be investing in building out the necessary StreamInsight operational components.

For this scenario, StreamInsight is the best choice.

Building the solution

In this solution, we will be constructing an application that embeds the **StreamInsight Server** in-process and pulls data from two separate feeds of data. Specifically, we are designing a very loosely coupled process where we use MSMQ as the medium between the event producers and the StreamInsight CEP engine. Each web server will send its machine event log entries to one MSMQ queue, and all the web click events will be distributed to a different MSMQ queue.

We will build MSMQ adapters for StreamInsight in a way that events are loaded into the CEP server as soon as they hit the queue. Our first LINQ query aggregates server log events per application, and keeps a sum of each type of event over one-minute intervals. Then we will add another LINQ query which uses the first query as input and joins to the click stream events for each website. When a particular website starts acting up, the "abandon cart" events should be amplified and we can make sure to immediately court those departed customers.

This flow is better explained in the following figure:

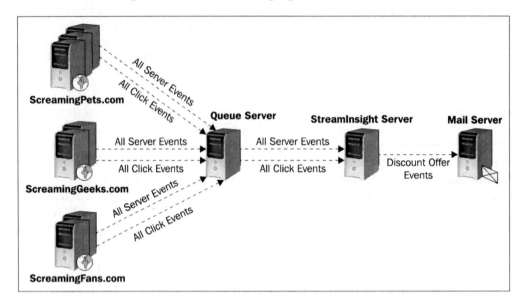

Note that we could also build an "Event Log" adapter to extract server events from each web server. This would be a good choice if we were in an environment where pushing of such data was not possible and pulling was the only viable option. In our case, we have Event Log entries being pushed into the StreamInsight engine, but the architecture does not differ much in the polling-based scenario.

Also, in reality, we would probably be interested in putting our enterprise integration bus at the end of this sequence flow, so that we have the option to fan out the discount offer event to multiple places (such as the marketing department, executive dashboards, e-mail recipients, and so on). The combination of StreamInsight for event receipt/filtering/enrichment and BizTalk for enterprise routing of relevant events is an enticing combination that leverages the best of both platforms. Consider this when constructing EDA solutions in the future.

Set up

Our solution uses MSMQ queues to store events, so we start this solution by creating two queues. Within the Windows Server 2008 Server Manager, expand the **Features** node and expand the **Message Queuing** node. Right-click the **Private Queues** folder and select **New | Private Queue**. Set the queue as transactional and name it `websiteaction`. Create one more transactional queue and name it `websitelogentry`.

A project solution has already been created and can be found in the `<Installation Directory>\Chapter13\Begin` folder. This solution contains two projects: `Chapter13.WatsonMedia.EventTypes`, which holds the three event payload structures used by the solution, and `Chapter13.WatsonMedia.EventPublisher`, which includes the application that populates the two MSMQ queues with website click and server log events. A StreamInsight event payload is simply a .NET object demonstrated as follows:

```
<summary>
/// Event payload definition for web server log events
</summary>
public class WebEventLogEntry
{
    public string SiteName { get; set; }
    public string EntryType { get; set; }
}
```

If you have not done so, ensure that you have installed the StreamInsight application. You can download this from the Microsoft website. Register the application by using your SQL Server 2008 R2 license key.

Creating an adapter

Now we are ready to build the solution. The first thing to create is an MSMQ input adapter. When deciding how to build an adapter, there is a choice of constructing a typed or untyped adapter. A **typed** adapter expects a specific event payload from the source system or device. An **untyped** adapter can accept any event data structure from the source. As you might expect, it takes some effort to build an untyped adapter because the inbound event must be properly serialized to a known event type and published to the StreamInsight engine. Our solution requires us to talk to multiple message queues, so the most efficient strategy is to build a single untyped adapter, and leverage it for each source queue.

We are also going to only build "point" adapters, as each event going through our engine will deal with point-in-time events, as opposed to interval or edge events, which contain a given duration length. For instance, a server log event is a **point event** as it is something that occurs at a single instant in time. An **interval event** has a specific start and end time, and the payload is only valid during that period. An example of this might be gambling odds for a sporting event, where the particular betting line is only valid for a certain time. Finally, an **edge event** is like an interval event where the payload is tied to a specific time window. However, it differs because the end time is unknown when the event is received by the engine. An example here may be an event indicating how long a truck driver has been on the road where the initial event is received when driving begins, but will not close until the driver clocks out.

Now, we can begin building our untyped point adapter as follows:

1. Right-click the **Visual Studio .NET solution** and choose to add a new class library project named `Chapter13.WatsonMedia.MsmqInputEventAdapter`.

2. Right-click the project and choose to add a reference. Include the StreamInsight components **Microsoft.ComplexEventProcessing** and **Microsoft.ComplexEventProcessing.Adapters**. Also add a reference to **System.Messaging**, so that we have access to MSMQ-specific objects. Finally, add a project reference to the `Chapter13.WatsonMedia.EventTypes` project contained within our solution. Recall that this project contains the .NET data objects that represent the event payloads used by StreamInsight.

3. Add a new .NET class file to this project and name it `MsmqInputConfig.cs`. Create a .NET structure in this class that will hold the runtime configuration properties that the CEP server passes into the adapter.

    ```
    public struct MsmqInputConfig
    {
      public string QueueName { get; set; }
      public string QueueDataType { get; set; }
      public List<string> InputFields { get; set; }
    }
    ```

4. Add a new .NET class to this project and name it `MsmqUntypedPointInput.cs`. This class holds the typed StreamInsight adapter for MSMQ.

5. Add the following six `using` statements to the top of the class:

    ```
    using System.Messaging;
    using Microsoft.ComplexEventProcessing;
    using Microsoft.ComplexEventProcessing.Adapters;
    using Chapter13.WatsonMedia.EventTypes;
    using System.Reflection;
    using System.Collections.ObjectModel;
    ```

6. Set the `MsmqUntypedPointInput` class to inherit from the `PointInputAdapter` interface. If we were building a typed adapter, then we would inherit a different object where we would specify a distinct data type as the adapter payload.

```
public class MsmqUntypedPointInput : PointInputAdapter
{
  public override void Resume()
  {
    throw new NotImplementedException();
  }
  public override void Start()
  {
    throw new NotImplementedException();
  }
}
```

7. Add a variable of type `MessageQueue` to the class. This object holds the pointer to the MSMQ queue used by our adapter. We also add variables to hold the base StreamInsight CEP event type (`bindTimeEventType`), a collection of fields contained in our runtime event (`eventFields`), the .NET type of the event (`eventClrType`), and an object used during the read from the active queue (`lockObj`).

```
//pointer to MSMQ polled by the adapter
private MessageQueue targetQueue = null;
//store reference to CEP event
private CepEventType bindTimeEventType;
//holds list of fields in the event
private List<string> eventFields;
//hold the late bound Clr type for the event
private Type eventClrType;
//used for prevent queue read overlap
private object lockObj = new object();
```

8. Now we add the additional constructor for the adapter class, which accepts a configuration information parameter, sets member variable values, instantiates our queue object, and registers the queue's event handler with our adapter.

```
public MsmqUntypedPointInput(MsmqInputConfig configInfo,
        CepEventType eventType, Type eventClrType)
{
  this.bindTimeEventType = eventType;
  this.eventFields = configInfo.InputFields;
```

```
    this.eventClrType = eventClrType;
    try
    {
      //create queue pointer
      targetQueue = new MessageQueue(configInfo.QueueName);
      //set the formatter to know about the message type
      targetQueue.Formatter = new XmlMessageFormatter
                    (new Type[] { eventClrType });
      //register with queue receive event
      targetQueue.ReceiveCompleted +=
    new ReceiveCompletedEventHandler (targetQueue_ReceiveCompleted);
      Console.WriteLine("Listening to the target queue named "
                    + configInfo.QueueName);
    }
    catch (Exception ex)
    {
      Console.WriteLine(ex.Message + ex.StackTrace);
      Console.ReadLine();
    }
  }
  void targetQueue_ReceiveCompleted(object sender,
                              ReceiveCompletedEventArgs e)
  {
    throw new NotImplementedException();
  }
```

9. The next step is to add code that adds a given event to the StreamInsight
    engine. The following code demonstrates how to create a point event and
    add the MSMQ message as its payload. The function takes the untyped object
    that came in from the queue and loops through its properties in order to
    create a StreamInsight event object.

```
private bool enqueueMessage(object queueEvent)
{
  //Ensure that the adapter is in the running state
  if (AdapterState.Stopping == AdapterState)
    Stopped();
  if (AdapterState.Running != AdapterState)
    return false;
  //Allocate a point event to hold the data for
      the incoming message
  //If the event could not be allocated, exit the function
  PointEvent currEvent = CreateInsertEvent();
```

```
if (currEvent == null)
  return false;
try
{
//Map data from the message into a
    CepEventTypeField structure (key/value pairs)
foreach (var pi in eventClrType.GetProperties())
  {
    //see if field in event includes field from typed class
    if (eventFields.Contains(pi.Name))
    {
      //create and add CEP field to event
      CepEventTypeField evtField =
          this.bindTimeEventType.Fields[pi.Name];
      currEvent.SetField(
        evtField.Ordinal,pi.GetValue(queueEvent, null));
    }
  }
//Assign the event timestamp - note; this could also come
    from a message property, or the time the message was
    delivered to the MSMQ queue
  currEvent.StartTime = DateTime.Now;
//If the event cannot be enqueued, release the memory and
    signal that the adapter is ready to process more events
    (through Ready())
  if (EnqueueOperationResult.Full == Enqueue(ref currEvent))
  {
    ReleaseEvent(ref currEvent);
    Ready();
  }
}
catch (Exception ex0)
{
  Console.WriteLine("Error in event enqueue: " +
                    ex0.ToString());
  Console.ReadLine();
}
return true;
}
```

10. Next up, we call this operation from the event handler we registered in the adapter's constructor. The event handler reads the message from the queue, calls the `enqueueMessage` operation we created earlier, and begins listening to the queue for the next message.

```
void targetQueue_ReceiveCompleted(object sender,
                            ReceiveCompletedEventArgs e)
{
  try
  {
    //create object that will hold inbound queue message
    object queueEvent = new object();
    //set the formatter on the inbound message
    e.Message.Formatter = new XmlMessageFormatter
                            (new Type[] { eventClrType });
    //deserialize the queue message
    queueEvent = e.Message.Body;
    // Synchronize enqueue message to avoid overlapping calls
    lock (lockObj)
    {
      // Enqueue the object
      enqueueMessage(queueEvent);
    }
    //start receiving again
    targetQueue.BeginReceive();
  }
  catch (Exception ex)
  {
    Console.WriteLine(ex.ToString());
  Console.ReadLine();
  }
}
```

11. Finally, we have to populate the "start" and "resume" operations that are required by the referenced StreamInsight interface.

```
public override void Start()
{
  //listen for next queue message
  targetQueue.BeginReceive();
}
public override void Resume()
{
```

```
    //listen for next queue message
    targetQueue.BeginReceive();
}
```

12. With the adapter completed, we create a new class file named
    `MsmqUntypedInputFactory.cs`, that returns the correct adapter based on
    the factory input. As we have a single untyped adapter, there is no decision
    logic necessary to instantiate the correct adapter.

13. Add the following three `using` statements to the top of the class:

```
using Microsoft.ComplexEventProcessing;
using Microsoft.ComplexEventProcessing.Adapters;
using System.Reflection;
```

14. Our public class implements the `IInputAdapterFactory` interface that
    requires us to implement the operations used by the StreamInsight engine
    when instantiating event publishing adapters. The code for the required
    `create` operation is included as follows:

```
public class MsmqUntypedInputFactory:
            IInputAdapterFactory<MsmqInputConfig>
{
  public InputAdapterBase Create(MsmqInputConfig
     configInfo, EventShape eventShape, CepEventType cepEventType)
  {
    //grab CLR type from CEP event type to be used by
                 adapter for MSMQ message typing
    CepObject o = (CepObject)cepEventType;
    Type clrType = Type.GetType(o.ShortName);
    //create and return the adapter
    InputAdapterBase adapter = default(InputAdapterBase);
    adapter = new MsmqUntypedPointInput(configInfo,
                 cepEventType, clrType);
    return adapter;
  }
  public void Dispose()
}
```

15. The StreamInsight Server works on application time versus system time. This means that the engine relies on the source applications to publish their application time in order to advance the event timeline. Applications send **Current Time Increment (CTI)** events, which tell the StreamInsight engine that no business events will arrive with a "start time" after the CTI timestamp. This allows the StreamInsight engine to flush any computed events by verifying that the timeline up to now will not change. While developers can explicitly enqueue CTI events to the StreamInsight engine, the easier option is to use the declarative model offered by the StreamInsight API. Update the `MsmqUntypedInputFactory` class declaration by implementing the `IDeclareAdvanceTimeProperties` interface.

```
public class MsmqUntypedInputFactory :
                 IInputAdapterFactory<MsmqInputConfig>,
                 IDeclareAdvanceTimeProperties<MsmqInputConfig>
```

16. This interface requires us to implement a single operation, which the adapter uses to publish CTI events after a given number of business events and with a particular timestamp.

```
public AdapterAdvanceTimeSettingsDeclareAdvanceTimeProperties
(MsmqInputConfig configInfo, EventShape eventShape,
                        CepEventType cepEventType)
{
  var atgs = new AdvanceTimeGenerationSettings
  (1,
 //after how many events should adapter advance time
  TimeSpan.FromTicks(-1),
  true);
  return new AdapterAdvanceTimeSettings(atgs,
                                        AdvanceTimePolicy.Drop);
}
```

17. We are ready to build our embedded server application which registers queries and leverages the adapter we built. StreamInsight also supports a shared infrastructure model where a common instance is provisioned and multiple clients can register and access queries and streams. In this scenario, we are taking advantage of the embedded deployment mode. Right-click the solution and create a new console application named `Chapter13.WatsonMedia.EventProcessingServer`.

18. Before starting to build the server application, right-click our new project and add a reference to the `StreamInsight.Samples.OutputAdapters.Tracer` DLL included in the StreamInsight SDK sample solution. This adapter either prints content to disk, or if the file name is empty, it outputs content to the console. For our purpose, this will serve as our output mechanism.

Also add references to `Chapter13.WatsonMedia.EventTypes`, `Chapter13.WatsonMedia.MsmqInputEventAdapter`, `Microsoft.ComplexEventProcessing`, `Microsoft.ComplexEventProcessing.ManagementService`, and `Microsoft.ComplexEventProcessing.Adapters`.

19. Open the `Program.cs` file and add the following `using` statements to the class. These statements cover CEP querying, business event payloads, our MSMQ adapter, the StreamInsight sample output adapter, console output, and thread synchronization.

```
using Chapter13.WatsonMedia.EventTypes;
using Chapter13.WatsonMedia.MsmqInputEventAdapter;
using StreamInsight.Samples.OutputAdapters.Tracer;
using System.ServiceModel;
using Microsoft.ComplexEventProcessing;
using Microsoft.ComplexEventProcessing.Linq;
using Microsoft.ComplexEventProcessing.ManagementService;
using System.Collections.ObjectModel;
```

20. Before defining the CEP query, let's add two utility operations that produce CEP streams out of our MSMQ adapters. Each operation accepts the `MsmqInputConfig` structure as input and returns a stream.

```
private static CepStream<WebEventLogEntry>
                                    CreateEventLogProducer()
{
  // Configure msmq input adapter
  var inputConfData = new MsmqInputConfig
  {
    QueueName = ".\\Private$\\websitelogentry",
    QueueDataType = "LogEntry",
    InputFields = new List<string>() { "SiteName",
                                        "EntryType" };
  };
  // Get a stream directly from the input adapter factory
  var inputDataStream =
      CepStream<WebEventLogEntry>.Create("LogInput",typeof
      (MsmqUntypedInputFactory), inputConfData, EventShape.Point);
  return inputDataStream;
}
private static CepStream<WebsiteAction>
                                    CreateSiteActionProducer()
{
  // Configure msmq input adapter
  var inputConfData = new MsmqInputConfig
  {
    QueueName = ".\\Private$\\websiteaction",QueueDataType =
        "SiteAction",InputFields = new List<string>() {
        "WebsiteProperty", "CustomerId", "ActionType" },
```

```
};
// Get a stream directly from the input adapter factory
var inputDataStream =CepStream<WebsiteAction>.Create
("SiteInput", typeof(MsmqUntypedInputFactory), inputConfData,
                      EventShape.Point);
return inputDataStream;
}
```

21. We can now populate the `Main()` function where we start up our server and define the queries. Then, we can optionally establish a WCF endpoint for the server that allows for the StreamInsight Debugger to attach to our server and its running queries.

```
//create embedded server
using (Server server = Server.Create("RSEROTER"))
{
  //Create a service host to expose the server's
      endpoint for management purposes
  ServiceHost host = newServiceHost
                (server.CreateManagementService());
  WSHttpBinding binding = new WSHttpBinding
                      (SecurityMode.Message);
  //make sure that your endpoint has the appropriate
      rights established through netsh
  host.AddServiceEndpoint(
  typeof(IManagementService),binding,"http://localhost:8089/
                                StreamInsight/RSEROTER");
  //If you want to run the debugger, start the host
  host.Open();
  //Next, the output adapter configuration needs to be defined.
  //create adapter configuration for output adapter
  var outputConf = new TracerConfig
  {
    DisplayCtiEvents = false,
    SingleLine = true,
    TraceName = "Chap13",
    TraceType = TraceTypeValue.Console
  };
```

22. Next up, we create an application in the server and instantiate our event streams through our MSMQ adapter.

```
//create application in the embedded server
  var myApp = server.CreateApplication("SampleEvents");
//instantiate the two CEP event streams
  var webActionStream = CreateSiteActionProducer();
  var webEventDataStream = CreateEventLogProducer();
```

23. Now, we are ready for the meat of the CEP application: the queries. The queries represent the standing questions we have about the data flowing through the server. The LINQ supported by StreamInsight enables queries that filter events (WHERE), correlate streams (JOIN), partition data (GROUP), rank (TOP), aggregate (AVG, SUM, COUNT), and more.

24. Any grouping computation such as doing a count of events or a ranking of events, leverages windows. A window is basically a period of time in which you are performing the computation. There are multiple types of windows all of which have different behaviors and event inclusion rules.

25. Our first query produces a count of event log "timeout" entries by website over a specific time interval. In our case, we leverage a Tumbling Window that has a distinct duration where events are aggregated and flushed after the interval passes. Any resulting aggregate events are put into a new event object called WebEventLogSummaryDetails.

```
//initial query which pulls all web server events that are
timeouts
var logEventQuery = from e in webEventDataStream
    where e.EntryType == "Timeout"group e by new { e.SiteName,
    e.EntryType } into oneMinuteGroup from eventWindow in
    oneMinuteGroup.TumblingWindow(TimeSpan.FromSeconds(60),
    HoppingWindowOutputPolicy.ClipToWindowEnd)
    select new WebEventLogSummaryDetails
{
  Website = oneMinuteGroup.Key.SiteName,
  Entry = oneMinuteGroup.Key.EntryType,
  EventCount = eventWindow.Count()
};
```

26. Our application only cares about scenarios where there are four or more timeout events in a given window. Another query is defined, which filters the results of the first query and only emits events when the aggregate count for the window exceeds four.

```
//filter the above web server events based on window count
var logEventCountQuery = from e in logEventQuery
            where e.EventCount > 4 select e;
```

27. Our other data stream consists of web clicks by our users. The clicks of interest are **Abandon Cart** events so we want to query that data stream and only return events that match our target condition.

```
//query of all website clicks related to abandoning cart
var webActionQuery = from e in webActionStream
            where e.ActionType == "AbandonCart" select e;
```

28. Finally, we are ready to join our queries. We want to find any abandon cart events for a given website that occur within a window where more than four server timeouts were observed for that website.

```
//final join query which merges server log and website click
    events when website is the same
var eventActionJoinQuery = from e in logEventCountQuery
    join f in webActionQuery on e.Website equals
        f.WebsiteProperty
select new
    {f.CustomerId,f.WebsiteProperty,e.Entry,e.EventCount};
```

29. Our final query gets bound to our adapter and started.

```
var query = eventActionJoinQuery.ToQuery(myApp, "Log Events",
        string.Empty, typeof(TracerFactory), outputConf,
        EventShape.Point, StreamEventOrder.FullyOrdered);
query.Start();
```

30. We wait for the user to halt the query and then execute the stop command.

```
//wait for keystroke to end
Console.ReadLine();
//end query
query.Stop();
```

31. Build the solution and launch the Event Publisher and Event Server applications, and notice that our Event Server is listening on two queues as shown in the following screenshot:

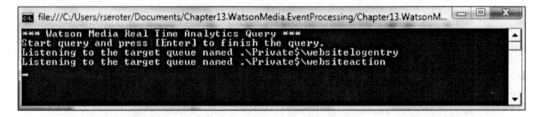

32. In the Event Publisher, we want to send in events, but particularly, we want to trigger timeouts for particular websites. Within our query, the timeout threshold is set to four, so until more than four timeouts occur in any one computational window, producing "abandon" events result no output events. Submit three timeout events for **Website A** and click the **Produce Timeout Events** button. Refer to the following screenshot:

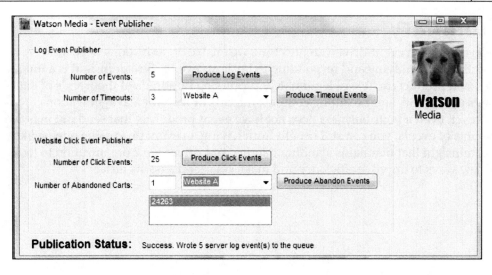

33. Produce any number of `Abandon Cart` events for that website, and observe that nothing is printed to the CEP Server output adapter. If within a short period of time (so as to fit into the window with the other events) you send more `Timeout` events, and then send more abandon events through, you should see the events output by the subscriber. The following screenshot shows the output of our timeout count and a series of customer IDs associated with abandoned carts:

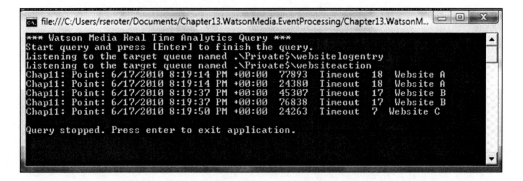

Summary

By leveraging an event-driven architecture, we enable organizations to be more proactive in identifying and responding to business events. StreamInsight is a unique Microsoft product capable of legitimately processing hundreds of thousands of data points per second, and executing complex filtering or incremental aggregations. However, even if your business does not have event producers that send out massive amounts of events, you can still benefit from having an event processing engine like StreamInsight that maintains standing queries, and drives your organization to look for new ways to improve efficiency and make smarter decisions faster.

14
Cross-Organizational Supply Chain

This chapter will discuss how to design and implement a Message Bus to exchange purchase order request and response messages within a supply chain.

Use case

Sam MacColl Commodities is a rapidly expanding commodity trading firm, which is a leader in the production of sustainable and ethical palm oil. Through rapid expansion and acquisition over the last 10 years, they have grown to be the largest palm oil plantation and milling operator in Papua New Guinea. Their core activity is the cultivation and processing of Palm Oil raw products into various derivatives for sale to domestic and international markets. The primary derivative they trade in is **Crude Palm Oil (CPO)**, which accounts from 70% of their yield. Their total output of CPO is approximately 500,000 tones.

Sam MacColl Commodities prides itself on being an environmentally friendly and efficient company; they only participate in sustainable production. Through strict adherence to international standards, they have also been able to increase the quality of their products. They were recently recognized for the low fatty acid levels of their palm oil.

Three years ago, the company floated on the Alternative Investment Market in the UK and with these funds they were able to accelerate their acquisitions and growth. By increasing size and through appropriate diversification, Sam MacColl Commodities were able to become the single supplier of choice for a number of large multi-national corporation customers. Coordinating the order and delivery of large amounts of commodities across the supply chain has been very challenging. Many of the individual units have their own individual supply chain systems. In one case, a huge order was could not be fulfilled because the commodity had already been sold by the subsidiary unit to another customer. Sam MacColl Commodities were threatened with legal action in this case.

Another challenge has been managing the credit limit of a large pool of customers. Previously, the individual sales reps in each subsidiary unit would approve transactions and seek unit-director level approval above a certain amount. Scaling this to a large organization is challenging and recently there have been a number of large transactions for which Sam MacColl Commodities (SMC) did not receive payment. This results in costly legal action and is extremely damaging to immediate cash flow and the firm's operations.

SMC's management realizes that they need to improve the quality of their customer experience to continue their long term growth strategy. They understand the need to consolidate onto a single set of processes and systems to avoid the direct and indirect costs associated with the issues we have highlighted. By addressing these challenges, SMC feel that they will be able to establish deep customer loyalty, which in turn creates a barrier to the entry for others and reduces their exposure to price sensitivity, which is notorious in the commodities industry.

SMC has brought in a new IT Director who has a lot of real-world experience building enterprise systems. His first priority is to ensure that all Customer PO Requests can be fulfilled with existing inventory before an acknowledgement is sent to the customer. His second priority is to establish a credit limit system. He intends to gradually migrate individual business units to this system.

SMC has grown through normal organic growth and acquisition as a company and therefore has a fairly homogenous set of core technologies. They are primarily a Microsoft "shop" utilizing ASP.NET for their web platform. They have numerous .NET developers on staff. Their primary database platform is SQL Server. They run a mixture of consolidated and dedicated environments depending on the business and technical requirements of the application. Some of their line-of-business applications require or run best on Oracle. Therefore, they also have a specialist Oracle support center. Because of the rapid growth of the organization and the margins that it provides, software purchases are often done in a best-of-breed manner instead of building or buying technology that cohesively integrates.

Key requirements

The following are key requirements for a new software solution:

- Provide a robust Message Bus for the SMC organization.
- Provide transport and transformation capabilities to connect to and consume multiple sources of data.
- Implement a loosely coupled design, which can extend and adapt over time.

Additional facts

There are some additional details gathered after the initial use case was shared with the technical team. These include the following:

- The project will need to demonstrate Purchase Order request/response and credit checking capabilities in an individual subsidiary unit of SMC first.
- Over time SMC management would like to on-board additional functionality into the system and have a single primary processor of transactional data. Therefore, the system must be able to scale to support up to 1 million business transactions per day (24 hour period).
- SMC is looking for a flexible solution, which can talk to a variety of systems.
- Along with immediate functionality for customer service needs, SMC would also like to understand how the system can be extended in the future to service additional customer and business needs which are identified.
- Reliability and speed are equally important here. Customers expect a response within 20 seconds for a real-time order as prices are volatile and they want to lock these in. A faster system will increase customer satisfaction but only if reliability is not compromised.

Pattern description

This solution calls for a Message Bus pattern. This subject is introduced in the book *Enterprise Integration Patterns* (Hohpe, Woolfe):

> *An enterprise contains several existing systems that must be able to share data and operate in a unified manner in response to a set of common business requests.*

The authors go on to say:

> *An enterprise often contains a variety of applications that operate independently but must work together in a unified manner. Enterprise Application Integration (EAI) defines a solution to this problem but doesn't describe how to accomplish it.*

Many companies that increase in size due to organic or acquisition growth find themselves in a position where the new enterprise consists of a large number of disparate systems that are responsible for managing their various products. Many times this causes inefficiency in the organization as sales reps/agents must log into multiple systems in order to get the answer to their question. This increases time and effort and the likelihood of mistakes. Over time, they may discover that it is inefficient so they may decide to implement a point-to-point integration. For example, one could create a consolidated web application GUI, which calls system A, B, or C as appropriate. One of the challenges for this is that as new GUI applications are added, each of them needs to perform this connectivity between the systems. In the majority of cases, the environment will be heterogeneous; even if they do manage to make all the applications work together, any change could stop it from working. For example, what happens if one of the systems is down, or if a system is upgraded or replaced? These two scenarios are illustrated in the following diagram:

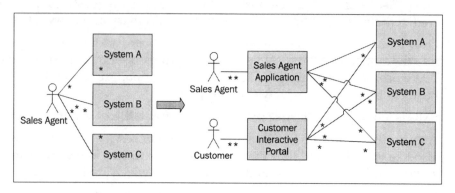

They could consider integrating the frontend application to all required backend systems, but this would dramatically increase the complexity of the application and if any other systems needed to connect to the same systems, that logic would need to be duplicated and maintained.

Rewriting all of a business's applications on a common platform is unrealistic and not practical from a financial point of view. Therefore, a Message Bus is an approach that is commonly implemented. This provides a communication infrastructure, adapter connectivity, and common command set. Companies that implement a Message Bus can use a universal connector between their various systems. A key requirement of a Message Bus is that it must be flexible and must be able to respond to change quickly, such as the addition of a new system or upgrade of a system. While the features of GUI systems may differ, the logic necessary to connect each of the backend systems is common and is encapsulated in the Message Bus and therefore can be reused by each GUI application. This enables applications to represent a unified view of their organization to their users, for example, sales agents, end customers, management, and so on.

By leveraging a Message Bus architecture, SMC will be able to provide an integration architecture that provides a common communication and messaging infrastructure to support communication between all systems across the enterprise. Let's revisit our previous example above and demonstrate how a Message Bus can be used.

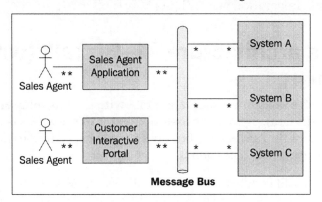

Here we have two GUI applications that are communicating with the **Message Bus**; the complexity of the integration that is required to connect to **System A, B** and **C** is handled by the Message Bus. The Message Bus is now responsible for routing messages to the appropriate systems and handling any necessary transport or transformation issues. This avoids the prohibitive costs of doing point-to-point, otherwise known as "spaghetti" integration. It also avoids the need for users to log onto multiple systems, thereby increasing productivity. A Message Bus is an example of a service-oriented architecture. The Message Bus acts as an intermediary across an enterprise's applications enabling them to be connected in a loosely coupled fashion. By standardizing on this approach and developing this integration capability, organizations are able to reduce the time to onboard new applications and offer new innovative composite services to their customers. This enables them to quickly react to changes driven either from customer demand or internal mergers, acquisitions, or re-orgs.

What Sam MacColl Commodities is looking to do is a close fit for Message Bus architecture. They have what are typically independent business applications built on top of heterogeneous systems. By establishing a common integration solution between them, they can achieve a business objective: establishing customer brand loyalty and demonstrating superior customer service during a period of growth, which in the long term will reduce their price sensitivity and will be a key source of competitive advantage. A key point of what they need is the ability to automate proper due diligence when confirming and fulfilling customer purchase orders in order to avoid disheartened customers.

Candidate architectures

We have two viable choices when looking to implement a Message Bus integration pattern across a supply chain. One of them is Windows Server AppFabric and the other is the BizTalk integration bus with the ESB Toolkit 2.1.

Candidate architecture #1–BizTalk (with ESB Toolkit)

BizTalk is Microsoft's Enterprise Integration tool with a robust messaging and workflow (Orchestration) engine. The assumption for this analysis is that SMC has a small installation of BizTalk Server, but does not have a common Message Bus platform or make use of the ESB Toolkit.

The ESB Toolkit 2.1 will be released with BizTalk Server 2010. At the time of writing, they are both in Beta release. The Toolkit provides a set of services, which build on the BizTalk platform and are useful for customers implementing a common Message Bus architecture. The term ESB stands for Enterprise Service Bus, which within the industry is seen as an evolution and mature view of the Message Bus concept. Two previous versions of the toolkit were released, 1.0, which worked on BizTalk Server 2006 R2 and 2.0, which worked on BizTalk Server 2009.

BizTalk is an established product from Microsoft for integration and processing of high-volume data streams. SMC is looking for a way to parse high volumes of data, perform any necessary transformation with various backend systems, and return a response to an end-user in seconds. BizTalk Server in combination with the ESB Toolkit provides an efficient high-performing way to build this capability for the SMC organization.

Solution design aspects

One of the key requirements of this solution is the ability to quickly and reliably process and provide pseudo-real time responses to purchase orders. The Message Bus needs to determine where to route the message and what transformations to apply to it. BizTalk is a pub-sub system, which fits naturally in this space. The ESB Toolkit adds additional components called resolvers, which extend the native BizTalk capabilities and make connectivity more dynamic. We will be dealing with lots of individual orders and a large number of backend systems. We need to assume that many of these factors can change over time, therefore the chosen solution must provide enough flexibility and extendability.

The services that the ESB Toolkit provides should be used as appropriate for the specific customer implementation. It is essentially a set of components and services that simplify implementing a Message Bus pattern with BizTalk. In the following table, I've provided a brief description of the main ESB services and an example of how they could be used to solve SMC's problems.

Service	Description	Uses in this scenario
Itinerary service	Uses XML metadata to route a message through Orchestration, transformation, or transmission services.	Compose the appropriate business logic depending upon the message received. Provide flexibility in the coupling of components. Itineraries are updateable without recompile.
UDDI service	Provides the capability to query UDDI repositories dynamically from other ESB services including Itineraries.	Dynamically update the endpoint information for new and existing systems as they are brought online in SMC's environment. This will remove unnecessary configuration relating to other systems in LOB applications.
Exception Handling service	Accepts standard fault messages, adds additional metadata, and provides a central portal for investigation and root cause resolution.	Provide a single unified framework and portal for SMC to manage exception data.
Transformation service	Provides the ability to execute BizTalk maps without using the underlying BizTalk messaging infrastructure.	Expose transformations that BizTalk provides via an endpoint that SMC LOB applications can call independently of other BizTalk services
Resolver service	Look up ESB endpoints (using UDDI, Business Rules Engine and other including custom resolvers) and provide all details of those endpoints.	Enables at runtime flexibility and determination of the route of a message within SMC. This is particularly useful when deploying a new version or onboarding new systems.
BizTalk Operations service	Provides runtime details about BizTalk hosts and deployed artifacts.	Provide uptime stats or dashboards to the business based on the information provided.

The following diagram illustrates how these services work together. The glue between all of these is the Itinerary, which is an XML document that provides the set of steps and tasks that the ESB Toolkit needs to perform to process the message.

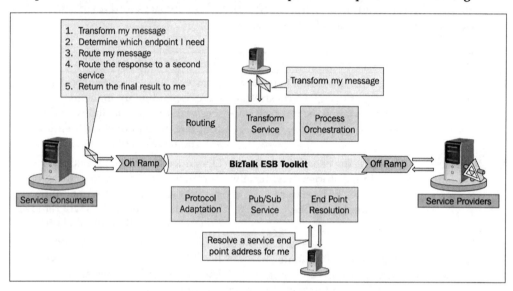

BizTalk Server is built to provide efficient, publish-subscribe messaging capabilities. By building on top of this platform, the ESB toolkit inherits this. Recent benchmarks have shown that BizTalk Server can scale to over 1,600 end-to-end messages per second, which equates to approximately 138 million messages in a 24 hour period. Given that SMC requires 1 million messages per day, we are confident that BizTalk Server provides sufficient margin of safety even with the overhead that the ESB toolkit components will introduce. We also need the ability to connect to a wide variety of sources in order to produce event streams. BizTalk Server has a well-understood adapter model where developers are free to use the out-of-the-box adapters for transport or LOB system connectivity. They can also build their own adapters using either the BizTalk Adapter Framework or the WCF Adapter SDK (the new de facto standard introduced in BizTalk Server 2006 R2). BizTalk's wide variety of out-of-the-box and available-to-buy adapters mean that the majority of connectivity in SMC should be possible without writing their own custom code or adapters. The fact that SMC can leverage the existing .NET capability if they do need to build adapters is a huge plus for them.

The loose coupling of BizTalk and the ESB toolkit enables a clean separation of artifacts and minimizes dependencies. The itinerary model also allows new and updated business processes to be deployed rapidly and for many BizTalk customers, this capability been a long time coming.

Solution delivery aspects

The ESB Toolkit is built on top of and leverages existing BizTalk functionality. It provides extensibility at all key points. The existing .NET skills that the SMC organization has are applicable as .NET or web service knowledge is applied at all extension points.

Despite the fact that the Toolkit is built on top of BizTalk Server, there is a learning curve. The ESB way of doing things is a paradigm shift for many developers. The 2.0 product has been released for approximately 12 months at the time of writing, so there is a community ecosystem, but it is still quite limited as it is a niche within a niche. Developers learning the ESB Toolkit should leverage the traditional Microsoft-provided documentation and samples as well as ad hoc internet searches to return relevant answers to problems.

SMC already has a small team of architects who have developed BizTalk Server applications, so they can build on and expand the capability of this team by choosing the ESB Toolkit. BizTalk developers are familiar with messaging concepts, so will find it easier to learn how to build solutions using the ESB services, when compared to someone with no integration experience. Over time, they will be able to effectively determine which ESB services to use and where. As with BizTalk, developers can install the ESB Toolkit and operate it locally on their existing BizTalk development installations before deploying the finished product to a more robust environment. As everything in an ESB Toolkit solution is contained within .NET projects, they can manage their code using the existing source-control repository that BizTalk uses.

Solution operations aspects

This is an area where the BizTalk Server product is well-established. There are no concerns over its ability to handle load and gracefully manage the required amounts of data. The story around high availability and support tooling is very strong. The ESB Toolkit's Exception Management portal and service provides the capability to determine how the engine is running. The Exception Management Service and portal is seen within the industry as one of the key reasons to adopt the ESB Toolkit into a solution. The portal interface can be extended and customized to display information specific to SMC. BizTalk and the ESB toolkit score very highly in this aspect.

Organizational aspects

The company is looking for something that can fill the immediate need while serving as a viable long term solution. BizTalk is an established product and the ESB Toolkit 2.0 has been released for some time and has been successfully adopted by a number of customers. With the 2.1 release, they will be able to take advantage of the features that BizTalk 2010, .NET Framework 4, and Visual Studio 2010 provide. We can only expect it to improve as it matures further in the marketplace. It leverages existing developer skill sets. The licensing costs for BizTalk are non-trivial but are not an adoption blocker for SMC. The extensibility that BizTalk and the ESB Toolkit provide enables SMC to create a well-thought-out Message Bus deployment, which can grow to meet future requirements. Building this functionality themselves would require a lot of architectural and development time and would pose a significant challenge for the organization.

Solution evaluation

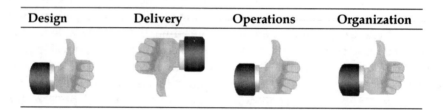

| Design | Delivery | Operations | Organization |

Candidate architecture #2–Windows Server AppFabric

SMC has an existing investment in .NET and the Microsoft platform. They have developed several applications that utilize WCF and WF and therefore Windows Server AppFabric could be leveraged here to build a Message Bus solution with custom-built components to meet SMC's requirements.

Solution design aspects

Windows Server AppFabric does not have a built-in publish-subscribe or Message Bus capability. WCF provides a basic routing service, but this in itself is not going to provide the enterprise-ready messaging and transformation capabilities that SMC needs. To build the required Message Bus architecture would require lots of custom code that would need to be developed and maintained. While the BizTalk Adapter Pack can be used within AppFabric (as long as you purchase a license for it), this only solves one piece of the puzzle (that is, connectivity). To build the rest of the capabilities will be a non-trivial and long-running challenge.

From a performance perspective, recent Microsoft performance labs have demonstrated that AppFabric can scale to meet the required loads. AppFabric can expose service contracts, which are represented by .NET 4 Workflow Services or traditional WCF services. There is no native transformation service within AppFabric and only a low-level exception handling capability is inherited from the framework. Making these generic services will require extensive and costly work.

Due to a combination of the technology being new and the requirement to build a lot of core complicated components, this is a negative aspect of the candidate solution.

Solution delivery aspects

AppFabric solutions are built primarily in Visual Studio.NET, so SMC developers are already familiar with constructing these projects and keeping the code in source-control systems. There is a lack of guidance available right now on how to best implement certain patterns. Because of the need to build some fairly robust custom code to handle the core Message Bus requirements, we will expect a longer development cycle more prone to slippages than if it was built on a typical messaging and integration platform. In addition to this, both the product and the underlying .NET 4, which it depends on, have only just been released. Therefore, development skills and experience in these technologies are difficult to find. It is likely that SMC would have to go with a team that had no successful deployments of this technology behind them. Even though they have a strong .NET capability within the organization, this is still a prohibitive factor.

Solution operations aspects

SMC already has an existing Windows Server 2008 and R2 infrastructure on which they can deploy AppFabric. This will mean that minimal training will be required in order to support the necessary AppFabric infrastructure for this application.

The product has a clear model for associating application components into a single manageable entity. Packaging and deployment of solutions is relatively straightforward, and the operations dashboard provides a clear look into the state of the server environment. Whilst the tooling is not as mature as for other platforms, as this is a version-one release, it is still not a major blocker to deployment.

The tracking functionality does introduce additional overhead. This would need to be carefully tested and they would need to determine if the tracking functionality met their operational data requirements if AppFabric was the chosen architecture.

Organizational aspects

SMC already has an existing Windows infrastructure that can support AppFabric. While this is a new technology and will require some training, it is not expected that this will be a significant burden. Therefore, AppFabric represents a good fit for the organization.

Solution evaluation

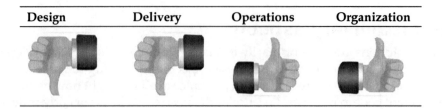

Design	Delivery	Operations	Organization

Architecture selection

Let's look at how these candidate architecture technologies stack up against each other. We can break down the primary benefits and risks of each choice as follows:

BizTalk Server 2010 with ESB Toolkit 2.1

Benefits	Risks
• High-throughput application • Proven deployments • Expertise available in core BizTalk platform • Existing components meet many requirements • Enterprise-class hosting infrastructure	• Management may view this as an ESB in a box • Limited proven expertise available on the ESB Toolkit • Ongoing support for ESB Toolkit, which is not officially part of the product

Windows Server AppFabric	
Benefits	**Risks**
<ul><li>Simple deployment and management model</li><li>Built on top of Windows Workflow 4</li><li>Expands on existing .NET development capabilities</li></ul>	<ul><li>Requires implementation of complicated custom components</li><li>No proven deployments using Message Bus pattern on this platform</li><li>Reinventing the wheel may not add value to the organization</li><li>Monitoring and tracking database functionality</li></ul>

A key benefit of a Message Bus implementation is the ability to reduce dependency on customized components and point-to-point integration from applications. In an AppFabric-oriented solution, each message flow would need to be statically defined through the AppFabric infrastructure. There is no pub-sub messaging capability to build upon; mimicking this introduces significant architectural and development risk. The current version of AppFabric is built for doing service aggregation and workflow and not complex Message Bus processing. In future versions, the gap is likely to decrease and Microsoft's messaging indicates they will be built on a common technology platform. But the customer needs to make a pragmatic and realistic decision now. Future roadmaps are volatile and may change over time. BizTalk and the ESB Toolkit are well-proven technologies. While AppFabric could be bent to try to fit this solution, it would be a less-than-ideal use of the product and the implementation would likely be sub-optimal. We would spend excessive amounts of time customizing and creating components for AppFabric that are already available today in BizTalk and the ESB Toolkit.

For this scenario, BizTalk and the ESB toolkit is clearly the best choice.

Building the solution

In this solution, we will be constructing a Message Bus pattern for processing Purchase Orders using BizTalk Server 2010 and the ESB Toolkit. We are implementing a single message flow to illustrate an example of how the ESB functionality can be leveraged. Our system will be loosely coupled and will use WCF-BasicHttp and WCF-WSHttp as the transport adapters of choice.

We will use the WCFTestClient tool to initiate PO Requests, which will then be processed by BizTalk/ESB Server. Our BizTalk/ESB Server will query the inventory server and customer server to determine whether the items requested are in stock and the customer meets the required credit limit. The credit limit is fixed across all customers and will be implemented within BizTalk. Based on the information received, BizTalk will approve/reject the purchase order appropriately. The main components are illustrated in the following diagram :

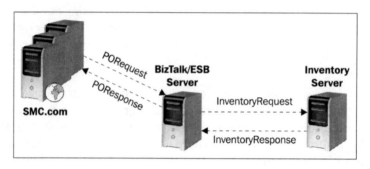

Setup

Before you start, you will need to have a working machine or virtual image that has the following components and any dependencies installed and configured:

- BizTalk Server 2010 (Beta used at time of writing)
- ESB Toolkit 2.1 (Beta used at time of writing)
- Visual Studio 2010
- SQL Server 2008/ R2
- UDDI Service
- IIS—this is necessary for the ESB web service and portal components
- Supported operating system; note that the UDDI component requires Windows Server 2008/R2

For detailed instructions please see the ESB Toolkit documentation available at `http://msdn.microsoft.com/en-us/biztalk/dd876606.aspx`. The central part of our solution is BizTalk/ESB Server. The first thing that we will do is define the Message Schemas that will be used to represent the following types:

- PORequest
- POResponse
- InventoryCheckRequest
- InventoryCheckResponse

This conforms to general contract-first SOA principles. These schemas have already been defined for you. They can be found in the `<Installation Directory>\Chapter14\Begin\Chapter14.SMCSupplyChain` folder. Open the **Chapter14.SMCSupplyChain.sln** solution file and you will see the **Chapter14. SMCSupplyChain.Schemas** sub-project. Within this, you will see schemas representing each of the types in the previous list.

Within the solution, you will find the following projects:

- `Chapter14.SMCSupplyChain.InventoryCheckService`
- `Chapter14.SMCSupplyChain.ItineraryLibrary`
- `Chapter14.SMCSupplyChain.Maps`
- `Chapter14.SMCSupplyChain.Orchestrations`
- `Chapter14.SMCSupplyChain.Schemas`

Some of these projects are already implemented for you.

Deploying and using a monolithic solution

We will now walk through and examine a monolithic implementation of this broker scenario that has already been completed for you. We will deploy this and use the BizTalk WCF Service Publishing Wizard to expose a monolithic implementation of this process as a WCF service that we can consume. Once we have done this, we will demonstrate how the ESB Toolkit can use the same artifacts in an agile manner through Itinerary. From the `Chapter14.SMCSupplyChain` solution, open the `Chapter14.SMCSupplyChain.Orchestrations` project. Open the `PurchaseOrderBroker.odx` Orchestration.

Your screen should now look like the following screenshot:

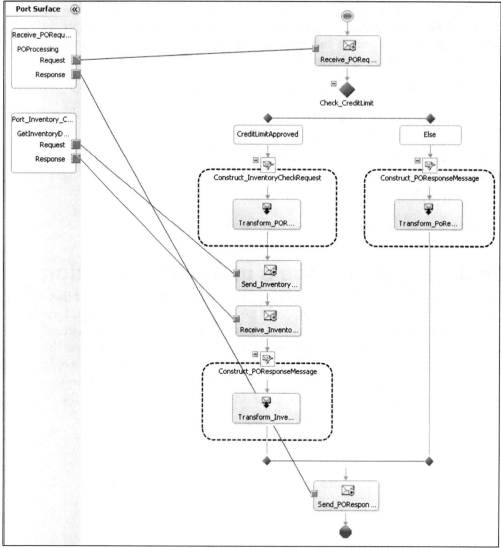

This is an example of a monolithic implementation of this chapters, use case. In particular, please note the following and examine these in Visual Studio:

1. The Decision Shape Check_CreditLimit has a conditional branch CreditLimitApproved, which uses the following static condition:

    poRequest.TotalDue<=500

2. Map usage is embedded into **Construct/Transform** shapes within the Orchestrations. See the **Construct_InventoryCheckRequest, Construct_POResponseMessage**, and **Construct_POResponseMessage** shapes.

3. The logical port **Port_Inventory_Check_Request** contains the operation name for the WCF service. Note that this is the **Identifier** property of the port; the value in this case is **GetInventoryData**.

Now let's deploy the required WCF service contained in the `Chapter14.SMCSupplyChain.InventoryCheckService` project and then the BizTalk assemblies.

4. Right click on the **Chapter14.SMCSupplyChain.InventoryCheckService** project in Visual Studio and select **Publish**. In the **Publish WCF Service** box that appears, click the ellipsis button circled in the following screenshot.

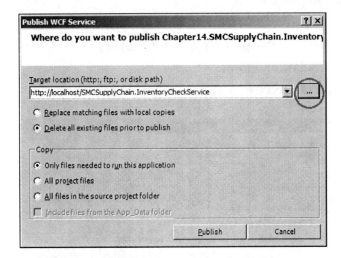

5. Select **Local IIS** and create a new Virtual Directory called **SMCSupplyChain. InventoryCheckservice**.

6. Follow the remaining steps of the wizard. Check that the target location is configured as `http://localhost/SMCSupplyChain. InventoryCheckService` and then click **Publish**.

We will now publish the BizTalk application and configure it.

1. Right-click on the `Chapter14.SMCSupplyChain` solution and click **Deploy Solution**. Check that no error messages appear and that the Deployment is successful.

2. Open the BizTalk Administration Console and verify that the solution is deployed in the **SMCSupplyChain** application.

3. To create the port required import the `InventoryCheckService_Customer.BindingInfo.xml` binding file, which is contained within the `Chapter14.SMCSupplyChain.Orchestrations` folder. This will create a WCF-Custom send port called `WcfSendPOrt_InventoryCheckService_WSHttpBinding_IInventoryCheckService_Custom`.

4. We now need to expose our `PurchaseOrderBroker.odx` Orchestration as a WCF service. Go back to your Visual Studio with the **Chapter14.SMCSupplyChain** solution open. Select **Tools | BizTalk WCF Service Publishing Wizard** from the **Tools** drop-down menu.

5. On the first **Welcome to the BizTalk WCF Service Publishing Wizard** screen click **Next**.

6. On the next screen, select the following options so that it is identical to the following screenshot:

7. **Service Endpoint**

8. **Adapter Name [Transport type]: WCF-WSHttp**

9. **Enable metadata endpoint**

10. **Create BizTalk receive locations**...: **SMCSupplyChain**

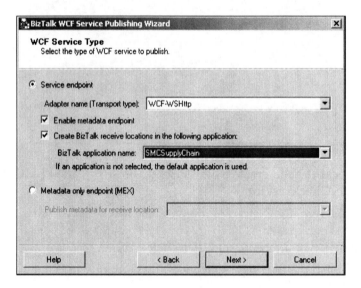

11. On the next screen select **Publish BizTalk orchestrations as WCF service** and click **Next**.

12. Now select the `Chapter14.SMCSupplyChain.Orchestrations.dll` from the build output location for the `Chapter14.SMCSupplyChain.Orchestrations` project. Click **Next**.

13. Leave the default settings on the next screen (**Orchestrations and Ports**).

14. On the next screen, **WCF Service Properties**, leave the default target namespace `http://tempuri.org`.

15. On the next screen, **WCF Service Location**, leave the default location: `http://localhost/Chapter14.SMCSupplyChain.Orchestrations`. Mark **Allow anonymous access to WCF Service** as **true** and click **Next**.

16. On the final **WCF Service Summary** screen click **Create**. Verify that there were no errors.

17. In the BizTalk Administration Console open up the **SMCSupplyChain** application **Receive Locations** section. You should see a new receive location which has been created.

18. Select the **Orchestrations** section, right-click **Chapter14.SMCSupplyChain.Orchestrations.Broker** and select Properties. Then click **Bindings** and configure the **Host**. For **Receive Ports**, specify the item generated by the Publishing Wizard, for the **Send Ports** specify the WCF-Custom Send Port created by the binding file which was imported. Click **OK**. Right-click on the **SMCSupplyChain** application and click **Start**.

 You will need to check that the `Chapter14.SMCsupplyChain.Orchestrations` Virtual Directory that was generated runs in an application pool whose identity (service account) is a member of the BizTalk Isolated Host Users Group.

19. We will now test this using the WCF Test Client. Open the WCFTestClient. exe located in `<Program Files Location>\Microsoft Visual Studio 9.0\Common7\IDE`.

20 Right-click the root node **My Service Projects** and select **Add Service**. Enter the endpoint address which points to the receive location you exposed as a WCF Service (I have not included it here because the default name is very long). Click **OK** to generate the proxy classes that the test client will use.

21. Expand the exposed Service Contract (Chapter14_SMCSupplyChain_Orchestrations_...). and double-click the **POProcessing** operation.

22. Enter the details for the Request as follows:

Field	Value
PurchaseOrderID	2
CUstomerID	2
TotalDue	499
Details	Length=1 Note: This will allow you to enter one product detail. Use values below:
ProductID	1
Quantity	1
ItemPrice	1

23. Select **Start a new proxy** and click **Invoke**. The first time you invoke it will take some time as BizTalk needs to load all assemblies and required cache information into memory.

24. You should receive a response that looks like the following screenshot. The key thing to note is that the **Status** field has a value of 200. I explain the status codes after this section.

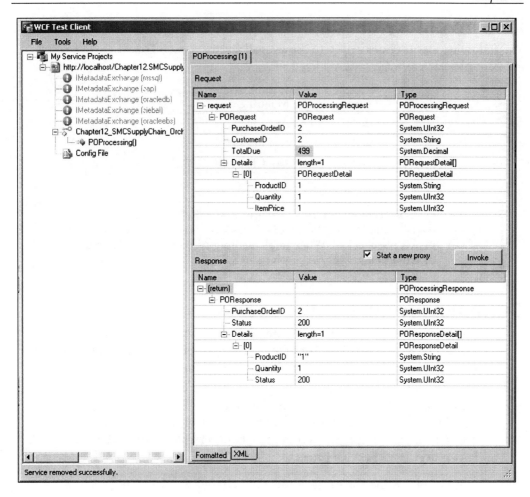

PO status codes

The following status codes apply to overall PO.

Code	Meaning
200	Approved
400	Rejected

Item inventory check status codes

The following status codes apply to the overall status of each **Detail**, for example, each item.

Code	Meaning
200	Approved
400	Not in stock
600	Not Checked

 600 is implemented for the scenario where the Total Due exceeds the permitted Credit Limit. In this case, the inventory status for each item is not checked. When implementing systems, it is a best practice to avoid unnecessary expensive service calls by using this technique.

Current behaviors of the system

- The maximum TotalDue is statically defined in the **PurchaseOrderBroker** Orchestration as 500. Any TotalDue value greater than or equal to 500 will return a response code of 400 and each Detail, that is, item in that PO, will have a Status of 600.

- If PurchaseOrderID is an even number and the TotalDue is less than or equal to 499 then the PO Status will be 200 and each item will be 200. This logic is implemented in the **Chapter14.SMCSupplyChain. InventoryCheckService** project.

Experiment by submitting the same request but change the following:

- **PurchaseOrderID:** change value to 3. The PO status should be 400 and each individual item Status should be 400, that is, not in stock.

- **PurchaseOrderID:** change value to 2 and **TotalDue** change to 501. The PO status should be 400 and each individual item Status should be 600, that is, Not Checked, due to TotalDue exceeding the statically defined credit limit.

 The rudimentary logic for the Inventory Service is implemented in the **Chapter14.SMCSupplyChain.InventoryCheckService** project.

Utilizing the ESB Toolkit

So far, we have seen one way to implement this solution and will now look at how the ESB Toolkit can make this solution more agile.

Using existing transformations within an ESB Itinerary

We will now extend this and use some of the existing BizTalk artifacts that were developed to meet this solution and demonstrate how the maps that we previously created can be utilized as an Itinerary. For simplicity sake, the itinerary will be implemented using file drops to facilitate easier testing. We will begin by implementing one of the transformations step by step, then expand and use another itinerary, which replicates the functionality of the Orchestration. This itinerary is transport independent so can be utilized from a different On-Ramp and Off-Ramp. The purpose of this section is to show you how the ESB Toolkit can be leveraged to use existing components.

1. From the <Chapter 14 files location>\Begin\ folder copy the **Filedrops** folder and all subfolders to the root of C:\. This structure will be used to receive and send files for the itinerary examples. If access to this location is not permissible on your system, adjust the location in the following instructions appropriately.

2. In the BizTalk Administration Console, open up the **SMCSupplyChain** application. Right-click on references and add a reference to the **Microsoft. Practices.ESB** application.

3. Open the **Receive Ports** section. Right-click and create a new one-way Receive port called **SMCOnRamp.OneWay**; this will be the on-ramp that BizTalk uses.

4. Within **the SMCOnRamp.OneWay** Receive Port Properties window, click on the **Receive Location** tab and select **New.**

5. Enter the name **SMCOnRamp.File** and specify the transport type as FILE. Click **Configure** and set the **Receive Folder location** to be C:\Filedrops\ SMCIn and leave the default **File mask** of *.xml.

6. Select the appropriate **Receive Handler** (default is **BizTalkServerApplication**). Select the **Receive Pipeline** as **ItinerarySelectReceiveXML**. Your screen should look like the following image:

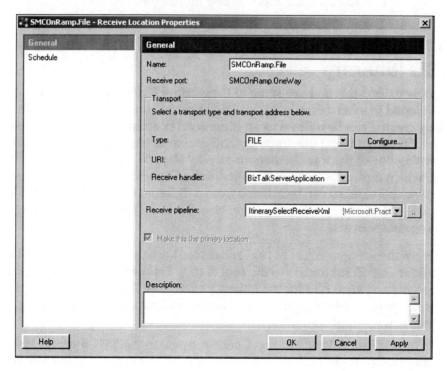

7. Click on the ellipsis button to configure the **ItinerarySelectReceiveXML** pipeline. You should set the **ItineraryFactKey** to **Resolver.Itinerary** and the **ResolverConnectionString** to **ITINERARY:\\name=SMCOneWaySimple**. This means that the Resolver will look up the value of the **SMCOneWaySimple** itinerary from the Itinerary store (which is a configured SQL Server Database). The following screenshot illustrates this:

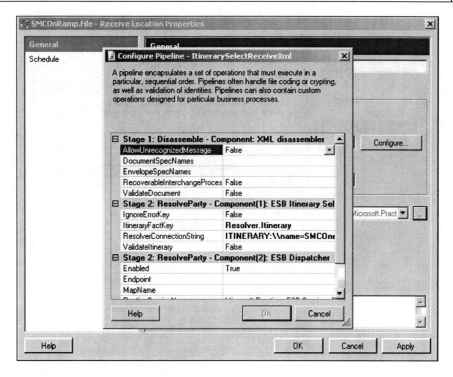

8. Note that there are other resolvers that can use the Business Rules Engine or UDDI v3 to resolve the Itinerary. In this case, we decided to specify this explicitly. As the itinerary resides in the database, we can change this at any time.

9. We now need to create a Dynamic Send Port within our application, which can subscribe to the messages that will be published by this Receive Port. Note the ESB terminology for this is an Off-Ramp. Expand **Send Ports** in the **SMCSupplyChain** application and create a **Dynamic One-Way** port called **SMCOffRampDynamicOneWay**. Set the **Send Pipeline** to **ItinerarySendPassthrough**.

10. Click **Filters** for this port and configure the following filters as per the next screenshot:

    ° `Microsoft.Practices.ESB.Itinerary.Schemas.`
      `ServiceName == SMCOffRampDynamicOneWay`

    ° `Microsoft.Practices.ESB.Itinerary.Schemas.`
      `IsRequestResponse ==false`

    ° `Microsoft.Practices.ESB.Itinerary.Schemas.`
      `ServiceState == Pending`

°   `Microsoft.Practices.ESB.Itinerary.Schemas.`
    `ServiceType == Messaging`

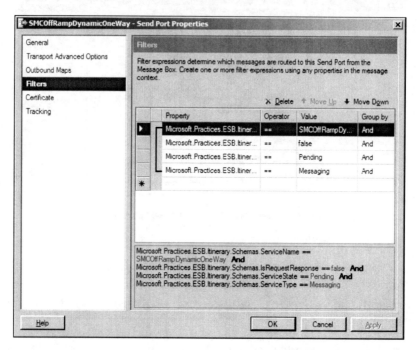

The BTS.ReceivePortName property can be used in the filter expression to match an Off-Ramp with a particular On-Ramp. Typically, I do not include this, as it keeps the Off-Ramp generic and reusable across different itineraries. Note that the GlobalBank ESB sample application also provides generic reusable On and Off-Ramps.

11. Now we will examine the itinerary **SMCOneWaySimple**, which we specified we would use in our On-Ramp. Open up the **Chapter14.SMCSupplyChain. ItineraryLibrary** project, which is contained within the solution. Open **SMCOneWaySimple.Itinerary** to open the Itinerary Designer, which was introduced in ESB Toolkit 2.0. Your screen should look like the following:

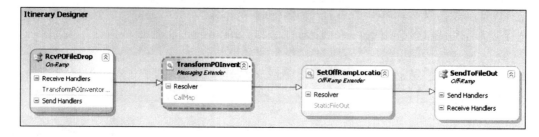

12. The Itinerary broadly consists of the following:

    ° On-Ramp: **RcvPOFileDrop** receives the message.

    ° Messaging Extender: **TransformPOInventoryRequest** executes during the receive pipeline stage (the container object specifies the BizTalk processing stage: either receive pipeline, Orchestration, or send pipeline) and invokes the previously defined map to transform the **PORequest** to an **InventoryCheckRequest**.

    ° Off-Ramp Extender: **SetOffRampLocation** uses a static resolver to specify the output location of `C:\filedrops\SMCOut\%MessageID%.xml`.

    ° Off-Ramp: **SendToFileOut** specifies the Dynamic Send port that we created earlier (our Off-Ramp). The previous resolver shape provides the transport type and location configuration in its static resolver.

13. First export the itinerary by clicking the Itinerary Designer surface and selecting **Export Model**. Save this in a convenient location as **SMCOneWaySimple.xml** and verify that it exports successfully.

14. We will now deploy this by opening a command prompt and changing to the directory `C:\Program Files\Microsoft BizTalk ESB Toolkit 2.1\Bin`.

15. We will use the tool ESBImportUtil, which is provided to deploy itineraries. Run the following command:

    ```
    EsbImportUtil.exe /f:"<Path to folder with Itinerary>\
    SmcOneWaySimple.xml" /c:deployed
    ```

16. Verify that you get the message :**The Itinerary <Itinerary location xml> was imported successfully successfully to database ....**

17. Now check that the receive locations, send ports, and required hosts are started.

18. Open the **PORequest_output.xml** file from the `<Chapter 12 files location>\Begin\SampleMessages` directory and once you have done this, copy it to `C:\Filedrops\SMCIn`.

19. Navigate to `C:\Filedrops\SMCOut` and verify that the folder contains a new message, whose format is of type **POResponse**. If you used the sample inbound message that I provided, your screen should look identical to the following screenshot:

```xml
<?xml version="1.0" encoding="utf-16" ?>
<ns0:POResponse xmlns:ns0="https://Chapter12.SMCSupplyChain.Schemas.POResponse">
  <ns0:PurchaseOrderID>10</ns0:PurchaseOrderID>
  <ns0:Status>400</ns0:Status>
  <ns0:Details>
    <ns0:Detail ProductID="ProductID_0" Quantity="10" Status="600" />
    <ns0:Detail ProductID="ProductID_0" Quantity="10" Status="600" />
    <ns0:Detail ProductID="ProductID_0" Quantity="10" Status="600" />
  </ns0:Details>
</ns0:POResponse>
```

Congratulations! You've now successfully deployed and used your first itinerary. Note that the deployment of the Itinerary was able to occur whilst BizTalk was still running. This means that your itineraries can change on the fly with zero downtime, which is one of the big benefits of ESB toolkit for BizTalk Server.

Using the itinerary service broker pattern to implement messaging-based routing with ESB

In this next example, we will show a way to use an itinerary to implement similar broker functionality to the **PurchaseOrderBroker Orchestration** we used earlier by leveraging the ESB toolkit. First, let us take a step back and recap on the functionality we implemented in the **PurchaseOrderBroker Orchestration** to meet our requirements:

- Receive a PORequest message.
- Evaluate the TotalDue promoted property.
- If the TotalDue is greater than 500, a map is called to construct a POResponse message with a status code that indicates that the order has not been approved. This response is sent to the appropriate location.
- If the TotalDue is less than or equal to 500:
    ° An InventoryCheckRequest is constructed by using a BizTalk map.
    ° A call is made to the Inventory WCF Service GetInventoryData operation.

- ° From the InventoryCheckResponse, which contains details of all the items requested in the original PORequest, a map is called to construct the appropriate POResponse.
- ° Send POResponse to appropriate location.

The BizTalk Orchestration engine is robust and proven. BizTalk is primarily targeted at and designed for integration scenarios, therefore, each Orchestration represents a tight coupling of components; it encapsulates a set of functionality from transformations to external system calls. To change the order of invocation of transformations we implemented in the **PurchaseOrderBroker Orchestration** would require recompilation and redeployment, which is not acceptable for some systems. Pub-sub messaging is configuration based so can be changed without recompilation and redeployment, but implementing the logic above in pub-sub would be challenging and would lose the view of the message flow that Orchestration provides. What we would really like is the functionality of Orchestration, with flexibility, and ease of configuration.

In version 1.0 of the ESB Toolkit, itineraries were a sequential set of steps modeled in an XML file. When the **Export Mode** is set to **Default** for an itinerary this is what happens under the covers. If this mode is changed to **Strict**, a number of items change in the XML output of the itinerary. This includes the addition of a number of attributes in the file that correspond to itinerary designer properties: specifically, a **Stage** attribute, which corresponds to the **Container** itinerary designer property; a **PropertyBag**; a **businessName** attribute, which corresponds to the **Name** designer property. Each **Service** also contains an **id** and a **nextId** value, as shown in the following image. This reflects internal changes that were made from ESB 2.0; the runtime now processes the itineraries as a linked list.

```
id="d90a2f8622b24aab8e9a3167cd441963" nextId="49953ce104ec40d491dc926ad301017e" businessName="TransformPOInventoryRequest"

id="49953ce104ec40d491dc926ad301017e" nextId="0763ddcc59b24b209f308052028fb9bd" businessName="ItineraryService6" />
```

The Itinerary Broker Service allows you to take advantage of this and implement rudimentary routing scenarios without an Orchestration. It is represented as two shapes in the toolbox: the **Itinerary Broker Service** and the **Itinerary Broker Outport**. The **Itinerary Broker Service** shape can be used with the **Context Resolver**, which enables us to access the BizTalk internal and schema promoted properties of the message. Recall that in our scenario TotalDue is a promoted property. We've already demonstrated transformation from within an itinerary, coupled with the access to the message context and the ability to route on it this looks promising.

In order to call the WCF service, we will require a two-way Off-Ramp, which we will implement as a BizTalk Dynamic Solicit-Response Port.

1. In the BizTalk Administration Console open up the **SMCSupplyChain** application. Right-click on **Send Ports** and select **New** then **Dynamic Solicit-Response Send Port**.

    In the **Send Port Properties** window set the following properties:

    ○ **Name**: SMCOffRampDynamicTwoWay

    ○ **Send Pipeline**: ItinerarySendPassthrough

    ○ **Receive Pipeline**: ItineraryForwarderSendReceive

2. Click **Filters** for this port and configure the following filters; these deliberately use the same context properties as the Off-Ramp we created earlier:

    ○ `Microsoft.Practices.ESB.Itinerary.Schemas.`
       `ServiceName == SMCOffRampDynamicTwoWay`

    ○ `Microsoft.Practices.ESB.Itinerary.Schemas.`
       `IsRequestResponse ==true`

    ○ `Microsoft.Practices.ESB.Itinerary.Schemas.`
       `ServiceState == Pending`

    ○ `Microsoft.Practices.ESB.Itinerary.Schemas.`
       `ServiceType == Messaging`

3. Now we will examine the itinerary **SMCOneWayBroker**, which we specified we would use in our On-Ramp. Open up the **Chapter14.SMCSupplyChain. ItineraryLibrary** project, which is contained within the solution. Open **SMCOneWayBroker.Itinerary**; your screen should look like the following:

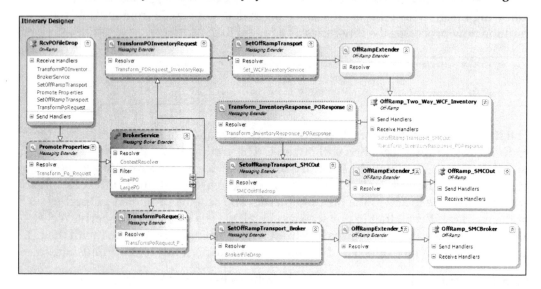

4. The first part of the Itinerary broadly consists of the following:

   ° **On-Ramp**: **RcvPOFileDrop** receives the message.

   ° **Messaging Extender**: **PromoteProperties** executes a map that maps itself, for example, PORequest to PORequest. This was implemented as a workaround to make the promoted property TotalDue accessible by the Context Resolver used by the BrokerService.

   ° **Messaging Broker Extender**: **Broker Service** evaluates the value of TotalDue, a promoted property within PORequest. This is implemented using two filters, **SmallPO** and **LargePO**. Filters are added using the **Itinerary Broker Outport** toolbox shape. **SmallPO** matches less than or equal to 500; **LargePO** matches TotalDue greater than 500. The first filter that evaluates true will be executed, in the same way as a Switch statement in C#.

5. If the **LargePO** filter evaluates true, the following will occur in order to return a rejected POResponse:

   ° **Messaging Extender**: **TransformPORequest_POResponse** executes a map, which generates the appropriate POResponse indicating it has been rejected.

   ° **Messaging Extender**: **SetOffRampTransport_Broker** uses a static resolver to specify the output location of `C:\ filedrops\SMCBroker\%MessageID%.xml`.

   ° **Off-Ramp Extender**: **OffRampExtender_SMCBroker** is a required component to invoke Off_Ramp.

   ° **Off-Ramp**: **OffRamp_SMCBroker** specifies the one-way Dynamic Send port that we created earlier (our Off-Ramp).

6. If the **SmallPO** filter evaluates true, the following will occur in order to check the inventory and return an appropriate POResponse:

   ° **Messaging Extender**: **TransformPOInventoryRequest** executes a map, which generates an InventoryRequest based on the details of the inbound PORequest.

   ° **Messaging Extender**: **SetOffRampTransport** uses a static resolver to configure the WCF properties.

   ° **Off-Ramp Extender**: **OffRampExtender** is a required component in strict mode to invoke Off_Ramp.

   ° **Off-Ramp**: **OffRamp_Two_Way_WCF_Inventory** specifies the two-way Dynamic Send port that we created earlier and uses this to call the Inventory WCF Service.

- ° **Messaging Extender: Transform_InventoryResponse_POResponset** executes a map to generate the appropriate POResponse.
- ° **Messaging Extender: SetoffRampTransport_SMCOut** uses a static resolver to specify the output location of `C:\filedrops\SMCOut\%MessageID%.xml`.
- ° **Off-Ramp Extender: OffRampExtender_SMCOut** is a required component in strict mode to invoke Off_Ramp.
- ° Off-Ramp: **OffRamp_SMCOut** re-uses the one-way Dynamic Send port that was used for the LargePO filter to send the POResponse to the folder specified in the resolver configuration previously.

As described above, this itinerary uses the Itinerary Broker Service to implement the functionality of the **PurchaseOrderBroker Orchestration**. Before running this sample, we will first examine some of the configuration properties and common gotchas required to make this type of scenario work.

- To configure the **Filter** for the **Itinerary Broker Service**, one **Itinerary Broker Outport** per filter is required. To access the context properties you should configure the **Expression** value to be: `//Property[@name='TotalDue']<=500` as shown in the following screenshot:

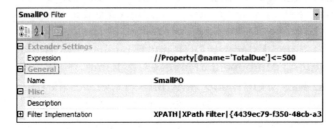

- When changing **Export Mode** from **Default** to **Strict** ensure that you have an Off-Ramp Extender before any Off-Ramp. **Strict** mode requires this.
- The **Static Resolver** is configured as follows to call the WCF Inventory Service:
  - ° **Transport Name: WCF-WSHTTP**
  - ° **Target Namespace:** `http://tempuri.org/IInventoryCheckService/`
  - ° **Action: GetInventoryData** This specifies the Operation from the Service Contract we wish to execute
  - ° **Transport Location:** <Path to .SVC file> path not included for brevity purposes

- The `SMCOneWayBroker` itinerary `Is Request Response` property is set to **true**. Even though we are using a one-way receive location, by setting this the runtime promotes the `TransmitWorkID` property to the Message Context. This is used by the `Itinerary Cache` component, which is contained within the `ItinerarySendPassthrough` pipeline as specified on our `SMCDynamicTwoWay` off-ramp. This enables the appropriate itinerary instance to be matched to the response.

- The `ItineraryForwarderSendReceive` is used in our `SMCDynamicTwoWay` off-ramp. When a message is received through a two-way receive port an instance subscription is created. This consists of the `EpmRRCorrelationToken` promoted property and a `RouteDirectToTP` promoted property. The Forwarder component contained within this pipeline sets the `RouteDirectToTP` property to **false** in the message content, hence ensuring that the itinerary can process the message; this is required in our scenario because we use a two-way off-ramp. Once the itinerary has completed it will set the property to **true**; if we had used a two-way On-Ramp, the response would therefore have been returned.

Now, we will test our itinerary and ESB tracing functionality to examine what is happening under the covers.

1. Open up the `Chapter14.SMCSupplyChain.ItineraryLibary` project, which is contained within the solution. Open `SMCOneWayBroker.Itinerary`.

2. Export the itinerary by clicking the Itinerary Designer surface and selecting **Export Model**. Save this in a convenient location as **SMCOneWayBroker.xml** and verify that it exports successfully.

3. We will now deploy this by opening a command prompt and changing to the directory `C:\Program Files\Microsoft BizTalk ESB Toolkit 2.1\Bin`.

4. We will use the tool ESBImportUtil, which is provided to deploy itineraries. Run the following command:

   ```
   EsbImportUtil.exe /f:"<Path to folder with Itinerary>\
   SmcOneWayBroker.xml" /c:deployed
   ```

5. Verify that you get the message **"The Itinerary <Itinerary location xml> was imported successfully to database ..."**.

6. Now check that the receive locations, send ports, and required hosts are started.

7. Now, we will enable tracing for the ESB Toolkit. Open your `BTSNTSVC.EXE.CONFIG` file, which is located by default in `C:\Program Files\Microsoft BizTalk Server 2010\`.

8. Add the following section to your `<Configuration>` block to configure a listener for ESB toolkit 2.1 that will write to the event log.

```
<system.diagnostics>
  <sources >
    <source name ="BizTalk ESB Toolkit 2.1" />
  </sources>
  <switches>
    <add name="BizTalkESBToolkit20"
              value="4"/>
  </switches>
  <trace autoflush="true"
       indentsize="4">
    <listeners>
      <add name="myListener"
         type="System.Diagnostics.EventLogTraceListener"
         initializeData="BizTalk ESB Toolkit 2.1" />
    </listeners>
  </trace>
</system.diagnostics>
```

9. From the BizTalk Administration Console, open the **SMCSupplyChain** application, expand receive locations, and right-click **SMCOnRamp.File** and select **Properties**.

10. Click the configuration ellipsis button for the **ItinerarySelectReceiveXML** pipeline. Set the **ResolverConnectionString** value to: **ITINERARY:\\ name=SMCOneWayBroker**.

11. We will now demonstrate that the Itinerary Broker Service filter functionality works. First copy the **PORequest_small.xml** file, which contains a TotalDue value less than 500, from the `<Chapter 12 files location>\Begin\ SampleMessages` directory and then copy it to `C:\Filedrops\SMCIn`.

12. Within the `C:\Filedrops\SMCOut` directory should be a new PORequest with a Status code of 200 for approved.

13. Copy the **PORequest_large.xml** file, where TotalDue is greater than 500, from the `<Chapter 12 files location>\Begin\SampleMessages` directory to `C:\Filedrops\SMCIn`

14. Within the `C:\Filedrops\SMCOut` directory should be a new PORequest with a Status code of 400 for rejected.

15. Open the Event Viewer Application Log and you will see events with source **BizTalk ESB Toolkit 2.1**. You will see events similar to the following. This particular event references a service **id** that corresponds to the **id** in our itinerary XML output file.

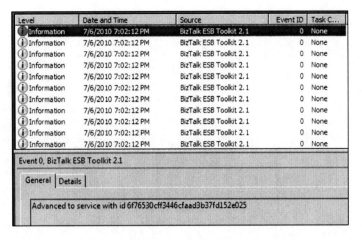

16. If we examine the output XML file for the itinerary, we can see that this **ID** corresponds with the **SMCOffRampDynamicOneWay** off-ramp that is defined in our itinerary.

```
- <Services xmlns="">
    <Service uuid="f0a0fa06d7cf4ee6a5586fef02d11ad6" beginTime="" completeTime=""
    name="SMCOffRampDynamicOneWay" type="Messaging" state="Pending" isRequestResponse="false"
    position="7" serviceInstanceId="" stage="sendTransmit" id="6f76530cff3446cfaad3b37fd152e025"
    nextId="00000000000000000000000000000000" businessName="OffRampExtender_SMCOut" />
  </Services>
```

Using the combination of ESB tracing and the exported XML file enables you to determine which route your itinerary took and where it stopped if a failure occurred.

Summary

In this chapter, we walked through how to implement a supply chain scenario using either an inflexible monolithic approach or a Message Bus-based approach by leveraging the ESB Toolkit 2.1 for BizTalk Server 2010. In particular, we demonstrated the Itinerary Broker Service functionality, which enables routing and can remove the need for Orchestration in some simplistic scenarios. We demonstrated the re-use of previously generated artifacts within different ESB itineraries. We deployed the itineraries easily without recompilation or redeployment of solution code.

We have scratched the surface here on the ESB toolkit functionality. It provides many additional capabilities including the abilities to use Orchestrations within itineraries, resolve itinerary based on Business Rules Engine (BRE) Policies, and a complex exception handling framework and management portal.

15
Multiple Master Synchronization

"The question is," said Humpty Dumpty, "which is to be master — that's all."

Through the Looking-Glass, by Lewis Carroll

It is a rare business that has one and only one version of truth for all of the data that it maintains. Instead businesses rely on a hodge-podge of diverse systems, all of which will identify the critical nouns of a business differently, and will often contain radically different versions of the definition of those nouns.

For example, in one system one of our authors might be labeled "Mike", in another "Michael", and in a third "That funny smelling, old guy." When one attempts to manage and reconcile these discrepancies one is presented with the same issue Humpty Dumpty presented to Alice in *Through the Looking-Glass*.

"When I use a word," Humpty Dumpty said in a rather scornful tone, "it means just what I choose it to mean—neither more nor less."

When trying to integrate and resolve these issues, you are potentially dealing with dozens of Humpty Dumptys, all of whom have attached different, nuanced meanings to the nouns they track. In this chapter, we will review how we keep the Red Queen from chopping off your head by reviewing a use case for a fictitious company, World Wide Widgets, and evaluating and reviewing portions of a potential solution.

Resolution of these issues will be complex and involve multiple, diverse technologies, even within the Microsoft stack. Here we will provide you a glimpse into the large world of master data management and the multiple methods for arriving at a single version of truth within a large diverse organization.

Use Case

World Wide Widgets (WWW) developed and patented multiple types of widgets for use in the brake and acceleration systems of automobiles and light trucks. They currently manufacture these system components in factories in North America, South East Asia, and Europe for sale to several auto manufacturers. Each manufacturer has insisted on slightly different designs of these components. WWW has sold the Widge-O-Stop brake system and the Widge-O-Go acceleration system, with modifications to the Toy O D'oh car company.

It was recently announced that Toy O D'oh will recall all 2009 and 2010 models for faulty brakes and gas pedals. Each of these systems uses WWW's patented Widge-O units. Regulatory authorities in Asia, North America, and Europe have all announced investigations and the legal department has warned management to expect long and protracted litigation around these issues.

You have been assigned the task of designing and building a system that will gather and characterize all of the company's records on the development of this system, as well as the sales and marketing of this system to Toy O D'oh. You must get all of the records, including un-structured and semi-structured data.

Key requirements

The system must correctly identify staff over time and correctly assign to them the roles they were in during particular times. This was a very long term effort. People left or joined the company, were promoted or changed roles, or changed names because of marriage or divorce. The project itself went through many code names. The trade name "Widge-O" was coined by the marketing department. The engineers, patent lawyers, and others involved in the research development and patents used numerous other terms.

Third-party consultants were also used as part of the development efforts. These include safety testing labs, software developers, and outside law firms for patent and regulatory work, all of whom should have (but perhaps did not) leave copies of their work product with WWW. Your system should identify gaps if they exist.

The company requires each staff person to maintain documents and work product on their local hard drives for seven years. Some staff have found this to be an onerous requirement so they have moved data onto other media. They will make that media available to you for searching and indexing.

Structured data that must be searched can be found in both Oracle systems and SQL Server systems. You must identify employees involved with the Widge-O. Data concerning these assignments can be found in the Oracle HR system. Data concerning safety testing can be found in SQL Server-based systems.

One of the biggest issues with any forensics type of project is the human factor. Here, the lawyers are involved and you must expect that everyone will be running for cover. They will be deleting documents and e-mails, moving material to USB devices and engaging in every imaginable effort to **CYA (Confound Your Assessment)**. Additionally, employees are not attempting to cover up or hide data, but they may inadvertently improperly store data.

During the normal course of events data and documents are altered over time. Versioning and the explanations for changes can be key evidence in law. You will need to track versions dates and revisions of data as part of any solution.

Additional facts

Given the risks and issues that would arise should this project fail, including legal liabilities and damage to the business's good name, we can assume that we will have more than adequate staffing and technical capabilities for this project. Moreover, this is an engineering company that understands the need for good design and competent software development, so they hire superior talent for both development and operations.

Pattern description

Like most enterprises, WWW has multiple databases each of which controls data for its specific area or business purpose, each of which is master of its own domain. Like most enterprises, WWW has no minimal tools in place to monitor and resolve differences between these data sources. For the purposes of this litigation, these differences must be identified and brought to the attention of the business so that they can be resolved or explained.

In master data management (MDM) situations such as this one, we gather the key data, often called the key nouns of an organization, identify data disparities, and reconcile those disparities. For example, a key noun for any organization would be "customers". The same customer might be identified as "Mike" in one system and "Michael" in another or may have different mailing addresses and phone numbers in those systems because of a move. One would reconcile these disparities in any MDM system using appropriate business rules so that the company can properly service the customer and has an accurate picture of its customer base. One rule might be "the most recently reported address is deemed to be the correct address", for example.

MDM in this situation serves the key role of gathering evidence for analysis by the legal team.

WWW needs to gather all of its data concerning its interactions with Toy oh D'oh, identify any discrepancies, then reconcile those discrepancies or feed them into a human workflow so that they can be investigated.

Candidate architecture

There are several tools that we need, to handle the issues presented.

1. We must extract existing data from multiple relational systems and load it into a clean environment where we will track data access and changes.

2. We must manage the definitions of key business nouns across multiple environments.

3. We must track metadata concerning various documents, spreadsheets, and other objects.

4. We must use unstructured and semi-structured data as a source for data mining and data analysis tasks by storing metadata concerning these objects in SQL Server.

5. We must search through and index semi-structured and un-structured data across the enterprise. This will include every server, every laptop, and all of the miscellaneous storage devices.

These needs cannot be met with any single product or technology in the Microsoft catalog. Rather, we will need to incorporate several technologies into our solution to gather, index, store, and present data to end users.

Solution design aspects

Here, we will review all of the technologies that we can bring to bear on the problem at hand.

SSIS

We have already discussed the use of SSIS in Chapter 5. Here we have "classic" ETL issues—the very issues SSIS was designed to deal with—as well as extracting data from "non-traditional" sources, such as documents, e-mails, and spreadsheets. SSIS does not typically come up on an architect's radar when faced with these data sources. Nevertheless, SSIS is an excellent tool for extracting metadata and other information from these objects.

Master Data Services

The key functionality of Master Data Services that we will illustrate here is the creation of a master data hub—a single source for all master data regardless of source system. We will ensure data consistency by treating each master data change as a transaction and logging the date, time, and user making the change.

Search Server Express

We must search and index documents across the enterprise. These documents can be in numerous formats. Microsoft released Search Server Express in 2008. We might also consider FAST ESP; however, Search Server provides the functionality we seek here and has the advantage of being free.

Solution operations aspects

WWW already has SQL Server in place. At most, we are simply leveraging the functionality of the latest release of SQL Server. While Search Server Express may be new technology for this enterprise, it has an easy, light, and intuitive administrative interface and should not provide any significant issues for WWW operations staff.

Organizational aspects

Simply put, this project must get done and must get done correctly. The risks to the very existence of the company should they lose any litigation, along with the adverse publicity arising from taking the blame for product failures, is simply too great. The organization will get the resources needed to be successful. In this case, that should be a simple task. For the most part, we are extending products already in use with a staff very familiar with the Microsoft stack.

Solution evaluation

Unlike other scenarios, we have discussed throughout this book, here we have no single magic bullet technology that can solve all of our issues. Instead, we will need to deploy multiple technologies that can meet the wide-ranging requirements presented here.

Design	Delivery	Operations	Organization
👍	👍	👍	👍

Architecture selection

Let us consider the components that make up this candidate architecture.

SQL Server, Master Data Services, and SSIS	
Benefits	**Risks**
• Easily deployed and extensible ETL tool	• Need to build sophisticated error handling systems
• Designed to handle batch processing of large files, exactly the task at hand	• Does not handle unstructured data well
• No additional licensing costs – comes with SQL Server	
• Can be built and maintained by current staff	
• Can build business rules to resolve data conflicts	

Search Server	
Benefits	**Risks**
• Indexes unstructured data	• Not clear if staff has the skills to support product
• Can review administrative shares (such as C$) on desktops	• Still possible for users to "hide" relevant documents on portable devices

This is an extraordinarily complex data management task as it touches on all of the data held by the organization in every possible format in which the organization holds it. You must get data in both the organizations "approved" formats as well as in any format that might be held by a key staff person that they obtained from outside sources (such as through internet research). In this case, the combination of a SQL Server-based solution along with Search Server will serve this organization. More complex organizations will need to consider FAST.

Building the solution

We will need to deal with both structured data stored in relational databases and unstructured data stored in file systems of various sorts (for example, marketing documents, engineering design drawings). We will manage conflicts between the relational systems using master Data Services, ETL using SSIS, and file system indexing using Search Server and SSIS.

The Electronic Discovery Reference Model (`http://edrm.net/`) refers to six phases of handling data:

1. Information management
2. Identification
3. Preservation and Collection
4. Processing, Review, and Analysis
5. Production
6. Presentation

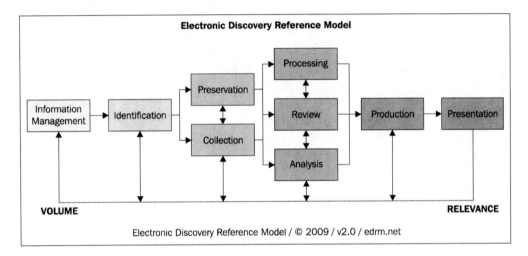

Our tasks focus on steps 1 through 3 while providing a firm foundation for steps 4 through 6, which can be handled using SharePoint, SQL Server Reporting Services, and Power Pivot.

In order to execute on these tasks we will need to have two data constructs, one for document and other source metadata and a second to hold relational data for analysis. While we could use two schemas for this purpose we have elected to go with two separate databases. First, this will optimize performance for what is expected to be two very different reporting criteria. Second, it will minimize confusion for both users and system operators. Third, it will allow us to secure the data properly, particularly if we need to extend the metadata system to include comments or other attorney work product, which should not be distributed outside the organization.

You can get a basic understanding of attorney client privilege and attorney work product rules at `http://www.lectlaw.com/files/lit16.htm`.

From a high-level logical view our system will look like this:

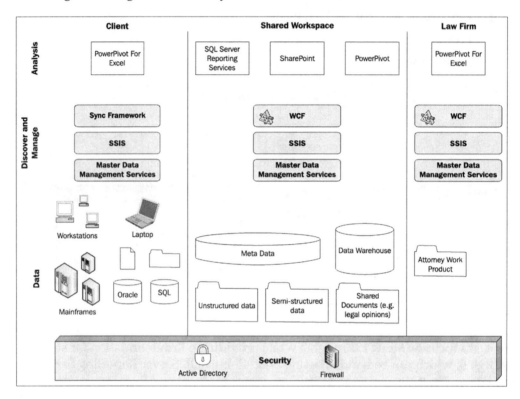

Fetching relational data

To borrow a phrase from cheap detective novels, we will need to know the who, what, when, where, and how for the development and production of the Widge-O. The "who" can be ascertained from the HR system. Here, we will use the HR schema provided to us in the Oracle 10G express edition as it is already populated with data. We have written out the employees and department tables to comma-separated files. As we covered the SSIS objects we will use in the debatching data chapter, we will not review the details again. We have created two parallel data flows, each of which pulls data from a comma-delimited ASCII file, converts the data to an appropriate data type, and loads the data into the correct tables in the HR schema of the metadata database we previously created.

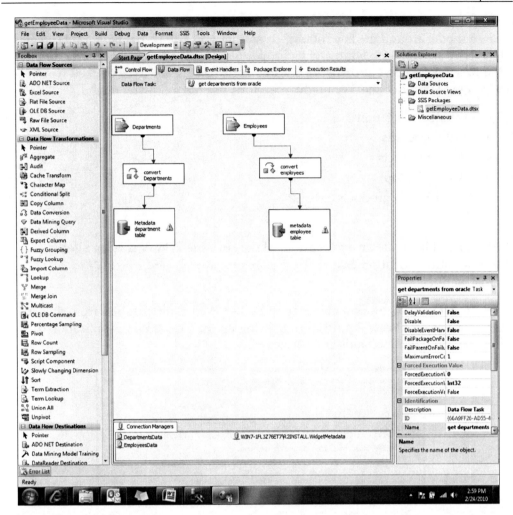

Master Data Services

Since this is a new technology with SQL Server 2008 R2, we should briefly discuss its setup. Master Data Services installs from its own MSI and is not part of the "standard" SQL Server install. The install program can be found at `<DVD Drive>:\MasterDataServices\x64\1033_ENU`. Upon completion of the install, the Master Data Services configuration manager will open. Follow the wizards and the installation instructions you can obtain from Microsoft to install the MDS database and configure the website to handle the web services that will be used to perform the actual data management between the MDS hub and the various databases we will be integrating.

Once you have completed the installation and configuration, your next step will be to create a model around the key "nouns" or entities you will be tracking. MDS creates a hierarchy around each noun and its properties. This is a hierarchical structure that organizes the data. In our scenario, one key entity that needs to be tracked would be the Widge-O product line. We might, therefore, use the following model:

- WidgeO Litigation
- Auto products
- Brake products
- Widge-O Stop
- Acceleration products
- Widge-O Go

We will need to create an application. Make sure the WWW service allows Windows authentication. See `http://support.microsoft.com/kb/942043/` for instructions.

Open the MDS configuration manager and select **Web Configuration** from the left panel. Next select **Create Application** to bring up the Create Web Application dialog. Fill in the configuration fields and select **OK**.

Next, you will need to select a database for the application. Click on the **Select** button that appears under the "Database" group box to bring up the "Connect to Database" dialog. Make the appropriate selections for your databases security context, and select **OK**.

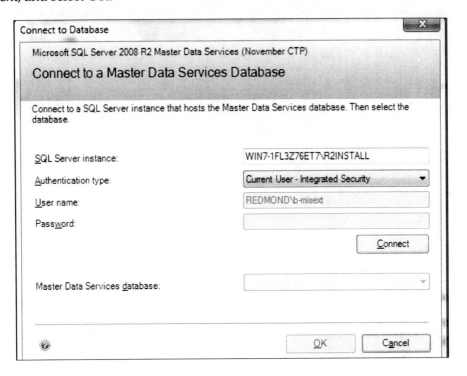

Your Configuration manager should now appear similar to the following screen:

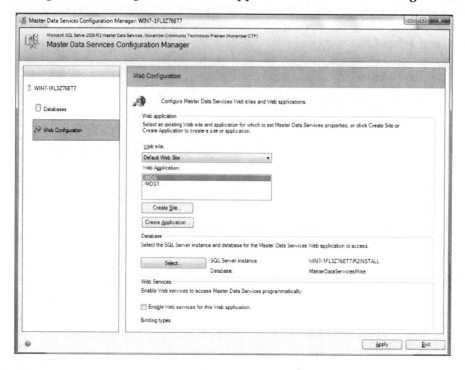

Select **Apply**. You should see the success dialog box. Select the "Launch Application in the Browser" checkbox to begin the actual work.

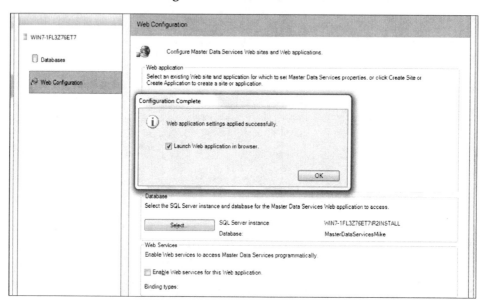

This will bring you to your default management page in your browser.

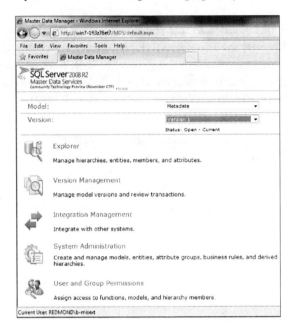

It will quickly become apparent that navigation through the MDS interface is not particularly intuitive. A cheat sheet is available at `http://msdn.microsoft.com/en-us/library/ee633735(SQL.105).aspx`. Open the "System Administration" link. We need to create a new model as described previously, so click on **Models**, then click on the icon with the "+" symbol.

Enter **WidgeO litigation** in the text box and leave the defaults and click on the **Save** icon.

We will now need to add entities to our model. You can think of entities as levels in the hierarchy or as dimensions in a snowflake schema. Select the **Manage** menu item then select **Entities**. Once again select the green "+" icon and add **Auto products** and select **No** from the **Enable explicit hierarchies and collections** drop down. Repeat the process for "Brake products", "Widge-O Stop", "Acceleration products" and "Widge-O Go".

Entities have attributes, which are... well attributes. They are similar to attributes in an XML file or the fields in a table. Once you have completed the creation of the entities, you should see the manage entities screen, looking like the following image:

When you select one of the entities, a number of icons will appear, as you can see displayed in previous image. We will limit our attribute creation to the Widge-O Go and Widge-O Stop leaf levels. Highlight **Widge-O Go** and click on the pencil icon. You will be taken to the edit entity page. Note that there are already two attributes, name and code. We will add "version" and "data source" to the attributes. Click on the green "+" symbol. The Add Attribute page will appear. Type "data source" in the name field and accept the remaining defaults. Repeat the process for "version" then repeat these steps for the Widge-O Stop. Click back through the save icons to reach the entity maintenance page and save your work.

Next, we will need to relate the entities through domain-level attributes. So, for the "Brake Product" entity, add a Widge-O Stop domain attribute and tie it with the Brake Product entity. For the acceleration products entities add a Widge-O Go domain attribute and tie it to the acceleration products. For the auto products entities, add a brake products and acceleration products domain attribute and tie it to auto products.

In order to complete our hierarchy, add a domain-based attribute "Products" to the WidgeO Litigation entity and point it towards the WidgeO Litigation entity in the **Entity** drop down.

Navigate back to the main menu. You can use the bread crumbs path appearing next to the SQL Server graphics in the upper left of the page. You will need to make sure that the correct model appears in the model menu, and then select "version_1" from the versions drop down.

Now (finally) we create our hierarchy. Select "System Administration" from the home page, then manage derived hierarchies from the menu. The derived hierarchy is derived from relating domain attributes.

Select **WidgeO Litigation** from the drop down and click on the green "+" icon. Name the hierarchy **WidgO ToyOdoh litigation** and click save. The hierarchy editing page will appear.

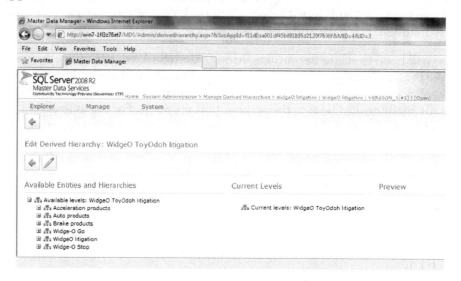

Simply drag the auto products line from the left to the right and the hierarchy is created. We have now completed our hierarchical structure to use to manage relational data concerning the product lines.

Next, we will need to create the infrastructure required to manage unstructured and semi-structured data, such as the material contained in Word files, e-mail, PDF files, or spreadsheets.

Unstructured data

A significant portion of a company's data is not held in structured relational databases. Instead, it is held in multiple, unstructured, or semi-structured formats. Think of how much day-to-day activity you, dear reader, carry out using relational databases and how much is carried out with e-mail. Indeed, you might even consider code and comments to fit the definition of semi-structured data.

Here the litigation teams need all of the documents concerning the Widge-O lines of products. "All" does not mean "most"—so every document, marketing graphic, engineering design, and sales spreadsheet must be found and indexed.

For purposes of this exercise, we want to capture the metadata concerning all relevant documents. For purposes of illustration, we will create a single directory to crawl. In the real world, you would need to crawl the administrative partitions and associated directories of each computer on the network (for example, \\computer1\ C$, \\computer1\D$, \\ComputerN\C$) searching for any file with a relevant extension (for example, docx, xls, pdf).

Create a directory labeled "WidgeO" then open your SSIS project for this chapter. For purposes of illustrating this effort, simply load it with a random assortment of files you now have on your system. Create a variable named **path** with a string data type, then drag a **Foreach** container onto the package.

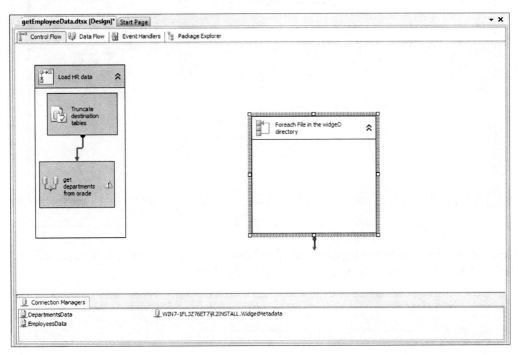

Open the `Foreach` loop container and select the **Collection** dialog from the left. We will be using a "For each file" enumerator. Browse to the WidgeO directory you created earlier.

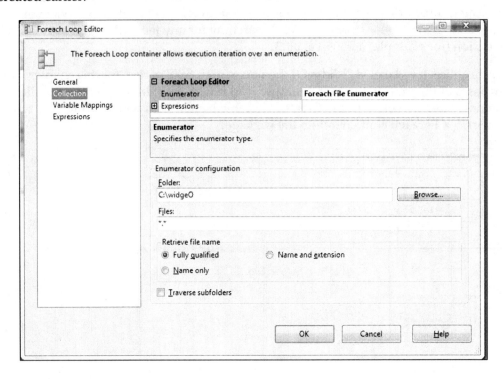

Next, select the variable mapping and select the `User::path` variable we created earlier. This should be mapped to the 0 index. Click **OK**.

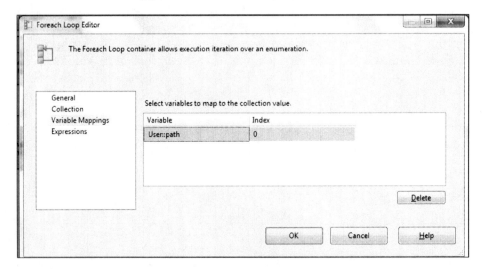

Click **OK** to accept your work.

The Foreach loop will loop through each file in this directory. We will be creating a script to fetch the metadata and loading the results into our database.

In order to handle that task, create additional string variables createDate to track the date of creation, DocName for the document name, and lastModDate to track the last modification date. You can create other variables to track other properties as you choose.

Drag a script task into the Foreach container and label it getDocData. You can create some artificial data for purposes of this exercise by copying random files into the widgeO directory.

Open the execute script object. We need to map the variables correctly. The path variable should be entered as read only, while the DocName, createDate, and LastModDate are mapped as read-write. Select the values from the drop downs.

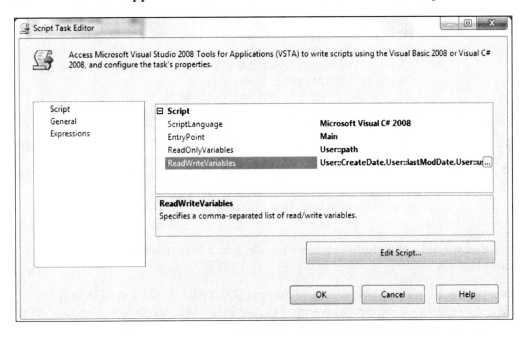

There are many ways we can get this data from the Dts variables collection into the database. Here we will choose to build an insert statement string and pass it to an execute SQL task, mostly because the author is about to start vacation and wants to get this done in the fastest and easiest way possible. To that end, create a variable "insertSQL" and add it as a read-write variable. We will then simply concatenate the string to create the insert statement.

You are now ready to actually write code!

You will need to add a USING System.IO line, then the following code in the Main():

```
public void Main()
{
    string path = Dts.Variables["path"].Value.ToString();
    //remember that the variable name is case sensitive.
    //for test
    //MessageBox.Show(path, "path", MessageBoxButtons.OK);
    System.IO.FileInfo fileInfo = new FileInfo(path);
    Dts.Variables["CreateDate"].Value =
                        fileInfo.CreationTime.ToString();
    Dts.Variables["lastModDate"].Value =
                        fileInfo.LastWriteTime.ToString();
    Dts.Variables["DocName"].Value =
                            fileInfo.Name.ToString();
    //MessageBox.Show(Dts.Variables["DocName"].Value.
            ToString(), "DocName", MessageBoxButtons.OK);
    //build the sql
    string SQL = "INSERT INTO Documents.DocumentTrace
    (DocName,DocPath,CreateDate,LastModifedDate,CreatedBy,
    ComputerID) VALUES ( " + "' ";
    SQL = SQL + Dts.Variables["DocName"].Value + "' " + ",
                        " + "' " + path + "' " +", ";
    SQL = SQL + "' " + Dts.Variables["CreateDate"].Value + "'
     , " + "' " + Dts.Variables["lastModDate"].Value + "' ,";
    SQL = SQL + "133, 1)";
    //MessageBox.Show(SQL, "SQL", MessageBoxButtons.OK);
    Dts.Variables["insertSQL"].Value = SQL;
    Dts.TaskResult = (int)ScriptResults.Success;
}
```

Note that we did not include any error handling as a best practice for this example shell.

Once your code is complete, drag and execute SQL task into the ForEach loop. We will use the same connection as we used earlier in the chapter. Select "Variable" from the SQL Source Type drop down and select User::insertSQL as the Source Variable.

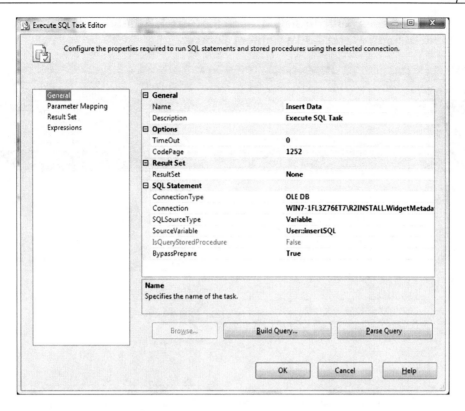

We have previously populated some the tables with data using SQL inserts included in the source code. This statement will insert the data into the `DocumentTrace` tables so that we have the correct metadata for relevant documents. You can now run the code and test it by selecting off the `DocumentTrace` table.

Search

Like most companies, the "working knowledge" at WWW is often not contained in formal, relational data structures. Instead it is in documents, e-mails, spreadsheets, and a host of other types of files that are used in every company for day-to-day interaction and collaboration.

You will need to work with a system that has SharePoint installed. Download and install Search Server Express from Microsoft using the install wizards. We will only work with crawling data on the local machine hosting SharePoint, as most of our corporate masters would take a dim view of us crawling production networks and colleagues' computers as a training exercise. We will also focus on Search Server Express as it allows you to familiarize yourself with the basic tasks associated with indexing and searching for unstructured data without incurring any licensing costs. Free is good.

Once you have Search Server installed, open the **Search Administration** page, then select **Content Sources** and **Add a Content Source**.

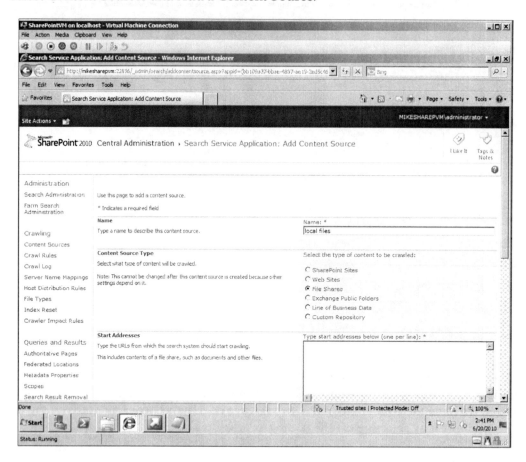

Name the crawl **local files** and select the **File Shares**. For the **Start Address** enter the absolute path for the machine you are working with along with the directory you wish to crawl (for example, \\MyMachine\SomeShare). Select "Crawl the folder and all subfolders of each start address" and, if you wish, create a schedule for both the full and incremental crawls. Check the "Start full crawl of this content source", click **OK** and away you go. You will be brought back to the **Manage Content Sources** page where you will see the status of your crawl.

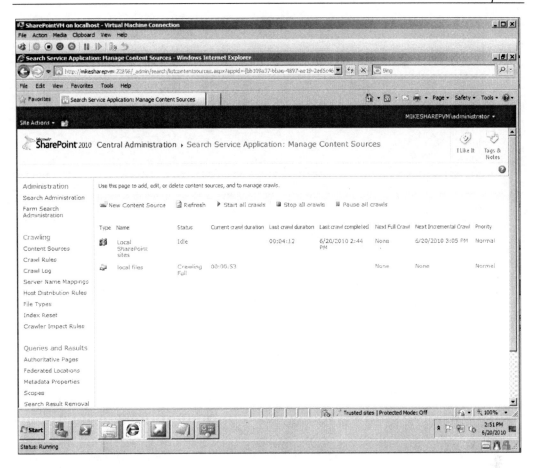

Once the crawl is complete, you can check the results in the crawl log. You can also enter a search term in the SharePoint site and see the results. For our particular scenario, this makes the content available quickly and easily to the lawyers and others who will need to work with it.

Summary

Here we have scratched the surface of the myriad issues surrounding master data management and the use of unstructured data in enterprise data management systems. There are, of course, additional tools and methods that we simply do not have the space to cover. Here we have used the basic tools of master data services and SSIS to handle some of the tasks associated with this problem.

16
Rapid Flexible Scalability

How often have you looked at the logs that are monitoring a system's usage and seen minimal use of memory, CPU, or other system resources? Servers are built to handle anticipated peak loads. Normal practice and the natural tendency to anticipate the worst and/or cover your behind usually mean that the highest peaks that a server can handle are almost never encountered. This is expensive, both in terms of capital costs for hardware and licenses and operational costs such as electricity, cooling, floor and rack space costs, support staff and other incidental costs. It also imposes significant burdens on the operational staff supporting the machines. The more machines one uses, the more likely it is that one of them will break. In keeping with Murphy's Law, this break will, of course, occur at 4:55 PM on the Friday before a holiday weekend.

The solutions associated with cloud computing have been around for some time but have typically been seen as immature. Certainly, they were never robust enough for enterprise-level applications such as small data marts or other applications with lower data storage needs (for example, small "stove pipe" applications supporting a single department in your company). With the introduction of Hyper-V and Azure, Microsoft has moved the cloud and virtualization story forward so that it can now support a flexible environment that scales seamlessly and allows for rapid application deployment to a secure environment.

In this chapter, we will expand on the use case of Chapter 15 involving WWW and Toy O D'oh automobile brakes and accelerators.

Use case

In Chapter 15, our use case involved World Wide Widgets (WWW) and their sale of brake and accelerator parts to Toy O D'oh. As a result of the problems with both the brakes and accelerators in Toy O D'oh vehicles, WWW has been sued in ten US states and is facing investigations by federal authorities in the United States, provincial and central government agencies in Canada, and several government regulators in Europe and Asia. Additional litigation is expected in other US states, as well as several provinces in Canada. The Italian government has attributed one death to problems with the braking system and has launched a criminal investigation. WWW has retained multiple law firms in each of these jurisdictions to handle these matters. Each jurisdiction has different rules of evidence and requirements for producing documents or other evidence. Each law firm has been retained for its capabilities in various areas of law. While each matter will have much in common, the differences in law require that each firm have a separate, walled off environment for collaboration with WWW.

WWW requires a consistent public face for these matters so that it can control adverse publicity and so that inconsistencies are not exploited by opposing attorneys. WWW also needs to control costs, so the firms must share work with each other so that WWW will not need to pay for the same efforts more than once.

WWW must quickly spin up a common collaboration area for all law firms as well as multiple, separate collaboration applications for each individual matter. WWW cannot afford the overhead and does not have the physical capacity to host individual database and application servers for each matter. Each matter is expected to be resolved relatively quickly, so the collaboration applications will need to be available for a period of six months for the US regulatory matters to three years for the state court tort litigation. At the close of each matter, the data will be archived and the collaboration application shut down. Therefore, WWW would like to keep hardware costs to a minimum.

One complicating factor that must be considered is the issue of attorney-client privilege and the differing rules that may apply to the privilege in different jurisdictions and legal systems. (For a general overview of the privilege, see `http://en.wikipedia.org/wiki/Attorney-client_privilege`.)

The development team will need to work closely with the user community, in this case the lawyers, to make sure you are meeting their very precise requirements for securing these privileged communications. Your failure to secure this data properly could result in a waiver of attorney client privilege and potentially harm WWW's position in court or with the public.

Candidate architectures

We have two viable options for implementing our business requirements.

Candidate architecture #1–Windows Azure / SQL Azure

There are several key requirements that Microsoft's cloud computing offering, Windows Azure, can meet easily. First "new" instances of any application can be spun up easily and then configured or customized. Each application scales transparently. As usage peaks, for example when filing or other court deadlines approach, the Azure platform scales transparently. As usage falls off, costs are reduced under the "pay for what you use" pricing model offered by Microsoft.

Cloud-based solutions will not require extensive capital expenditures for servers or delays imposed by the need to build, ship, and install hardware. One simply goes to Microsoft, activates the appropriate sized solution, and starts to build the application. The management of Toy O D'oh wants to put this matter behind them, as it has given them an enormous public relations hit. Given the possibility that many of these cases will be resolved quickly (for example, through settlement) it would be unwise to make a large capital investment for multiple servers that may be decommissioned long before their expected lifespan has expired.

Solution design aspects

Windows Azure offers a simple resource that meets the business requirements for a rapidly deployed, relatively inexpensive, and highly secure environment. Azure scales transparently, so during peak usage periods you have no need to worry about capacity, yet you will not need to pay for or support that additional capacity in the valleys of demand.

The issue of attorney-client privilege is potentially complicating. Azure stores data on hardware owned and controlled by Microsoft or its partners, so you are putting privileged communications on a medium not controlled physically by the attorney or the client. Some have noted the potential for loss of privacy rights such as attorney-client privilege (*State v. Bellar*, 231 Or.App. 80, 217 P.3d 1094 (Sept. 30, 2009)). Make sure to explain to both the internal corporate legal staff and outside attorneys precisely how data is moved and stored in a cloud environment so that they understand and sign off any potential risks.

Solution operations aspects

Windows Azure provides an easy operational framework because the application is abstracted from the hardware and operating system. WWW will not need to specify servers, order them, await delivery, place them in racks, build them out to corporate specifications, make sure you are in compliance with licenses for the operating system and other software, install software, test, etc. all before a single line of code is written or any customization of applications is started. One simply goes online with Microsoft, orders the appropriately sized environment and you are up and running that day. Software developers can therefore focus on what they do best, developing software, instead of worrying about hardware and operating system configurations.

Of course, it does not follow that one can simply throw garbage code up to the cloud and expect it to run well. Indeed, because it is a shared environment, Microsoft may well shut down SQL queries that takes "too long" to run, uses tempDB "too much" or otherwise behaves boorishly with respect to system resources. A developer will still want to performance test a system to make sure the code is not a bottleneck. The point here is that your focus is now on the code and only the code, not on the myriad details of supporting a rack of servers.

Organizational aspects

WWW has a sophisticated IT organization that is faced with the need to get application infrastructures up and running quickly, securely, and with a minimum of headaches so they can get on with supporting the business during a time of crisis. Azure distils these tasks to their essence, allowing the staff to get on with the application side of extracting WWW from the mud hole they are currently stuck in.

Solution evaluation

Design	Delivery	Operations	Organization

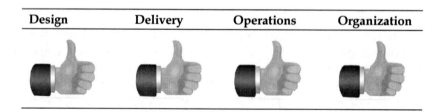

Candidate architecture #2–Hyper-V

Hyper-V is a virtualized server environment that will allow WWW to host multiple solutions in their own environment. They will have control over all aspects of their data in a Hyper-V environment, including physical control over the data storage. While this would solve potential issues around waiver of the attorney-client privilege, it has all of the downsides of hosting the environment at WWW (capital and operational costs, and so on). Like Azure, new instances can be brought online quickly after the initial server build is complete. Hyper-V is easy to administer and well within the capabilities of any senior server administrator and DBA.

Solution design aspects

Like Windows Azure, Hyper-V offers an easy-to-configure environment where base installs and configurations can be completed within hours once the host server is installed and configured. As no third party is involved in any aspect of this architecture there will be no issue of waiving any privilege. WWW does not keep spare, rather powerful servers and extra Windows Server operating system licenses just lying around, however, so there will be capital expenses associated with these purchases, as well as day-to-day operational costs associated with the systems maintenance.

Solution operations aspects

Hyper-V also provides for an operating system that is abstracted from the underlying hardware. It is not, however, infinitely scalable. It is limited to four virtual processors, 64 GB of memory, and has other limitations (see `http://technet.microsoft.com/en-us/library/ee405267(WS.10).aspx` for details). For the purposes of this application, for WWW, we should be well within the limits of Hyper-V. This application will have a limited number of users and is not expected to be processor intensive.

Organizational aspects

As with the other technologies discussed, we can expect the IT staff to pick up Hyper-V quickly and have no issue with the underlying technology. There are, however, cost, time, and expense issues that need to be considered and balanced with the legal issues presented. Moreover, the need for a Hyper-V solution will be over, long before the hardware has reached its end of life. The server could be re-purposed to other applications after these legal matters have settled, but we do not have any strategic requirements that would match this hardware.

Solution evaluation

Design	Delivery	Operations	Organization

Architecture selection

Windows Azure / SQL Azure

Benefits	**Risks**
• Pay as you go, so no capital license cost • No need to purchase hardware or deal with rack space, cooling systems or other hardware operations • Rapidly deploy applications • No "unused" capacity (for example, idle servers)	• Learning curve for WWW staff • Potential waiver of attorney-client privilege

Hyper-V

Benefits	**Risks**
• Rapidly deploy applications • Completely control environment, including physical access to the servers and data • Integrates easily with WWW AD security • Licensing is based on physical processors, so license costs are lower than "bare metal"	• Delays in roll out caused by vendor delays in delivering hardware • Licensing and hardware capital costs • Limited scalability • Must use SQL Server 2008 and Windows Server 2008; will not work well with any legacy licenses

In this case, we have two potentially conflicting requirements. The first is to keep capital costs and operational costs to a minimum while quickly bringing up applications as required. This requirement points strongly towards a Windows Azure solution. On the other hand, a Windows Azure solution could form the basis for adverse judicial rulings on assertions of attorney-client privilege. That would be bad, to say the least.

A mixed solution would be highly recommended here.

As a first step, we would need to obtain from the attorneys a list of jurisdictions where the use of Windows Azure would be too risky relative to the costs involved. We would then architect a Hyper-V solution that meets the anticipated peak needs of those jurisdictions. Presumably, the hardware itself will be smaller and present lower costs than a server built for all jurisdictions. Remember when pricing this model that Microsoft licenses software based on physical processors, so we can create as many virtual servers as the physical limitations of the server and network environment can handle. Ultimately, this means our licensing costs would be lower for a partial Hyper-V solution.

All of the other environments would be built on Windows Azure. You should expect this to be an iterative process along the following lines:

You: Here is what it would cost to have all 50 US states on Hyper-V.

Business: That Much?!?!?! Too expensive! Take off these 10 states!

Repeat until resolved.

Building the solution

We will focus our efforts here on building a cloud-based solution and the data portion of a cloud application.. Cloud computing requires a significant shift in how one thinks of building applications, particularly in the case of database professionals. Those of us who spend hours each day worrying about issues like I/O, disk contention, backup and recovery, storage and partitioning, or other similar issues related to hardware now have no worries. The effect can be a bit scary, similar to removing the training wheels from a child's bike. Sure you can go wicked fast, but how do you keep your balance?

If you have not already done so, go to `http://www.microsoft.com/windowsazure/` and set up your Azure account. As of this writing, Microsoft is offering a free version to help you get started. As a first step, we will want to create a database and populate it. One thing each of the lawyers will need is data on employees and their jobs, so they can ascertain who was involved with each technology and contact them if needed. In addition, this data will tell us which employees should have their local systems and occasionally connected storage devices (for example, flash drives) searched for relevant material.

Go to your Azure portal and navigate to the SQL Azure database tab and click the "Create Database" button. As each of these applications is focused on cases or enforcement actions in individual jurisdictions, we will plan on creating at least one database for each. Certain jurisdictions, simply because of geographical size, population, or other issues may require more than one. Here, we will create a database for **Colorado** with a size of **1 GB**. We used this size because that is free.

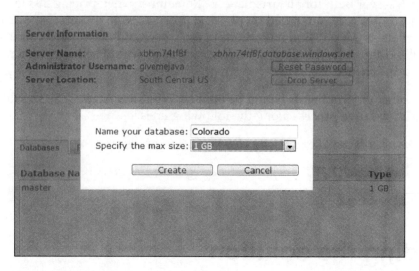

Press the create button and the database will be created. There is no need to set the path for your data files, create separate transaction log files, worry about file groups, set database level options, or do any other task that one would normally do when creating a database on a server in your local data center.

DBAs, are you feeling verklempt?

We will want to create unique users and logons for each of our individual applications so that the security requirements are met. Fire up the SQL Server management studio and connect to SQL Azure as described in the Azure primer chapter. Create a new logon and user with simple SQL statements such as the ones that follow:

```
CREATE LOGIN ColoradoUser
  WITH PASSWORD = '1nYourDre@ms'
GO
use Colorado
go
CREATE USER ColoradoUser
  FOR LOGIN ColoradoUser
  WITH DEFAULT_SCHEMA =   dbo
GO


-- Add user to the database owner role
EXEC sp_addrolemember N'db_owner', N'ColoradoUser'
GO
```

With respect to security, SQL Azure will force you to use strongly typed passwords. This is, of course, a best practice that we should be using at all times.

Next, we will need to create tables to store relevant data. We will demonstrate data loading from the Oracle HR schema shipped with Oracle Express using SSIS.

Create the relevant tables using the accompanying scripts. These are extremely simple Create Table statements. Again, since we have abstracted our application from the underlying physical storage, we do not need to worry about a host of parameters we would need to worry about if we were placing the table on storage in the corporate data center. Hence, we do not see keywords such as "ON" or references to fill factors.

Integrating SSIS with SQL Azure

In the coming discussion, you will note something quite profound about the difference between using SSIS as an ETL tool with SQL Azure and SSIS as an ETL tool with SQL Server on "bare metal" living in your corporate data center. That profound difference is that there is no difference.

Well, truthfully, that is an oversimplification, but not by much. The steps you take when designing and building a solution, the decisions on whether to do data transformations on the database or within SSIS, and similar considerations do not change at all. Set operations should still be done on the database side; "non-set" or cursor operations should still be done on the SSIS. SQL Azure does not support CLR as of this writing. In cases where you would consider a CLR stored procedure, use script objects in SSIS or create an application in the Application Fabric and use it to manipulate data instead.

SQL Azure will tend to be less forgiving of sloppy or poor coding practices. With SQL Azure you are sharing a resource, so long running transactions, acquisition of too many locks, excessive TempDB usage, or other sloppy practices will generate errors in the Azure environment.

The logic of a shared resource, abstracted from the underlying hardware, also means that certain transact SQL features are not supported. For example, global temporary tables, access to system tables, most features related to data storage (for example, filegroup management) and distributed transactions are all not supported. Check MSDN for a full listing.

One item that is a bit counter-intuitive is the fact that SQL Azure does not support heap tables. For you to do inserts, and for the table to be useful by any practical measure, it must have a clustered index. There are some papers and blog posts indicating that the need for clustered indexing arises from the way Microsoft replicates data across physical environments and otherwise maintains storage of your data.

Clustered indexes are, of course, easily created and do not require any new primary keys for the purposes of this application. For example, on the HR.Employees table we created earlier, we would simply execute the following:

```
Create clustered index IX_Employee_ID
on HR.Employees(Employee_ID)
GO
```

Again, the index is abstracted from the underlying storage, so we do not need to worry about storage options. Like the creation of the tables, we do not concern ourselves with fill factors, padding or other arguments that concern where or how to physically store the data. We just create the index and let SQL Azure figure out the rest.

Specific to SSIS, you cannot use OLEDB to connect to SQL Azure. So our first step will be to create an ADO.NET connection to our SQL Azure database shown as follows. The more observant reader will note that we are running SSIS on a virtual machine using Hyper-V. This is because some of our authors just like showing off.

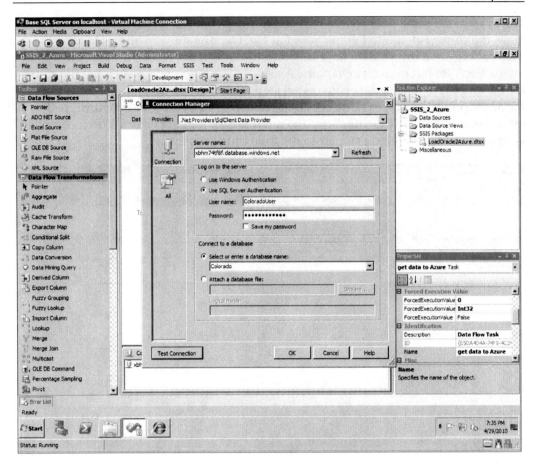

Other than the use of ADO.NET, there is nothing very different between connecting to SQL Azure and connecting to any other database.

We will use the same data source we used in prior chapters to load the employees table, the comma-delimited employees flat file. Once again we will create an SSIS package and drag a data flow task into it. We will not repeat the specific instructions set out in earlier chapters. As shown next, you will need a flat file source for the employee data, a data conversion step to convert the data from ASCII to the appropriate data types (Unicode, date, numeric(9,2), and four byte unsigned integers), an ADO.NET destination, and a flat file for logging errors. When complete, your data flow should look similar to the following image:

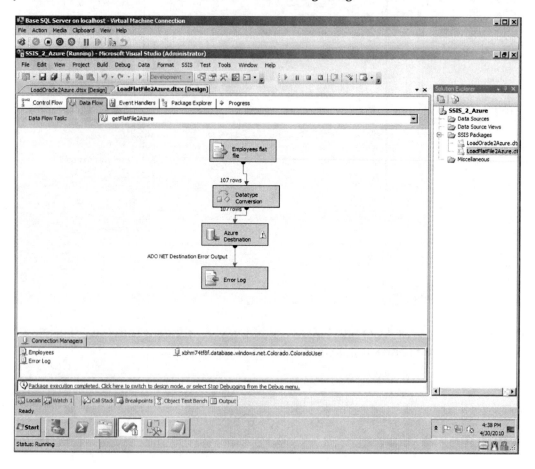

Summary

As you can see, SQL Azure allows us to deploy scalable applications rapidly in response to a business crisis and provides the security we need for even the most sensitive data and corporate relationships. By running our ETL on Hyper-V, we further conserve resources and save on licensing and hardware costs.

17
Low-Latency Request-Reply

In a fast-paced web-based world, the need for up-to-the-minute information from external sources is critical in maintaining an effective web presence. From real-time inventory checks, to stock trades, to banking transactions, to large batch data processing, low-latency processing is essential. This chapter's use case will focus on low-latency message flow, which is a common pattern for data access with external systems following a **Service Oriented Architecture (SOA)**-based topology.

When interacting with external data sources, it is vital to produce efficient service calls that return external data without significant delay. Building a core foundation of enterprise services and aggregating results effectively can result in faster response times and greater end-user satisfaction. For a front end web-based application, the goal is to have a web page load for the user without a noticeable delay. This is typically thought of a less than 100 millisecond response time for an end-to-end web page load time. While the connection the user has with the site cannot be guaranteed, the response time and logic inside the web page and external service calls can be optimized while preserving a well-constructed and reusable architecture.

Use case

AllFriends Media is an online retailer specializing in selling DVDs online through a successful retail store. The key to the success of the online store has been a social networking experience through other sites allowing users to write detailed reviews on movies, suggest movies to friends, and tag items that other friends might be interested in.

As competition increases with the online DVD market and with the introduction of video download, margins are slim and sales are down. In fact, the business has realized that sometimes they are not the lowest price for an item they sell. They see an increasing trend of users searching the site, reading reviews, and going to buy the DVD elsewhere or buying it on-demand.

Rather than losing all the revenue from these users, the business would like to capitalize on this experience by offering users the ability to buy titles and direct downloads from other vendors directly on the website.

In order to do this, the business would like to add real-time calls from the website to outside services that return pricing and availability information from other vendors. This should happen with limited impact to the user experience. The number of external vendors will be fixed initially at four but others may be added over time.

A mock up of the screen is shown next. The AllFriends Media graphics department will add pictures and coloring at a later time.

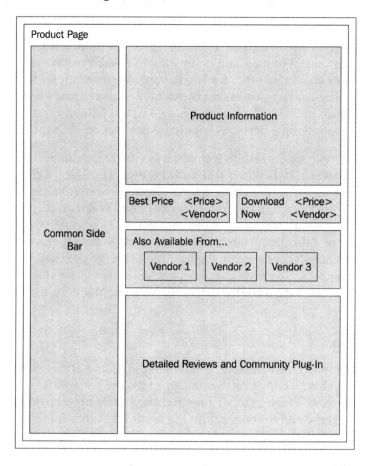

AllFriends Media is primarily a Microsoft shop and delivers all IT projects internally leveraging an existing pool of technologists. Given the fast-paced and ever changing world of web-based technologies, AllFriends Media thinks of itself as a forward thinking company willing to bet on new technology offerings.

Key requirements

The following are key requirements for a new software solution:

- The website will make calls out to external services and format the response information to be displayed on the screen.

- It is acceptable that adding a new vendor in the future will require a code change.

- If a call to the external vendor fails or takes too long, no external vendor information should be displayed on the page for that vendor — in limited cases, this is acceptable.

Additional facts

There are some additional details gathered after the initial use case was shared with the technical team. These include the following facts:

1. All participating external vendors will expose web services and contracts for easy interaction.

2. The performance and availability of vendor-exposed services cannot be guaranteed.

3. Hardware, network, firewalls, and distance to external vendors are optimized for low latency.

4. While every page will make this service call, network bandwidth internally is adequate to handle the traffic.

Pattern description

The goal of every Service Oriented Architecture is to build reusable, scalable, and abstracted solutions that can be re-used enterprise-wide to solve common problems. Solutions commonly take the form of request-response services. With many SOA-based solutions, latency of the calls becomes a top issue in the mind of business stakeholders as this directly relates to the quality of a user's experience. This is evident when working with request-response messages with an end user waiting for the response on the other end. In our case, if a poor user experience is encountered, then that user may end up going to another site.

When talking about latency related to an end user's experience on a website, latency is thought of as the round-trip time that the page requested by the user takes to load. The goal is to achieve no noticeable latency in the user experience, which is commonly thought of as a round trip in less than 100 milliseconds. It is important to note that the connection the user has to the server can be a significant bottleneck in the process but assumptions need to be made on the quality of this connection.

Latency can exist in many forms. They are as follows:

1. **Application latency**: The amount of time it takes the process doing something to load and execute.
2. **Firewall latency**: The time through the firewall.
3. **Router latency**: The time to read the headers and route the packets to the next destination; packages may end up queuing up under heavy load.
4. **Dropped packets**: The time needed to retry packets dropped due to poor network connections.
5. **Internet latency**: The connection quality and speed the user has to the remote server.
6. **Distance**: It is one of the basic laws of physics; the closer to the server the better — even at the speed of light.

No talk about latency is complete without talking about throughput. Throughput is generally measured by bandwidth as bits per second. This determines the size of the pipeline that data can flow though. From an application perspective, generally optimizing latency comes at the cost of greater throughput.

This scenario will focus on reducing the application latency given the assumption that other types of latency are nearly identical for each proposed architecture. Also, application latency is commonly something we have direct control over and the low hanging fruit when it comes to solving latency issues. In general, some of the items to consider when designing a low latency application are the following:

- Reduce or eliminate latency in initial service start up time
- Ensure external calls have appropriate timeouts with compensation logic
- Optimize payload size for network conditions
- Turn off any overhead like logging or tracking
- Reduce serialization on the wire
- Ensure optimal hardware

Candidate architectures

We will look at three possible solutions to the low-latency scenario outlined in the use case as follows.

Candidate architecture #1–BizTalk Server

BizTalk is Microsoft's Enterprise Integration tool and with AllFriends Media being a largely Microsoft-based technology firm, chances are BizTalk is already in use in one form or another. For the purpose of this analysis, the assumption will be that BizTalk is already in use and has the capacity to handle the additional load of this scenario.

We can take a look at the decision framework as it relates to BizTalk to see if a BizTalk-based solution is a fit for this use case.

Solution design aspects

BizTalk Server can easily perform web service aggregation using an Orchestration (that is, business process). BizTalk has the ability to expose an Orchestration as a WCF Service. A simple request-response schema would need to be created to detail the contract for this interaction. Inside the BizTalk Orchestration, each external vendor call will need a separate send port, several maps, and schemas. After all the messages have been returned from the external vendors, a .NET component or a multi-message mapping would be needed to build the final response message.

The main concern with this solution is the use of the publish and subscribe architecture that is the cornerstone of BizTalk Server. This architecture results in increased latency because each message is persisted in a SQL Server Database. Another concern is the use of an Orchestration to aggregate the return results because most Orchestrations contain a series of persistence points. Persistence points are spots inside the BizTalk Orchestration that save all the state information of the running Orchestration to SQL Server. This can be minimized through proper design of the Orchestration. While these message and state data persistence features of BizTalk are desirable in many cases, it is not ideal in a low-latency request-response scenario.

Solution delivery aspects

AllFriends Media is a web-based company with a pledge to keep up on current technology trends or risk being left in the dust by the competition. The assumption is they already have BizTalk running so adding an new solution to support this vendor-lookup process is possible.

With existing solutions at the company using BizTalk Server, the skills exist to build out this scenario within the company. It also means they have resources that understand how a messaging-based solution would work using BizTalk.

Solution delivery would not be a negative factor in using BizTalk Server for this scenario.

Solution operation aspects

AllFriends Media is an existing Microsoft shop with BizTalk in house. This means they already have procedures in place to monitor and support BizTalk. If this was not the case, this could be a factor in the decision given the ramp-up cost to build skills in supporting BizTalk Server. Supporting BizTalk Server is a unique endeavor and not like standard web-based technologies.

Solution operations are not a negative factor in using BizTalk for this use case.

Organizational aspects

The company understands what it takes to build a BizTalk solution, because of the existing investment in BizTalk Server. This is not a negative factor in using BizTalk for this use case.

Solution evaluation

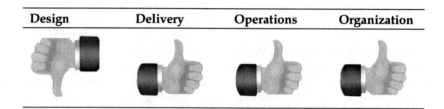

Design	Delivery	Operations	Organization

Candidate architecture #2–Windows Server AppFabric

Windows Server AppFabric is made up of enhancements to Windows that provide first class hosting for WCF and WF applications. A Windows Server AppFabric-based solution would leverage .NET 4.0 technologies to support this use case. The solution would use a .NET 4.0 Workflow Service to expose endpoints to the client, in this case the frontend website, through WCF.

This Workflow Service would be a service aggregator. It would make various calls to the outside vendors and consolidate all the results back to the client. This would all be done in workflow to allow for easy development using the mostly drag-and-drop design experience. A small set of custom activities would be needed to transform vendor-specific request-response messages into generic formats for the frontend client. Using the **Parallel Action** shape inside the workflow, an overall timeout can be set for all the external calls. This will ensure a maximum wait time for external calls.

See Chapter 2 (*Windows Communication Foundation and Window Workflow 4.0 Primer*) and Chapter 3 (*Windows Server AppFabric Primer*) for more specific information on using WCF, WF, and Windows Server AppFabric.

Now, we can take a look at the decision framework as it relates to .NET 4.0 and Windows Server AppFabric to see if it is a fit for this use case.

Solution design aspects

This use case can be solved using .NET 4.0 and Windows Server AppFabric for a single Aggregator Workflow Service. This service would do the following:

1. Expose the request-response schema to the frontend

2. Know what external vendors to call

3. Know how to call each external vendor and translate the various formats back into the expected response format

4. Ensure a timely execution to external vendors ensuring calls are made as fast as possible

5. Avoid persistence of the data to ensure a quick execution

While a single Workflow Service could be used, each specific vendor call will be segmented out into its own project. This ensures that changes made to vendor calls are abstracted from the workflow logic. Also, if other systems down the road need to make calls to this same vendor the code could be reused. Since the workflows are .NET-based, adding Service References to multiple external services is straightforward. This would allow for consuming information from various sources with no issues. This would be done by creating a new workflow for each vendor. Communication between the Core Workflow and the Vendor Workflows will be done via defined Data Contracts. The Vendor Workflows would be required to format all vendor request-response messages into the common format. Transformation of the vendor data will be done via custom activities.

While retry and persistence are not needed for this solution, Windows Server AppFabric has the flexibility to add these features to other solutions as the need arises.

Solution delivery aspects

AllFriends Media is a leading-edge web-based company. They have a staff of skilled resources that would be able to pick up the new design experience of .NET 4.0 and Windows Server AppFabric. Furthermore, building on Server AppFabric would ensure that we are using the best and most current technology Microsoft has to offer.

Using the Workflow Designer, developers would be able to reduce the coding effort to build this application since very little custom code would be needed. This should result in faster development and reduce overall testing time.

The timeline in not a factor given expected completion time using this technology is low compared to a custom-written C# solution.

Solution operation aspects

AllFriends Media runs an existing website with backend systems largely based on Microsoft technology. This would lead to the conclusion that a new solution based on .NET 4.0 and Windows Server AppFabric would fit in well in the landscape.

One of the assumptions is that the internal network bandwidth and hardware can support the additional load of real-time calls made to the Workflow Service. Given this assumption, the .NET 4.0 and Windows Server AppFabric-based solution would work for AllFriends Media.

Organizational aspects

Organizationally, AllFriends Media is on the cutting edge of technology. While Windows Server AppFabric is new and they do not have existing skills in this area, it would be easy for the existing team to learn the technology.

Solution evaluation

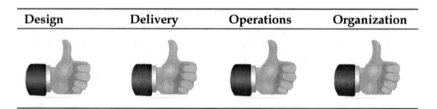

Design	Delivery	Operations	Organization

Candidate architecture #3–Windows Azure platform

Windows Azure is Microsoft's cloud-based service offering. We will take a look to see if this offering with work for this low-latency based scenario. In addition to latency concerns, the website code will need some changes to be hosted in and make calls into Windows Azure.

Solution design aspects

All the operations of the website that need inputs will be performed in a set of web roles while all the external web service calls and query matching will be performed in a worker role. All the headless computing will be performed in a set of worker roles. In order to maintain a good user experience, the web application can queue user requests and quickly return control back to the user. The set of worker roles will read the queue, match responses, and return results to the user. The user screen will be populated with results as-and-when the external web service calls complete. The user can perform other activities on the website in the meantime. The external addresses of vendor websites will be maintained in a configuration file, which will be used by the worker roles.

The core concern with this approach is the latency between the onsite hosted website and the remotely hosted Azure services, since the website would need to return data from an Azure Service call. In addition, the Azure services would have additional latency in the calls out to the external vendor sites.

From a security standpoint, the design will allow a seamless authentication and authorization model to support all users (AllFriends Media enterprise users and internet users) using the Windows Azure AppFabric Access Control Service.

Solution delivery aspects

AllFriends Media Technologies currently has a staff made up of both proficient .NET developers and administrators well versed in Microsoft server product deployments. The learning curve to develop the solution on Windows Azure and the new deployment model will be very easy.

The developers can deploy the Windows Azure development fabric on their development machines for easy debugging and troubleshooting. Usage of the existing Microsoft set of tools will be seamless to move from an on-premise development to Microsoft Azure development model.

The timeline is flexible. Given the solution outline above this should be easily accomplished in that timeline.

Solution operation aspects

A portion of the daily operations work is now offloaded to Windows Azure. Hence fewer members of the AllFriends Media operations team will work full time to support this solution. This team will now focus on monitoring and making sure the system is meeting their performance bar. They will be able to tweak the elastic aspects of the Windows Azure deployment based on the system load.

Once the developers complete a major milestone, the golden build will be uploaded to the staging area where the test teams will stress-test the integrated components. Optionally the team will open up the staging solution to some online users to get real-time validation before deploying the solution to the production servers.

Such a framework allows an agile development and deployment environment, helping the teams to focus on key operational metrics and not to worry about the servers being up, which is guaranteed by the Azure SLA.

Organizational aspects

Given that Microsoft Windows Azure has released recently, AllFriends Media is adopting a new wave of technology perceived as risky by the operations team. The team is taking a guarded approach with regards to a full rollout replacing the older website. So initially the team will continue to support both their existing solution and the new Microsoft Azure deployment.

The Azure platform is supported by the Microsoft team, which means a strong SLA for server availability—which is a big reassurance to the AllFriends Media management.

One of the key benefits is that AllFriends Media is able to leverage their existing investments in Microsoft tools and technology concepts. Given the elastic aspects of the windows Azure, AllFriends Media is able to keep the costs within the current budget.

AllFriends Media management does understand that Microsoft Azure provides an easy elastic model thus paving the way for faster solutions for the market

Solution evaluation

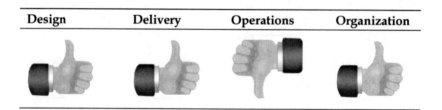

Architecture selection

Below are some key benefits and risks related to each of the architectures reviewed in the section above.

BizTalk Server	
Benefits	**Risks**
• Out of the box support for integrating with outside parties though various adapters	• MessageBox database that ensures messages do not get lost also slows down the solution
• Ability to aggregate messages together and return a single response	• Additional quality-of-service features around guaranteed delivery are unnecessary in a request-reply consumer transaction
• Extensive tracking and monitoring	

Windows Server AppFabric	
Benefits	**Risks**
• Robust hosting for .NET 4.0 workflow and WCF services	• Unproved scalability and track record
• Provided at zero cost with a Windows license	• Additional hardware may be needed to support the load
• Simple IIS hosting and user interface	• New offering so skills will need to be learned
• Basic support for tracking and monitoring	

Windows Azure	
Benefits	**Risks**
• Scalable, cloud-based approach with no additional hardware costs	• Possible latency issues with more distributed components
• Geo-located with operations around the world	• Less flexibility
• No additional environment support and monitoring	• New offering so skills will need to be learned

Architecture selection

After reviewing the decision framework and the proposed solutions using BizTalk, Windows Server AppFabric, or Azure, the best solution for this use case is a solution based on Windows Server AppFabric.

The key driving factors for this decision are the flexibility around instance persistence and the ability to host the solution locally and reduce distance latency.

Windows Server AppFabric will leverage a .NET 4.0 Workflow Service exposed via WCF to allow easy interchanges from the website. The workflow calls to the external vendors will be encapsulated into separate projects to provide further abstraction. This solution will be optimized for low latency WCF calls by doing the following:

- Enabling service auto-start (Available in IIS 7.5) to ensure the service is warmed up and ready to run optimally before the very first call.
- Set a low timeout value on the Parallel Activity inside the workflow with compensation logic to return whatever results the service has received in a given amount of time.
- Configure the service to not do any tracking or logging, although this is highly optimized in AppFabric.
- Payload sizes are already small so nothing is needed to reduce the service call size.
- For simplicity, this sample uses basicHttpBinding. If endpoints support it, moving to netTcpBinding would reduce latency in serialization.

Building the solution

This solution will be made up of a Core Workflow Service to handle the request-response messages from the web frontend. This service has a defined data contract for receiving the request and sending the response. This is defined in the **DataContracts** project in the following solution. These contracts have been simplified to focus on the concept rather than contract logic.

In order to support a growing site that may expand to other vendors down the road, a separate workflow project will be created for each vendor interaction. This will also allow for changes to individual vendors with no impact to other deployed solutions. Communication with this workflow will be done via defined contracts. In this case, the input is a product identifier and the response is a generic vendor result. Translation will be needed to convert the specific vendor results into the generic results.

The Core Workflow collects all the various generic response elements and constructs the response message to return to the calling application. All this is done with a handful of lines of custom C# code. All in all, very few lines of custom C# code are needed to build out this entire solution.

Setup

Initial setup is needed to simulate calls to the external vendors. For demo purposes, the vendor calls will exist on the same box as the other code in the solution. We will set up four simulated vendors named **Vendor A**, **Vendor B**, **Vendor C**, and **Vendor D**. Each simulated vendor has a unique request-response data structure as they would in reallife.

1. Launch Visual Studio.NET 2010 and open the **Chapter17_VendorApps.sln** solution in the `<Installation Directory>\Chapter17\Begin` folder. When prompted to create the virtual directories click **OK**.

2. Launch Visual Studio.NET 2010 and open the **Chapter17.sln** solution in the `<Installation Directory>\Chapter17\Begin` folder. This contains the projects to help get started building the solution.

Building the vendor-specific and aggregate workflows

Once the simulated external vendor services are installed, it is time to build out the Vendor A Workflow and Core Workflow Service that we consume when calling this service and aggregate the results.

The following projects are included in the Begin Solution:

- **Chapter17.CallVendorB**: This is the workflow and service details specific to Vendor B.

- **Chapter17.CallVendorC**: This is the workflow and service details specific to Vendor C.

- **Chapter17.CallVendorD**: This is the workflow and service details specific to Vendor D.

- **Chapter17.DataContracts**: This is the data contracts used by the core workflow service exposed to the frontend website. It also contains the generic Vendor Result used to exchange data between the workflows. It is worth taking a look at how the Data Contracts are defined. The response is designed to return an Array of generic vendor result messages.

- **Chapter17.TestApp** : This is a simple Windows Form used to test the final workflow solution.

We will be adding the missing projects to complete the end-to-end solution.

1. Launch Visual Studio.NET 2010 and open the **Chapter17.sln** solution in the `<Installation Directory>\Chapter17\Begin` folder. You will see several projects already in the solution for you. They are outlined above. We will add the missing components to call Vendor A and aggregate the results.

2. Create a new **Activity Library** project (located under the Workflow templates under C#) named **Chapter17.CallVendorA**.

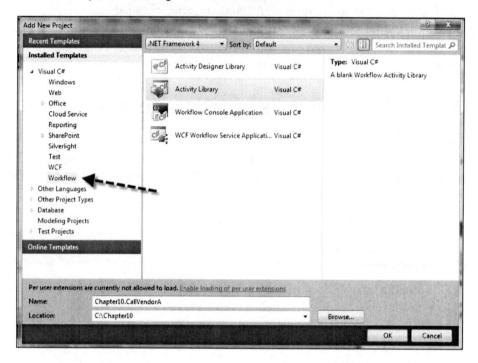

3. Rename the default file from `Activity1.xaml` to **VendorA.xaml**.

4. Right-click on **VendorA.xaml** and go to **View Code**. Update the Class name from **Activity1** to **VendorA** shown as follows:

5. Add a **Service Reference** to `http://localhost/Chapter17.VendorA/ MovieDownloadSrv.svc` by right-clicking on the **Chapter17.CallVendorA** project and select **Add Service Reference**. Name the reference **VendorAService**. Adding the service reference will create a Toolbox item for the service call that can be dragged and dropped onto the workflow surface. The name of the item is the Service Method name; in this case it will be called **GetMoviePrice**.

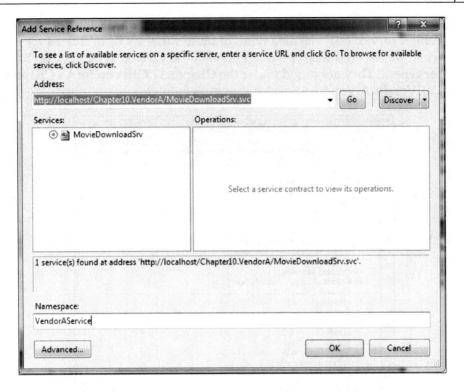

6. Add a reference to the **Chapter17.DataContracts** project. This will be used to formulate the **Vendor Result** message to return to the Core Workflow.

7. Build the project. This will allow the added service reference to be used later on.

8. Once all the initial groundwork is done, it is time to begin to build out the workflow. Open **VendorA.xaml** by double-clicking on it. Drag and drop a **Sequence** shape (under **Control Flow**) from the Toolbar onto the surface. Rename the shape to **Vendor A**.

9. When the Vendor A **Sequence** shape is selected, click on **Variables** at the bottom of the screen.

10. Variables are needed to create the request and response parameters for the vendor service call. The data types of these variables were created for us when we added the service reference. For the variable type, click on **Browse for type....** They are found under the **Chapter17.CallVendorA - Chapter17. CallVendorA.VendorAService** shown as follows:

11. Create the following variables at the **Vendor A** scope.

Name: **VendorRequest**
Type: **MovieDownloadRequest**
Default: **New MovieDownloadRequest()**

Name: **VendorResponse**
Type: **MovieDownloadResponse**

12. The end result is shown as follows:

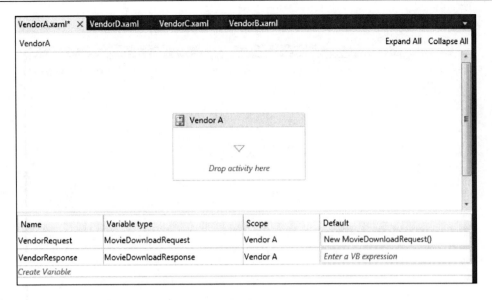

13. Click on **Variables** to close the window. Next, we need to define the arguments for the workflow. These are the values we want to pass into and out of the workflow in the same way that we define input and output parameters in a standard .NET class operation. In our case, the parameters are ProductId for input and VendorResult for output. Click on **Arguments**. Add the following two arguments:

Name: **ProductId**
Direction: **In**
Type: **String**

Name: **Result**
Direction: **Out**
Type: **VendorResult** (Select this from the **Chapter17.DataContracts** project reference.)

14. At the end, it should look like the following image:

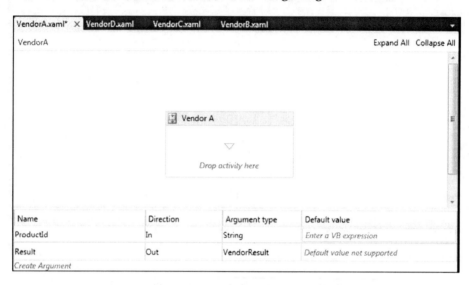

15. Create a Custom Activity used for mapping the vendor in (this case Vendor A) specific response to the standard Vendor Response message. This is needed to ensure the generic response is returned out of the workflow to the Core Workflow. Add a new item to the project. Under **Code**, select **Class**. Name the new file **VendorAToVendorResult.cs**.

16. Add the following `using` statements to the existing `using` statements. Leveraging the `System.Activities` reference will allow the class to inherit from `CodeActivity` as required to create a custom activity.

```
using System.Activities;
using Chapter17.DataContracts;
using System.Threading;  // Used for testing only
```

Add the following code inside the namespace tags to complete the custom activity.

```
    public sealed class VendorAToVendorResult : CodeActivity
    {
        // Create the IN parms.  In this case it will be the
           Vendor A Response
        InArgument<VendorAService.MovieDownloadResponse>
vendorResponse;

        public InArgument<VendorAService.MovieDownloadResponse>
VendorResponse
        {
```

```
        get { return vendorResponse; }
        set { vendorResponse = value; }
    }

    // Create the OUT parms. In this case it will be the
       generic Vendor Response
OutArgument<VendorResult> vendorData;

    public OutArgument<VendorResult> VendorData
    {
        get { return vendorData; }
        set { vendorData = value; }
    }

    // Override the Execute method with our specific logic
    protected override void Execute(CodeActivityContext
context)
    {
        // Create a new instance of the Response
        VendorResult oResult = new VendorResult();

        // Mapping
        oResult.BuyURL = this.VendorResponse.Get(context).URL;
        oResult.Price =this.VendorResponse.Get(context).Price;

        // These are not returned from the Vendor A
           Service call.
        // They are hard coded here as they are the same for
           every call to this Vendor.
        // This is a download only Vendor so items are always
           in stock and download.
        oResult.InStock = true;
        oResult.IsDownload = true;
        oResult.Vendor = "Vendor A - Thread ID " +
            Thread.CurrentThread.ManagedThreadId.ToString();

        // Return the result
        context.SetValue(VendorData, oResult);
    }
}
```

17. Build the project. As a result of the build, the new activity will show up in the Toolbar and is named **VendorAToVendorResult**.

18. Next, add all the workflow activities needed to complete this workflow. Add the following items, in order, inside the Vendor A **Sequence** activity.

   ° **Assign**: Rename it to **Assign Product ID**. This shape is found in the Toolbar under **Primitives**.

   ° **GetMoviePrice**: Found on the Toolbar. This was created by the add service reference and makes the call to the external vendor service.

   ° **VendorAToVendorResult**: From the Toolbar. This is the custom activity created earlier.

19. The end result is shown as follows:

20. The assign shape is used to set the input argument of **ProductId** to **VendorRequest.SKU**.

21. Click on the **Assign** shape and view the properties of the shape in the **Properties** window (press F4 if the window is not visible). Set the **To** value to **VendorRequest.SKU**. Set the **Value** to **ProductId**. Visual Studio.NET IntelliSense should recognize both these values.

22. On the **GetMoviePrice** shape, set the following properties. Set **GetMoviePriceResult** to **VendorResponse** and **Movie** to **VendorRequest**.

23. On the **VendorAToVendorResult** shape, set **VendorData** to **Result** and **VendorResponse** to **VendorResponse**.

24. Build the project. It should build with no errors.

25. This process was followed for each of the other three vendors. Small changes were made to support the various vendor-specific contracts of each of the vendors.

26. Next, the Core Workflow used to aggregate the individual results will be created. Create a new project in this same solution. Right-click on the solution and select **New Project**. Select **Workflow, WCF Workflow Service Application** and name the project **Chapter17.CoreWorkflow**.

27. Right-click on the **CoreWorkflow** project and go to **Properties**. Click on the **Web** tab. Select the **Use Local Web Server** selection and click the **Create Virtual Directory** button using the default address of http://localhost/ Chapter17.CoreWorkflow. This will create a virtual directory in IIS for this project.

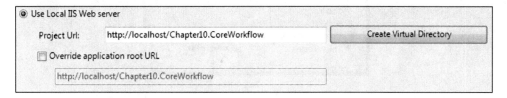

28. Rename the existing Service1.xamlx file to ProcessExternalData. xamlx. Next, set both the **ConfigurationName** and **Name** properties to **ProcessExternalData** by clicking on the workflow surface and viewing the properties in the **Properties** window (if it is not shown, press F4).

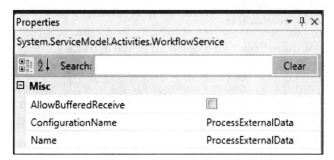

29. Click on the **ReceiveRequest** shape and ensure the **CanCreateInstance** checkbox is checked.

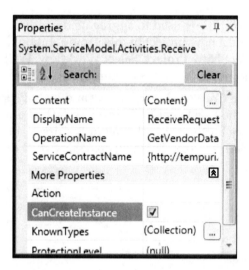

30. Add reference to the following items projects via project references by right-clicking on **Chapter17.CoreWorkflow** project, **Add Reference...**
    Chapter17.CallVendorA
    Chapter17.CallVendorB
    Chapter17.CallVendorC
    Chapter17.CallVendorD
    Chapter17.DataContracts

31. Build the solution. This will ensure all of the activities inside the referenced projects are made available on the Toolbox inside Visual Studio.

32. Define the input and output messages for the Core Workflow. These will be exposed though the WCF Endpoints of this service. Click on the **Variables** tab at the bottom of the workflow surface. Delete the **data** variable. Add the following four variables:

    Name: **ExternalDataRequest** (this is the WCF Service Request)
    Type: **ExternalProductDataRequest** (located inside the DataContracts Reference)
    Default
    Name: **ExternalDataResponse** (this is the WCF Service Response)
    Type: **ExternalProductDataResponse** (located inside the DataContracts Reference)

    Default: **New ExternalProductDataResponse()**

Name: **EndLoop** (this is used to end processing of the parallel shape when the end of the delay is reached)
Type: **Boolean**
Default: **False**

Name: **ReturnCount** (this is also used to end processing of the parallel shape when all four external vendor calls are completed)
Type: **Int32**
Default:

The end result is as follows:

Name	Variable type	Scope	Default
handle	CorrelationHandle	Sequential Service	*Handle cannot be initialized*
ExternalDataRequest	ExternalProductDataRequest	Sequential Service	*Enter a VB expression*
ExternalDataResponse	ExternalProductDataResponse	Sequential Service	New ExternalProductDataResponse()
EndLoop	Boolean	Sequential Service	False
ReturnCount	Int32	Sequential Service	*Enter a VB expression*
Create Variable			

33. Set these variables as the request and response messages for the service by changing the content on the **ReceiveRequest** and **SendResponse** shapes. Click on **ReceiveRequest** and rename the operation to **GetVendorData**. Click on **Content**. Under **Message** set the **Message Data** to **ExternalDataRequest** and **Message Type** to **Chapter17.DataContracts. ExternalProductDataRequest**.

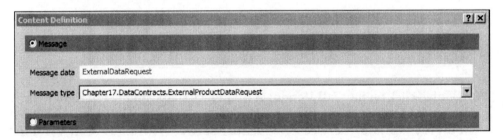

34. Click on **Content** on the **SendResponse** shape. Set the **Message Data** to **ExternalDataResponse** and **Message Type** to **Chapter17.DataContracts. ExternalProductDataResponse**.

35. Add a **Parallel** shape between the **Receive** and **Send** shapes. Inside the **Parallel** shape add five **Sequence** shapes. Four of the sequence shapes will each contain the logic to make the calls to the external vendors. The last sequence shape will be used as a timeout. In the event of any of the calls to the outside vendors taking longer than the timeout, the workflow will stop processing the other parallel branches and return the results received to the caller.

36. Ensure the **Parallel Shape** is selected and under **Properties** set **CompletionCondition** to **EndLoop Or ReturnCount = 4**.

37. The Parallel shape in .NET 4.0 does not guarantee that each action will run on a separate thread. In the case of asynchronous operations, delay shapes, or messaging activates separate threads will generally be created. If any of the branches in the parallel shape set the **CompletionCondition** (a Boolean expression), the other branches will no longer be executed. Name each of the five sequences shapes as follows: **Call Vendor A, Call Vendor B, Call Vendor C, Call Vendor D, Timeout**. It should look like the following:

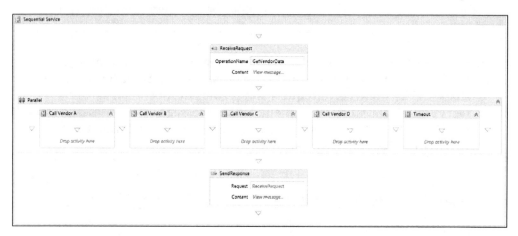

38. Double-click on the **Call Vendor A Sequence** shape on the top right to drill down into it. The breadcrumb trial on the top of the workflow surface should now say **WorkflowService > Sequential Service > Parallel > Call Vendor A**. Drag and drop from the Toolbar the **VendorA** shape and place it inside the **Call Vendor A Sequence** shape. The **VendorA** shape appears in the Toolbox as a result of adding the reference to the **Chapter17.CallVendorA** project.

39. Add an **AddToCollection** shape directly under the **VendorA** shape. This is located under the **Collection** selection from the Toolbar. The **AddToCollection** shape is used to add the response from Vendor A to the result collection. The result collection is what is returned to the calling website. Add an **Assign** shape under the **AddToCollection** shape.

40. With the **Call Vendor A Sequence** shape selected, click on **Variables** and create a new variable local to this scope. This variable will only be at this **Call Vendor A** scope.

    Name: **VendorDataResponse**
    Type: **VendorResult** (from the Data Contract reference)
    Default: **New VendorResult()**

41. At this point, the activity will look like the following:

Name	Variable type	Scope	Default
VendorDataResponse	VendorResult	Call Vendor A	*Enter a VB expression*
handle	CorrelationHandle	Sequential Service	*Handle cannot be initialized*
ExternalDataRequest	ExternalProductDataRequest	Sequential Service	*Enter a VB expression*
ExternalDataResponse	ExternalProductDataResponse	Sequential Service	New ExternalProductDataResponse()
EndLoop	Boolean	Sequential Service	False
ReturnCount	Int32	Sequential Service	*Enter a VB expression*
Create Variable			

42. Now set the parameters on the **VendorA**, **AddToCollection**, and **Assign** shapes using the variables that have been created.
On the **VendorA** shape set **ProductId** to **ExternalDataRequest.ProductId** and **Result** to **VendorDataResponse**.

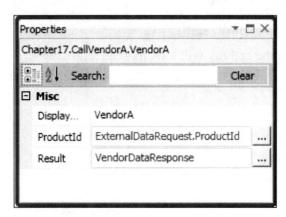

43. On the **AddToCollection** shape, set **TypeArgument** to **Chapter17. DataContract.VendorResult**, **Item** to **VendorDataResponse**, and **Collection** to **ExternalDataResponse.Result**.

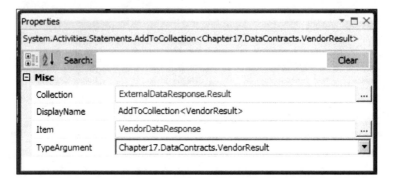

44. On the **Assign** shape set **To** to **ReturnCount** and **Value** to **ReturnCount + 1**.

45. Repeat this process for the other three **Vendor Sequence** shapes that were added to the **Parallel** shape.

46. Return to the main workflow surface by using the breadcrumbs at the top. Double-click on the **Timeout Sequence** shape to drill down into it.

47. Drag a **Delay** shape and **Assign** shape from the Toolbox, both from the Primitive section.

48. Set the **Delay** to **New Timespan(0,0,0,0,65)**. This will set up a 65 millisecond delay on this shape and ensure the service does not wait any longer than 65 milliseconds for an external vendor call.

49. On the **Assign** Shape, set **To** to **EndLoop** and **Value** equal to **True**.

50. The end result should look like the following:

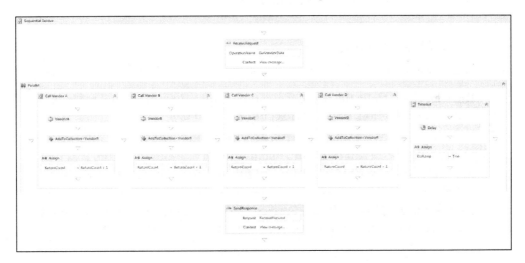

51. Open the **app.config** file for each of the **Chapter17.CallVendor** projects. Copy the binding information under **<basicHttpBinding>** into the **Web.config** file of the **CoreWorkflow** project. All four **<binding>** nodes should exist under a single **<basicHttpBinding>** node in the **Web.config** file. Do the same for the **<endpoint>** node under the **<client>** section. All four **<endpoint>** nodes should exist under a single **<client>** node. This is needed so that the CoreWorkflow has the necessary binding and endpoint information to make the WCF calls to the external vendor sites. Check the End Solution to see the **App.Config** file for the final solution.

52. Configure the services in IIS for low-latency calls by turning off monitoring and enabling Auto-Start. This will greatly reduce the latency created by the first call to a service and reduce processing time by not collecting any service metric data.

    Inside IIS, right-click on the **Chapter17.CoreWorkflow** Virtual Directory. Go to **Manage WCF and WF Services** section, **Configure....**

    Select the **Monitoring** tab. Uncheck the **Write events to the database** checkbox.

    Select the **Auto-Start** tab. Select **Enable**.

Testing the solution

Launch the **TestApp**, which is a simple application form that contains three buttons.

1. **Run Service**—Calls the Service one time. This returns the total records, vendor information, and total execution time.

2. **Run Service – 25**—Calls the Service 25 times. Returns vendor information, minimum service call duration, maximum service call duration, and the average. Removes the minimum and maximum values prior to calculating values.

3. **Run Service – 250**—Calls the Service 250 times. Returns minimum service call duration, maximum service call duration, and the average.

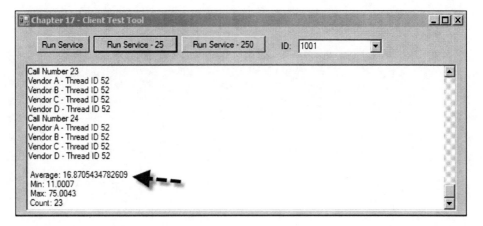

Play around with changing sleep values in the simulated external vendor services and changing the delay time inside the Core Workflow. See how this affects the results.

Summary

In this chapter, we looked at several different types of latency. The focus was on how best to reduce Application Latency, which is the latency we developers have the most control over. We looked at how BizTalk, Windows Server AppFabric, and Azure all could work in a low-latency environment but we chose a final architecture based on Windows Server AppFabric. This architecture uses a fast, non-persistent .NET 4.0 Workflow to aggregate various vendor response messages and to return a single result to the client.

18
Handling Large Session and Reference Data

In this chapter, we will look at how to handle large session and reference data sets and how implementing a caching tier is beneficial. We will showcase the usage of the best suited Microsoft technology for this task.

Use case

WinOrBow Games is an interactive online gaming company which has a varied set of games ranging from tic-tac toe to blackjack. When a user registers with the system, as part of the social experience they can create a set of personas, subscribe to news feeds, modify the look-and-feel of their portal page, and more. All of these settings are tracked as part of their online user profile. Once users log into the system they can play with other online users or play against the online system also known as WinGuru. Optionally, users can also team up with their online friends and play against WinGuru. In this mode, the users share a social experience by sharing messages about game strategy and working together. Users playing in practice mode can look up game rules, review finished games, and strategize their next move. Users can pause a game, log out, and resume it at a later point. This convenience feature is a big hit among the registered users. The company is also looking to extend the games to mobile users who will interact with the web applications as part of the "on the go" experience.

WinOrBow has about 800,000 registered users, of which, 250,000 users are logged onto the system at any point in time. It is projected for the user base to grow over 5M in the next three years.

WinOrBow Games is primarily Windows platform where most of the packaged applications and programming tools are predominantly Microsoft technologies. ASP. NET is used for building the web applications. At the back end, the system also uses a set of .NET applications to monitor online user activity. These applications perform computations and then store the results to specific databases across different backend platforms. They do have a sizable number of .NET developers and own some of Microsoft's server platforms like SQL Server. Developers use the Visual Studio and Team Foundation Server system for all their development and testing efforts.

WinOrBow has adopted a "build versus buy" strategy where they prefer to leverage platform components and build custom solutions instead of buying high priced enterprise solutions.

Key requirements

The following are key requirements for a new software solution:

- Improve the current performance (latency) of the website.
- Architect a solution that can scale for the increased growth of the company.
- Implement high availability across all tiers of the solution.
- Minimize the impact on the mission critical systems by offloading temporal workloads to medium end servers.

Additional facts

There are some additional details gathered after the initial use case was shared with the technical team. These include the following:

1. Reasonably cheap boxes will be used to run the non-mission critical workload.

2. Chosen technology must have security and manageability knobs making it easy for the operations team.

3. Users will connect to any web server in the farm, so the data has to be accessible from any machine.

4. The customer is looking to design all components to be pluggable instead of taking a hard dependency.

Pattern description

Application objects are constructed from combining different backend data sources such as databases and web service calls. When users repeatedly access the same application object, there is increased stress on the system to regenerate the individual responses. For example, consider a popular online forums website that shows a list of topics, various posts for each topic, and then the related threads for each post. The backend data could be organized across several tables such as `Forum_Topics`, `ListOf_Posts`, `Post_RelatedThreads`, and `User_Response`. On each user visit, the page load needs to visualize data joined from all these tables. Initially, the website might perform well with most data in the database server memory but slowly as the users and content increase, there may be disk access that affects the overall latency. Most of the time, the access might be for such read-only objects.

When using the traditional three tier system (web, business logic, and data tier) without caching, such repeated access of reference data that goes over the network requires additional resources. In such cases, the performance can be optimized when the cross machine and network access is avoided. This happens when the data can be stored on the webserver and returned immediately. In addition to the web server impact of database-heavy sites, there is also stress on the database servers which could affect other core transaction processing systems using the database servers. When some sort of caching is implemented, the latency can be low across all user requests. Even as the backend data changes with new topics and user responses, one can limit the object lifetime in the cache to minimize any consistency issues, which may be a lesser concern. In such workloads, the application objects access can be viewed as lookups of `<key, value>`.

Let us consider another scenario: online travel search. When a user searches for airfare, hotel accommodation, and places to visit in Italy, for example, the website needs to respond instantly with the relevant results. A large portion of the results, such as places to visit or list of popular hotels for a zip code is reference data. In addition, there are a couple of other access behaviors which are interesting. A user could submit a set of such queries for different cities for which the website will have to perform several backend computations. The website could be interacting with a set of different external systems. One could be an external airline system, a set of systems for hotel availability and places to visit with reviews. Upon receiving responses, the website would combine the results, filter them, apply any particular user preferences (for example, sorting) and then visualize the results for the end user. In order to do this, the website will need a temporary storage for computing results. Ideally, a cache will be extremely useful both from a performance and maintenance standpoint. As all the data is held in memory, there is no additional data storage or persistence related maintenance operations required.

This is especially useful when the user decides to run the query all over again for a new city or come back at a later time. Further, as the user makes selections, updates are made to the shopping cart tracked as part of the session. The session data is available for both reads and writes as the user traverses the website and it needs to be available as long as the user is active on the website. As the user adds different items to the shopping cart and accesses it from several web pages, the website needs to ensure high availability in addition to performing well.

Broadly, data access in this workload pattern can be viewed as reference (used primarily for read only access across all users) and activity (single user read-write) data. For example, catalogs of books or flight arrival information are treated as reference data. Such data does not change often and will be used by several users accessing the website. Activity data is specific for each user, for example, purchasing vehicle insurance from a website using a shopping cart application. Another related workload is resource data where the data is shared across a set of users where read and write updates are allowed. In an airline system, the tickets inventory constantly changes based on the purchase activity in the system. In such cases, some sort of concurrency control mechanism across all users would be required.

Candidate architecture

We are looking at a single candidate for this solution. While the Windows Server AppFabric Cache is the best choice for this scenario, we will also discuss the alternatives for accessing reference data.

Candidate architecture #1–Windows Server AppFabric Cache

Usage of distributed caching technology is common when implementing this pattern. Before talking about it, let us look at a couple of other options available – database servers and ASP.NET (session and application caching). Let us use the data from the use case and key requirements to see how the options stack up.

In large enterprises, SQL Server or any database server is a huge investment used by many critical applications. In this pattern, the reference data could be accessed repeatedly from the database tables which may become inefficient and obtrusive to other transaction processing systems sharing the database instance or the network. As we have seen in the previous section, when the workload is essentially lookup-based like `<key, value>`, it does not require core database functionality such as querying, data management, logging, indexing, and so on. When temporal computations are performed, it does not benefit from writes batching and large I/O optimizations that database servers do so well. Similarly, session data does not really require durability, it only needs to be available while the user session is active.

Overall, here are some challenges when only using a database server to store reference data:

1. Increased maintenance operations to manage the data growth.
2. Additional resources stress (CPU usage, network bandwidth) on the database server box.
3. Impacting performance of other database applications.

SQL Server will perform reasonably well for this workload but would need the company to plan for the challenges above. In addition, when the resource stress increases there will be additional investment required to scale up the hardware resources. We will discuss usage of SQL Server as part of the solution, just not for session and reference workloads. In our use case, given the projected growth of the company (5M users) and the kinds of social interaction the website allows, SQL Server usage for session data and reference data access will not be appropriate.

ASP.NET has support for application caching as well as user session state management. Using this, each web server can cache reference data but not in a central manner. This would imply that the data is replicated in each web server node. As the need for caching reference data increases, this will hinder the scaling of the solution – either more memory is needed on each web server or application requests go directly to the backend for certain requests. In the case of session state management, ASP.NET has an easy mechanism both from a programming model and configuration knobs. As users connect in a web farm, they can be load balanced to any web server. Even though, session state can be stored in a common state server accessible to all web servers, the state server can very soon become the bottleneck for scaling the application. Another downside is the inability to protect against the state server failures.

In summary, here are the challenges when using ASP.NET caching and session features for our use-case:

1. Replicating reference data across all web servers.

2. Machine failures affecting session state management.

3. Usage of central session state server could become a bottleneck with increased user load.

Neither direct SQL Server access nor ASP.NET caching is the right choice here. Let us analyze the key requirements and see how Windows Server AppFabric Cache stacks up against our decision framework.

Solution design aspects

At the core of the requirements of the use case is the fact that the application has to scale linearly for the long term. This essentially would require a scale out architecture where one can add servers on demand based on capacity requirements. In order to avoid making changes to host information, it will be easier if the application communicates with a logical server farm and doesn't need to know all the individual server names. This way, it would be a truly distributed application where users can connect to any cache server in the farm, and the system handles data partitioning by keeping it transparent to the application. Under the covers, Windows Server AppFabric Cache shares the core fabric layer with SQL Azure and is built to scale for large number of servers. The application servers (acting as cache clients) just need access to one server in the cluster and can then access all servers in the cluster. However, it is recommended that the application servers reference as many cache servers in the app.config or web.config as possible. When an application server connects to any cache server, it gets a routing table which has the mapping of partitioned data access to the actual cache servers. This design ensures that new servers are automatically accessible to the application servers.

A key aspect is to maintain low latency for all user requests including the login experience, exchanging messages with other online friends, loading of the last stored game, history of previous games, and so on. Accommodating this request would require an ability to partition the dataset for each user in memory with the ability to access them individually or all at once. In addition, when multiple users are playing together, their common strategies such as game moves can be co-located and available as bulk access to minimize network latency overhead. Another common design would be to avoid network overhead wherever possible by having data cached at the client side (on the web servers).

In our use case, reference items such as the news feed, information about the logged on users, and the collection of on-going games are some common items across all users which will benefit from being maintained on the web servers themselves. As this data changes, it will be useful to refresh it at configurable intervals. Windows Server AppFabric Caching provides logical data containers including named caches and regions. Named caches can be used to partition data for different objects and they are automatically striped across the entire cluster. It is also possible to set separate policies for each named cache. Regions allow co-location of objects with an ability to bulk fetch. Local cache is another feature that lets caching of objects on the cache client application (web or application servers). It has knobs to expire an object after a configurable **TTL (time to live)** or automatically synchronize object changes via notifications when data changes in the cache cluster. The latter is implemented by cache client application polling the cache servers for the set of changes over a configurable interval.

One of the main goals of the solution is to build it for high availability scenarios. From the use case requirements, the session data and some of the user profile data will need to be stored with additional replicas to protect against machine failures. The application should not have to worry about managing the high availability configuration. In Windows Server AppFabric Caching, the High Availability option is available at a named cache level and is just a configuration knob. The system identifies primary and secondary servers for the replicas and monitors their availability. In case of a server failure, new replica servers are elected automatically.

The application should have control to store and remove objects, change the amount of cached time in the cache tier, and control the client side caching. User sessions will need to be available from any web server and will need replicas to protect against machine failures.

As all the content in the cache tier is in memory, SQL Server will be used as the data repository in the solution. The application must have control to access the data explicitly from SQL or from cache as appropriate.

Solution delivery aspects

Windows Server AppFabric Cache exposes a set of .NET based client API and the solutions can be easily built using Visual Studio, making it a natural fit for WinOrBow application developers. The product just depends on .NET 4.0 and runs on the Windows 7 or Vista platform for development purposes. Developers can use Event Tracing for Windows (ETW) and performance counters for debugging purposes. In particular, the integration with ASP.NET is pretty straightforward and can be done via configuration. Many of the behaviors for the caching API such as the cache server information and local cache usage can be set up via configuration or via code.

It is important to note that this is a new product from Microsoft and hence availability of detailed patterns and guidance is limited. It is expected that design patterns and performance guidelines will improve in the future. Developers can use the product documentation and leverage the online community for specific guidance discussions. The product uses the channel model net.tcp transport of WCF, which has several resources available online. Overall, this should make it easy for WinOrBow developers to deliver the solution in weeks rather than months.

Solution operations aspects

The administration tool for managing Windows Server AppFabric Cache is based on PowerShell. It exposes command-lets to configure and administer the cache cluster and getting/setting named cache properties. The hardware configuration allows usage of medium range servers (quad core) with 8-16 GB memory that play well to keeping the overall costs low. The product is integrated with ETW and the Operations team can use existing tools from the Windows resource kit (tracelog, trace.rpt) to collect diagnostic data for debugging purposes. The product also provides a set of rich performance counters for collecting steady state information, identifying capacity issues or application object access failures across the deployment. The WinOrBow operations team can also leverage the System Center Operations Manager management pack for proactive management by configuring specific rules.

At this time, there are no rich, GUI-based tools available as part of the product. Leveraging the community for availability of additional tools is one possible option. The current security model for authorizing client applications is based on domain and only at a cache cluster level which works for the WinOrBow deployment. The operations team also would need to build expertise and extend their tools to work with PowerShell.

Organizational aspects

WinOrBow is looking at a solution that can satisfy their current requirements and continues to get better in-line with the company's long term. Given that Windows Server AppFabric is an important part of the overall strategy for Microsoft, the cache feature will continue to evolve with the next set of releases. The cache integration programming paradigm allows the solution to enable or disable the cache via configuration which minimizes the risk. The product support falls under the traditional Microsoft support which again minimizes the risk for WinOrBow. Windows Server AppFabric Cache is part of Windows Server SKU and saves significant licensing dollars when compared to other competing products.

Architecture selection

As mentioned earlier, Windows Server AppFabric Cache is the best choice. Here is a quick summary of the evaluation:

Windows Server AppFabric Cache	
Benefits	**Risks**
• Built for high performance and scale • Easy integration using ASP.NET session provider and simple .NET based APIs • Available as part of Windows Server SKU	• Lack of extensive community code/resources given V1 product • High Availability feature supports 2 replicas, however all data is still held in memory

Building the solution

Here is the high-level architecture of the solution:

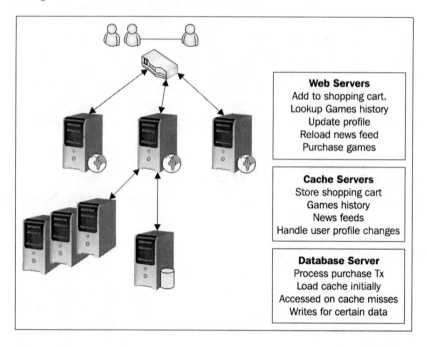

The solution built using Windows Server AppFabric Cache along with SQL Server as the durable store will scale for WinOrBow needs. The application will use a cache-aside pattern – the application accesses the cache for lookup data and if it is not found, would execute the query against the database server. After the application receives the object, it would populate the cache server for the subsequent set of accesses. In some cases, the cache can be front loaded with the common reference data, such as finished game information and news feed data, prior to any user request coming into the system. When games complete, the history can be updated in the cache tier. Updates to a user profile that needs to be durable can be made directly against the database server. Another approach could be leveraging notifications in the cache cluster when items are modified—the recipient of the notification can then store the object in SQL server.

All the ASP.NET session data (shopping cart) could be stored in the cache servers by just modifying the `web.config`.

In this solution, we will be building a portion of the application to demonstrate usage of the cache. The WinOrBow Project will modify an existing ASP.NET application to leverage the cache for both session and reference data. All the cache related interactions are isolated as part of the `CacheUtilities.cs` class file.

1. We will set up and configure the cache cluster to include all the application needs.

2. We will modify `web.config` to provide some information about the cache cluster under the `datacacheclient` configuration section.

3. We will then add AppFabric Cache provider as the custom ASP.NET session provider under the "sessionState" section. In this sample, we use the session provider that shipped with the V1 release. An enhanced version that supports partial session updates is now available on codeplex - `http://aspnet.codeplex.com/releases/view/46576`

4. We will then create `CacheUtilities.cs` and then add code to use it from `Login.aspx` and `MyPage.aspx`.

Setup

A project solution `AppliedArchitecture.Chapter18.Caching` has been created in `<Installation Directory>\Chapter18\Begin` folder. This solution contains the WinorBow ASP.NET project.

Before beginning the lab, you must have Windows Server AppFabric Cache service, client and admin feature installed and configured on your machine. The pre-requisites for configuring the cache features are .NET 4.0 RTM and PowerShell v2. In your development environment, both Windows 7 and Vista OS platforms are supported. For production deployment, the cache servers need to be on Windows Server 2008 SP2 or Windows Server 2008 R2 OS platform. If required, please refer to Chapter 3 for more installation instructions.

1. If you don't have the product set up already, install the RTW version of Windows Server AppFabric from the following location. It is possible to do a standalone install of the Cache feature. You can check the download section from this link: `http://www.microsoft.com/downloads/en/results.aspx?freetext=Windows+Server+AppFabric&displaylang=en&stype=s_basic`

2. Run the Cache Administration Windows PowerShell Tool to start the cache cluster.

3. Using the same administration tool, create the following named caches–
   SessionCache, HeadLineNewsCache, and GamesHistoryCache. The named
   caches will be set up with different policies (expiry time, eviction settings,
   High Availability) based on application access needs.

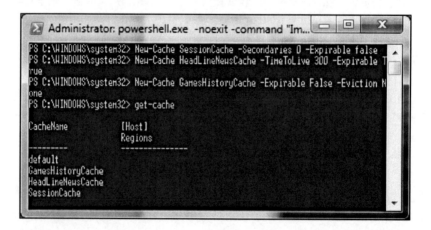

In a production system, one could deploy SessionCache in High Availability mode with Secondaries as 1. Such a configuration would require the cache servers to run Enterprise or Data Center edition. For this lab, if you set up the Secondaries as 1 on your development environment (on client OS), the cache service will crash and fail to restart. Here is the error you would see in ETW:

AppFabric Caching service crashed. {The High Availability feature of Windows Server AppFabric caching features requires all nodes in the cache cluster to be running Windows Server Enterprise Edition or higher. Please confirm that all High Availability cache nodes are running on a supported.

To recover, you would have to export the cluster configuration using `Export-CacheClusterConfig` commandlet to a file, and then modify the file by changing the named cache properties for "SessionCache" and then import the cluster configuration using the `Import-CacheClusterConfig` command. After this, starting the cache cluster will succeed.

4. Set up the cache cluster security appropriately so that the user account under which the web application is running has access to the cache cluster. This can be done by using the commandlet `Grant-CacheAllowedClientAccount <domain\user>`. Alternatively, for this development solution, you can disable security in the cluster by using the commandlet `Set-CacheClusterSecurity None`.

Integrating with Windows Server AppFabric cache

Next up, we actually build the solution that uses the cache.

1. Launch Visual Studio.NET 2010 and open the `ApliedArchitecture.Chapter18.Caching.sln` from the `<Installation Directory>\Chapter18\Begin` folder. You should see the WinOrBow VS project.

2. The WinOrBow ASP.NET website project has two web pages—`Login.aspx` and `myPage.aspx`. These two pages contain the logic for playing the simple "TicTacToe" online game.

3. Add a reference to **Microsoft.ApplicationServer.Caching.Client** and **Microsoft.ApplicationServer.Caching.Core** DLLs.

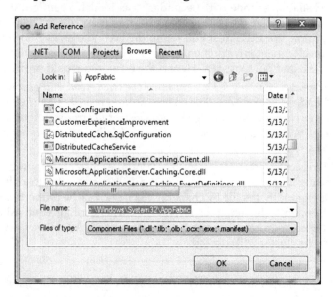

4. Modify the `web.config` to add the AppFabric dataCacheClient and ASP.NET session provider sections.

```
Web.config ×
    <?xml version="1.0"?>
    <configuration>
      <configSections>
        <!-- AppFabric Cache related configuration -->
        <!-- required to read the <dataCacheClient> element -->
        <section name="dataCacheClient"
                 type="Microsoft.ApplicationServer.Caching.DataCacheClientSection,
                 Microsoft.ApplicationServer.Caching.Core, Version=1.0.0.0,
                 Culture=neutral, PublicKeyToken=31bf3856ad364e35" allowLocation="true"
                 allowDefinition="Everywhere"/>
      </configSections>
      <system.web>
        <compilation debug="true" targetFramework="4.0"> </compilation>
        <authentication mode="Windows"/>
        <!-- AppFabric Cache related configuration -->
        <sessionState mode="Custom" customProvider="DataCacheSessionStoreProvider">
          <providers>
            <add name="DataCacheSessionStoreProvider"
                 type="Microsoft.ApplicationServer.Caching.DataCacheSessionStoreProvider,
                 Microsoft.ApplicationServer.Caching.Client, Version=1.0.0.0,
                 Culture=neutral, PublicKeyToken=31bf3856ad364e35" cacheName="SessionCache"/>
          </providers>
        </sessionState>
        <!-- <pages controlRenderingCompatibilityVersion="3.5" clientIDMode="AutoID"/> -->
      </system.web>
      <!-- AppFabric Cache related configuration -->
      <dataCacheClient requestTimeout="10000" channelOpenTimeout="3000" maxConnectionsToServer="1">
        <hosts>
          <host name="raramani-laptop" cachePort="22233"/>
        </hosts>
        <securityProperties mode="None" protectionLevel="None"/>
      </dataCacheClient>
    </configuration>
```

> Even though the *cacheName* specified in the providers section appears as an error (attribute is not allowed) it will work fine. It is used by the AppFabric Cache ASP.NET session state provider to store the objects in the specified named cache. The named cache must have been created earlier. If this is not specified, the session data will be stored in the default named cache.

5. Add a new .NET class named `CacheUtils.cs` to contain all the cache specific interaction and at the beginning, add the following set of `using` statements:

```
using System;
using System.Collections.Generic;
using System.Linq;
using System.Web;
using Microsoft.ApplicationServer.Caching;
```

6. Declare the following set of variables:

```
// channel factory that uses net.tcp binding
    private static DataCacheFactory dcf;
    // handle to named caches
    private DataCache dc, gamesHistorydc;
    private static string newsCacheName = "HeadLineNewsCache";
    private static string gamesHistoryCacheName =
"GamesHistoryCache";
    public bool useCache = false;
```

7. Add code to the `Setup` method.

```
public void Setup()
        {
            try
            {
                if (dcf == null)
                {
                 // Instantiation will setup connections to all
                    cache servers specified in <hosts> section in
                    web.config
                    dcf = new DataCacheFactory();
                }

                // Get handles to the named caches used by the
                    application for reference data
                dc = dcf.GetCache(newsCacheName);
                gamesHistorydc = dcf.GetCache(
                                gamesHistoryCacheName);
```

```
            useCache = true;
        }
        catch (DataCacheException dcexp)
        {
            useCache = false;
        }
    }
```

8. Add code to fetch the Header News feed data.

```
public object GetNewsFeed()
    {
        try
        {
        // Get the latest Headlines to display during
           login
            object item = dc.Get("HEADLINES");

        // In case the cache servers are not available/
           reachable or the object has been expired,
        // item will be null

            return item;
        }
        catch (DataCacheException dcexp)
        {
            return null;
        }
    }
```

9. Add code to the completed set of games as this will be used in the portal page for the users.

```
public object GetGamesHistory()
    {
        try
        {
        // Get the games that have completed, for simplicity
           this will be stored as a single item
        // Alternatively, can create separate Regions for each
           day and use Bulk API to get the history
        // In case the cache servers are not available or
           reachable or the object has been expired,
        // item will be null
            object item = gamesHistorydc.Get(gamesCacheKEY);
```

```
            return item;
        }
        catch (DataCacheException dcexp)
        {
            return null;
        }
    }
```

10. Add code to update the Games history. When a user completes an online game, this will be invoked to update the games history.

```
public void UpdateGamesHistory(string updatedGames)
    {
        try
        {

            gamesHistorydc.Put("GAMES", updatedGames);
            // In case the cache servers are not available/
               reachable or the object has been expired,
            // this will fail

        }
        catch (DataCacheException dcexp)
        {

        }
    }
```

11. In the `Login.aspx.cs` class, declare a static reference to a `CacheUtil` instance. This means that all the users accessing this web server will share the connections made to the cache servers.

```
private static CacheUtils cacheUtil;
```

12. Set up the instance and add code to access the cache contents during the login process.

```
protected void Page_Load(object sender, EventArgs e)
    {
        if (!Page.IsPostBack)
        {
            if (cacheUtil == null)
            {
                cacheUtil = new CacheUtils();
            }
            try
```

```
                          {
                                cacheUtil.Setup();
                          }
                          catch (Exception excp)
                          {

                          }
                    }
      newsItem.Items.Clear();
                    try
                          {
                                // populate the news items
                                object item = cacheUtil.GetNewsFeed();

                                if (item != null)
                                    newsItem.Items.Add(item.ToString());
                                else
                                    newsItem.Items.Add("Nothing to show");
                          }
                          catch (Exception excp)
                          {
                                if (cacheUtil.useCache)
                                    newsItem.Items.Add("Headline News not
                                                        available");
                                else
                                    newsItem.Items.Add("Headline news being
                                                        populated");
                          }

                    }
```

You may notice that the News is not populated in the login page. In this solution, we are not populating the named cache with any items. If you write a service to periodically populate the `HeadLineNewsCache` by adding an object, the login page will update as users login into the system.

13. Modify the `myPage.aspx.cs` page and declare a static reference to a *CacheUtil* instance. This will also ensure that all users accessing this web server share the cache server connections and do not instantiate new connections.

```
private static CacheUtils cacheUtil;
```

14. Modify the `Page_Load` method for the first page load to set up the `cacheutil` instance. Then access the cache to get the list of past games and load in the page.

```
if (cacheUtil == null)
{
cacheUtil = new CacheUtils();
}
try
{
    cacheUtil.Setup();
}

try
{
object val = cacheUtil.GetGamesHistory();
    string finishedGames = "";

    if (val != null)
    {
        finishedGames = (string)val;
        // finished games are delimited by ':'
        char[] separator = new char[] { ':' };
        string[] strSplitArr = finishedGames.Split(separator);
        foreach (string arrStr in strSplitArr)
        {
        PastGames.Items.Add(arrStr);
        }

    }


    finishedGames = finishedGames + String.Format(": User {0}
Date {1} Game {2}", UserName, DateTime.Now.ToShortDateString(),
"TicTacToe");
                    cacheUtil.UpdateGamesHistory(finishedGames);


}
catch (Exception excp)
{  }


}
```

15. Build and run the application.

16. Enter an identical username and password "test1" on the Login.aspx page and click the "Log in" button. You will be redirected to myPage.aspx, where you should choose **TicTacToe** as the chosen game. Then make a couple of moves. Your screen should look something like the one shown next. Then click **Disconnect** to simulate a user losing connectivity.

17. Then log back in with the same credentials, and your session should resume (similar to when a session does not expire). The dropdown with past games should show the current game.

18. Now, you can now create a website using the project, register the application, and load test the application by creating a set of test clients.

19. You can monitor the cache statistics from the admin tool.

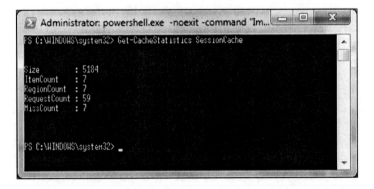

20. You can also monitor the cache cluster the set of Perfmon counters under 'AppFabric Caching: Cache' and 'AppFabric Caching: Host' counter groups.

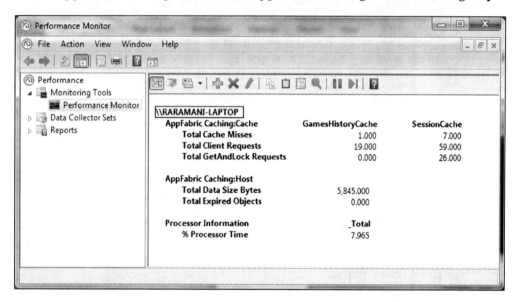

Summary

In this chapter, we looked at how an online gaming application with a social experience and a growing user base can build a scaling solution by leveraging a caching tier. This is a typical use-case of how more and more applications really need a caching tier which must be scalable, highly available, offers excellent performance, and provides easy tools for the operations team. Windows Server AppFabric caching is a fitting choice that can be used by web and mid-tier applications.

19

Website Load Burst and Failover

In this chapter, we'll look at how to leverage the cloud for load burst and failover scenarios. We will discuss the pattern and a set of implementation candidate options. Finally, we will showcase the implementation using the Windows Azure platform.

Use case

HomeUtiliiesOnline is the new generation home utility research and services company that allows their customers (individuals or apartment complexes) to research, manage, and schedule payments for all services regarding their home. The company is in a growing phase at this point with about 1 million subscribers, about 70% of whom own a single family home. The remaining 30% are a combination of apartment complex managers and residents. The company is also affiliated with a set of utility service providers. The company provides a portal where users can make payments to the utility providers – gas, electricity, phone, and cable. Users also visit the site to research the utilities spending pattern and look at ways to reduce their monthly costs.

Currently, the company has one main data center on the US West Coast and an additional site in the East Coast primarily for disaster recovery scenarios. A central global traffic routing product monitors the status of servers in the data centers and load balances appropriately. The global traffic routing product always routes users to the closest data center and also gracefully handles scenarios where one of the data centers is down.

The solution is a three tier architecture which is comprised of the website, business logic, and a backend database system. The business logic, which is implemented as a set of WCF services, is used for both the internal processing and interaction with the 3rd party web services. The backend database has the user sensitive information and transactions secured for authorized access, unlike the consolidated utility consumption and researchable data sets. Within each data center, there are two sets of clusters for each tier—web, database, and business logic. In most situations, the website provides good responses to customer requests. However, in spite of the current setup for load balancing, it is noticed that during sudden spikes, the servers in both the data centers are running close to maximum capacity. In a recent outage that affected both the data centers, the entire site was down for over three hours.

The company management is debating adding another data center for failover and load burst scenarios, cognizant of the fact that servers across all the data centers may not be fully utilized.

HomeUtiliiesOnline is built primarily on the Windows platform where all the tiers and programming tools are predominantly Microsoft technologies. ASP.NET is used for building the online web system. In the middle tier, there are a set of WCF services that route the requests to the external utility service or access data from the backend database. SQL Server, which serves as the enterprise database, manages the data set required for both the user-specific transactions as well as the consolidated usage pattern queries. Most of the developers use .NET, Visual Studio, and Team Foundation Server tools for all of their development and testing activities.

The company has adopted a "buy versus build" strategy where they prefer to leverage readily available solutions instead of building customizable in-house ones.

Key requirements

The following are key requirements for the new software solution:

- Building a solid infrastructure which is resilient and handles the increased and irregular workload.
- Keeping the operational expenses (OPEX) to a minimum.
- Enabling the operations team to react in an agile manner.

Additional facts

There are some additional details gathered after the initial use case was shared with the technical team. These include the following:

- Technology choice should ideally build on top of the existing applications framework and not require too much of a drastic redesign or re-write.

- The design should scale well for the company's current and future workload requirements.
- Ability to apply failover semantics to different portions of the various tiers.

Pattern description

This pattern essentially has two different parts – handling failover and handling load burst. Failover is the ability to switch over to another "ready" system when an abnormal termination occurs. This is usually automatic when the system detects the termination and assigns control to the ready system. One of the key goals when designing failover is to make this transparent to the end users. Users might need to reconnect, but application state or data may be centralized so that the "ready" system can pick up where the failed one ended. Deciding capacity requirements for a system is again a systematic and scientific computation process — different metrics such as the number of transactions, required response time, and the number of concurrent users may be used. In the end, a decision needs to be made and this number would be higher than the average of the metrics but lower than the occasional peak. A load burst is a sudden increase or spike in workload possibly just for a period of time. When this happens, application performance can degrade and in some cases recover at the end of the period; in other cases, the application can terminate.

You can break down the system into various layers. First, there is the physical infrastructure such as server machines, network routers and switches, storage systems, and so on. Next is the actual platform such as application servers, database servers, web servers, and so on which run on the physical infrastructure. Finally, there is the custom application or services (unique to each company) that run on top of the platform. In order to build systems that are highly available (that support failover), a key aspect is to make sure that the infrastructure has redundant machines that can continuously handle user requests. In traditional systems, this has required additional hardware resources such as high end server boxes, robust network infrastructure, and shared storage, to name a few considerations. Then, there is a need to extend the same capabilities to the platform which would require running high end software SKU licenses and extra effort from the operations teams for getting the platform components (such as the database server, application servers) all set up and configured correctly. Finally, it comes down to the custom applications and services that need to incorporate aspects of high availability. If you think about it, the final piece is really the crux of what really matters.

The custom applications and services software layer is the one that drives business value and the rest of them are merely in place for supporting it. Depending on the platform choice and how the actual software is designed, the actual application and services can be made adaptable to failover with minimal effort or require extensive design. Given all these moving parts, traditionally building failover has always been a "special" aspect used by high end enterprises. In addition, the current on-premise failover approach has required spending money well in advance for setting up and testing the system end to end. And all this "special" handling is for the corner case when some part of the system breaks down. I am not trying to trivialize this corner case; indeed, it can have a big impact on the business surviving in case of a viral social networking site, for example. However, this system failure is indeed a corner case usually with a low frequency of occurrence.

On a similar note, scaling up to handle load burst scenarios requires similar attention but is slightly more challenging. In the case of failover preparation, it could be as simple as mirroring the setup in another system and overall doubling the total infrastructure. When dealing with load burst, it may be difficult to predict exact peak and prepare for it in advance. In some cases, this could involve repeatable analysis to get closer to a reasonable peak workload and might be a "wait and watch" method. Typically, this needs agility to spin up new resources on demand. Ideally, this needs to happen with minimal impact on the deployment which is also hard to achieve. Again, the spike can be a corner case. For example, in our use case, one might expect increased activity during the beginning and end of every month when a lot of payments activity happen – users issuing utility payments, partner companies running monthly reports, and so on. However, there might be external factors that trigger more activity on the website. For example, when there are adverse weather conditions, home owners might perform a lot more research for precautionary home projects or to buy supplies. Such scenarios get harder to predict and prepare for the IT team.

Traditionally, the stance has been for capacity to be maintained at slightly higher than average workload to account for such scenarios. In addition, it also requires for streamlining the operations process which might include a set of IT operations teams to be available on pager duty every day.

Such an approach has the following challenges:

- Constant increase in operation expenses or need for additional resources.
- Inability to predict guaranteed SLA and risk calculations.
- Affecting company growth.

Chosen architecture

The first approach that is usually considered is some sort of virtualization technology deployed within the enterprise and thus create a type of private cloud. This naturally builds on top of existing systems in place providing an efficiency model that pools all the physical infrastructure components. In this case, an operations team might be able to spin up additional virtual machines on-demand and be more agile in responding to the needs. However, it does not solve all the other problems. The company still has to own, set up, and manage the various layers. The sharing of the pooled resources just helps to optimize the usage but managing the system, responding to environmental changes, and the onus of maintaining SLAs still need to be handled in-house, which continues to be a main challenge.

Public cloud technology provides some unique advantages – out-of-the-box high availability, really high SLAs guarantees (99.99 uptime), elastic scale across "infinite" resources, and a consumption-based pricing model. Leveraging the public cloud for load burst and failover scenarios is an interesting choice to consider.

Just like we broke down the constituents of an on-premise system into physical infrastructure, platform, and the custom applications or services, the public cloud can be viewed in a similar manner. One approach is to leverage some of the infrastructure pieces (physical machines, storage, and network) in the cloud and allow the operations team to deploy and manage everything on it. This does reduce the workload of the in-house teams with agility and SLA guarantees provided by the hosting provider. But it still requires the in-house operations team to make sure the platform and software services are scaled appropriately for incoming workloads.

Finally, the approach that would seem ideal is one where both the infrastructure and platform aspects are readily taken care and the focus for the company is on developing the solution, and the operations team's responsibility is for monitoring the deployment. The operations team can check to make sure the production deployment is in good health and raise alerts to the cloud platform provider, who has the onus of maintaining SLAs, physical machine health, environmental changes for applying software updates, and so on. The in-house team can dial up or dial down the usage based on their needs. In our use case, they can pro-actively increase the cloud resources for the beginning and end of the month or increase the configuration at run-time when the situation requires it. This would be the ideal choice that lets *HomeUtiliiesOnline* focus on building valued services and applications for their customers without having to worry about how the system handles the scenarios for failover or load burst.

Let's look at how Microsoft Windows Azure stacks up against our decision framework. Note that only the decision criteria most pertinent to this use case are included here.

Solution design aspects

One key decision is to design systems to work with large volumes of data but provide fast response times. So it is critical to understand which portions of the architecture need this performance aspects and how they will be affected when using the on-premise versus cloud deployment model.

Next, one needs to decide the kind of data that needs to be moved to the cloud. In scenarios where sensitive data or transactions need to flow only from on-premise systems, it is typical for the read-only or consolidated reporting portions to be made available in the cloud. In the case of *HomeUtiliiesOnline*, the capability to research utilities consumption and look at consolidated utility spending patterns may be moved over to the cloud system. Users can schedule payments from the cloud hosted application but actual lookup of sensitive data stored in the on-premise system may be via a service hosted in the cloud or completely done by the on-premise system. Usage of the Windows Azure AppFabric (Service Bus and Access control services) may be applicable here.

Analyze if and how each tier in the architecture can have a corresponding representation in the cloud. To start off, making the web tier available in the cloud is usually straight forward. In most cases, the same web solution developed for the on-premise deployment can be easily modified for deployment in the cloud with some minor changes to a website's `web.config` file. Stateless web applications will work seamlessly. In the case that in-flight web connections get failed over, usually this would require a restart of the user request submissions. For making the database tier available in the cloud, the various artifacts (schema, stored procedures, indices, and so on) of the on-premise data tier need to be replicated on the cloud database as well. It is possible that the cloud database system lacks many of the robust on-premise database systems, so portions of the applications that use the minimal functionality across both systems may lend well to moving to the cloud. Synchronization between the cloud and on-premise systems needs to be handled out of band. For example, in the current release, the sync framework is not supported in SQL Azure. Finally the business logic tier may need some modifications to expose the services as cloud service endpoints. Hosting the set of WCF services as a web or worker role will need some configuration and code changes.

Next, choose the allowable interactions between the various tiers deployed across on-premise and cloud. For example, should the cloud hosted components be a tight inter-operable unit or can the cloud hosted web application access the on-premise database system? In the case of Windows Azure, the various tiers are separate silos — so allowing a mixed model will work as long as there is no state that needs to span across these systems. Building the components in such a modular fashion is useful, especially if things need to be changed in the future.

The security model becomes a critical choice when using a combination of cloud and on-premise models –access control services can help federate security and are a required component for the cloud based services, whose equivalent on-premise security model could have just leveraged an ADFS model. The security model for web users and database users is a little simpler. ASP.NET applications can continue to use the provider model. For example, the security can be in a custom implementation or a database. So now, the custom provider would need to ensure that the various resources are available for authenticating users. Database users can continue to specify user credentials in the SQL connection string.

In summary, there are a varied set of criteria that can skew the design choice based on the factors outlined above.

Solution delivery aspects

The Windows Azure platform development environment leverages the typical Microsoft Visual Studio .NET environment. Since *HomeUtiliiesOnline* has a large team of .NET developers, it will be very easy for them to pick up this technology. The platform comes with a set of developer deployment and debugging tools, making it easy to build the system on a single developer machine.

Solution operation aspects

One of the key value-adds of the Windows Azure platform is the ability to elastically scale and maintain the SLA for increased load or fail over scenarios. This helps to limit the number of touch points the operations team needs to monitor and control the system. However, the management story is probably not as rich as the on-premise equivalent. The set of management tools and API is limited. Even though the Windows Azure Service Management APIs are REST based APIs that can be used to automate the deployment, management, and scaling of applications, it may still need further validation to support additional run-time requirements such as increasing capacity. On-premise tools such as Systems Center Operations Manager used for pro-active monitoring are also missing for the cloud today. SQL Azure databases need to be managed from SQL Management Studio, since the online portal only allows basic operations.

Organizational aspects

Even though the Microsoft cloud platform is a V1 offering, it is a core part of the company's strategy as it moves to the online model. Just recently in 2010 Q2, there are more than 10,000 customers who have deployed solutions to production on this platform. By adopting the Windows Azure platform, *HomeUtiliiesOnline* will continue to leverage their existing .NET investments and can continue to build upon for the future.

Solution evaluation

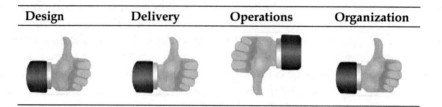

Design	Delivery	Operations	Organization

Windows Azure Platform	
Benefits	**Risks**
Supports elastic scale for large data sets	Lack of extensive community code/ resources given a version1.0 product
Easy integration using Visual Studio and existing skillsets	Many of the operational aspects will continue to evolve and don't yet have the rich tools
Choice of pure cloud versus mixed model	

Building the solution

This section will build out a portion of the solution to demonstrate the implementation on the Windows Azure platform. The solution contains three projects – the ASP.NET web tier, a small portion of the WCF business logic, and finally the Windows Azure Cloud Service project. The database aspects of the solution are left out; please refer to the SQL Azure section of Chapter 6 of this book for understanding its design and deployment model. Here is a quick summary of the steps we will use:

- We will add ASP.NET code for the web role of the cloud services project. For the ASP.NET page design and code, we will use the ASP.NET Webtier project that is already present in the starter solution.

- Within the same web role, we will then create and host a WCF service. For the WCF service creation, we will use the WCFServiceTier project which again is already present in the starter solution.

- After updating the web role project, we will modify it to host the WCF service within ASP.NET and wire up the logic to invoke the WCF service from ASP.NET.

- We will build and test the solution on the development machine and use the Development Fabric.

- Finally, we will deploy and host the solution on Windows Azure.

Setup

A project solution AppliedArchitecture.Chapter19.HomeUtilitiesOnline.
sln has been created in the <Installation Directory>\Chapter19\Begin folder.
This solution contains the three projects that we will be using in this exercise. The
cloud services project will be deployed and tested. This project was created using the
"Windows Azure Cloud Service" template that is installed as part of the Windows
Azure SDK. If you need to understand how to create such a project and include
the various roles, please refer to the solution that is part of Chapter 6, which is the
Windows Azure primer chapter. That lab solution has screenshots that show wiring
up the various roles.

The other two projects, **Webtier** and **WCFServiceTier**, exist as a head-start for
creating the service and ASP.NET logic for the cloud service. These two projects will
not be deployed or tested.

Before beginning the solution, you must have the latest Windows Azure SDK and
Windows Azure tools installed on your development machine. You can access them
from http://www.microsoft.com/windowsazure/windowsazuresdk/ and set
them up for your environment. Also make sure all the system requirements and
instructions to install any latest hotfixes have been followed. These labs have been
developed using Visual Studio 2010 and the Windows Azure Tools for Microsoft
Visual Studio 1.2 (June 2010).

As part of the SDK installation, you should get the Windows Azure Cloud Services
Visual Studio project template, the development fabric, and the development storage
fabric on your machine. The development fabric simulates the cloud environment
locally by simulating a hosting environment for the web and worker roles part of the
project. From the task bar, you can start or shut down the development fabric.

If you need to host the solution on Windows Azure, then you need
to register on the Windows Azure portal and have an account set up.
Please refer to *Chapter 6, Windows Azure Platform Primer* to get further
instructions. For this exercise, this step is not a necessity and you can run
our solution on the local development fabric until step 5 in the "Testing
and Deploying the cloud service" instructions as follows.

Adding the WCF portion to Cloud Service

1. Launch Visual Studio.NET 2010 and open the `AppliedArchitecture.Chapter19.HomeUtilities.sln` in the `<Installation Directory>\Chapter19\Begin` folder. You should see the empty cloud services project, the **WCFServiceTier** project, and the **Webtier** project.

2. Right-click on the **Web Role1** project and add a new item. From the Visual Studio designer, choose **WCF service** from the set of installed templates and give **Service1** as the name for this service.

3. Next, add code to **IService.cs** and **Service1.svc.cs** using the equivalent files from the **WCFServiceTier** project.

4. Additionally, in **Service1.svc.cs**, at the beginning add the following using statement:

   ```
   using System.Collections;
   using System.ServiceModel.Activation;
   ```

5. Next modify `Service1.svc.cs` by adding the following lines of code right before the service declaration:

   ```
   [ServiceBehavior(AddressFilterMode = AddressFilterMode.Any)]
   [AspNetCompatibilityRequirements(RequirementsMode =
       AspNetCompatibilityRequirementsMode.Allowed)]
   ```

6. At the end of this operation, your **WebRole1** project should be as follows:

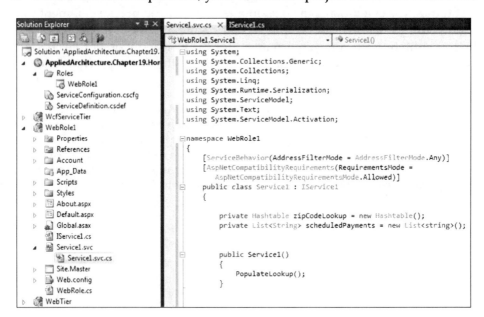

7. Then open the project's `web.config` and add the following section for the new behavior to support hosting on Windows Azure. You can find this under the `system.servicemodel` section of the configuration file.

```
<behavior name="httpAzureBehavior">
  <serviceMetadata httpGetEnabled="true" />
  <serviceDebug includeExceptionDetailInFaults="false" />
  <useRequestHeadersForMetadataAddress>
    <defaultPorts>
      <add scheme="http" port="80" />
      <add scheme="https" port="443" />
    </defaultPorts>
  </useRequestHeadersForMetadataAddress>
</behavior>
```

8. Build the project to make sure there are no errors. With this step, you are done adding the basic WCF business logic to the project.

Adding the ASP.NET portion to Cloud Service

1. From the Web role project, now open `Default.aspx` and design the page similar to the page in the **Webtier** project. You can actually copy the files if it is easier. If you do copy, make sure that the namespace in `Default.aspx.cs`, is **WebRole1** and the `Default.aspx` source view is set up correctly to refer to **WebRole1** and not instead to **Webtier**.

2. We are using the web role to host both the ASP.NET and WCF service so that they will be deployed on the same virtual machine on the cloud. Another design option could be to host the WCF service as a separate role, if there are other clients that could access it.

3. Remove the projects **WebTier** and **WCFServiceTier** since they are no longer required.

4. Rebuild the solution. View `Default.aspx` in a browser window to make sure the page gets loaded correctly.

5. Open `Default.aspx.cs` and add the following piece of code:

```
private static Service1 invoker;

        protected void Page_Load(object sender, EventArgs e)
        {
            if (invoker == null)
                invoker = new Service1();

        }
```

6. For the **GetUtilProviders** button click event, add the following code snippet:

```
string zipcode = "98052";
int index = zipCodeDropDown.SelectedIndex;
if (index < 0)
    index = 0;

zipcode = zipCodeDropDown.Items[index].ToString();
string providers = invoker.GetProviders(zipcode);

OutputListBox.Items.Add(providers);
```

7. For the **GetExpensePatterns** button, add the following bit of code:

```
string zipcode = "98052";
int index = zipCodeDropDown.SelectedIndex;
if (index < 0)
    index = 0;

zipcode = zipCodeDropDown.Items[index].ToString();
string output = invoker.GetExpensePatterns(zipcode);

OutputListBox.Items.Add(output);
```

8. For the **SubmitExpenses** button, add the following code snippet:

```
string zipcode = "98052";
string user = UserTxtBox.Text;
string utilityProvider = UtilityProviderTxtBox.Text;
int expenseAmount = Convert.ToInt32(ExpenseAmoutTxtbox.Text);

int index = zipCodeDropDown.SelectedIndex;
if (index < 0)
    index = 0;

zipcode = zipCodeDropDown.Items[index].ToString();

invoker.MakePayment(user, zipcode, utilityProvider,
expenseAmount);
```

9. Build the solution and now you are done with the code changes. We will test the solution on the development AppFabric and finally deploy it to the cloud.

Testing and deploying the Windows Azure Cloud Service

1. In Visual Studio, click on `ServiceConfiguration.csfg` and modify the instances count to 3.

2. Then, bring up the Development Fabric UI by right-clicking on the task bar and choosing the option **Show Development Fabric UI**.

3. From the Visual Studio solution explorer, select the **AppliedArchitecture. Chapter19.HomeUtilities** project and hit *F5*.

4. If you click on the instance ID under **WebRole1** for the service named **AppliedArchitecture.Chapter19.HomeUtilities**, you can see the multiple role instances running and the development fabric doing the status checks.

5. There should be a browser window that loads `Default.aspx`. On the browser window, provide some test values to see that the application is performing. Some sample output is shown as follows:

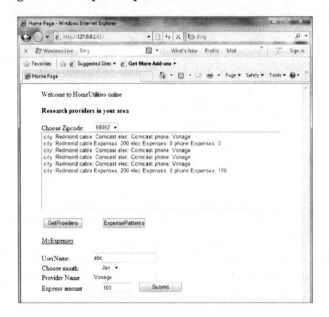

When using multiple instances, the logic to store the expenses should be moved to either SQL Azure or to Windows Storage. If you maintain the in-memory state within the service (for example, in a hash table), when these role instances get deployed to different virtual machines, the output will be incorrect.

6. Next, we will modify the solution to host it on Windows Azure. You can reduce the number of Web role instances to 1. Go to `https://windows.azure.com/Cloud/Provisioning/Default.aspx`, click on your project, and then click on **Create a new service**. Choose **hosting service** and give a friendly name to your service with the publically accessible URL.

7. Now, you are ready to publish the solution to Windows Azure. Before doing this you will need to associate your solution with a certificate and upload the certificate to the portal. This is done to ensure that the right security is in place to access your online account. If you don't have a certificate already, this is how it needs to be created. Right-click on the `AppliedArchitecture.Chapter19.HomeUtilities` project and select **Publish**. From **Credentials**, select **Add**; this will bring up a pop-up which is shown as follows:

8. From the drop down shown in **(1)** in the picture above, click on **<Create>**. This will create a new certificate on your machine.

9. Next, click on **Copy the full path** of the certificate and then click on **Developer Portal,** which will open up a browser window. You might need to run the browser in administrator mode.

10. From the developer portal, choose your Project name, then pick the correct hosted service and then choose the **Account** tab on the top. Then click on **Manage My API certificates**. You should see an option to upload the certificate file from local storage. Click on **Browse** and paste the certificate path that was copied in the earlier step. Upload the certificate to the portal. Then from the **Account** page, copy the **Subscription ID**.

11. Now go back to the Visual Studio window and paste the Subscription ID in step 3 shown in the screenshot above and continue with the Publish process. At the end of this process, your window should look similar to the following screenshot:

12. From Visual Studio, you can monitor the progress of the publish process.

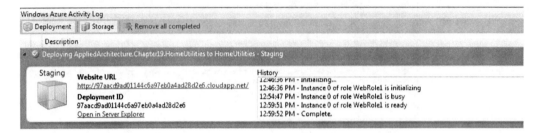

 Instead of doing the complete publish process from Visual Studio, alternatively you can choose to just create the deployment package from Visual Studio and then upload the package from the Windows Azure portal.

13. Now from the Windows Azure portal, you can move the deployment from staging to production and test the application.

Summary

With the advent of the Windows Azure platform, it is increasingly becoming the platform choice for handling load burst and failover scenarios. With the support for the various features such as out of the box high availability, really high SLAs (99.99) guarantees, elastic scale across "infinite" resources, and importantly, consumption-based pricing model, it now becomes compelling for enterprises and small medium businesses to leverage it for lowering TCO. However, there are a set of design criteria and corporate policies that need to be considered to allow mixed access patterns where the various tiers—web, business, and data tier can access the on-premise or the cloud hosted logic. Such a mixed deployment model lets companies leverage their existing infrastructure and complement it with the elastic aspects of the Windows Azure platform, thus lowering the operation costs.

20
Wrap Up

In this book, we sought to provide direction to those trying to figure out when to use a particular Microsoft application platform product. Microsoft has provided architects and developers with a vast array of solution choices, but it often takes years of experience before we truly understand the ideal use cases and nuances of the products being offered. My fellow authors and I have put forth a methodical approach that looks at a full spectrum of aspects to consider when selecting the appropriate product for a solution. The Decision Framework outlined key categories that covered architecture quality attributes as well as strategy, delivery, and operations. Assessing all of these dimensions will allow us to make an informed and confident choice.

One thing we did not include in our Decision Framework is a weighting mechanism. That is, we all know that all requirements are not created equal. Some requirements are "must have" and others are "nice to have." It is the role of the architect to identify and amplify the solution needs that are crucial for success and ensure that those needs are at the top of mind when assessing implementation choices. This can help prevent "analysis paralysis" where your team goes round and round over product evaluations and cannot seem to come to a conclusion. By focusing on the key solution (and organizational) needs, and which product best addresses them, you can move forward with a peace of mind. This means not looking at every principle in the Decision Framework as a deal-breaker. What if low latency processing is absolutely critical, but the best choice fails to have an ideal product administrative function? Which is most important? Classify the questions you ask by priority of need.

What did we find?

We learned through the process of writing this book that some of our preconceived notions about what products can (or cannot) do was out of date. BizTalk is not the only solution for message routing and processing, but at the same time, BizTalk Server still represents the leading choice for doing enterprise-class reliable messaging on the Microsoft stack. We learned that the SQL Server stack of products is really maturing and tools like Service Broker and StreamInsight warrant our architectural attention. We found that Windows Server AppFabric made hosting WCF and WF services in IIS a viable enterprise solution with enough management and durability to satisfy many organizational requirements. The Microsoft cloud services, while admittedly in a "version 1" state, do not just duplicate on-premise capabilities but also offer inventive ways to solve old problems. The biggest thing that we learned is that even though there is a clear overlap amongst the application platform technologies, there are also clear differentiators and ideal use cases for each.

Where to go next

As we stated back in the introduction, this book is not a tutorial on the Microsoft application platform. Nor does it provide you with a cookie-cutter checklist for each and every technology problem you encounter. Rather, I hope that you walk away from this book and do three things:

1. **Take a more holistic approach to selecting the underlying technology for your solutions**. Investigate your use case and aggressively pursue functional, non-functional, and derived requirements in order to get the full scope of the problem at hand. Then assess the software platform components against the key dimensions of evaluation.

2. **Customize the decision framework to meet your organizational needs**. While we think that our four categories of consideration (design, development, operations, and organization) sufficiently cover your key stakeholders, this model is not set in stone. Look for ways to add/subtract/ modify the qualifying questions that make up each decision area and personalize it in a way that suites your team.

3. **Commit to establishing more technical depth on one unfamiliar Microsoft platform technology**. There are not enough hours in the day to go off and become a rock star for each technology highlighted in this book. What you CAN do is look for your biggest area of weakness, and dedicate time to fully understanding the solution space and patterns for that product.

Writing this book was a valuable exercise for us, and hopefully reading it was a beneficial one for you. We look forward to continuing this discussion with you and improving the practice of architectural assessment.

Index

clients 45
Cloud Service, HomeUtiliiesOnline
  ASP.NET portion. adding 491, 492
  WCF portion. adding 490, 491
complex event processing (CEP), Watson
        Media Properties
  about 335, 336
  BizTalk Server 338
  description 335, 336
  StreamInsight 336
compute layer, Windows Azure
  about 122
  web role 122
  worker role 122
Connectors collection 107
construction considerations, solution
        delivery aspects
  aspectssoftware criteria 21
content-based routing pattern, McKeever
        Technologies
  candidate architecture 189
  description 189
  router service, adding 210-213
  setup 197, 198
  solution, building 197
  workflow, building 198-209
content-based routing service 33
Content Delivery Network (CDN) 125
contract, WCF configuration 31
core workflow, Bowl For Buddies
  Assign shape 271
  Assign shape, dragging 267
  building 258-260
  Send Email activity 264
  Send Email Error Notification sequence
        activity 272
  Send Email sequence activity 265
  SendNotificationResponse property 271
  SendReplyToReceive activity 269
  Send Success Notification sequence activity
        270
  TextEventLog property 273, 274
  top-level flowchart 262
CREATE TABLE command 133
Crude Palm Oil (CPO) 357
currentCustomer 170
Current Time Increment (CTI) events 350

Customer 172
customer list, Bowl For Buddies
  creating 276-278

D

Dallas, project 138
databases, BizTalk
  about 76
  BAMArchive 76
  BAMPrimaryImport 76
  BizTalkDTADb 76
  BizTalkMgmtDb 76
  BizTalkMsgBoxDb 76
  BizTalkRuleEngineDb 76
  SSODB 76
data formats 67
data integration considerations, Solution
        design aspects
  software criteria 15, 16
data publisher, LarHans Pharmaceuticals
  configuring 237-240
David Chappell's Whitepaper, URL 32
debatching bulk data, Big Box Stores
  encryption 318, 319
  solution, building 317
  target system 320
decision framework
  applying 26
  architecture strategy, deciding 13, 14
  input sources 11
  need for 10
  recommendations 10
decision framework, dimensions
  organizational considerations 14, 24, 26
  solution delivery 20
  solution design 14, 16
  solution development 14, 21
  solution operations 14, 22, 23
decision framework, input sources
  derived requirements 12
  functional requirements 11
  non-functional requirements 12
  organization direction 13
declarative model 34
DeploymentDiagnosticsManager class 126

Thank you for buying
Applied Architecture Patterns on the Microsoft Platform

About Packt Publishing

Packt, pronounced 'packed', published its first book "Mastering phpMyAdmin for Effective MySQL Management" in April 2004 and subsequently continued to specialize in publishing highly focused books on specific technologies and solutions.

Our books and publications share the experiences of your fellow IT professionals in adapting and customizing today's systems, applications, and frameworks. Our solution based books give you the knowledge and power to customize the software and technologies you're using to get the job done. Packt books are more specific and less general than the IT books you have seen in the past. Our unique business model allows us to bring you more focused information, giving you more of what you need to know, and less of what you don't.

Packt is a modern, yet unique publishing company, which focuses on producing quality, cutting-edge books for communities of developers, administrators, and newbies alike. For more information, please visit our website: www.packtpub.com.

About Packt Enterprise

In 2010, Packt launched two new brands, Packt Enterprise and Packt Open Source, in order to continue its focus on specialization. This book is part of the Packt Enterprise brand, home to books published on enterprise software – software created by major vendors, including (but not limited to) IBM, Microsoft and Oracle, often for use in other corporations. Its titles will offer information relevant to a range of users of this software, including administrators, developers, architects, and end users.

Writing for Packt

We welcome all inquiries from people who are interested in authoring. Book proposals should be sent to author@packtpub.com. If your book idea is still at an early stage and you would like to discuss it first before writing a formal book proposal, contact us; one of our commissioning editors will get in touch with you.

We're not just looking for published authors; if you have strong technical skills but no writing experience, our experienced editors can help you develop a writing career, or simply get some additional reward for your expertise.

[PACKT] PUBLISHING enterprise
professional expertise distilled

SOA Patterns with
BizTalk Server 2009
Implement SOA strategies for BizTalk Server solutions

Richard Seroter   PACKT

SOA Patterns with BizTalk Server 2009

ISBN: 978-1-847195-00-5   Paperback: 400 pages

Implement SOA strategies for BizTalk
Server solutions

1. Discusses core principles of SOA and shows
   them applied to BizTalk solutions

2. The most thorough examination of BizTalk and
   WCF integration in any available book

3. Leading insight into the new WCF SQL Server
   Adapter, UDDI Services version 3, and ESB
   Guidance 2.0

MySQL 5.1 Plugin
Development
Extend MySQL to suit your needs with this unique guide into the
world of MySQL plugins

Sergei Golubchik   PACKT open source
Andrew Hutchings

MySQL 5.1 Plugin Development

ISBN: 978-1-849510-60-8   Paperback: 288 pages

Extend MySQL to suit your needs with this unique
guide into the world of MySQL plugins

1. A practical guide with working examples
   explained line by line

2. Add new functions to MySQL with User
   Defined Functions

3. Export information via SQL using the
   INFORMATION_SCHEMA plugins

4. Search within PDFs, MP3s, and images;
   offset user typing errors with fulltext
   parser plugins

Please check **www.PacktPub.com** for information on our titles

WCF Multi-tier Services Development with LINQ

ISBN: 978-1-847196-62-0   Paperback: 384 pages

Build SOA applications on the Microsoft platform in this hands-on guide

1. Master WCF and LINQ concepts by completing practical examples and apply them to your real-world assignments

2. First book to combine WCF and LINQ in a multi-tier real-world WCF service

3. Ideal for beginners who want to build scalable, powerful, easy-to-maintain WCF services

Programming Microsoft Dynamics NAV 2009

ISBN: 978-1-847196-52-1   Paperback: 620 pages

Develop and maintain high performance NAV applications to meet changing business needs with improved agility and enhanced flexibility

1. Create, modify, and maintain smart NAV applications to meet your client's business needs

2. Thoroughly covers the new features of NAV 2009, including Service Pack 1

3. Focused on development for the three-tier environment and the Role Tailored Client

4. For experienced programmers with little or no previous knowledge of NAV development

Please check **www.PacktPub.com** for information on our titles

Lightning Source UK Ltd.
Milton Keynes UK
UKOW020726280513

211353UK00001B/1/P